Preface

The book ***Paint Pigment Varnish & Lacquer Manufacturing*** contains most valuable informations & technologies including various formulations to manufacture Paints and Enamels, Solvents and Plasticisers, Thinners, Advances in the Production of Powder Coatings, Bituminous Paints, Synthetic Enamel Paints, Emulsion Paints, Distempers, Nitrocellulose Lacquers, Pigments & Extenders, Varnishes & Media, Formulatiions of Paints & Varnishes & Typical Formulations of Ready - Mixed and Stiff Paints, Insulation Varnishes and Wire Enamels, Testing and Evaluation of Paints & Details of Plant & Machineries and the Addresses of Plant and Machineries and Raw Materials Suppliers.

An attempt has been made to improve this book in all the respect as compare to the available books in the market related with this subject. For the new entrepreneurs, we have made certain project profiles especially on the topic Paint Varnish and Lacquers, so that they can easily find out the investments to be made in this industry. Apart from these profiles we have also included a Directory Section for the new ventures just to obtain the Machineries & Equipments as well as Raw Materials.

It is hoped that this book will serve as a ready referencer to all those who are engaged in the field of Paint Pigment Varnish & Lacquers Industry, be it is a technologist, a corporate planner or a business man planning to setup a new projects.

Director
ENGINEERS INDIA RESEARCH INSTITUTE
Nai Sarak, New Delhi.
Fax : 91-11-291 6431

CONTENTS AND SUBJECT INDEX

Chapters	Page No.

PAINT PIGMENT VARNISH & LACQUER MANUFACTURING

With Directory of Machinery & Raw Material Suppliers

A complete encyclopaedia on Paint Pigment Varnish and Lacquer Manufacturing which deals with new technologies, processing, formulaes, project profiles and directory section. The book is covering with the 20 detailed chapters including directory section & details of machineries & equipments for Paint Pigment Varnish and Lacquer processing industries.

Written By :

EIRI CONSULTANTS & ENGINEERS

and

Compiled By

SUDHIR GUPTA

A WORLD RENOWED CONSULTANTS WORKING OVER 21 YEARS

ENGINEERS INDIA RESEARCH INSTITUTE

4449, Nai Sarak, Main Road, New Delhi - 110 006

Phones : 291 8117, 291 6431, 292 0361 Fax : 91-11 - 291 6431

PRINTED & PUBLISHED BY

ENGINEERS INDIA RESEARCH INSTITUTE

Regd. Office : 4449, Nai Sarak, New Delhi - 110 006 (INDIA)
Tel : 291 8117, 291 6431, 292 0361 • *Fax* : 91-11-291 6431

DISTRIBUTED BY

SMALL INDUSTRY RESEARCH INSTITUTE
New Delhi (INDIA)

ISBN : 81- 86732 - 16 - 0
Printed in New Delhi (INDIA)

Rs. 450

Printed & Published by Sudhir Gupta for "Engineers India Research Institute" and Laser Type Set by **Puneet Malhotra** at **Engineers India Research Institute,** and printed at **'Sanjeev Offset Printer', Krishan Nagar, New Delhi - 110 051**

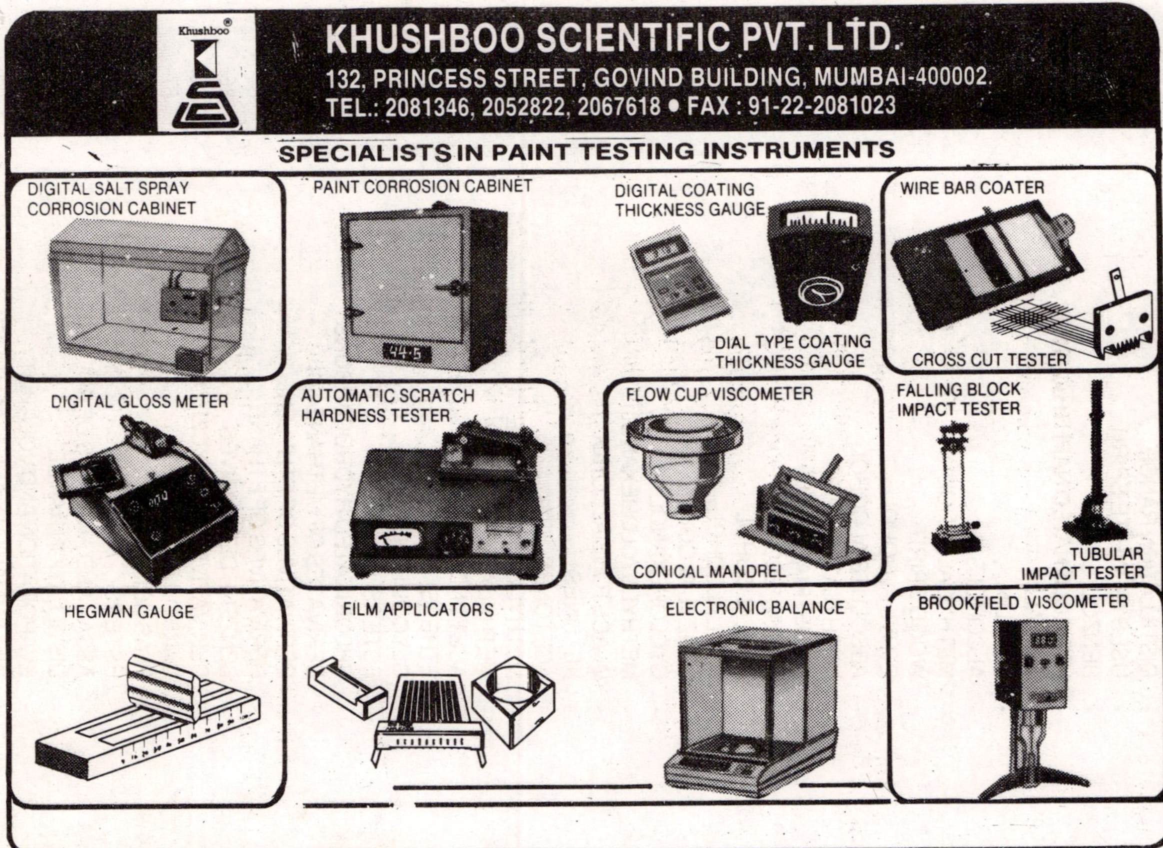
KHUSHBOO SCIENTIFIC PVT. LTD.
132, PRINCESS STREET, GOVIND BUILDING, MUMBAI-400002.
TEL.: 2081346, 2052822, 2067618 • FAX : 91-22-2081023
SPECIALISTS IN PAINT TESTING INSTRUMENTS
DIGITAL SALT SPRAY CORROSION CABINET
PAINT CORROSION CABINET
DIGITAL COATING THICKNESS GAUGE
DIAL TYPE COATING THICKNESS GAUGE
WIRE BAR COATER
CROSS CUT TESTER
DIGITAL GLOSS METER
AUTOMATIC SCRATCH HARDNESS TESTER
FLOW CUP VISCOMETER
CONICAL MANDREL
FALLING BLOCK IMPACT TESTER
TUBULAR IMPACT TESTER
HEGMAN GAUGE
FILM APPLICATORS
ELECTRONIC BALANCE
BROOKFIELD VISCOMETER

Emulsions Paints 136-182

Varnishes 255-276

Paints Formulaes 277-297

Varnishes Formulae 298-320

Insulating Varnishes and Wire Enamels 330-352

Testing & Evaluation of Paints 358-367

1

PAINTS AND ENAMELS

Introduction

Considered in its broadest sense, the term paint embraces all materials of this nature, whatever may be the manner in which the pigment is fixed to the surface, and may be subdivided according to the nature of the vehicle used. The various methods of painting may be classified thus ;-

Oil Paint, in which the vehicle is essentially composed od a drying oil; on exposure to air this solidifies by chemical change, forming an elastic insoluble film.

Enamel, in which the vehicle consists of a polymerised drying oil ; or a combination of drying oil and resins giving a similar type of film but more lustrous and less elastic.

Water Colour, in which the vehicle is a solution of gum, which hardens by evaporation of the water, producing a film freely soluble in cold water.

Distemper, in which the vehicle is a solution of glue, which hardens by evaporation of the water, producing a film insoluble in cold but soluble in warm water.

Tempra, or **Washable Water Paint,** in which the vehicle is an emulsion, generally of a drying oil and some form of glue, which hardens by evaporation of the water and oxidation of the oil, producing a film more or less waterproof.

Fresco, in which the vehicle is lime water, which hardens by conversion into carbonate of lime, producing a film insoluble in water, but readily destroyed by weak acids.

Of these, the first is by far the most important in modern practice, and by common consent the term paint is taken to signify oil paint unless mention is made to the contrary.

Oil Paints

Whilst an oil paint of the very best quality, such as is used by artists, will consist entirely of a single pure pigment and a drying oil, the paints employed for industrial purposes are more complicated in composition, and may contain :-

1. **Pigment**

   (a) Stainers or body colours (such as chrome).
   (b) An opaque white, to reduce the strength of colour and increase the cpacity
   (c) White base, such as barytes, to modify the character and reduce the cost.

2. **Vehicle**

   (a) Drying Oil
   (b) Drier
   (c) Volatile solvent, to adjust the working quality

The proper composition of paint is at present a very conteneious point. As regards the pigment, it was generally held formerly that paint should contain only a single pigment, except in the case of pale tints, where a considerable proportion of an opaque white, such as White lead or zinc oxide, is essential.

More recently, however, the view has been put forward on scientific grounds, that no single pigment is so satisfactory as a combination of pigments, and that especially in the case of white paints a mixture of white lead and zinc oxide, or titanium oxide and zinc oxide produces a better paint than any one of these pigments used by itself.

The addition of any of the mineral whites is a still more debated point. Barytes, for example, was regarded until recently as purely and solely an adulterant, whereas it is classed to-day by the majority of colour chemists, in common with other materials of the same category, as an *"inert extender"*, and regarded as playing a legimate part in the composition of paint.

It is now generally conceded that those mineral whites which are chemically inert and unaffected by acids or other destructive agencies, do not impair the durability of the paint. Even if such pigments serve no actively useful function in the paint, as is contended by many, their presence is only detrimental in so far as they reduce the opacity. Where great opacity is required, their presence is objectionable, but for many purposes where this is not essential they merely have the effect of diluting the pigment, and so reducing the cost considerably.

This, however, does not apply to such of the mineral whites as are not inert or chemically stable. Such materials as terra alba and Paris white can only be looked upon as adulterants, because they decidedly impair the durability of the paint — the former is decidedly soluble in water, whilst the latter, although insoluble in water, is hygroscopic, and readily destroyed by acids, and moreover has a tendency to contain free lime, which may attack and decompose the oil in the vehicle.

The proper physical condition of the pigments is also a matter of controversy — some investigators hold that uniform fineness of particles is ideal to be aimed at, whilst others maintain that a proper blending of fine amorphous particles and coarse crystalline particles results in the most satisfactory and durable material, a more continuous surface free from voids being thereby produced.

It would be outside the scope of this book to discuss such controversial points, but it may be stated generally that no hard and fast rule can be laid down to cover all cases; much depends on the nature of the work and the condition of exposure, for it has been clearly shown that a paint that is perfectly satisfactory in one situtation may prove a failure in another where the atmospheric conditions are different, and so on.

As regards the vehicle, again, there is considerable divergence of opinion as to its precise composition, and much depends on circumstances. The following points may, however, be mentioned as a rough indication of generally accepted principles :-

1 The vehicle should be free from non-drying oils, which can only be regarded as adulterants, and which seriously impair the strength of the film.

2. Excessive addition of driers should be rigorously avoided — other things being equal, a slow-drying paint is more durable than a quick-drying one, for the reason that the oxidation of the oil does not stop when the film has hardened, but continues (at a less rapid rate) until eventually the film loses its elasticity, and becomes hard and brittle. Excess of drier, therefore, in hastening the initial stages hastens also the final disintegration, and results in the paint soon cracking.

3. The additon of "thinners" should be restricted to the minimum amount necessary to secure proper working consistency. Excess results in undue thinness of the film and lack of continuity, which impairs the life of the paint.

The relative consistency of the paint itself. or the proportions of pigment and vehicle in the paint, which determines its consistency may vary to a large extent according to circumstances. Thus, for the highest class of furniture painting thin washes of hard-drying paint are undoubtedly best, whereas ordinary woodwork, which is to be finished in oil colour, requires paint of a medium consistency. The fluidity of paints should also vary in certain cases with the number of the coat. Thus priming paints for wood or stone should always be thin, and contain excess of oil to stop the suction and provide a key for subsequent coats.

The points to be observed in selecting the various ingredients have been discussed in considering them individually, but the value of the paint depdends upon more than merely selecting suitable materials; a great deal depends on the care and skill with which they are combined to produce the finished paint. This fact has only been generally recognised since the manufacture of paint received the attention of chemists, and from being a matter of rule of thumb became a branch of applied science.

Until quite recent times it was only considered necessary to put the various ingredients together in a pail and stir them up with a palette knife or stick, but investigation has shown that this practice, besides being wasteful of material, involves two fundamental errors which detract from the efficiency of the paint.

In the first place, it is difficult under such conditions to ensure uniformity of composition, even in the hands of a trained mixer working on definite instructions; and when, as is frequently the case, the proportion of the various ingredients is left to the discretion of the painter a great element of chance is introduced. In the second place, it is well established that there is a vast difference both in the working quality and the durability of a paint mixed in a rough and ready way and one which pigment and vehicle are intimately and uniformly incorporated by specially designed machinery; in the latter case, the pigment will be reduced to a state of uniform fineness, and each particle of pigment will be surrounded by a film of the vehicle. The result is that the paint works smoothly and evenly in the brush, and a coat is produced which, on drying, forms a uniform and unbroken film offering great resistance to decay.

In the former case, the paint is more or less irregular in texture, because, although the pigment used may consist of fine particles, these tend to agglomerate together when stirred into the vehicle, owing to the surface tension of the latter, and unless more labour is bestowed in mixing than is usually the case the paint will be by no means unoform, and the pigment will be largely present in the form of minute lumps or aggregations of particles; moreover, a great deal of air will be carried into the paint, entangled between the particles of pigment, or mechanically introduced during the mixing. As a result, the paint neither works so freely nor covers so large a surface unless an excess of "thinners" is employed, and film produced on drying is neither uniform in character nor of the most efficient nature to resist deacay.

Paste Paints

It is a common practice amongst decorators, especially in the north, to obtain their paints in a semi-prepared condition, the pigments being ground in oil to a stiff paste by the manufacturer, and the requisite thinners and driers added by the painter to suit the particular work in hand.

This has decided advantages in the hands of a skilled craftsman, enabling him to adjust his paint to special conditions, but it is open to the objection that the paint is not so uniform in composition, or so perfectly blended, as in the case of paints prepared entirely on a maufacturing scale.

The normal consistency of a paste paint is that characteristic of putty, in which the proportion of oil is just sufficient to be absorbed by the pigment to form a composition which is perfectly plastic, but does not adhere to the fingers. The preparation of such pastes forms the first step in the manufacture of all paints, the manufacturer usually keeping a stock of pastes ready either for sending out as such, or conversion into ready mixed paints or enamels. There is a great advantage in storage of the paste before use in this way , as a more stable mixture of pigment and oil is obtained owing to air and voids being reduced to a minimum, and the particles of pigment becoming more uniformly dispersed in the oil. In the manufacture of the highest grades of enamel, for instance, it is no uncommon thing for the paste to be matured for several months before being thinned.

The proportions of oil required to convert different pigments into paste is a function of the oil absorption, and varies from 8 percent in the case of pigments like white lead to 150 percent in the case of carbon blacks. The actual amount of oil required for a given weight of pigment does not correspond exactly to the oil absorption figure, but is invariably lower, owing to the great pressure employed. By making a preliminary experiment on a works scale with a pigment of known oil absorption the relation between the two can be readily calculated however, and a working factor established by which the amount of oil required by a batch of any pigment can be calculated from its oil absorption. The writer has many times calculated for paste paints in ton batches from a laboratory sample in this way with satisfactory results.

Tube colours, used for high-class decorative work, are paste paints of high quality, consisting of pure pigments very finely ground in linseed oil and put into collapsible tubes.

Artists colours, are prepared in the same way, poppy oil being largely used as the vehicle on account of its pale colour and slow drying.

Ready Mixed Paints

The tendency of modern practice is for paint to be supplied to the painter mixed ready for use, being prepared by the manufacturer according to definite formulae and manufactured with the aid of specially designed plant. Such ready mixed paints are supplied under hundreds of proprietary names, but they conform in general to the following principles.

Gloss paints are prepared by thinning down previously prepared paste paints with a vehicle such as 4 parts of refined linseed oil to 1 part of turpentine or white spirit, the drying being adjusted by the addition of liquid driers.

Flat paints for undercoatings etc., are prepared by reversing the proportions of oil and volatile solvent in thinning the paste, so that there is only sufficient oil to bind the pigment.

Priming paints are oil paints modified in the following particulars for preparing new woodwork for painting :-

1. A pigment of pronounced drying action, notably lead, is used, to ensure quick and hard drying.

2. A thin consistency is obtained by adding excess of oil, in order to stop the suction of the wood and provide a good key.

3. The volatile solvent should contain solvent naphtha to ensure ready penetration of the wood. This solvent also preserves the wood by sterilising it from the attack of destructive organisms.

Enamels

This type of finish combines the function of paint and varnish, containing a limited amount of pigment to give opacity, but *"flowing"* during drying so as to give a brilliant surface free from brush marks.

The finest types of enamel are invariably supplied to the decorator ready for use, and are prepared by thinning a finely ground and well-matured oil paste with a highly elastic mixing varnish prepared from stand oil, or a long-oil varnish containing a hard resin. The content of pigment is lower than that of oil paints, rarely exceeding 6 lbs. to the gallon, as excess of pigment impairs the flow and gloss. Such enamels have, therefore, only moderate opacity, and they dry slowly, 16 to 24 hours being a normal time. They produce a tough elastic film of great smoothness and lustre and extreme durability.

Hard Gloss Paint

This name has come into general use during the past few years to signify a product intermediate in character between a straight oil paint and an enamel

The pigment concentration is sufficiently high to give good obliteration and the vehicle is usually a wood oil varnish. It dries more rapidly than enamel and gives a higher gloss and harder film than an oil paint.

Flat Enamels are made with an excess of volatile thinner like flat paints, from which they differ in possessing the property of flow, drying with a smooth satin-like surface.

Special Paints

Apart from the main types of paints used in ordinary decorartive work, innumerable modifications are used for particular purposes, to which only the briefest reference can be made.

Anti-fouling paints, to protect ships bottoms, are made with pigments such as oxide of iron in a quick-drying Tung oil varnish, usually thinned with solvent naphtha, and containing poisonous ingredients such as *mercuric oxide* and *copper rosinate*.

Anti-corrosive paints, for the preservative of iron and steel are prepared with rust-inhibiting pigments, such as red lead, lead chromate, and graphite, and the medium is specially prepared to afford the maximum resistance to moisture.

Anti-acid paints are prepared with pigments of great chemical stability, such as titanium oxide, and a medium containing a maximum of hard resin.

Damp-resisting paints, and *"petrifying liquid"*, are composed of a vehicle formed by dissolving paraffin wax, rosin, bitumen, and gutta percha in various proportions in mineral solvents, with the addition of *Tung Oil*.

Metallic Bronzes and Bronze Paints

Bronze Powders consist of metals in a state of fine division; the *gold bronzes*, ranging from deep copper to pale lemon, are alloys of copper with varying proportions of zinc or aluminium, and silver bronze is pure aluminium.

They are prepared by casting the alloy into ingots, which are rolled and hammered into a fine powder by a series of stamping machines. The powder is sifted and air-floated into uniform fineness, and then polished in a drum fitted with revolving brushes, a small quantity of stearine or hard wax being added to give a high gloss and prevent adhesion.

Preparation of Bronze Paints

Bronze are made into paint by mechanical mixing with a vehicle without grinding, which would alter their structure. As the particle of bronze are necessarily somewhat; large, the paint does not readily remain in suspension, and must be constantly stirred during preparation and use to ensure uniformity. The medium used should be strictly neutral in reaction, as the slightest acidity causes discolouration of the metal, and is also liable to cause bursting of the containers by the pressure of the gas generated by the reaction. In the case of bronze paints for inside use, where durability is not of importance, this is generally ensured by using a neutral hardened rosin or ester gum, dissolved in white spirit, as the medium. For exterior use, an elastic oil varnish is employed, the free acid being neutralised by shaking with slaked lime allowing to stand before adding the bronze.

The following is an example :-

Copal varnish	5-1/2 pints
Turpentine	1-1/2 pints
Terebine	1 pints
Slaked lime	2 ozs
Bronze powder	7 lbs

Bronze paints are also largely made with a medium prepared from a high viscosity nitro-cellulose.

The following is an example :-

Bronze powder	5-1/2 lbs
Nitro-cellulose	5 lbs
Damar	5 lbs
Industrial spirit	1-1/2 lbs
Benzol	25 lbs
Butyl acetate	58 lbs
	100 lbs

The nitro-cellulose solution is generally prepared separately and the bronze added just before application, as it is liable to cause the solution to gelatinise on storage. This effect is most pronounced in the case of copper bronzes, which react rapidly with nitrocellulose solutions, causing them to set up to an unworkable jelly in a very short time. Zinc powder has a similar action, and in both cases the effect is intensified if the bronzing liquid has any degree of acidity.

Properties

The value of bronze paints is due to their exceptionable opacity and light-reflecting power. This is due partly to the molecular structure of the metal itself, and partly to the shape and size of its particles. The particles of bronze powder are not crystalline or spherical, as in the case of most pigments, but in the form of minute flakes. When mixed with the vehicle these flakes tend by a surface tension phenomenon to flocculate on the surface and form what is known as a *"leaf"* effect, the individual particles overlapping to form a structure analogous to the arrangement of the tiles on a roof, with the result that practically perfect opacity is produced. This peculiar structure has a double effect. In the first place, it prevents the penetration of light into the film, which is one of the most potent factors in the disintegeration of paint. Secondly, it is claimed that the overlapping structure provides a maximum resistance to the penetration of moisture, and consequently secures the maximum protection from the weather. This accounts for the fact, well recognised in practice, that bronze paints have remarkable protective properties.

When bronze powders are kept mixed with vehicle for a considerably length of time the tendency to form this peculiar structure is gradually destroyed, probably owing to the complete wetting and partial penetration of the flakes by the medium. On this account it is good practice to mix bronze paints on the job, and not to supply them ready mixed.

The property of *"leafing"* is shown to the best advantage with aluminium, owing to its low specific gravity. The efficiency of bronze paints from the point of view of durability is reduced somewhat by the addition of materials of similar structure but lacking in opacity, such as powdered mica, which is sometimes used as an extender. Where the bronze is used purely for its decorative effect, however, such addition is not a great disadvantage, as the low specific gravity of the mica assists the formation of the leafing, and keeps the bronze on the surface. It is, therefore, more useful in the case of the copper than the aluminium bronzes.

The combination of graphite with aluminium has the reverse effect. Graphite has a structure similar to that of metallic bronze, and is one of the exceptional pigments that possess great opacity with low specific gravity. Its use in connection with bronzes is, therefore, beneficial from the point of view of durability, but, on the other hand, its dark colour and lack of brilliancy impairs the bronze from the decorative point of view.

The great drawback to the metallic bronzes, and particularly aluminium, is that their protective action is largely discounted by the corrosion of the metal itself on exposure to the weather. Aluminium is popularly supposed to be free from oxidation because it does not rust like iron, but the fact that it remains bright in moderately dry air is not due to its being entirely resistant to combination with oxygen, as in case of platinum or gold. Aluminium oxidises, in fact, so rapidly that immediately it is exposed to the air it becomes covered with a thin film of oxide, which, being colourless and transparent, is not visible. This serve to protect the metal from further action in moderately dry air, but if kept in the damp for any length of time it soon becomes covered with a white deposit of alumina. Aluminium is also rapidly attacked by both alkalies and acids, the immediate effect of which is to turn the surface black, with ultimate corrosion. Consequently aluminium paint on exposure to the weather, especially in towns, soon loses its brialliancy and becomes dull and unsightly.

Copper bronzes suffer from the same defect to a more marked

extent — they rapidly tarnish by oxidation and by the action of sulphur gases, whilst traces of acid attack them with the formation of green verdigris.

Water Paints

Washable Distemper

This type of paint is largely used in modern interior decoration and also for priming woodwork prior to the application of oil paint. The medium used is a material such as a drying oil which is insoluble in water, but can be emulsified and rendered miscible with water by conversion into a lime soap. On the evaporation of the water this forms a binder for the pigment, which hardens on exposure and becomes more or less insoluble.

Manufacturers of washable distempers have their own ideas as to proper composition of the emulsion, and one can only say in general terms that the binding material of washable distempers varies widely in different cases, some using an alkaline solution of casein , others casinate of lime, others again a more complex emulsion of linseed oil. The body of the paint is barytes, Paris white, or lithopone, the tints being produced by the addition of a small percentage of stainers, which in all cases must consist of a pigment or pigments unaffected by alkali.

The following are some typical examples :-

1. **Paste Washable Distemper**

Glue	15 lbs
Soft soap	2 lbs
Pale boiled oil	5 gallons
Varnish foots	4 gallons
Lithopone	1 cwt
Paris white	2 cwt
Barytes	1 cwt

The glue and soft soap are dissolved in water containing 1 percent of phenol in a steam-jacketed pan, the oil and varnish added to the solution, and heated until emulsified. This emulsion is then mixed with the pigments in a pug mill and water added to form a stiff paste. The paste is finally ground with a small proportion of stainers, according to the tint required.

2. **Powder Distemper**

A mixture of Paris white 2 parts and barytes 1 part, is blended with stainers to the required tint in an edge runner, and a small proportion of linseed oil added. 70 lbs. of this mixture is then ground to fine powder with :-

Casein	8-1/2 lbs
Lime	5 lbs
Borax	1/2 lbs

For use, this powder is mixed with hot water to the consistency of thin cream.

3. A mixture of gum thus, 10 parts, and stearic acid, 1 part, is made into an emulsion with a weak solution of ammonia and ground into a stiff paste with the following mixture :-

Paris white	2 parts
Casein	4 parts
Lime	1 parts

This forms the white base, which is tinted by the addition of a small quantity of pigment and thinned with water to the required consistency for use.

2

SOLVENTS AND PLASTICISERS

Introduction

Solvents are used in paints and lacquers to reduce the viscosity or consistency of the material and facilitate the application of a uniform coating. They must be compatible with the oil or resin present. After application the solvent is no longer required and should evaporate completely from the film.

Another class of organic liquids used in paint industry is plasticisers; their function is to remain permanently in the film of paint or varnish after application in order to impart elasticity and proper adhesion to it. In contradistinction to the volatile solvents, plasticisers should be perfectly non-volatile, and should also be chemically stable, and not after in properties on prolonged exposure.

Solvents

Paint and lacquer solvents are volatile organic liquids which can be classified into well-defined chemical groups. Their solvent power and general physical properties vary over a wide range. The important properties of paint solvents are the following :

1. Solvent power 2. Volatility

3. Stability
4. Toxicity
5. In flamibility and flash point
6. Colour

The following properties are also of importance as indicators of purity.

1. Specific gravity
2. Moisture content
3. Acidity or alkalinity
4. Non-volatile matter.

General Properties of Solvents

1. Solvent Power

The film forming materials used in paints and lacquers are usually organic in nature and possess no crystalline structure. When treated with suitable solvents they dissolve to give solutions the viscosity of which increases with increasing concentration. There is no solubility limit, as in inorganic solutions, but problems of application, limit the concentration used.

It is well known that certain types of resins or oils are soluble only in certain types of solvents. A number of theories have been put forward to explain solvent action. One of the theory is based on popularity, according to which there is a tendency of polar molecules to form associated groups of molecules by attraction. Polar solids such as cellulose nitrate dissolve readily in polar solvents such as esters and ketones but are insoluble in non-polar hydrocarbons.

In each of these clases there are variations in solvent power or strength of the individual solvents. Thus in the non-polar solvents, the aromatics give solution of oils or resins of lower viscosity than those in aliphatic hydrocarbons.

Kauri Butanol value is a criteria applied to solvent to be used in varnishes and paints. A good solvent is indicated by a high K.B. value.

2. Volatility

This property is of fundamental importance in the selection of a solvent for a particular use, and investigations are made as to

(a) the rate
(b) the uniformity
(c) the completeness of evaporation, or freedom from residue.

Whilst the rate of evaporation is generally considered to be proportional to the boiling point the term *'high boiler'* used to signify a solvent evaporates slowly; this is only true with in limits. In solvents of the same type, such as the various petroleum distillates, the rate of evaporation is approximately proportional to the distillation range. This does not hold, however, with solvent of different classes. The fundamental factors which control evaporation are the specific heat of the material and the latent heat of evaporation, and these can differ considerably in different classes of solvents. As an example, the evaporation rate of tetrachlorethane with a boiling point of 147°C is considerably higher than that of water with a boiling point of 100°C.

3. Stability

By stability of a solvent it is implied that the solvent must be inert to the ingredients with which it is mixed in a paint formulation. It is must be stable during the processing of the paints and should not produce adverse effects of any kind during processing as well as during application. Its function is only to dissolve partially some of the ingredients of paint.

4. Toxicity

The vapours of all volatile materials are toxic to some degree if they are inhaled in sufficient concentration over a long period. The concentration of vapour in the air will be related to the volatility so that high boiling point solvents and plasticisers are not likely to give dangerous concentrations. For many industrial solvents there is a *"maximum allowable concentration"* in parts per million by volume and concentrations above this are considered dangerous.

Some or these solvents are known to be very harmful and their absorption into the system can result in chromic illness. Among the most harmful are benzol and chlorinated hydrocarbon. .

5. Flash Point and Inflamibility

The great majority of organic solvents are inflammable to an extent roughly proportional to their boiling point and a fire risk is therefore associated with their use. When these liquids are heated, the concentration of vapour in the air above their hydrostatic level increases with temperature until it will flash on application of a flame. The lowest temperatures at which this phenomenon occurs is known as the flash point of the liquid.

The flash point of a mixture of two solvents of different flash points can lie between or below their individual flash points.

Flash points of solvents can be raised in several ways. The first and obvious way is to eliminate wholly or in parts constituents of low flash-points, this generally entails eliminating the low boilers. A second method is to choose low boilers which do not form mixtures of low boiling point. A third method is to increase the proportion of high boilers at the expense of the medium boilers. Fourthly, low boiling non-associated liquids may be replaced by associated liquids of similar boiling *e.g.* alcohol for benzene. Last and best, a small proportion of highly volatile non-inflammable liquids such as methylene chloride, ethylene chloride, carbon tetrachloride *etc.*, may be used.

6. Colour

With the exception of the heavy coal-tar naphthas, most solvents have very little colour. In majority of instances colourlessness of a solvents is a very important property. If a solvent is slightly coloured due to the presence of some impurities it must be decolourised before use.

Classification of Solvents

1. Petroleum Hydrocarbon

A considerable number of very useful and widely used solvents are obtained either by distillation of crude petroleum or by thermal cracking of petroleum gases. The products obtained by distillation are mainly paraffin hydrocarbons containing small amount of aromatics. The thermal cracking processes are designed to give solvents with high aromatic contents.

(a) Low-boiling petroleum fractions

Petroleum ethers are marketed under several grades according to the boiling range. Three most common boiling ranges are 40 to 60°C; 60 to 80°C and 80 to 120°C.

(b) Special boiling point solvents

These are produced in six or more boiling ranges between 30 and 160°C.

2. White Spirit

It is produced from petroleum fractions distilling in the temperature range of 150 and 190°C.

High-aromatic Solvents from Petroleum

These solvents conatin from 73 to 93 percent of aromatics. The specific gravity ranges from 0.833 to 0.883. They are supplied in graded boiling ranges between 100 and 210°C and are marketed under proprietory names.

2. Solvents from Coal-tar

Coal-tar distillation gives a range of solvent fractions of increasing temperature of distillation.

The solvents of this class are :

(i) Benzol
(ii) Toluol or Toluene
(iii) Xylol or xylene.

At high temperature distillations coal-tar after the removal of benzol yield coal-tar naphthas. Two grades of coal-tar naphtha, that are used as solvents are solvent naphtha and heavy naphtha.

(a) Solvent naphtha

It is also known as 90/160 naphtha *i.e.* 90 percent distills below 160°C. It is widely used as a solvent for rubber, but for paint it is not as good as heavy naphtha.

(b) Heavy naphtha

It is also known as 90/190 naphtha *i.e.* 90% distills below 190°C. It is an excellent solvent for a wide range of resins used in chlorinated rubber paints, anti-fouling composition and as an additive in primers for wood. It is also used widely as the solvent in bituminous paints.

3. Terpene Solvents

(i) Turpentines

These solvents are obtained from the resinous materials present in pine and other coniferous trees. For the last so many years it had used as the standard thinner for paints and varnishes, but it has now been replaced by other solvents due to the introduction of alkyds and other synthetic resins

(ii) Dipentene

This solvent is prepared by a modification of the distillation process for wood turpentine. It has a distillation range of 175 to 195°C. It is an excellent solvent for many synthetic resins and finds use in improving the wet-edge time of decorative undercoats and finishes.

(iii) Pine Oil

It is usually obtained with turpentine and is separated by fractional distilation. It has a higher boiling range *(200-230°C)* than turpentine. It is used as a de-odourant in paints. It possesses some germicidal properties also.

Various alcohols used as solvents in paint industry include methyl alcohol, ethyl alcohol, n-propyl alcohol, iso-propyl alcohol, n-butyl alcohol, iso-butyl alcohol, di-acetone alcohol, *etc.*

5. Esters

A number of esters used as solvent in paint industry include ethyl acetate, n-butyl acetate, ethyl lactate, *etc.*

6. Ethers

Various ethers *e.g.* glycol ethers and glycol ether-esters used as solvent include di-isopropyl ether, ethylene glycol, monoethyl ether or 2-methoxyethanol, ethylene glycol, monoethyl ether or 2-ethoxyethanol, ethylene glycol monobutyl ether or 2-butoxyethanol, ethylene glycol monoethyl ether acetate or 2-ethoxyethyl acetate.

7. Ketones

Ketones used as solvents in paint industry are acetone or dimethyl ketone, methyl ethyl ketone, methyl iso-butyl ketone, cycloh-exanone *etc.*

8. Chlorinated hydrocarbons

Important solvents in this group are methylene chloride, ethylene chloride or 1 : 2-dichloroethane, trichloroethylene, and perchlor-oethylene *etc.*

Petroleum Hydrocarbons

1. Low-boiling Petroleum Fractions

(a) Petrol

It is a partially refined fraction of petroleum crude with a distillation range between 75° and 160°C. It is not generally used in the paint industry but is occasionaly employed as a thinner in certain types of paints where rapid evaporation is required.

(b) Ligroin *(Petroleum Spirit)*

It is the fraction coming over between 60°C and 100°C consisting of about 75 percent paraffin hydrocarbons, chiefly hexane and heptane, the remainder being mainly olefins with a small and varying amount of aromatic hydrocarbons depending on the source from which it is obtained.

(c) ***Benzine*** is the name generally given to a re-distilled and purified petroleum spirit, free from sulphur and other impurities, which evaporates completely without leaving any trace of residue. It is the fraction distilling between 60°C to 120°C.

(d) Petroleum Ether

It consists mainly of hexane, and heptane with a boiling point below 60°C and specific gravity below 0.670. It is used as an alternative to ether as an analytical extracting agent for oils and fats and similar purposes.

2. White Spirit *(Mineral Spirit)*

White spirit is an extremely important petroleum product which may be regarded as the next product distilled over after the Special Boiling-Point Spirits

The boiling range is mainly between 150° and 190°C although a small percentage may boil up to 210°C. The composition of commonly used white spirit is as follows.

Boiling range	Up to 155°C	10% max.
	Below 195°C	90% min.
	Max. Boiling Point	210°C.
	Flash point	34°C min.

The characteristic odour of white spirit is due to mainly to impurities and aromatics. White spirit possesses moderate solvent power and is miscible with most organic solvents. it dissolves raw and refined oils, light and medium stand oils etc. It is, however, not a good solvent for highly polymerized stand oils and blown oils.

White spirit is a thinner usually in outside house paints. It evaporates after application leaving behind the non-volatile vehicle to bind the pigment particles to each other and fix the entire film as a continuous coating to the surface to which it is applied. It has been estimated that white spirits account for 75% of all hydrocarbon solvents in the surfece coating industry and for about 98% of all solvents in architectural finishes. Mineral spirit is particularly suitable as a solvent in all types of architectural finishes, including house paints and enamels based on oleoresinous or alkyd resins because of its good volatility range, clean evaporation and good brushability. Mineral spirit is also the solvent for thinning varnishes and alkyd resins immediately after the cook. Another purpose for which white spirit is used extensively is as a cleaning agent in paint, printing inks etc.

3. High Aromatic Solvents from Petroleum

These solvents range in specific gravity from 0.833 to 0.833 and contain 73 to 93 percent of aromatics. Their boiling range is between 110° and 210°C.

They possess high solvent power and can be replace many of the coal-tar solvents. They have faint and not unpleasent odour and some of them are preffered to the coal-tar naphthas.

These petroleum aromatics generally find use in the surfece coatings, inks, polishes, insecticides, and solvent extraction where their ready-availability, consistency of quality, attarctive price low odour and accurately known distillation range can be used to tailor-make a product for almost any requirement.

II Solvents from Coaltar

1. Benzol

Benzol is a clear, colourless liquid with a peculiar smell, due to the presence of small quantities of impurities; their approximate composition is as follows .

Benzene	60-75 percent
Toluene	24 percent
Light hydrocarbons	4 to 6 percent
Carbon bisulphide etc.	2 percent

Its principal use in the paint industry is as a thinner or diluent for cellulose ester products. It is employed as a solvent for oil-soluble dyes in the preparation of stains for wood work, owing to its high penetrative power; it is also used as an ingredient and diluents for paint removers, and is sometimes added in small proportion to paint thinners to increase their solvent power.

Benzene

Benzene is a pure compound — C_6H_6; the fundamental member of the aromatic series of hydrocarbons, the impure distillate described above being known as Benzol for distinction. It is obtained from benzol by treatment with sulphuric acid and fractional distillations and is colourless, limpid liquid, with a high refractive index, and a characteristic unobjectionable odour. It solidfies at 5.5°C and boils at 80.5°C. Pure benzene contains traces of sulphur, H_2S and undissolved water. It gives off a highly inflammable vapour at ordinary temperatures, the flash point being 8°C. It is practically insoluble in water, but soluble in the lower and higher alcohols and most other organic solvents.

Benzene can be used as a diluent in lacquers or adhesive based on cellulose nitrate, cellulose aceto-butyrate, cellulose acetate, vinyl copolymers and some acrylics; it may be used as a prime solvent in ethyl cellulose, styrene, and styrene copolymers, some acrylics and rubber-based products. It is a valuable constituent of thinners intended for use with any of the foregoing and it is a solvent for most oils, fats, waxes, alkyd resins, and many natural resins. It is a solvent for a number of other cellulose esters and ethers, in particular, cellulose dinaphththenate, dilaurate, dipalmitate, distearate, dinitrolaurate dinitropalmitate diacetyl laurate, and diacetyl palmitate. If mixed with alcohol it will dissolve benzyl cellulose and other ethers. It is a solvent for most oils and for ester gums, benzyl abietate, copal ester, polystyrene, polyisobutylene, polyvinyl acetate, colophony, elemi, fluid silicones, vegetable oils, phosphorous, iodine, gammabenzene hexachloride 29%, coumarone, benzyl resin, mastic, raw rubber, guttapercha resin, thio-urea resins, chlornaphthalene resin, and naphthalene formaldehyde resin. It does not dissolve cellulose acetate or nitrate, sandarac, manila or copals, and is nonmiscible with water, aqueous solvents and glycols, monochlorohydrin, monacetin. It attacks polythene, polyvinyl chloride, and methyl methacrylate but not nylon.

2. Toluol *(Commercial Toluene)* $C_6H_5CH_3$

It is the most extensively used diluent for cellulose nitrate lacquers. It is not a solvent for cellulose nitrate, but solutions in true solvents will tolerate greater additions of toluol than any other hydrocarbons. It has an important bearing on the cost of the lacquer. Toluol is a solvent for a large number of resins and is miscible with drying oils and most other solvents. It does not dissolve PVC, copals or shellac.

Toluene is the next homologue in the benzene series of hydrocarbons *viz;* benzene with one hydrogen replaced by methane ($C_6H_5CH_3$). It has a lower solidifying point than benzene, below 95°C., and the boiling point, *(with the usual rule that the boiling point rises with the complexity of the hydrocarbon)*, is 111°C. Toluene is a solvent for ethyl cellulose, ester gums, resins and its many variations, like epoxy resins, amino resins, alkyd resins, cyclohexanone resins, sulphinamide resins, polyester resins, gum copal ester, raw rubber: chlorinated, cyclized and semirized rubber, butadiene/styrene acryonitrile rubber, gutta percha resin and mastic, and most acrylic or alkyd methacrylic resins, polystyrene, polyvinyl acetate, polyisobutylene, chlorinated polyvinyl chloride chlorinated polypropylene, chlorinated diphenyl and chlorinated paraffin, natural synthetic waxes, oils, bitumen gilsenate. It is not a solvent for shellac, sandrac, polyvinyl chloride, polyethylene, cellulose acetate and cellulose nitrate, nylon, polytetrafluorethylene and moulded phenolic resins. It is miscible with oils, hydrocarbons, and other solvents including pure ethyl alcohol, but not with industrial methylated spirits, monochlorohydrin, glycol and water; it can be emulsified with water, with a wide range of emulsifying agents, or with hydrated isopropanol.

Toluol or commercial toluene contains some sulphur compounds and methyl thiophenes, having the boiling range between 110°C and 120°C.

3. Xylol *(Commercial xylene)*

It is a mixture of three isomers in which the meta-isomer predominates.

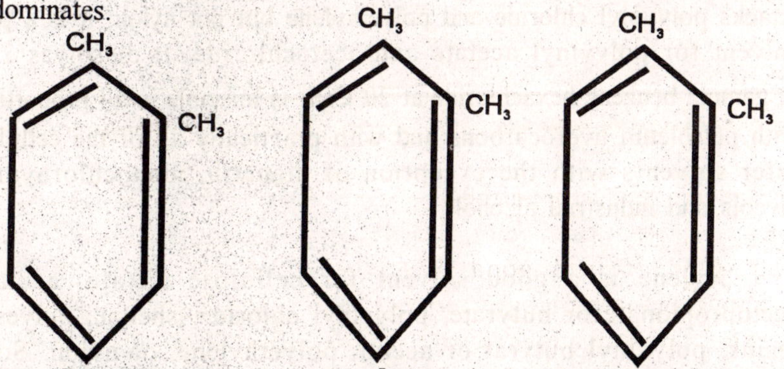

o-xylene	m-xylene	p-xylene
b.p.144.2°C	b.p.139.1°C	b.p.138.3°C

In some grades small quantities of other aromatic solvents are also present.

Xylol is now one of the most important solvents used in the paint industry because of its high solvent power for a very wide range of resins used in both stoving and rapid air-drying coatings together with a convenient rate of evaporation. The solvent power is increased appreciably on addition of 10 to 20 percent n-butanol and this mixture is very widely used in stoving finishes. The rate of evaporation is too great for use in brushing finishes.

Xylol is used as a diluent in cellulose nitrate lacquers and as the main solvent in lacquers based on polystyrene, polymethyl methacrylate and chlorinated rubber. It is an excellent solvent for asphaltic bitumen and petroleum pitch.

Xylene

It is the next member of the series, $C_6H_4CH_3.CH_3$ having three isomers *viz;* ortho, meta and para-xylene.

Xylene is a solvent for ethyl and benzyl cellulose, ester gum, copal ester, benzyl abietate, rubber, gutta percha resins, polystyrene, methyl methacrylate, polyisobutylene, rubber chloride dammar, elemi, coumarone, colophony, fluid silicones, melamine formaldehyde, and urea formaldehyde resins, castor, linseed, and other oils. It attacks polyvinyl chloride and polyethylene but not nylon; it is a poor solvent for polyvinyl acetate and acetochloride. It dissolves 25% of gamma-benzene hexachloride at 20°C. It is miscible in all proportions with petroleum hydrocarbons and with practically all of the cellulose ester solvents with the exception of diacetin, monochlorhydrin, glycols, and industrial alcohols.

Xylene is a good solvent for cellulose nitrate, acetate, acetopropionate or butyrate, polyvinyl chloride, shellac, polyester resins, polyvinyl butyral or acetal, polyethylene, or nylon. Some grades of the cellulose nitrate can be dispersed in specific mixtures with anhydrous ethyl alcohol, and cellulose acetate of the soluble variety absorbs about 5% of meta-xylene at 25°C whilst flexible polyvinyl chloride can also be softened by prolonged contact with xylene.

Terpene Solvents

1. Turpentines

This group of solvents is obtained from the *'oleoresin'* contained in various species of pine and other coniferous trees. If a cut is made in the trunk of one of these trees a gummy material is exuded and can be collected in cups attached to the trunk. Distillation of this material yields the volatile gum-turpentine. Steam distillation of wood or of the stumps of pine trees yield wood or stump turpentine.

Composition and Properties

The turpentines consist of mixtures of members of the turpene group of unsaturated cyclic hydrocarbons. The mixture consist chiefly of alpha-pinene, Beta-pinene, carene, sylvestrene, and dipentene and the properties vary with the source of the turpentine. Alpha-pinene is the main constituent of gum-turpentine whilst the wood-turpentines consist mainly of dipentene.

The turpentines are clear, colourless liquids with characteristic pungent odour. Long exposure to the vapour can cause headache and nausea.

They evaporate uniformly but, due to unsaturation, oxidation and polymerization of a part of turpentine takes place at the same time. The product so formed is non-volatile but miscible with dry oils and resins and therefore become part of the film.

The physical characteristics of the turpentines are as follows:

	Gum Turpentine	*Wood Turpentine*
Specific gravity	0.862 - 0.872	0.859- 0.875
Distillation range	150 - 180°C.	150-170°C.
Refractive index (20°C)	1.469 - 1.478	1.463 - 1.483 .
Flash Point	30 - 37°C	34 - 36°C.
Non-Polymerizable material	Not more than 11%	Not more than 16%

Properly prepared gum-turpentine is a clear, colourless liquid, any pronounced colouration indicating impurity. Turpentine is inflammable, but not *'highly inflammable'*. It evaporates uniformly at a rate which renders it satisfactory as apint and varnish thinner; it does not evaporate completely, always leaving a small residue. Being an unsaturated compound, it is chemically active and oxidizes and polymerises on exposure to air. This property gives it exceptional value as a thinner; under the conditions that exist in the drying of paints and varnishes it acts as a carrier of oxygen to the oil, absorping oxygen from the air and giving it off again in contact with the oil, and thus facilitating the drying of the film. It has good solvent power. The acid value of turpentine ranges from 1 to 3.

2. Dipentene

This solvent is prepared by a modification of the distillation process for wood turpentine. It has a higher distillation range *(175 to 195°C)* and an appreciably lower rate of evaporation. It is also possesses some anti-skinning properties. The physical characteristics of dipentene are as follows :

Specific gravity	0.844 - 0.850
Boiling range	175 - 195°C.
Flash Point	54°C.
Kauri-Butanol value	105

It is as solvent for rubber, rubber chloride, ester gum, coumarone, colophony, metallic driers; it does not dissolve cellulose acetate or nitrate with most of the usual resin-oil combinations for which it is a good dispersing medium and with which it reduces *'skining'* and gelling and also retards initial hardening.

3. Pine Oil

Pine oil is usually obtained with turpentine and is separated by fractional distillation. The chief constituent is terpineol. It has a higher boiling range *(200-230°C)* than turpentine and a much lower rate of evaporation. The specific gravity ranges from 0.932 to 0.945.

Pine oil has an agreeable pine-like odour and is used as a reodourant in paints and disinfectants. It also possesses some germicidal properties. It is an excellent solvent for most resins.

Alcohols

1. Methanol, CH_3OH

Methanol alcohol or methanol is an important solvent. It is prepared by both, destructive distillation of wood and synthetically by the hydrogenation of carbon monoxide. Its physical properties are as follows:

Specific gravity (20°C)	0.792
Boiling range	95% between 64 and 67°C
Flash Point	6°C.

Methyl alcohol has pronounced toxic properties and is used as a denaturant for the ethyl alcohol in methylated spirit. It is a cumulative poison. Pure methyl alcohol dissolves neither cellulose acetate nor high viscosity nitrate but the presence of small proportion of acetone renders it a potent solvent for the nitrate and to a less degree, for the acetate. It is a solvent for ethyl cellulose, polyvinyl acetate, colophony, shellac, benzyl-abietate, castor oil, and is miscible with aromatic hydrocarbon. It partially dissolves mastic and soft copals. It is non-miscible with linseed oil and with petroleum hydrocarbons. It doesnot dissolve polyvinyl chloride or chloracetate.

2. Ethanol, C_2H_5OH

The grades of ethyl alcohol used most extensively in surface coating are specially denatured alcohol and methylated spirit. Pure anhydrous ethyl alcohol has the following characteristics:

Specific gravity	0.7937
Boiling range	78.3°C
Flash Point	14°C

The solvent properties of alcohol rapidly decrease with increasing proportions of water; alcohol containing 5% of water is practically a non-solvent for all forms of cellulose nitrate. An addition of 20 to 30% of benzene renders it a solvent for benzene cellulose, ester gum and coumarone. It dissolves ethyl cellulose and solutions up to 16% can readily be made.

It is a solvent for certain synthetic resins such as soft lakdites, polyvinyl acetate, low viscosity silicones, acrolein resin, furfural resin, and cyclohexanone resin, and cyclohexanone form aldehyde resin. It is miscible with castor oil and hydrocarbons. Industrial Methylated Spirit *(IMS)* consists of ethyl alcohol 95 percent denatured with 5 percent methyl alcohol. It dissolves a number of natural resins including shellac with which it forms several spirit varnishes. It also dissolves some synthetic resin such as polyvinyl acetate and cyclohexanone resin. It is completely miscible with water, hydrocarbons and castor oils.

3. n-Propyl Alcohol ($CH_3.CH_2.CH_2.OH$)

N-propyl alcohol is similar to isopropyl alcohol in properties and is superior as a lacquer diluent on account of its higher boiling point, which makes it less likely to cause chilling. It is miscible with all the usual solvents and with water in all proportions. The physical constants of the pure alcohol are as follows:

Specific gravity	0.8052
Boiling Point	97.2°C
Flash Point	22°C

It is a solvent for rosin, shellac, ester gum, urea-formaldehyde resins, and castor oil. When hot it dissolves cotton seed and linseed oils. It doesnot dissolve celulose esters, but has a solvent action on some cellulose ethers.

4. Iso-propyl Alcohol

It has the formula

$$\begin{matrix} CH_3 \\ CH_3 \end{matrix} > CH.OH$$

Isopropanol is widely used as a substitute for ethyl alcohol in the surface coating industry. It can be prepared by the hydration of propylene.

Pure iso-propanol has the following physical constants.

Specific gravity (20°)	0.7925
Boiling Point	97.2°C
Flash Point	22°C

Pure isopropyl alcohol is not a solvent for cellulose esters, but has distinct latent solvent properties, the presence of a relatively small quantity of an esters rendering it a solvent for cellulose nitrate. It dissolve cyclohexanone-formaldehyde resin, colophony, shellac, *etc.* It doesnot dissolve polyvinyl chloride, acetate or chloroacetate.

It has the advantage over industrial alcohol in that it is anhydrous and therefore less likely to cause water blush.

5. n-Butyl Alcohol

Four alcohols are derived from butane, differing slightly in their properties — normal, iso, secondary and tertiary. The butanol of commercial importance is n-butanol. It possesses the following physical constants :

Specific gravity (20°C)	0.811
Boiling Point	118°C
Flash Point	37°C

It dissolves a number of natural resins and the following synthetics — urea-formaldehyde, melamine-formaldehyde, polyvinyl acetate. It is miscible with hydrocarbon solvents, and linseed oil. It does not dissolve celllulose esters or ethers, PVC, polyvinyl chloride acetate or rubber chloride. n-Butanol is used extensively in conjuction with xylol in stoving finishes where it appears to act as a very efficient latent solvent.

6. Isobutyl Alcohol $(CH_3)_2$ CH. CH_2 OH

It has found application in the manufacture of cellulose nitrate lacquers, in stoving and catalysed finishes containing animo-resins, and in wash primers. It also behaves satisfactorily in phenol-formaldehyde coatings, PVC emulsions, epoxy primers, and any coatings where a medium boiling alcohol is required.

7. Secondary Butyl Alcohol

It has the following physical constants.

Specific gravity	0.806
Boiling Point	99°C
Flash Point	21°C

It is extensively used as a medium boiling solvent in lacquers and is a latent solvent for cellulose nitrate.

8. Di-acetone Alcohol $CH_3COCH_2C.(OH)(CH_3)_2$

It is a colourless, odourless liquid with the following physical properties:

Specific gravity	0.942
Boiling Point	167°C
Flash Point	37°C

It is a good solvent for cellulose nitrate and is a useful high-boiling solvent for cellulose acetate lacquers.

V Esters

Esters are produced by the general reaction between an alcohol and an acid according to the equation

$$R.COOH + R'OH === R.COOR' + H_2O.$$

The reaction will proceed forward if the water formed is removed by any means.

The esters have a general similarity of properties, differing mainly in the distilation range and rate of evaporation, according to the complexity of the molecule.

Esters in general possess characteristics aromatic odours resembling those of various fruits. This is especially characteristic of acetates, the pungency increasing with the complexity of the molecule.

Butyl and amyl acetates are far the most widely used of the series.

This is the most widely used medium boiling solvent for cellulose nitrate lacquers. It is sufficiently volatile to leave the film readily but does not cause chilling of the film with consquent blushing. It is an excellent solvent for many other resins and oils viz.,ester gum, benzyl abietate, polystyrene, Polyvinyl acetate and chloride and copolymers, cyclohexanone-formaldehyde resin, gutta-percha resin; it is miscible with castor, linseed and other oils, also with hydrocarbons.

2. Amyl Acetate

Amyl acetate is the doyen of the cellulose nitrate solvents. Its one great disadvantage is its powerful, but harmless, '*banana*' odour which to some extent is objectionable.

Amyl acetate is a good solvent for cellulose nitrate, ethyl cellulose, ester gum, colophony, benzyl abeitate, cyclohexanone formaldehyde resin, polyvinyl acetate and aceto-chloride, rubber chloride *etc.* It partly dissolves shellac and copal ester; it attacks polythene, methyl-methacrylate resin and polyvinyl chloride; it doesnot dissolve cellulose acetate. It is miscible with castor, linseed and other varnish oils.

Ethers

These are generally inert towards the majority of chemicals and are useful solvents for oils and a number of natural resins. Among them glycol ethers are most important.

Glycol Ethers

Several of less volatile ethers formed by the combination of monohydric with polyhydric alcohols have come into industrial use as they form powerful solvents for cellulose esters. The most important of these is formed by the union of ethyl alcohol and ethylene glycol.

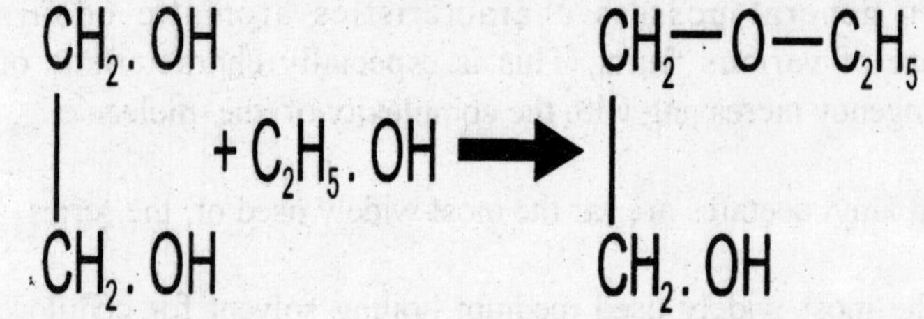

Ethylene glycol   Ethylene - glycol - mono - ethyl ether

It has the advantage of combining a suitable distillation range *(126-137°C)* and high flash point *(104°C)* with chemical stability and a faint and not unpleasent odour. It is a solvent for many natural resins and synthetics such as alkyds and epoxies.

Ketones

Ketones are a class of compound characterised by the presence of the carbonyl group >C=O. The lower members of the class are very volatile and highly inflammable liquids and are soluble in water. The following ketones are among the most important paint and lacquer solvents.

1. Acetone CH_3COCH_3

It possesses the following characteristics

Specific gravity	0.790
Boiling Point	56.2°C
Flash Point	16.5°C

It is one of the most powerful organic solvents and is used as a low-boiling solvent in some cellulose acetate and nitrate lacquers. The great solvent power renders it an attractive ingredient for paint strippers. It dissolves cellulose acetate, tripropionate, benzoate, nitrate, aceto-nitrate, aceto-propionate, auto-butyrate, ethyl cellulose, glyceryl phthalate resins, thiourea resin, cyclohexanone-formal-dehyde resin, polyvinyl acetate, and chloro acetate *etc.* It is miscible with castor, linseed, china wood, cotton seed, palm, olive and other polymerised oils and with most hydrocarbons. It attacks benzyl cellulose, polyethene, polyvinyl chloride, methacrylate *etc.*

2. Methyl-Ethyl Ketone $CH_3COC_2H_5$

It is commercially known as ***MEK***. It is quite similar to acetone except that it has higher flash point and lower rate of evaporation. The physical constants are as follows :

Specific gravity	0.805
Boiling Point	79.6°C
Flash Point	7°C

MEK is used widely as a resin solvent, especially for cellulose nitrate, cellulose aceto-butyrate and for ethyl cellulose. It is not a good solvent for cellulose acetate.

Chlorinated Hydrocarbons

The hydrogen atoms in both saturated and unsaturated hydrocarbons can be replaced by chlorine and may of these substitution products are useful solvents.

1. Methylene chloride CH_2Cl_2

It is a highly volatile liquid with boiling point 41°C and specific gravity 1.336. It is a very powerful solvent and is a major component of many non-inflammable paint strippers.

2. Ethylene Dichloride, $ClCH_2CH_2Cl$

It boils at 84°C and has a specific gravity of 1.44. It is also a powerful solvent and is used in paint strippers.

3. Trichlorethylene $Cl_2C=CHCl$

It boils at 87°C and has a specific gravity of 1.48. It is a powerful solvent and evaporates rapidly. It is a sole solvent in a dipping paint.

4. Chloroform $CHCl_3$

It is perhaps one of the most effective solvent but due to its highly narcotic nature it does not find wide application as a lacquer solvent.

5. Carbon Tetrachloride CCl_4

It is one of the most widely used solvents of this group. It is a colourless, non-inflammable liquid. It is dangerous toxic and generates poisonous gases. Its boiling range is 76-77.5°C, sp. gravity — 1.601 to 1.607.

It dissolves some varieties of cellulose acetate and dinaphthenate but not the nitrate or propionate; it is a good solvent for ethyl cellulose, benzyl resin, polystyrene, rosin, ester gum, thiourea resin; it does not dissolve shellac, hard copal, polyvinyl chloride and chloroacetate.

Plasticizers

The function of a plasticizer in paints and varnishes is to remain permanently in the film and improve its flexibility without impairing its other properties. The ideal plasticizer is a substance completely compatible with the other ingredients, non-volatile, and chemically stable and inert. The important classes of plasticizers are the following:

1. Esters

These comprise the largest class. The boiling points of esters increase with increasing molecular weight until the volatility of the material decreases to the point where it can be used as a plasticizer.

The following list comprises a few of the many ester plasticizers in common use with their boiloing points and the materials for which they are satisfactory plasticizers.

Plasticizer	*B.P.°C (760 mm)*	*Plasticizer for*
Triacetin	280	Cellulose acetate Cellulose nitrate
Dimethyl phthalate	284	Cellulose acetate
Dibutyl phthalate	340	Cellulose nitrate Ethyl cellulose vinyls
Di-octyl phthalate	230 at 5mm Hg	Cellulose nitrate, vinyls
Tributyl phosphate	290	Cellulose nitrate
Tricresyl phosphate	365	Cellulose nitrate

2. Castor Oil

It is a non-drying oil, completely non-volatile and remains permanently in the film.

3. Blown Castor Oil

It is a high viscosity material and is used as a plasticizer in cellulose undercoats and primers.

4. Camphor

Camphor was the first plasticizer to be incorporated into cellulose nitrate. It is ring ketone of the terpene family and possesses the structure :

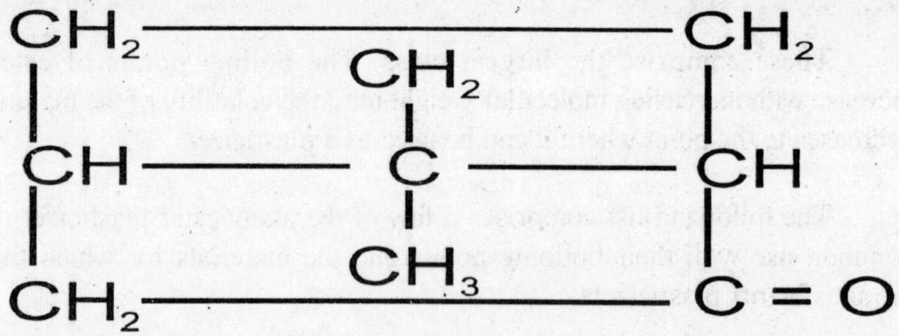

Camphor is a solid with specific gravity 0.992 and melting point 178°C. It is used to a small extent as a plasticiser in spirit varnishes and lacquers, and largely as a plasticizer for cellulose esters.

5. Chlorinated Waxes

A range of liquid plasticizer, derived from hydrocarbon waxes, and are completely non-volatile and are used as plasticizer for vinyls and cellulose nitrate.

Liquid or solid paraffins in the C_{10} and C_{30} range can be chlorinated in the presence of light to a chlorine content of 40-70% giving either viscous liquids or solids which have a variety of applications. The average physical property of chlorinated paraffin waxes depends on :

(a) *The nature of paraffin raw material*

(b) *The extent of chlorination*

(c) *The conditions of chlorination, especially the temperature.*

The chlorine content in the commercially available chloro paraffin is designed after the trade name. Thus CEECLOR 48 *(an ICI product)* means that this chloro paraffin has 48% chlorine in it.

Properties and Uses

These are lightly yellow to amber colour, viscous liquids or solids. The specific gravity of liquid chlorinated paraffin wax increases with increasing chlorine content.

The chlorinated paraffin waxes *(CPW)* of the middle range *i.e.*

around 40-45% chlorine content find their most important usuage as a plasticizer because of their compatiblity with a large variety of resins and plastics. The major use of chlorinated paraffin wax (CPW) is as a secondary plasticizer for PVC resins. CPW is also used as plasticizer or plasticizer-extender for other plastics like synthetic rubber, chlorinated rubber, nitrocellulose and polystyrene *etc.*

6. Chlorinated Diphenyls

Chlorinated diphenyls consist of non-volatile plasticizers of varying chlorine content and molecular weight. They are used as plasticizers for chlorinated rubber, vinyls and cellulose nitrate. Their use is somewhat restricted by slight toxic properties. These plasticizers are permanently thermoplastic, have low volatility are non-corrosive to metal, non-oxidizing, and are not hydrolysed by water or alkalies.

The chlorinated diphenyls are also used in transparent strippable protective coatings where they produce compositions of considerable rigidity, with good tensile strengths but low impact strengths.

3

MORE OTHER IMPORTANT DETAILS ON SOLVENTS AND PLASTICISERS

Introduction

Organic liquids are largely used in the manufacture of paints and kindred products, their principal function being as volatile solvents or thinners, to lower the viscosity of a paint or varnish temporarily, to facilitate application. After the material has been applied to a surface the thinner is no longer required, and the essential feature of this type of a solvent is complete volatility at ordinary temperatures.

Another class of organic liquid is used as *plasticisers*, the function of which is to remain permanently in the film of paint or varnish after application in order to impart elasticity to it. In contradistinction to the volatile solvents, plasticisers should also be chemically stable, and not alter in properties on prolonged exposure.

Volatile Solvents

Until some fifty years ago turpentine and alcohol were the only volatile solvents of any importance, but the number has increased considerably, particularly in the past fifteen years. The materials now available fall into several distinct groups, namely :-

Turpentines Petroleum distillates Coal-tar distillates. Hydrocarbons chlorides and sulphides.	Alcohols. Ketones. Esters

Turpentines

The solvents in this group are mainly derived from the resinous exudations of various species of pine and other coniferae. They consist essentially of mixtures of various members of the group of aromatic hydrocarbons known as terpenes, which all have the empirical formula $C_{10}H_{16}$. These differ amongst themselves mainly in the grouping of the atoms in the molecule, and are closely similar in properties.

The chief terpenes occurring in the varieties of turpentine are :-

	Specific Gravity	Boiling Point °C	Refracti--ve index	Optical Activity	Chief Source
alpha-Pinene (Dextro-pinene, or australene,)	0.858-0.860	156-160	1.4655	+21	American Turpentine
ß-Pinene (Leavo-pinene, or terebenthene	0.858-0.860	156-160	1.4655	-40	French Turpentine
Dipentene,	0.845	178	1.4731	nil	Elemi
Sylvestrene,	0.848	176	1.4757	+66	Russian Turpentine

The resinous exudations from the different species of pine trees contain these and other terpenes in varying proportions in combination with solid resins. The name turpentine was originally applied to such resinous exudations, which were collected and used as varnishes in their original state.

It was soon found, however, that the value of the materials was considerably enhanced by subjecting it to distillation, when it was separated into a volatile liquid and a solid resin. This process became an established industry, the solid resin being known as *"colophony"* or *"rosin"*, and the liquid portion as *"spirit of turpentine"* or *"Oil of turpentine"*. This name is now-a-days very generally contracted to *"turpentine"* and popularly, contracted further to *" turps"*. As the name *"oleo-resin"* forms a distinctive term for the natural product, it is a convenient practice to use the name turpentine as a generic term for the volatile spirit obtained by distillation of the oleo-resin from any species of pine.

For technical purposes the turpentine may be grouped into four main types :-

American, obtained mainly from the long leaf pine *(pinus paulstris)*, and produced chiefly in the southern United States - notably Virginia and Carolina. This is the predominant type of turpentine used in this country.

S.European, obtained largely from the maritime pine. *(Pinus maritima)*. It is produced chiefly in the South of France, also in Spain, Portugal, Greece, and Austria, and is the chief type used on the continent, comparatively small quantities being imported into this country.

Indian, obtained principally from the chir pine *(Pinus longifolia)*, The industry is of recent development, and the product is mainly consumed in the East, little being available for export.

Scandinavion, obtained from the Scotch fir *(Pinus sylvestris)*. The bulk of this is not a true turpentine, but corresponds more to a tar spirit, being obtained by the destructive distillation of the wood. Some is now prepared, however, by steam distillation.

The production of turpentine is an industry of considerable dimensions. The consumption increased rapidly towards the end of the nineteenth century, and reached a maximum just prior to the war, when the world output of all grades approximately to 170,000 tons.

The relatively amounts produced annually in the various countries of origin are appproximately :-

United States,	100,000 tons
Greece,	3,000 tons
France,	30,000 tons
India,	1,000 tons
Spain	6,000 tons
Miscellaneous	3,000 tons

The imports of turpentine into this country amount to from 30,000 to 40,000 tons annually.

Manufacture

The method of obtaining the crude oleo-resin for distillation is the same in principle in all countries, with minor differences of detail. Incisions are made in the tree, and the oleo-resin exuding from these is collected.

In most countries the trees growing naturally in the forests are tapped in this way, and as the process in time kills the tree, the forests gradually become depleted. In france, the outstanding features of the industry are the systematic planting of the trees and the working of them in sections, so that the supply is continuous and there is no wast or destruction of the forest. The permanency of the supply is safeguarde by the systematic replanting of the forests in proportion as the trees die or are felled.

The turpentine was originally extracted from the oleo-resin by dry distillation, but this gives a very inferior product, and was replaced by steam distillation. about 100 years ago. In the more modern types of plant steam distillation under reduced pressure is practiced, whilst dry distillation in *vacuo* is employed in the production of : *"English distilled turpentine"* by the refining of Scandinavion pine oils.

Composition

The several types of turpentine have vertain peculiarities by which they can be identified, of which the most characteristic is the odour, this being due to a small proportion of essential oil, which differs in composition in each species of pine.

The differences in composition and properties are shown in the following table :-

	American	S.European	Indian
COMPOSITION:-			
Australene (alpha–pinene),	72%	37%	60.8%
Terebenthene (ß-pinene),	28%	63%	-----
Carene and longifolene,	-----	-----	10.2%
PHYSICAL PROPERTIES :-			
Optical rotation,	+8 to16	-18 to 40	-2 to 6
Specific gravity,	0.860 - 0.880	0.857-0.872	0.865-0.880
Flash Point,	90°- 95°F,	86°- 90°F	99°F
Distillation range,	150°- 180°C	155°- 170°C	165°-175°C
Refractive index,	1.466-1.478	1.468-1.478	1.481

Properties

The main properties of all true turpentines, distilled from oleo-resins, are practically identical, and there is no technical ground for preferring one to the other. The preference for american in this country is based purely on prejudice, owing to the unfamiliar smell of other varieties. In france and central Europe, S.European turpentine is regarded as the standard type, and preferred to american. It cannot be regarded as in any way sophistication to supply french or spanish as geniune turpentine, and undoubtedly a considerable quantity of this type comes over here and is used by varnish makers as American.

Colour :

Turpentine in general is a clear limpid liquid, and when properly prepared should be perfectly colourless. Carelessness in preparation will result in a distinctly coloured product, and some samples are liable to develop colour on exposure to sunlight. In order to ensure uniformity, definite standards have been agreed upon, and specifications usually require the turpentine to pass the standard for *"water white"*.

Odour :

The smell of turpentine is not unpleasent in small quantity, but prolonged exposure to it is distinctly objectionable. Its effect varies very greatly with different persons, some being rapidly affected with headache and sickness, where as others suffer no inconvenience at all. It is this physiological action of turpentine vapour which is largely responsible for the popular objection to the *"smell of paint"* It may be said in passing that whilst the unpleasent effects are by no means imaginary, and extreme cases of suspectibility have been known to occur where definite illness has been caused by the vapour, the effect is in general merely temporary inconvenience during exposure. Painters constantly working with it soon acquire immunity and suffer no ill effects whatever from constant exposure to the vapour. The smell of turpentine was at one time regarded as the hallmark of a good paint, but with the recognition of the value of other thinners this is becoming less general.

Distillation Range

Being a substance of complex composition, turpentine, in common with most other hydrocarbon solvents, has a variable boiling point, the recognised distillation range being from 150° to 180°C. These limits are fairly constant and any marked variation indicates impurity. The regularity of fractions coming over between this range varies somewhat in different samples, but not to the same extent as with the petroleum distillates.

Turpentine is readily inflammable, burning with a smoky flame which deposits soot in large flakes, a peculiar order being evolved during the burning.

Evaporation

When exposed to the air in a thin film turpentine evaporates almost completely, leaving no stain if tested by the usual method of pouring a few drops on to clean filter paper and allowing it to stand for half an hour.

If the test be carried out under more critical conditions, however, it will be found that the evaporation is not absolutely complete, a slight trace of residue remaining. This is due ro the fact that during the evapration in presence of large excess of air a chemical reaction takes place, the common experience that turpentine develops a sticky film on the neck of a bottle in which it is kept for any length of time being due to this action. If turpentine is evaporated under carefully controlled conditions it will be found that a definite residue is obtained on evaporation, The amount varying according to the length of time the turpentine has been stored.

Apart from this polymerisation, the evaporation of turpentine is perfectly regular and uniform.

These evaporative properties of turpentine account for its great popularity and unique position as a thinner for paints, and more particularly for varnishes and enamels. There is considerable evidence for thinking that under the conditions which obtain in the drying of paints and varnishes the turpentine acts as a carrier of oxygen to the oil, absorbing oxygen from the air and giving it off again in contact with the oil, and thus facilitating the drying of the film. Any non-volatile residue formed during the evaporation becomes part of the film and acts in conformity with it, ultimately hardening to a solid resin by further poymerisation . This property of polymerising on drying is characteristics of the turpene group of solvents, and is shared only by the partially saturated hydrides of naphthalene described in a later section.

The ***solvent power*** of turpentine exactly answers to the requirements of a paint and varnish thinner. That is to say, it dissolves readily all vegetable and mineral oils, but does not dissolve the linoxyn formed by the drying of a paint film, so that a fresh coat of paint and varnish made with it can be put on a previous coat after drying without bringing it up. It dissolves soft resins, but only dissolves the copals and hard resins after they have been *"run"* and subsequently combined with oil. As a solvent for mineral waxes it is not quite so good as the coal tar hydrocarbons, but it forms a good solvent for animal and vegetable waxes and a solution of bees wax in turpentine is largely used as a furniture polish.

Turpentine is practically insoluble in water, but water is soluble in it to a slight extent, and it is generally contains traces. It mixes in all proportions with the monohydric alcohols and other organic solvents.

Chemical Reactions

Turpentine, being an unsaturated body, is chemically active. If kept in an iron or steel container for any length of time the metal will corrode, particularly along the surface of the liquid, which develops a reddish colour due to colloidal oxide of iron This action can be prevented by protecting the inner surface of the container with a lacquer of shellac or synthetic resin, and storage in iron tanks so protected has given satisfactory results. Zinc or galavanised iron containers cannot be used unless protected in the same way, as the exposed metal is attacked with formulation of zinc salts which give a turbid appearance to the turpentine. The most common practice is to use either wooden or tinned iron vessels for storage.

Like other unsaturated compounds, turpentine absorbs halogens readily; the reaction is very vigrous, and can take place with explosive violence. The absorption of iodine is utilised as a test for the purity of turpentine in the same way as for oils; the iodine value recorded by different observers varies from 282 to 380.

Turpentine also reacts with sulphuric acid, polymerising to form terbene and colophene ($C_{20}H_{32}$). As most of the substances, such as petroleum, used as adulterants for turpentine, are not acted upon by sulphuric acid, this reaction forms a useful method of determining the purity. This test was first elaborated by Candless and has been adopted in most official specifications.

Specifications - B.S.I. specifications, No. 244, for Turpentine, Type 1, refers to the true turpentine described above, distilled from the oleo-resin, irrespective of the country of origin.

This contains the following provisions :-

Appcarencc

As free as possible from colour, and free from water and visible impurities.

Specific Gravity at 15°C - 0.862 to 0.872.

Distillation Range

Not more than 1 percent below 150°C and not less than 95 percent below 170°C.

Residue on Evaporation

Not exceeding 2 percent, which must be wholly organic.

Refractive Index (D, 20°C.) — 1.469 to 1.478.

Polymerisation Residue

Not exceeding 11 percent by volume, with a refractive index not less than 1.490.

Flash Point

Not below 90°F.

Rectified Oil of Turpentine

This is a purified turpentine, prepared by treating it with an alkali to neutralise the free acids and redistilling with steam.

Fat Turpentine

If turpentine is kept at a temperature of about 80°C or is exposed for a considerable period to air and sunlight, it undergoes a gradual combined process of oxidation and polymerisation, ultimately changing into a liquid of syrupy consistency. This was used formerly by artists, and is still employed to a small extent as a medium in pottery and glass painting and in certain photographic processes.

Oxidised Turpentine

In the manufacture of synthetic camphor, pinene is extracted from turpentine, and the residue containing the other terpenes mixed with various chlorine derivatives is left as a by-product and used under this name. It resembles pine oil, but has a higher boiling point and slower evaporation.

Terbene is a mixture of dipentene and other hydrocarbons prepared by mixing turpentine with sulphuric acid and shaking. The treatment is repeated until the turpentine is optically inactive, and the product is then steam distilled.

It is a colourless liquid of characteristic odour, of the same general character as turpentine, slightly soluble in water. The boiling point should approximate to 160°C but ranges from 156° to 180°C, and the specific gravity at 15°C ranges from 0.862 to 0.866. When freshly prepared it is quite neutral, but on exposure to light and air it changes in a similar manner to turpentine, becoming acid, acquiring a yellow colour, and gradually resinifying.

American Wood Turpentine

This name is given to the variety of turpentine obtained from the stumps left in the ground on the felling of the pine trees.

When these stumps were first utilised as a source of turpentine they were subjected to destructive distilltion, which produced a very inferior turpentine they were subjected to destructive distillation, which produced a very inferior turpentine of bad colour and smell and contaminated with methyl alcohol and acetic acid; a product, in fact, which was not really turpentine, but more of the nature of tar spirit.

The modern plants employ a process in which the wood is reduced to powder and subjected to live steam in a digestor to extract the turpentine and pine oil and then boiled with petroleum spirit to dissolve out the rosin. This extraction is carried out in series, each charge of wood after steaming being washed with several charges of solvent on the multiple extraction system. After the extraction is completed the charge is finally steam distilled to recover the solvent.

The operation of the steam distillation process, although apparently simple, requires considerable skill and experience to produce a uniformly satisfactory product. The more carefully it is conducted the more closely does the product approximate to that obtained from the oleo-resin.

As now prepared by this steam distillation process, wood turpentine is closely similar to ordinary American turpentine, the main differance between the two being that the wood turpentine contains a material proportion of dipentine and a proportion of limonene and terpinene. This gives it a smell distinct from that of ordinary turpentine, but has the advantage of increasing its solvent power.

The physical data for this type of turpentine as given in B.S.I. specification, no. 290 are :-

Specific gravity	0.859—0.875
Distillation range	Not more than 1 percent, below 150°C Not more than 70 percent, below 170°C Not more than 90 percent, below 180°C
Residue	Not exceeding 2 percent.
Refractive index	1.463- 1.483
Polymerisation residue	Not above 16 percent.
Flash Point	Not below 90°F

Russian Turpentine also known as Polish, Swedish, or Finish turpentine is obtained from the scotch fir *(Pinus sylvestris)*, immense forests of which are found in Russian, Poland, Finland, and Scandinavia. It is produced by destructive distillation of the wood, and is charactercised by an extremely pungent and penetrating odour, which produces unpleasent effects on the user. The composition is complex and variable. The principal constituent is the terpene, sylvestrene, which is present to the extent of about 70 percent. Dextro-pinene forms from 10 to 15 percent, and there is a similar proportion of cymol, the balance being small quantities of creosote and hydrocarbons of high boiling point.

Russian turpentine is rarely obtained water-white like true turpentine, but generally has a decided straw colour, which deepens on storage, particularly if exposed to light. It evaporates rather more slowly than wood turpentine, and leaves a high percentage of residue. It absorbs oxygen more freely than true turpentine, and rapidly increases in viscosity on standing.

The physical properties are :-

Boiling range	160° — 180°C.
Specific gravity	0.862 — 0.875
Flash Point	95° — 100°F
Refractive index	1.476
Optical rotation	+24

Tar Spirit

If the crude tar obtained by the destructive distillation of wood is re-distilled, a volatile spirit is obtained which is employed to some extent as a solvent. The principal source is Stockholm tar, and a similar product is obtained as a by-product in the production of wood turpentine by the destructive distillation process. When freshly prepared, tar spirit is a light straw colour, but it is gradually darkness on exposure to light, ultimately turning to a dark brown viscous liquid.

It has mild but penetrating odour of creosote, and is extremely complex in composition, containing terpenes, cresote, acetone, vand various phenolic bodies. The physical constants are very variable but the boiling range usually runs from 160° to 270°C, and the specific gravity from 0.9 to 1.0.

It evaporates rather slowly and leaves a slight non-volatile residue, on account of which the odour persists for a long time. It is, in fact, closely allied to Russian turpentine, which is smetimes sold as tar spirit.

On account of its content of ketones, tar spirit has a strong solvent power, and is useful for the penetration of black stoving varnishes, being a good solvent for pitches.

Pine Oll

It is a by-product of the wood turpentine industry, coming over with the turpentine, from which it is separated by fractional distillation. It is also obtained as a by-product in the manufacture of wood pulp by the sulphite process.

It is a light straw-coloured oil with a pleasent odour resembling that of pine needle oil.

The physical data are :-

	R.C. Palmer	Teeple
Specific gravity at 15°C,	0.932- 0.935	0.935-0.947
Refractive index at 20°C,	1.4798-1.4815	1.4830
Boiling point,	190°- 195°C	206°C
Distillation range,	90 Percent between 190°-218°C	75 percent between 206°-218°C
Acidity,	Below 0.1 percent	-----
Moisture content,	Below 1.25 percent	3-4 percent
Flash Point,	76° F.	-----
Optical rotation,	-----	-11

It is used as a slow-drying solvent, being an excellent solvent for gums and resins, and is useful for many purposes on account of the powerful and very agreeable smell it imparts. It has the exceptional property of being actively germicidal, although non-poisous to human beings. On accout of this lack of toxicity, combined with its pronounced smell and unpleasent taste, it has been suggested as a denaturant for alcohol.

Rosin Spirit

It is produced by the destructive distillation of low-grade rosin, coming off before the rosin oil. The crude distillate is treated with caustic soda to neutralise the free acid. and re-distillate to produce the commercial rosin spirit.

This refined rosin spirit is an almost colourless liquid. somewhat resembling turpentine. but differing in physical properties. The smell is quite characteristic and quite different from that of any of the turpentines. When properly refined, and entirely free from non-volatile rosin oil, rosin spirit froms a good solvent for oils, and it was largely used at one time as a cheap substitute for turpentine. It does not form a really satisfactory thinner for paints, as it evaporates in an irregular manner, leaving a viscous residue which dries badly and hinders the oxidation of the oil. With the advent of the abundant supplies of petroleum solvents and the introduction of the other modern solvents and the introduction of the other modern solvents, its use has considerably decreased, and it is little used in the paint industry at the present time.

Petroleum Distillates

White Spirit

The first to recognise the petroleum of a petroleum distillate as a solvent in the paint industry appears to have been Samuel Banner, who introduced it as Patent Turpentine in 1885. For many years it was regarded as a cheap adulterant for turpentine, and generally known as *"Turpentine substitute"*. As its use developed, however, it attained recognition as a distinct solvent, and name *"white spirit"* became established.

Manufacture

The raw material for white spirit is the middle portion obtained in the preliminary refinement of petroleum intermediate between the light motor spirits and the burning and lubricating oils.

As the white spirit manufacturer is concerned chiefly to produce a satisfactory article for use as a solvent, a great deal depends in the first instance on the choice of his raw material, the chief point to consider being to obtain an oil containing the highest possible content of the aromatic series, which have a greater solvent power than the paraffin series. The best white spirit is obtained from Borneo petroleum , but an excellent quality is also made from Roumanian oil.

Starting with the semi-refined oil delivered from the wells, this is first treated to remove impurities; the chief of these are thiophenes and other sulphur compounds, which are very objectionable in the finished product, and unsaturated hydrocarbons of the olefine series. The complete removal of both these classes of impurities is essential to a first class, sweat-smelling product. The purified spirit is then discharged into stills fitted with steam coils, where it is heated by steam at a pressure of about 110 lbs., superheated to about 540°F., and distilled off under reduced pressure.

By careful regulation of the temperature and pressure of the steam, the distillate is separated into fractions of different boiling range. In order to render this separation more complete the vapour coming from the still passes first through a fractionating column, and then through a dephlegmator, the design of which varies in different works, but generally consists of a vertical steel cylinder in which are fitted a number of copper tubes through which a flow of water is maintained. The vapour from the fractionating column passes round these tubes, and any portion of the distillate boiling above the required limit is condensed and returned to the fractionating column by means of a return pipe in the bottom.

From the dephlegmator the vapour passes into condensers, consisting of coils immersed in a tank through which a steady stream of cold water is circulated, the condensed liquid from the condensers being discharged into storage tanks.

Properties :

The odour of white spirit is one of its most useful properties. If not properly prepared it may retain traces of olefines and sulphur compounds, and is then liable to have a persistent and unpleasent smell, but if properly prepared it has a characteristic smell, less pungent and less unpleasent to work with for prolonged periods than that of almost any other organic solvent.

Colour

White spirit should be perfectly colourless, and should easily pass the test for water-white. It should also be perfectly clear and free from any trace of suspended matter.

Distillation Range

The essential requirement for white spirit is that it must be completely volatile, but on the other hand must not evaporate with extreme rapidity. It must, therefore, be free from highly volatile spirits, and also from the non-volatile paraffins used as burning oils.

The limits to which all white spirits should confirmed are :

The initial boiling point should not be be below 140°C.

The end point should not be above 230°C.

Flash Point

This is closely propotional to the boiling range and ranges from 75° to 100° F. The essential point is that it must be above 73°F. (23°C) in order to comply with the regulations as regards inflamability for transport and shiping.

Within these limits the requiremens of consumers as regards the volatility and flash point will vary somewhat in different industries and at different times. Most distilleries offer three or four standard grades of white spirit, to suit the requirements of different consumers. The following are the standard grades of one of the following producers :-

Grade	Specific Gravity	Boiling Range	Flash Point
Special (extra light),	0.784	143-180°C	74°F
No.1 (light),	0.787	145-200	80
No.2 (medium),	0.790	158-200	90
No.3 (heavy),	0.794	160-210	100-105
No.4 (extra heavy),	0.807	180-220	125

For use as a paint and varnish thinner, a medium grade is required. The initial boiling point should not be below 150°C. ; a lower boiling point indicates the presence of hydrocarbons which evaporate too rapidly and cause the paint to have a tendency to commence setting before it is properly brushed out. On the other hand, the end point must not be above 210°C., as a higher limit implies a *"tail"* of non-volatile hydrocarbons which retard the drying and tend to cause a weak film. The bulk, in fact at least 90 percent, should distill between the limits 160° and 200°, and it is of real advantage if the fractions come over evenly between these two limits.

The **evaporation rate** is of considerable practical importance. For most purposes it is essential, not only that the spirit shall evaporate entirely in a reasonable time at ordinary temperatures, but that it should be evaporate at an even rate.

Illingworth has published the result of careful experiments on the evaporation of white spirit in relation to its boiling range, from which it is abudantly clear that for paint manufacture 90 percent. should distill below 200° and all at 218°C., and that in a spirit showing any content boiling above 200°C. the evaporation is unoform up to this point and then exihibts a marked drop or *"tail"*.

The effect of such a *"Tail"* is not only to retard the drying of the paint, but to produce a soft, tacky film, for it must be remembered that the position is complicated in practice by the fact that the spirit is evaporating from a solution in oil, which oil is oxidising and increasing in viscosity at the same time. Under such condition it is well establised that even in the case of a highly volatile solvent the last traces become enmeshed in the drying film and only escape very slowly. The tendency of the *"tail"* is therefore, to remain permanently in the film. This effect is found to a still greater extent in varnishes and it is in this respect that the inferiority of white spirit to turpentine as a varnish thinner becomes apparent. Although turpentine ehibits a similar *"Tail"* on evaporation, this is due to the fact that it partially polymerises and oxidises during evaporation; the residue left in the film continues this action and ultimately hardens in conformity with the oil itself, becoming part of the film, whereas any residue from white spirit remains a more or less permanent source of weakness.

The absence of such a non-volatile residual is generally determined by the "*spot test*", which is carried out by placing five drops on a dry filter-paper and allowing it to stand for half an hour at ordinary atmospheric temperature, when the spirit should completely evaporate, leaving no trace of greasy mark on the paper. A more reliable method. is to place one drop of the sample under examination and one drop of a standard sample side by side on a clean sheet of plate glass, and note the relative time of evaporation to dryness and the absence of any greasy residue.

The **solvent power** of white spirit may be described as moderate. It mixes freely with all mineral and vegetable oils, and is, therefore, quite satisfactory as a paint thinner, but is an indifferent solvent for oxidised oils such as blown oils, stand oils, and thickened tung oil. Cases frequently occur, particularly with gold size made from wood oil and rosin, where the addition of white spirit will cause precipitation of the resin and polymerised oil on standing for some time. Similarly, a blown oil will often dissolve in white spirit, but separate out again on keeping for some days. The same thing happens characteristically with the metallic salts of fatty acids such as lead linoleate and cobalt linoleate. Liquid driers prepared by dissolving such metallo-organic compounds are very liable to separate out on keeping, particularly if chilled, unless very carefully prepared. Linoxyn is practically insoluble in white spirit, and a throughly hardened paint film is not affected by it.

Freshly prepared rosin is freely soluble in white spirit, but rosin which has matured for some time and suffered the chemical changes which take place on storage is only partially soluble, leaving a considerable amount of insoluble residue. The soft resins such as Damar and Manila are moderately soluble, but generally form cloudy solutions, and have a tendency to drop out of solution on storage. Hard resins are practically insoluble, except after melting and combining with oil. Oil varnishes can be thinned with white spirit, but the solution formed is not so stable as that made with such solvents as turpentine.

White spirit is insoluble in water, but mixes in all proportions with most organic solvents. Methyl and ethyl alcohols are exceptions, but the addition of a higher alcohol — butyl or amyl— causes a mixture of white spirit and alcohol to become mutually soluble.

As it consists essentially of fully saturated and cylic hydrocarbons, white spirit is chemically very stable and does not act as an oxygen carrier in the manner characteristic of turpentine. The drying of paints and other preparations made with it is purely a matter of evaporation as far as the thinner is concerned, and it does not affect the drying of the oil in any way.

White spirit made from a suitable oil which has been efficiently refined prior to distillation should be practically free from sulphur compounds. An inferior or improperly refined product is, however, liable to contain small percentages of various organic sulphur compounds. The presence of these is extremely objectionable, as they react with metalic compounds such as lead, cobalt, or manganese salts used as driers in paints and varnishes, causing discolouration. Such discolouration is noticed, for instance, when a varnish is thinned with a white spirit containing sulphur.

Uses

The principal use of white spirit is as a volatile solvent or thinner in paints, boot polishes, metal polishes, and floor and furniture polishes. For this purpose it has taken a recognised place, and is used extensively and in large quantities. For the purpose of a thinner, where uniform and complete evaporation on exposure to the air is the essential requirement, it is perfectly satisfactory, and has advantage over such solvents as turpentine of being low in cost and having the comparatively mild odour reffered to. Where other considerations have to be taken into account, however, the case is different. The relative merits of white spirit as compared with turpentine as a thinner for high-class varnishes and enamels are a subject of frequent controversy but in the present writer's opinion white spirit is essentially a thinner for paints rather than varnishes. Its solvent power for oils is practically equivalent to that of turpentine, but its solvent power for resin is distinctly inferior. In varnishes also its chemical inertness is a disadvantage, for it lacks the oxygen-carrying properties of unsaturated hydrocarbons such as turpentine and tetralin, which facilitate the hardening of the film and exercise a certain bleaching effect on the oil.

Another purpose for which spirit is extensively used is as a cleaning agent in paint, printing ink, and similar factories, and for cleaning off oil from machinery etc. It is also preferable to turpentine for washing out painter's brushes, etc., as it evaporates without the oxidation and consequent resinification characteristic of turpentine, which tends to leave the brush slightly sticky and promotes the condition known to the painter as *"lousy"*. For such cleaning purposes, it is waste to use a paint-maker's grade of white spirit.

The heavier grades with an end point up to 230°, which are cheaper to produce, are actually more efficient for the purpose, as the less volatile constituents remain on the article cleaned for some time after evaporation of the bulk as an extremely slight film, sufficient to retard the rusting of the metal containers, etc., and to keep the hairs of brushes in a flexible condition.

Specification :

The B.S.I. specification for white spirit, for paints, contains the following provisions :-

Description

Wholly a petroleum product, *"water-white"*, clear free from water and solid matter.

Distillation Range :

Not more than 10 percent below 150°C. Not less than 80 percent below 190°C.

Freedom from Grease — Determined by spot test.

Residue on Evaporation

Not to Exceed 0.2 percent, and to be wholly organic.

Reaction — Neutral

Freedom from Sulphur Compounds — Determined by copper strip test.

Volatility — Similar to that of turpentine.

Flash Point — Not below 78°F.

Petrol

This is obtained from the *"Tops"* or first distillation of petroleum — the portion coming over below 160°C.; it is mainly used as a motor spirit, and to certain extent as a solvent. It is not so good a solvent for most purposes as the equally volatile benzol obtained from coal tar, but it is useful for the preparation of certain types of enamels where rapid evaporation is desired and the pungent smell of solvent naphtha is objected to.

By further distillation petrol is refined into fractions with a very close boiling range of any desired volatility, such as :-

Petroleum Ether

It consists mainly of hexane (C_6H_{14}) and heptane(C_7H_{16}) with a boiling point below 60°C and a specific gravity below 0.670. It is used as an alternative to ether as an analytical extracting agent for oils and fats and similar purposes.

Petroleum Spirit

The fraction coming over between 60° and 100°C., consisting of about 75 percent paraffin hydrocarbons, chiefly hexane and heptane, the remainder being mainly olefines with a small and varying amount of aromatic hydrocarbons depending on the source from which it is obtained.

Benzine

It is the name generally applied to a re-distilled and purified petroleum spirit, free from sulphur and other impurities, which evaporates completely wothout leaving any trace of residual. By careful fractionation the distillers produce benzine to any specific boiling range between 60° and 120°C. to suit the particular purpose for which it is to be used.

Shale Naphtha is a product similar to petroleum spirit, obtained by the distillation of bituminous shales.

Coal-Tar Distillates

When coal-tar is distilled in the same manner as petroleum, a series of products are obtained, of which the following are used to some extent as volatile solvents :-

Benzol :-

It is a clear, colourless liquid with a peculiar smell, due to the presence of small quantities of impurities, the approximate composition being :

Benzene	60-75 %
Toluene	24 %
Light hydrocarbons	4-6 %
Carbon bisulphide	2 %

It is mainly being used in the paint industry is as a thinner or diluent for cellulose ester enamels. It is employed as a solvent for oil-soluble dyes in the preparation of stains for woodwork, owing to its high penetrative power; it is also used as an ingredient and diluent of paint removers, and is sometimes added in small proportion to turpentine substitutes to increase their solvent power.

Benzene is the pure compound C_6H_6 the fundamental member of the aromatic series of hydro carbons, the impure distillate described above being known as benzol for distinction. It is obtained from benzol by treatment with sulphuric acid and fractional distillation, and is a colourless, very limpid liquid, with a high refractive index, and a characteristic unobjectionable odour. It solidifies at 5-5°C. and boils 80.5°C. It gives off a highly inflammable vapour at ordinary temperatures, the flash point being 8°C.

It is practically insoluble in water, but soluble in all proportions in the lower and higher alcohols and most other organic solvents.

Solvent Naphtha is the next fraction in the distillation of refined coal-tar naphtha after the removal of the benzol. It owes its pronounced solvent power, combined with great volatility, to the presence of a large proportion of xylenes and cumenes, but has an exceedingly complex and variable composition, including, in addition to the above, a proportion of paraffin hydrocarbons and a small content of naphthalene.

It is generally separated into two fractions :-

1. Light Solvent Naphtha, which distills 90 percent below 160°C. This grade is mainly used as a solvent for rubber, for which it is almost the only solvent of industrial importance.

2. Heavy Solvent Naphtha, distilling between 160°C and 190°C and usually specified 90 percent below 90°C. It is mainly used as a solvent and thinner for quick-drying paints such as anti-fouling composition, and as a solvent for pitches. It is also used, in conjuction with white spirit, as a thinner for priming paints for wood work. Its value in this direction is partly due to the fact that it has a greater penetrative power for wood than other solvents, and it is particularly useful for the priming of sappy or resinous woods. In addition to this, it has considerable toxic and germicidal properties. It, therefore, tends to preserve the wood by sterlising it and destroying any mould spores or insect eggs it may contain which facilitate its decay. It is also used as a thinner for cellulose ester lacquers.

Toluene, or methyl-benzene, is the next homologue in the benzene series of hydrocarbons, and consists of benzene with one hydrogen replaced by methane, having the formula C_6H_5 CH_3.

It has a lower solidifying point than benzene, below —95°C, and the boiling point, following the usual rule that the boiling point rises with the complexity of the hydrocarbon is 111°C.

An almost pure toluene is obtainable commercially with a nearly constant boiling point. Less pure commercial toluene is generally known as "*toluol*" for distinction, and is manufactured on a large scale. The boiling point of this should range between 110° and 120°C.

Toluene is employed for many industrial purposes, but is not extensively used as a solvent in the paint industry, except as a thinner for cellulose ester lacquers.

Xylene, the next highest member of the series, $C_6H_4(CH_3)_2$, is used to a considerable extent as a solvent for asphaltum, and also in the printing industries for certain processess where a very even evaporation is essential.

Hydrogenated Naphthalenes

These are synthetic products, prepared by the action of hydrogen on naphthalene. Naphthalene is a highly unsaturated substance, containing five double bonds, and, theoretically, the hydrogenation of naphthalene can take place in five stages according to the number of double bonds in the molecule which are saturated. All these five possible derivatives have been prepared experimentally — namely, the di-, tetra-, hexa-, octa-, and deca- hydronaphthalenes. Only two of these compounds are produced industrially; the tetra-hydride, known as tetralin for short, and the deca-hydride, or dekalin; in these one and both of the benzene rings are saturated respectively, thus :-

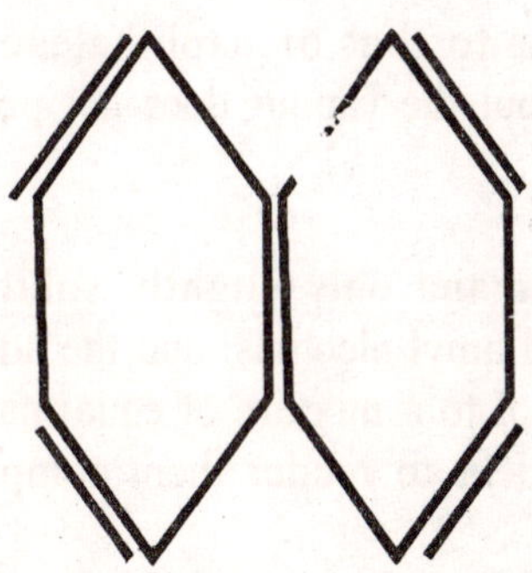

Naphthalene, $C_{13}H_8$

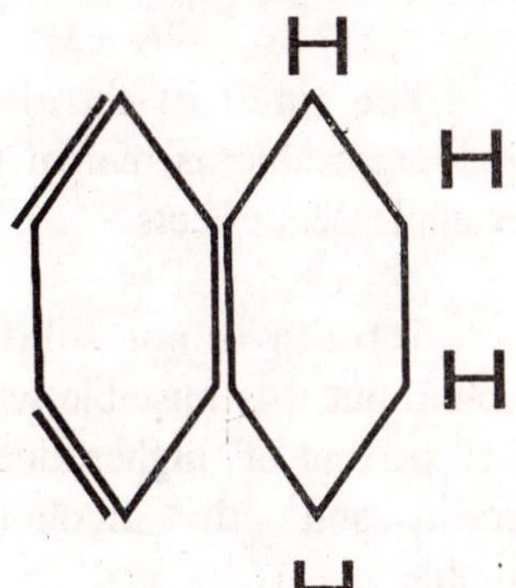

Tetrahydronaphthalene, $C_{10}H_{12}$, Tetralin, or Tetranap

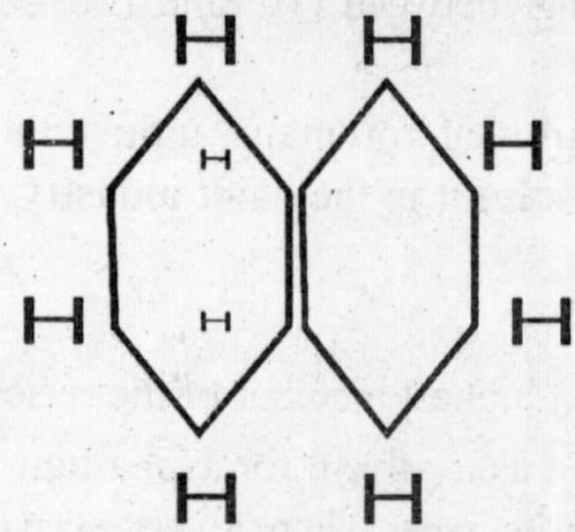

Decahydronaphthalene, $C_{10}H_{18}$, or Dekalin

Tetralin

It is prepared by heating pure naphthalene with hydrogen under pressure in an autoclave in presence of a catalyst, such as finely divided nickel. It is prepared commercially in a practically pure state, having a nearly constant boiling point of 205°C. Being only partially saturated, it is closely similar to turpentine in its chemical properties. It is, for instance, capable of autooxidation in the same way; a sticky film develops on the neck of a bottle in which it is kept for any length of time the liquid gradually acquiring a pale straw colour. A similar occurs if it is evaporated over a water-bath at low temperature, when it turns yellow and ultimately resinifies.

The smell of tetralin is similar to that of naphthalene, and not so agreeable as that of turpentine, but the vapour does not produce any unpleasent effects.

Tetralin is not soluble in water and only slightly soluble in alcohol, but it is miscible with butyl and amyl alcohols, and the addition of 10 percent of higher alcohol or benzol to a mixture of equal parts of tetralin and ethyl alcohol is sufficient to render them completely miscible.

Tetralin ranks as one of the most powerful solvents for oils and resins. It not only dissolves all vegetables oils, but has a decided solvent action on linoxyn, and for that reason is too powerful to use by itself as a paint thinner as paint made with it would be liable to siften the undercoats. It does not act like alcohols in its solvent action, and does not dissolve shellac and similar substances which are soluble in methylated spirit.

The rate of evaporation is considerably slower than that of turpentine, and this, combined with its strong solvent action, renders it very useful in the preparation of paint removers. By using a mixture of tetralin and acetone one obtains a very powerful solvent, beacause the acetone attacks the film, which is then held in solution by the tetralin and kept soft for a sufficient time to enable it to be worked upon. At the time, it evaporates completely in a few hours, leaving a dry and clean surface for repainting.

Dekalin

If turpentine is re-treated with hydrogen in presence of a catalyst under higher temperature and pressure than those required for its formation from naphthalene, it is converted into the fully saturated deca-hydride, the name of which is contracted for convenience to dekalin.

The further hydrogenation is accompanied by a further change in properties, the boiling point falling to 190°C., the specific gravity to 0.890, and the refractive index to 1.4672. The odour of naphthalene entirely disappears, dekalin possessing a peculiar characteristic smell of its own, quite different from that of tetralin, and resembling that of damp straw.

Being a fully saturated body, it is chemically more stable and does not react to the same extent as tetralin . It does not resinify on evaporation, for example, amd may also be kept for prolonged periods without showing any change of properties. Its vapour appears to be quite without physiological effect either on animal or insect life. Its solvent power is considerably less pronounced than that of tetralin; according to the author's experience, it is practically equivalent to turpentine in this respect, as it mixes in all proportions with fatty oils and dissolves waxes and soft gums like damar, mastic and manila in equivalent proportions to turpentine. It doesnot, however, dissolve hard gums like kauri and copal, nor does it attack linoxyn.

It is practically insoluble in water and alochol, but mixes with other organic solvents. The rate of evaporation is rather quicker than that of tetralin, and as there is no oxidation during evaporation, it leaves no trace of non-volatile residue.

Alcohols

The alcohols are a large and important group of organic compound derived from hydrocarbons by the substitution of hydroxyl for one or more of the hydrogen atoms in the molecule.

They compare, very broadly speaking, with the alkalies and other inorganic hydroxides in their ability to combine with organic acids to form compounds, analogous to salts, known as esters.

Ethyl alcohol is by far the most important of the alcohols from the practical point of view, so much so that it is convenient and well-established practice for the term alcohol, when used without any qualification, to imply ethyl alcohol, other members of the group being always distinguished from it by giving the full name. Modern practice tends to establish distinctive names for the higher and lower homologues of ethyl alcohol in industrial use.

Thus :-

Methanol signifies methyl alcohol	CH_3OH
Ethanol signifies ethyl alcohol	C_2H_5OH
Proponal signifies propoyl alcohol	C_3H_7OH
Butanol signifies butyl alcohol	C_4H_9OH

Methyl Alcohol

It was originally produced by the destructive distillation or wood, but it is now largely produced synthetically, by the hydrogenation of carbon monoxide, which is effected by heating the mixed gases under gases under a pressure of about 200 atmosphere in presence of a catalyst. The alcohol can be obtained practically pure by this process, whereas that obtained distillation requires repeated fractionation to remove impurities. The pure alcohol is a colourless liquid with a faint odour resembling that of ethyl alcohol. It boils at 66°C under normal pressure and is miscible with water in all proportions. It has pronounced toxic properties, more so than ethyl alcohol, as it is oxidised in passing through the system, with formation of formaldehyde and formic acid.

Wood Spirit *(wood naphtha, wood alcohol, espirit de bois)*

This is the commercial impure grade of methyl alcohol prepared by the destructive distillation of hard woods such as beech or elm. The crude wood alcohol thus obtained contains about 82 percent, methyl alcohol with varying amounts of acetone, methyl esters, allyl alcohol, aldehyde, methylamine, etc. This is further distilled over lime to prepare the refined product, which contains about 95 percent methyl alcohol, the balance being mainly acetone.

This spirit is largely used as an adulterant for alcohol to render it undrinkable, on account of its objectionable taste and its cheapness. It is an advantage for this purpose that it does not materially affect the properties of alcohol as a solvent.

Wood spirit is miscible with water, and is a solvent for many inorganic substances as well as for fats, oils, and soft resins. The proportion of acetone it consists assists it as a solvent and extracting agent.

It is a good solvent for shellac, and is largely employed in the preparation of spirit varnishes.

Ethyl Alcohol

This is produced when ever a ferment such as yeast is allowed to act on sugar solutions of moderate strength at temperatures between 50°F. and 90°F. In theory, the process consists of a simple spilitting up of the sugar into alcohol and carbondioxide, but the actual reactions are far more complicated.

Alcohol for industrial purposes is usually made from cereals, in which the starch has first to be converted into sugar by the action of another organism in the process known as *"malting"*, and this is subsequently converted into alcohol by fermentation or *"mashing"*. The fermented mass contains alcohol, water, and fusel oil, which latter is a mixture of higher alcohols together with amall quantities of acetic acid, aldehyde, and esters mixed with the solid and unfermentable portions of the original grain. The alcohol is separated from this mixture by distillation.

Absolute Alcohol

This is ethyl alcohol in a state of almost chemical purity, and, in particular, anhydrous. It is a colourless liquid almost without smell, very mobile, and having a strong burning taste.

It is decidely hygroscopic, gradually absorbing moisture from the air unless kept tightly sealed. On the addition of water in small proportion combination takes place with considerable evolution of heat. It is prepared by dehydration of spirits of wine by re-distillation over quicklime and final treatment with metallic sodium.

The absolute alcohol prepared industrially as an analytical reagent, etc., usually contains a small quantity of water, from a half to one and a half percent. Absolute alcohol is made on an industrial scale by an improved method of distillation, which enables it to be prepared at a cost sufficiently low for industrial use as a solvent. It is claimed that the removal of the last traces of water converts it into an active solvent for nitro-cellulose.

The solvent power of alcohol depends greatly on its freedom from water; thus linseed oil, which is quite insoluble in industrial spirit, is soluble to the extent of 3 percent in absolute alcohol.

Methylated Spirit (Denatured Alcohol)

This is alcohol adulterated for industrial use with some noxious substance so as to render it unfit for drinking and free it from excise duty. It is essential for the purpose that the added substance should not interfere with the use of the spirit as a solvent and for household purposes as a fuel, cleaning agent, etc. Wood naphtha in the proportion of 10 percent was originally used, but as this was easily removed by distillation, three-eigths of 1 percent mineral naphtha was added. The regulations for its composition have been altered from time to time to ensure rendering it undrinkable and at the same time as far as possible non-poisonous

The addition of a small quantity of methyl-violet, 1 oz. to 4,000 gallons, has been required in order to provide a further safeguard by giving it a distinctive colour.

Later, the use of crude pyridine prepared from bone oil has been legalised as the denaturant.

Methylated Finish is methylated spirit in which a proportion of rosin is dissolved in order to enable it to be sold without a licence. It must contain not less than 3 Ozs. to the gallon to pass the Excise.

Industrial Spirit

It is the grade of alcohol used as a solvent for manufacturing purposes. It is denatured in a similar manner to methylated spirit in order to prevent its use for drinking and allow it to be used free of duty, but the denaturing is not the carried to such an extent, in order to avoid interface with its technical properties.

It differs from ordinary methylated spirit in three respects :-

1. The petroleum spirit is absent.
2. It contains only half the quantity of wood naphtha (5%)
3. The colouring indicator is omitted.

The restrictions placed on the use of this spirit are that it cannot be sold by retailers, but must be obtained by consumers direct from the manufacturers in quantities of not less than 5 gallons at a time. Manufacturers must first obtain a permit from the excise authorities, stating the purpose for which it is intended to be used, and a register of its consumption must be kept available for inspection by the Excise Authority. Regulations are also made as to its storage in factories, to safeguard against fire.

Butyl Alcohol

Four alcohols are obtained from butane, differing slightly in their properties, normal, iso-, secondary, and tertiary. The butanol of commerce is the substantially pure normal alcohol. It is mainly produced, together with other alcohols and acetone, by the fermentation of maize by means of a bacillus discovered by Weiamann in 1915. It is a clear colourless liquid with a peculiar penetrating odour, which has a characteristic effect when inhalted, generally described as *"gripping the back of the throat"*. Like all the alcohols, it has considerable toxic effect, and produces distressing symptoms if inhaled for any considerable time. Its consumption is 98 percent butyl alcohols, the balance being traces of ethyl alcohol and acetone.

Unlike the lower alcohols, butanol is not miscible with water in all proportions, but is only soluble to the extent of 1 part of butanol to 12 parts of water, and the commercial article is practically anhydrous.

It is one of the few materials which act as a solvent for most types of resins, dissolving both shellac, soft resins like damar and Manila, and hard resins such as Congo.

As it is also a solvent for all types of oil, its use in the preparation of spirit varnishes enables drying oils to be used as plasticisers to increase the elasticity of the film, instead of resorting to non-drying oils such as castor oil, which are soluble in the lower alcohols.

By the solution of hard resins in mixtures of alcohol and butanol spirit paper and stoving varnishes can be prepared which give a much harder and tougher film then those prepared in the usual manner from soft resins. It has sufficiently to allow the varnish to flow to an even coat and also to allow the moisture to absorb the heat necessary for vaporisation.

Butanol, although not itself a solvent of nitro-cellulose, is used in a similar manner in cellulose ester lacquers. It is added in small proportion to the thinner to retard the evaporation of the low-boiling solvents which have a tendency to cause *"blushing"* of the film under favourable conditions of humidity by precipitating moisture from the air, which reacts with the nitro-cellulose, giving the film a milky appearance. Its addition also causes the film to flow out smoothly and prevents pinholing and similar defects.

In addition to its solvent power for resins and oils, butanol is also a powerful and rapid solvent for linoxyn and other oxidised oilo films. On this account it forms a very effective ingredient of paint removers. Its comparatively slow evaporation is an advantage from the practical point of view, whilst its high flash point renders it more safe in use than equally effective solvents like acetone, which on this account are subject to transport restrictions. Unfortunately, its value for this purpose is discounted to some extent by its irritating effect on the throat, which makes it difficult to work with in confined spaces.

This solvent action on linoxyn may also be taken advantage of by adding a small proportion of butanol to certain types of enamels which have a tendency to skin badly in a partly-filled can. The butanol evaporates into the air space in the can, and by keeping the oxidised oil in solution as it forms, prevents the skin from developing.

Amyl Alcohol

Pentane, C_5H_{12}, is capable of forming eight isomeric alcohols having the formula C_5H_{11} OH. A mixture of these, in which the predominant member is iso-amyl alcohol, is obtained by the distillation of fusel oil. This alcohol was first extracted from the spirit obtained by the fermentation of substance containing starch, hence the name amyl (from amylum, starch).

Fusel Oil is the residue obtained from the rectification of alcohol, containing all the higher alcohols, etc., produced in the fermentation. It is a body of extremely complex composition, which varies considerably according to the grain used for the fermentation. It is produced to the extent of about 0.5 percent in ordinary alcoholic fermentation.

The supply of amyl alcohol is dependent on the quantity of this fusel oil available from the alcohol distilleries, and is consequently limited, and at times not equal to the demand. The principal supply is derived from the potato spirit obtained as a by-product in the manufacture of whisky.

Commercial amyl alcohol is obtained from the crude fusel oil by shaking with slightly alkaline water to remove the ethyl alcohol. The aqueous extract is allowed to stand, when the amyl alcohol separates out on top of the lye. This is drawn off, dried over calcium chloride, and re-distilled. The product is a colourless, oily liquid, with a smell closely resembling that of butyl alcohol, and having the same curious effect on the throat.

It is only slightly soluble in water, 1 volume being soluble in 39 volumes of water. It mixes freely with other alcohols, and in its solvent power is equivalent to butyl alcohol. Its toxic effects are rather more pronounced than with butyl alcohol; inhalation of the vapour being poisonous. The toxic effects of drinking inferior spirits are mainly due to the presence of amyl alcohol.

It is largely used as a solvent for natural and synthetic resins and for the preparation of amyl acetate.

Benzyl Alcohol

This is the alcohol derived from toluene, thus :-

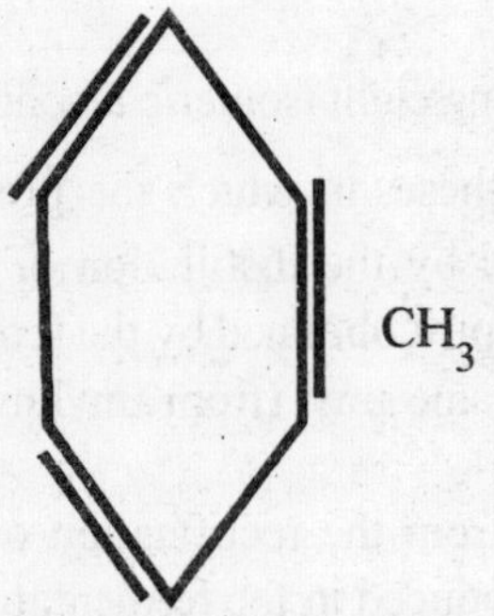

Toluene

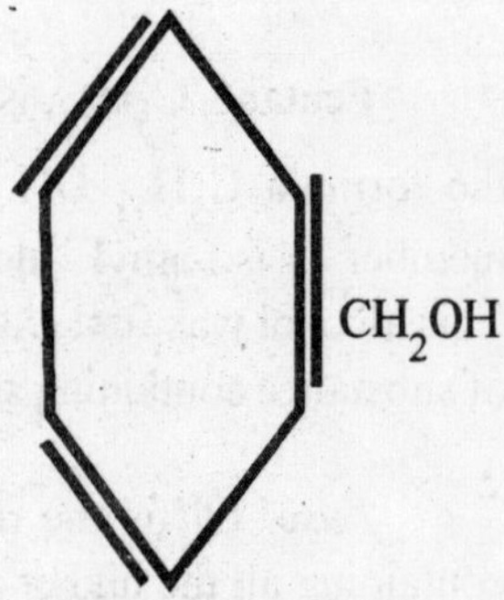

Benzyl alcohol

It was originally obtained from Peruvian balsam by extraction with caustic potash, but is generally prepared synthetically. The usual method of preparation is to treat toulene with chlorine gas and saponify the benzyl chloride thus formed by digestion with caustic soda. It is also prepared by boiling benzal dehyde with caustic soda.

Benzyl alcohol is used to a certain extent as a solvent, more particularly for cellulose acetate.

Cyclohexanol

This is the monatomic alcohol derived from cyclohexane, and is prepared by the hydrogenation of phenol, thus :-

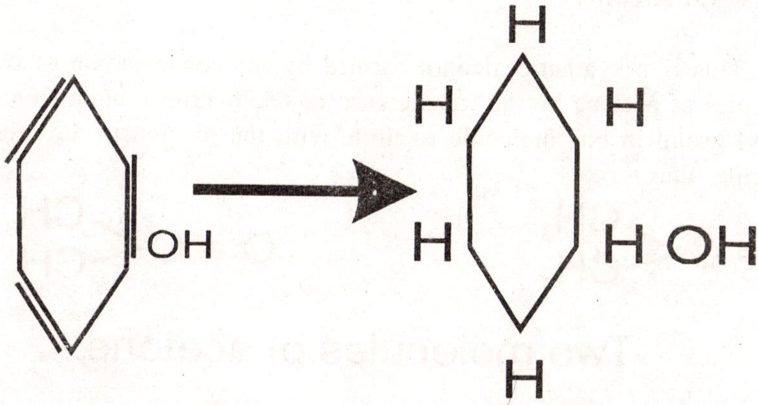

Phenol, C_6H_5OH **Cyclohexanol, $C_6H_{11}OH$**

It is technically known as Hexalin, or Sextol. The process of preparation is closely similar to that of tetralin. Cyclohexanol is quite neutral in character and has properties similar to those of an alcohol of high molecular weight. It is used not so much as a direct solvent as for promoting the solubility of substances in other organic solvents, and for lowering the surface tension between two liquids so as to render them miscible.

Although cyclohexanol does not itself dissolve cellulose esters, if a small quantity is added to a solution of nitro-cellulose in amyl acetate, a much more stable solution is formed, which can be diluted in any proportion with benzol or white spirit without precipitation.

Methylcyclohexanol (methyl-hexalin)

This bears the same relation to cyclohexanol as toluene does to benzene.

It is prepared by hydrogenating orhto-cresol, and is an only liquid with a rather unpleasent odour, which is not strong, but very persistent.

It is closely similar to cyclohexanol in its properties, but not quite so powerful in its action; it is, however, considerably cheaper to produce, and, therefore, takes its place for most industrial purposes.

Di-acetone Alcohol

This is a synthetic alcohol formed by the condensation of two molecules of acetone by the transference of one hydrogen atom from a methyl group in one molecule to unite with the oxygen in the other molecule, thus :-

Two molecules of acetone.

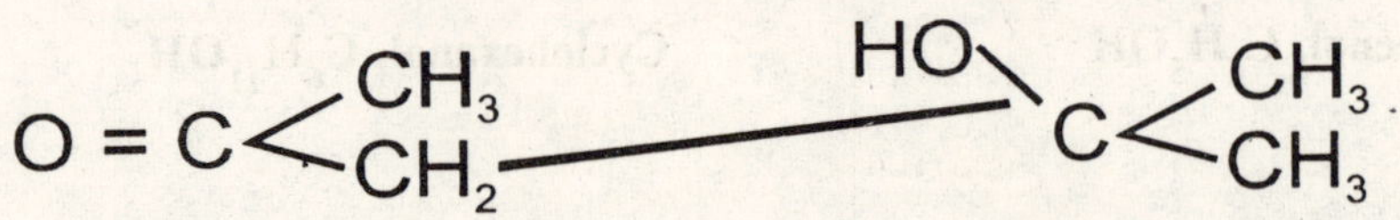

One molecule of Di-acetone alcohol

It was first prepared by Heintz in 1873 by distilling acetone over a concentrated solution of potassium hydroxide. Numerous other investigators prepared it subsequently by different methods, and several patents have been taken out for its manufacture on a commercial basis, the main principle employed being that of passing acetone over a catalyst such as granular calcium hydroxide.

Di-acetone alcohol is a water-white liquid miscible in all proportions with both water and alcohol, and also miscible with benzol up to 50 percent.

The pure substance has a boiling point of 163°C., but commercial samples normally contain a small proportion of acetone and show a variable boiling point. The substance is also liable to dissociate on storage, with the result that the percentage of acetone increases. Di-acetone alcohol is used in the preparation of cellulose ester products, being a good solvent both for nitro-cellulose, cellulose acetate, and resins. It is, in fact, closely similar in solvent properties to methyl ethyl ketone, but has a considerably slower rate of evaporation.

Ketones :

Ketones are a group of organic compounds closely similar to the aldehydes, resulting from the oxidation of secondary alcohols; they are intermediate, in fact, between the alcohols, and the fatty acids. The lower members of the series are neutral and highly volatile liquids of characteristic odour. With increasing complexity they become insoluble in water and the solidfying point rises, the higher members being solid and odourless.

Acetone

This is the most important member of the kerone group, and has the composition di-methyl ketone :-

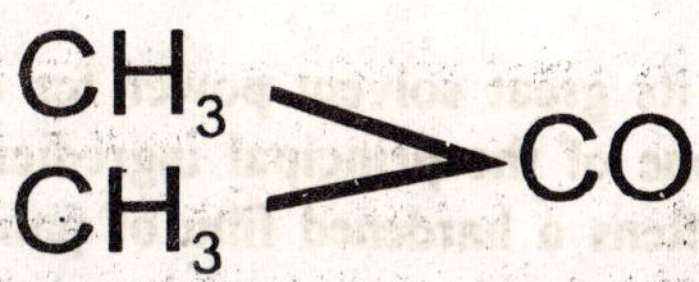

It was discovered early in the ninteenth century and investigated by Liebig and Dumas in 1832. It is formed in various ways, such as by the oxidation of alcohols, the distillation of the calcium salts of fatty acids, or the composition of organic chlorine derivatives.

Acetone has been employed industrially as a solvent for many years, and is used in large quantities. Numerous processes for preparing it on a commercial scale have been introduced from time to time, but substantially the whole of the acetone available is now prepared by :-

1. The distillation of wood (together with wood naphtha).
2. The fermentation of maize (together with butyl alcohol).
3. The condensation of acetic acid.

Acetone is obtainable in a state of great purity, a good sample showing 99 to 100 percent of di-methyl ketone, and distilling completely between 55° and 57°C. It is a mobile liquid, perfectly clear and water-white, with a mild and not unpleasant odour. A good sample should be practically anhydrous, and show no turbidity with distilled water and no residue on evaporation over the water bath. It is extremely volatile and inflammable, and flashes at ordinary atmospheric temperature, the flash point being well below 0°C. It mixes with water and alcohols in all proportions and with all other organic solvents.

The solvent power is extremely great, and covers a very wide range of substances. All animal and vegetable oils are soluble in all proportions, but mineral oils are only slightly soluble. It is one of the few solvents for the linoxyn formed by the oxidation of vegetable oils. Rosin and soft resins are completely soluble, and hard and fossil resins are soluble to a great extent, although not completely. Shellac is soluble to the extent of over 80 percent. Synthetic resins are not, however, soluble in acetone.

With the exception of amyl and butyl acetates, acetone forms the most active solvent for cellulose esters, and it is employed largely in the preparation of cellulose ester lacquers.

On account of its great solvent power for resins and oxidised oils, acetone forms one of the principal ingredients of most neutral paint removers. It softens a hardened film of paint and varnish with great rapidity, but its value in this connection is somewhat restricted by its extreme volatility, the surface hardening again in the course of a few minutes unless it is operated upon immediately after applicaton of the solvent.

Methyl Ethyl Ketone, ($CH_3 CO C_2H_5$)

This is produced with acetone in the distillation of wood, and is similar to it in properties, but superior in solvent power, and has the advantage of having a slower rate of evaporation and a higher flash point. A good sample is perfectly clear and practically colourless, and should contain not more than 0.01 percent of organic acid or 2 percent of water, and be entirely free from aldehydes. It should leave no trace of tarry residue on evaporation. It is employed on the continent as a denaturant for alcohol, the similarity of boiling points making separation by fractionation nearly impossible.

Methyl Acetone

This solvent is obtained as a by-product in the preparation of acetic acid, methanol, and acetone by the destructive distillation of wood. It is of complex composition, consisting mainly of acetone, methanol, and methyl acetate. The proportion in which these are present vary very considerably in the products turned out by different distilleries, according to the conditions under which the refining of the crude product is conducted, and also vary in the same works from time to time according to the relative demand for the various constituents.

The following is a typical analysis :-

Acetone	45.05 %
Methyl acetate	21.46 %
Methanol	32.09 %
Minor constituents	1.40 %

Methyl acetone should be practically neutral, the acidity, calculated as acetic acid, not exceeding 20 parts per million. When properly prepared the colour is water-white, and it should be quite anhydrous. Methyl acetone is an extremely useful solvent for many purposes on account of its composite nature. There are many substances which are only completely dissolved by the combined action of two or more different solvents, in either of which they are only partially soluble. Some grades of cellulose nitrate, for example, are more readily dissolved by methyl acetone than by one of its constituents alone.

Acetone Oils

In the preparation of acetone by the wood distillation process a dark liquid as a by-product which is of variable composition, but always contains a large proportion of higher ketones and aldehydes. This is separated by further distillation into heavy acetone oil and light acetone oil. The latter, which comes over between 70° and 130°C., is a straw coloured liquid, containing methyl ethyl ketone as the principal constituent, which is used to some extent as a solvent for cellulose nitrate. Its use is limited by its pronounced odour and variable composition and solvent power.

Cyclo-hexanone is the ketone derived from cyclo-hexanol by the introduction of the *CO* group. It is prepared by heating a mixture of cyclo-hexanol and phenol in presence of a catalyst and subsequent oxidation with bichromate. It is prepared industrially as a solvent for cellulose nitrate as it forms solutions which are stable on dilution with thinners such as toluene. It is also a solvent for cellulose acetate, the softer natural resins, and most synthetic resins.

The distillation range is 154°-156°C., the specific gravity 0.945 and the flash point 156°F.

Methyl-cyclo-hexanone is a higher homologue with the same general properties, but the distillation range (160°-170°C) and the flash point (127°F) are higher.

Mesityl Oxide is an unsaturated ketone obtained by the dehydration of diacetone alcohol. It is a powerful solvent with a strong and objectionable odour which limits its use. On account of its solvent power for both cellulose esters and oxidised oils it is used to some extent as a constituent of paint removers.

Ethers

Ethers are derived from alcohols by combination of two molecules with elimination of water. In ordinary technical work the name implies the most important member of the group, ethyl ether, which has the composition—

$$\left.\begin{matrix} C_2H_5 \\ C_2H_5 \end{matrix}\right> O$$

This is produced by distilling alcohol with strong sulphuric acid, and it was supposed, before the days of systematic chemistry, that the ether was derived from the sulphuric acid in this process. Hence the original name *"sulphuric ether"*, which should be regarded as obsolete.

The sulphuric acid first attacks one molecule of alcohol, forming ethyl hydrogen sulphate, and this reacts with a second molecule, forming ether and water, and releasing the sulphuric acid for further action, so that a small quantity of acid is capable of converting a large quantity of alcohol.

Ethyl ether is a colourless, extremely limpid liquid, exceedingly volatile and inflammable, and having a characteristic pleasent odour. Owing to its extreme volatility, it is not often used as a solvent in industrial preparations. In combination with alcohol it forms a good solvent for cellulose esters; this combination is too volatile for use in nitro-cellulose lacquers, but is employed in the manufacture of collodion and explosives. Ether is largely employed in the paint laboratory as a solvent for the separation of the pigment and vehicle preparatory to analysis. Its extreme volatility combined with solvent power renders it particularly useful for such purposes, as it enables separation to be obtained quickly and the pigment to be obtained quite dry.

Glycol Ethers

Several of the less volatile ethers formed by the combination of monohydric with polyhydric alcohols have recently come into industrial use they form powerful solvents for cellulose esters. The most important of these is formed by the union of ethyl alcohol and ethylene glycol. Thus :-

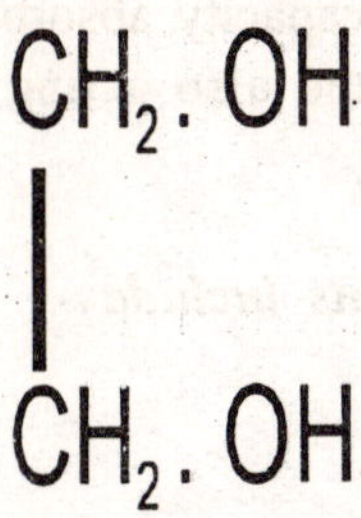

Ethylene glycol

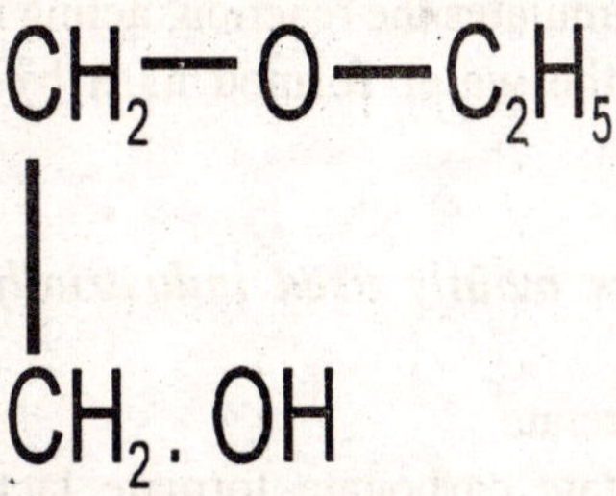

Ethylene - glycol - mono - ether

This ether is commercially known as *"cellosolve"* for short on account of its efficiency as a solvent for cellulose nitrate. It has the advantage of combining a suitable distillation range (126°-137°C) and high flash point (104 °C) with chemical stability and a very faint and not unpleasant odour. The corresponding methyl and butyl ethers are also used to a less extent for adjusting the viscosity and rate of evaporation of cellulose lacquers.

Esters

Mention has been made of the fact one of the characteristic properties of alcohols is their reaction with acids to form esters. The esters formed in this way with organic acids form a group of solvents which have come into way with organic acids form a group of solvents which have come into prominence in the past few years owing to their value in the preparation of cellulose ester products, as they provide a series of slow-evaporating solvents which readily dissolve both the cellulose esters and the resins with which they are combined.

They are all formed by the same general reaction, the alcohol being heated with the acid or one of its salts and the resulting ester distilled off.

The reaction may be expressed thus :-

$$C_2H_5OH + CH_3\ COOH = CH_3\ COO\ C_2H_5 + H_2O$$

Alcohol **Acetic acid** **Ethyl acetate**

In industrial practice a proportion of sulphuric acid is added to the mixture : this stimulates the reaction, acting in a double capacity, absorbing and removing the water formed as a by-product, and also acting as a catalyst.

The esters mainly used industrially as solvents include :-

Methyl acetate
Ethyl acetate, carbonate, formate, lactate.
Propyl acetate
Butyl acetate, butyrate, formate, lactate.
Amyl acetate, formate, lactate, propionate.
Benzyl acetate
Glycol acetate.

These esters have a general similarity of properties, but vary in distillation range and rate of evaporation according to the complexity of the molecule. ***The figures for these are given in the mentioned table given in the last of this chapter.***

Esters in general possess characteristic aromatic odours resembling those of various fruits. This is especially characteristics of the acetates, the pungency increasing with the complexity of the molecule. Whilst the odour of methyl acetate, for instance, is mild, that of amyl acetate, although pleasant, is so powerful as to be a handicap to its use.

The lactates have a very much less prounounced odour but are liable to decomposition.

The solvent power for cellulose esters is greater with the esters of the lower than the higher alcohols, but, on the other hand, the value of the lower members as solvents is discounted by their greater volatility and their relative chemical instability. Esters such as methyl and ethyl acetate are decidedly hygroscopic and liable to hydrolyse in presence of moisture, whereas the butyl and amyl esters are relatively stable.

Butyl and amyl acetate are by far the most widely used of the series at the present time; they form the staple solvents for cellulose nitrate, as they do not readily hydrolyse with water, and their rate of evaporation is quick enough to ensure reasonably quick drying, but not so rapid as to cause chilling of the surface, and consequent deposition of moisture, or *"blushing:*. The two are practically equivalent in their properties, and in practice they are often interchanged, butyl acetate being supplied as amyl and vice versa according to the fluctuations in the price of the respective alcohols.

Chlorinated Hydrocarbons

The substitution of hydrogen by chlorine in various members of the paraffin and olefin series of hydrocarbons produces a number of useful solvents which form a group having the same general characteristics. These differ in the following respects from those of all other groups of solvents previously considered, the difference being mainly due to the content of chlorine :-

1. *High specific gravity* : they are invariably heavier than water.
2. *Low inflammability* : in most cases they are completely non-inflammable. The less chlorinated members of the series can be ignited, but they burn with such a low heat of combustion that the flame is rapidly extinguished.

3. *Low heat ˆ vapourisation.* such that their volatility is high in proportion to the boiling point. Thus tetrachlorethane, which has a boiling point of 147°C., evaporates very much more rapidly than water.

4. *Liability to decomposition* on exposure to sunlight or in presence of moisture, with formation of hydrochloric acid. They deteriorate if kept in clear glass bottles exposed to the light, and are liable to corrode iron vessels unless perfectly free from moisture.

5. *Pronounced anaethetic* properties, and in some cases decided toxic effect.

6. Pronounced and characteristic odour.

The first three of these distinctive properties, combined with the fact of their high solvent power for a very wide range of organic substances, render this group of great value for many industrial purposes. It is unfortunate that their usefulness is discounted for many purposes by the pronounced toxicity. Were it not for this they would undoubtedly take first rank as industrial solvents, particularly on account of the freedom from fire risks. A non-inflammable, non-poisonous solvent would obviously be of immense industrial value, and the demand for it is constant and insistent. Unfortunately, no solvent has yet been produced which combines these three properties of high solvent power, non-inflammbility and absence of toxicity.

Derivatives of Methane, CH^4. :-

Methylene chloride	$CH_2 CL_2$
Chloroform	$CHCL_3$
Carbon tetrachloride	CCl_4

Methylene chloride is a liquid of low boiling point, only slightly inflammable. It evaporates rapidly, and is a strong solvent for oils, resins, and rubber, and would form an excellent substitute for solvent naphtha. It is usually prepared by reduction from carbon tetrachloride or chloroform.

Chloroform is mainly prepared by the treatment of acetone or alcohol with bleaching powder.

Its most important use is as an anaesthetic, but it is also used largely as a solvent. It is the most effective solvent, for instance, for extracting the free sulphur from pigments such as untramarine and cadmium sulphide, where very pure sulphur-free grades are required for special purposes such as artists' use.

It is also a solvent for rubber and gutta percha and most resins. Only the hardest resins, such as amber, resist complete solution on prolonged shaking with chloroform. It is only soluble to the extent of 1 part in 200 parts of water, but mixes in all proportions with organic solvents and vegetable and mineral oils. Exposed for any length of time to light in presence of moisture, chloroform is liable to decomposition with formation of hydrochloric acid and chlorine. It is extremely volatile and lowers the temperature to such an extent by its rapid evaporation as to cause freezing. It is practically non-inflammable, but can be ignited with difficulty.

Carbon tetrachloride, the final member of the series, is prepared by the action of chlorine on carbon bisulphide. It closely resembles chloroform in general properties, but is distinguished from it by being quite non-inflammable. On this account it is largely used for *"dry cleaning"* of fabrics, and as an extraction agent.

It mixes with other organic solvents, is only soluble in water to a slight extent, and dissolves vegetable and mineral oils. It dissolves most of the resins in the cold, but the hard fossil copals only dissolve with difficulty. In common with all the chlorinated compounds, it is not a good solvent for shellac. A mixture of equal parts carbon tetrachloride and alcohol will, however, dissolve shellac to the extent of about 25 percent.

Derivatives of Ethylene, C_2H_4 :-

Dichlorethylene	$C_2H_2\ CL_2$
Trichlorethylene	C_2HCL_3
Perchlorethylene	$C_2\ CL_4$

These are all prepared from acetylene by progressive chlorination.

Dichloroethylene is a powerful solvent, and its usefulness lies in its low boiling point and rapid volatility, combined with low inflammability. For some purposes, such as the extraction of some dyes, perfumes, and other organic substances, which are only stable at temperatures below the boiling point of water, a solvent of very low boiling point is essential. Such solvents in general give off a dangerously inflammable vapour on evaporation, which is a series drawback for operations on an industrial scale.

Dichlorethylene is soluble in water, but mixes with alcohol freely. A mixture of industrial spirit and dichlorethylene forms a useful solvent for resins, such as shellac, which is considerably less inflammable than the pure spirit.

Trichlorethylene is extensively employed as a solvent for the extraction of oil from seeds; owing to its extremely low latent heat it evaporates very rapidly, and being a pure substance leaves no *"tail"* or residue.

On account of its non-inflammability it is used largely for the *"dry cleaning"* of fabrics and the degreasing of textiles etc.

It is an extremely powerful solvent, dissolving all oils, most resins, rubber, and many inorganic substances such as sulphur and phosphorous, and is particularly efficient because of its great penetrative power. It does not dissolve cellulose nitrate or acetate by itself, but in combination with phenol and particularly the hydrogenated phenols such as cyclohexanol it rapidly acts as a solvent for these substances. On account of its solvent power it is used as a cleaning agent, and in combination with soft soap (with which it forms a stable emulsion miscible with water) it is used in the preparation of solvent soaps.

Perchlorethylene is identical in properties with trichlor-, but has a slower rate of evaporation.

Derivatives of Ethane, C_2H_6

Tetrachlorethane	$C_2H_2CL_4$
Pentachlorethane	C_2HCL_5
Hexachlorethane	C_2CL_6

Tetrachlorethane is the best known of this series of solvents, and is technically very efficient. It is a water-white liquid with an odour closely resembling that of trichlorethylene, and is similar to the ethylene derivatives in many of its properties, although differing from them in some important respects. Its physiological action is much more pronounced for instance. In addition to the vapour having a pronounced anaesthetic effect, prolonged exposure to the fumes causes specific illness, as it attacks the liver. It is essential that it should not be used to any used to any extent in confined spaces, and unless care is taken to provide ample ventilation, serious and even fatal illness may be caused. It should be noted that, on account of its high specific gravity, the vapour is considerably heavier than air, and the ventilation of workshops in which it is used should accordingly be downwards and not upwards. If care is taken to provide adequate ventilation, carrying off the vapour in this way so that no great concentration exist at the level at which the air is inhaled by workers, it can be used freely withot danger.

Tetrachlorethane is the most powerful solvent of this group. It is insoluble in water, but mixes freely with alcohol and all organic solvents. It is a good solvent for all oils, fats, and waxes, and dissolves soft resins completely. It also attacks hard resins, but does not dissolve them completely in the cold in the same way as the higher alcohols. It also attacks oxidised oils, and forma a very efficient and rapid paint and varnish remover.

Tetrachlorethane is also a good solvent for pitches and bituminous substances. On account of its solvent power for resins, combined with its rapid rate of evaporation, it forms a useful thinner for paints for special purposes required to dry rapidly and give a hard and fairly tough film. Apart from the unpleasant effect of its vapour, it is too powerful a solvent for ordinary paints except for application by spraying, as the undercoat would be moved on the application of a second coat by the brush.

Unlike trichlorethylene, it is also a solvent for cellulose nitrate and cellulose acetate, and may be used for the preparation of non-inflammable cellulose ester lacquers. It is a solvent for many inorganic substances, notably sulphur and phosphorus.

Pentachlorethane closely resembles tetrachlorethane, and is mainly distinguished from it by its high boiling point and consequent slower rate of evaporation. It is only employed to a limited extent as an industrial solvent.

Hexachlorethane is a solid at ordinary temperatures, and is used as a non-inflammable plasticisers.

Benzene Derivatives :-

Two of the several possible chlorine derivatives of benzene. *Monochlorbenzene and Dichlorbenzene*, are prepared on an industrial scale for use as solvents.

The latter is a mixture of the ortho and para varieties in the approximate proportion of 75 and 25 percent respectively. Monochlorbenzene is prepared by the direct action of chlorine on benzene in presence of iron as a catalyst, the crude product being purified by the fractionation in *vacuo*. Both these substances dissolve soft resins, but damar is soluble only in mono-chlorbenzene. Copals and other hard resins are insoluble in either.

These substances are used to some extent as solvents, but are rather difficult to work with. Dichlorbenzene is not a good practical solvent for spirit varnishes, etc., as it does not give a good film on drying. The monochlorbenzene, however, gives a film which dries with a matt surface and is useful for preparing dull finishes.

Derivatives of Glycerol (or Glycerine), $C_3H_5(OH)_3$:-

These are known as chlorhydrins, the two used commercially being *dichlorhydrin* and *epichlorhydrin* :-

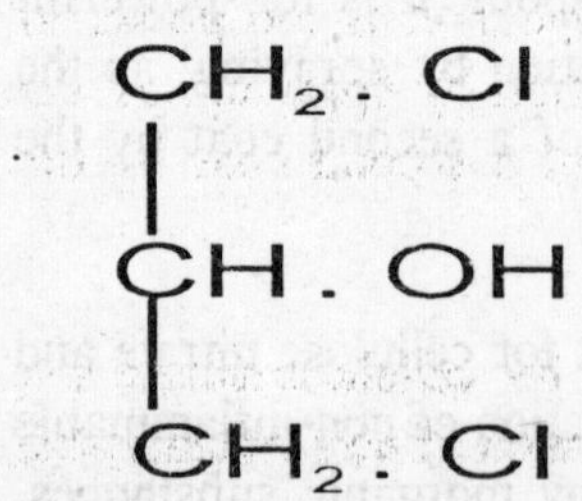

Dichlorhydrin

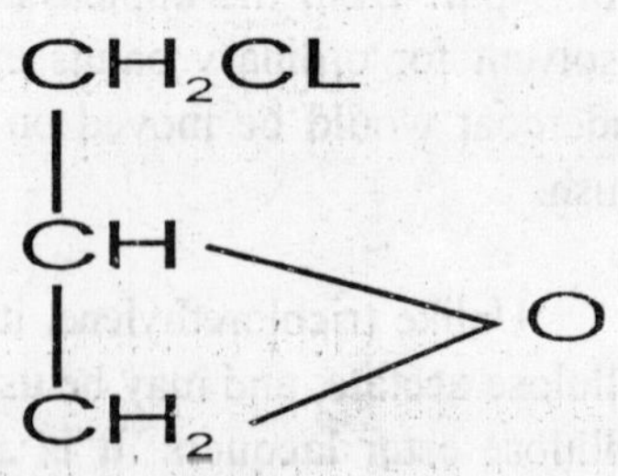

Epichlorhydrin

They are both powerful solvents, but are not used extensively at the present time.

Carbon Bisulphide

This is the only volatile solvent in industrial use which contains sulphur as an essential constituent, the composition being indicated by the formula CS_2. It was discovered in 1796 by Lampadius, and is prepared by the direct union of sulphur and carbon at a low red heat.

Pure carbon bisulphide is perfectly clear and water-white, and has a smell resembling that of chloroform, only much more pungent. The ordinary commercial article, however, is pale yellow in colour, with a penetrating evil odour, due to the presence of a small quantity of other organic sulphur derivatives.

In contradistinction to the chlorinated solvents, carbon bisulphide is highly inflammable, the flash point being — 20°C., and it is liable to spontaneous ignition on exposure to the air at a temperature approximating to the boiling point of water, whilst the vapour forms an explosive mixture with air at ordinary atmospheric temperatures. From the point of view of the fire risk, therefore, it is about the most dangerous solvent used in commerce.

The inflammability, combined with decided toxic action, limits its industrial uses, which is unfortunate, because as a solvent it is extremely useful. It dissolves readily, not only all oils, fats, and waxes, most of the resins, and organic substances such as camphor, tar, rubber, and guttapercha, but also many inorganic substances, including sulphur, phosphorous, and iodine.

It is decidely the most effective solvent for rubber known, and was at one time largely used in the rubber industry, particularly as a thinner for sulphur chloride in the cold cure process of vulcanisation.

Plasticisers

Castor Oil, obtained from the seeds of the castor oil plant, *Ricinus communis*, is the tri glyceride, or glyceryl ester, of ricnoleic acid. It is a non-drying oil of exceptionally high viscosity, and differs from most other vegetable oils in being readily soluble in alcohols and insoluble in petroleum distillates. On this account it forms a useful plasticiser for alcoholic spirit varnishes, and is extensively used for this purpose. It is also largely used as a plasticiser in many of the cheaper types of cellulose ester products. It is unsatisfactory for high-class nitro-cellulose enamels, as being a non-solvent for the ester it tends to produce an unstable film, which is liable to become sticky.

The physical constants are :-

Specific gravity at 15°C	0.959 to 0.968
Iodine value	82 to 90
Saonfication value	176 to 184
Acid value	1 to 4 %
Unsaponfiable matter	0.5 to 0.7 %
Acetyl Value	146 TO 150
Refractive index	1.477

GLYCERINE, or glycerol, is a tri-hydric alcohol of the composition :-

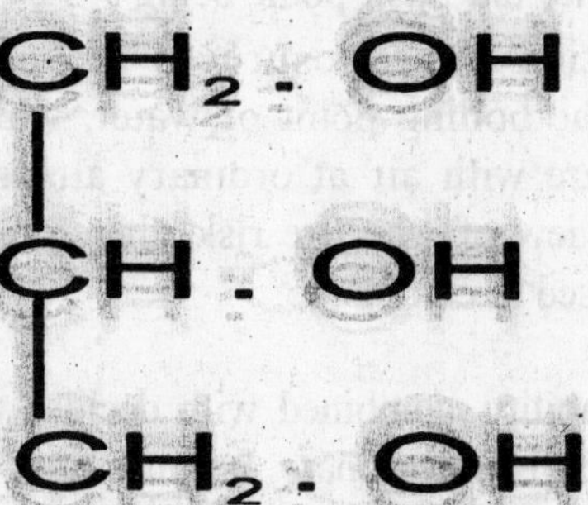

It is contained as an ester in all vegetable oils, and obtained as an ester in all vegetable oils, and obtained as a by-product in their decomposition by alkalies to form soap (saponification). It has the following constants when pure :-

Boiling point	**290°C**
Specific gravity at 15°C	**1.265**
Refractive index at 20°C	**1.473**

It is not appreciably volatile at ordinary temperatures, is freely soluble in water, and has very pronounced hygroscopic properties, absorbing up to 50 percent of water. If a mixture of equal parts of glycerine and water is exposed to the air in a thin film it remains constant, the tendency of the water to evaporate being just balanced by the absorption power of the glycerine.

Glycerine is consequently useful as a plasticiser for water soluble gums, and is largely emplyed for this purpose in artists' water colours, etc. to prevent hardening off before use.

Camphor is an aromatic ketone closely allied to the terpenes, having the composition $C^{10}H^{16}O$.

It occurs naturally in the wood of the camphor tree, found chiefly in japan and Borneo, and is also prepared synthetically by the action of hydrochloric acid on turpentine.

It is slightly soluble in water in water (about 1 part per 1,000), and freely in organic solvents such as acetone, and has the following characteristics :-

Specific gravity	0.992
Melting point	175°C
Boiling Point	204°C

It is used to a small extent as a plasticiser in spirit varnishes and lacquers, and largely as a plasticiser for cellulose esters in the production of *celluloid*. It is not used to any extent in modern practice in the production of nitrocellulose enamels and lacquers, as it does not fulfil the essential condition of stability, evaporating rapidly when exposed to the air.

Esters

As the molecular weight of the esters is increased, either by using a higher alcohol or a higher acid, the boiling point rises until a point is reached at which the substance is no longer volatile and can be used as a plasticiser. The distinction between a non-volatile plasticiser and a volatile solvent is difficult to draw in this case, the one class merging into the other, but it may be given as a general rule that an ester is not sufficiently free from evaporation at normal temperature to form a satisfactory plasticiser unless the boiling point is well over 250°C.

The following table of the principal esters used industrially indicates their relationship in this respect, the figures for those which may be regarded as plasticisers being in ordinary type and those for volatile solvents in *Italics*. The approximate boiling is given in degrees Centigrade.

Alcohol Radicle				Acid		
	Acetate	Oxalate	Phthalate	Tartrate	Stearate	Phosphate
Ethyl	75	185	295	-----	-----	-----
Butyl	125	245	315	290	360	-----
Amyl	135	265	340	400	360	-----
Glyceryl	260	-----	-----	-----	-----	-----
Phenyl	-----	-----	-----	-----	-----	410
Cresyl	-----	-----	-----	-----	-----	430

This group of plasticisers is largely used at the present time in the preparation of cellulose ester products.

Assay and Analysis of Solvents

Physical

Solvents are mainly identified and their purity judged by their physical properties. The determination of many of these, namely :-

Odour	Refractive index
Colour and appearance	Viscosity
Specific gravity	

Optical rotation

A useful means of identification is afforded by the fact that some solvents, notably turpentine, have the power of rotating a beam of polarised light either to the left (leavo-rotary or —) or right (dextro-rotary or +).

The appartus used for this test is the *polariscope*, in which a ray of polarised monochromatic light is passed through a column of the liquid of definite length, and the angle of rotation measured.

Distillation Range

This is perhaps the most important test for solvents, both as a means of identification and as an indication of purity or suitability for any particular purpose.

To obtain consistent results, it is of the utmost importance that distillation tests should be carried out under uniform conditions, as slight variations, such as in the dimensions of the distillation flask, materially affect the results.

Evaporation and Volatility

In the selection of a solvent for any particular purpose its evaporation properties are of fundamental importance, and investigation shlould be made as to (a) the rate, (b) the uniformity, (c) the completeness of evaporation, or freedom from residue.

Whilst the rate of evaporation is generally considered to be proportional to the boiling point, the term *"high boiler"* often being used to signify a solvent which evaporates slowly, it must be borne in mind that this is only true within limits. In solvents of the same type, such as the different petroleum distillates, the boiling range is a guide to the rate of evaporation. But this does not hold with solvents of different types, the real factors which govern evaporation being the specific heat of the substance and the latent heat of evaporation, which differ widely in different classes of compounds. Thus, to take an extreme case, tetrachlorethane with a boiling point of 147°C has a considerably quicker rate of evaporation than water with a boiling point of 100°C.

The rate of evaporation is determined against a standard by using two watch glasses or flat-bottomed dishes, and placing a filter paper in each. The papers are moistened with equal weights of the sample and the standard, exposed at ordinary room temperature, and weighed at intervals until no further loss in weight occurs. The residue on evaporation is found in a similar manner, by evaporating 10 c.c. of the sample in a shallow dish over a water bath or in a water oven, and determining the loss in weight.

Inflammability and Flash Point

The great majority of volatile solvents are inflammabe to an extent roughly proportional to their boiling point. Although this has little bearing on their technical value, the *flasn point*— that is, the temperature at which the liquid commences to give off a vapour which will ignite on exposure to a flame, is of importance from the point of view of fire risk. A liquid is generally regarded as *"inflammable"* when the flash point is below 150°F. When it lies with in the limits reached by atmospheric temperature in summer it is classed as *"highly inflammable"*, and subject to restrictions as regards transport. In this country the limit is fixed at 73°F., and in United States at 30°C.

The instruments used for the determination of flash points below 150°F. . The standard in this country is the *Abel* apparatus. In the *United States* the *tagliabue* appartus is the standard.

Chemical — The general tests for purity include :-

Acidity or Alkalinity

This is determined by titration with standard alkali or acid. For this purpose the sample must be made miscible with the aqueous solution of the reagent and an indicator for the titration must be used which is also soluble in the mixture. The procedure, therefore, varies with different solvents. Those soluble in water, such as acetone, are simply diluted with neutralised industrial spirit, using phenol phthalein as an indicator. Substances such as white spirit which have no tolerance for water, are shaken up with neutral distilled water to extract any acid, and the aqueous layer titrated, using a water soluble indicator such as methyl orange.

Moisture :-

The presence of moisture in a solvent, which is often a disadvantage, is detected by diluting the sample with another solvent which is miscible with it and has no tolerance for water. The usual diluents are benzene, petroleum spirit, and carbon bisulphide. Five c.c. of the sample are placed in a stoppered measuring cylinder and the diluent added in successive quantities until any water present is thrown out, indicated by the solution becoming turbid on shaking. The determination should be made at a standard temperature, 15°C. being usually specified, as the solubility of the water increases with rise of temperature.

Sulphur :-

The presence of sulphur compounds is now usually detected by the test introduced by H.A. Gardener, in which a strip of pure sheet copper is placed in a test tube with the solvent, which is then boiled for 30 minutes. The presence of sulphur in undesirable amount is shown by a pronounced blackening of the copper strip, a slight tarnish being disregarded.

This test can be conveniently carried out in conjuction with the distillation test the copper strip being placed in the distillation flask; this saves the time of making a separate test, and has the further advantage that the copper strip; produces more steady boiling and prevents *"bumping"*.

Where the presence of sulphur is indicated by this qualtative test, the amount may be determined quantitatively by burning a weighed quantity of the solvent, absorbing the products of combustion by aspiration through sodium carbonate, oxidising the sulphur compounds to sulphates, and estimating gravimetrically by precipitation as barium sulphate.

Special tests are employed for determining the purity of different types of solvents, or determining their amount when present in mixtures, of which the following may briefly indicated as being the most generally used :-

Coal-tar Distillates

The purity as regards freedom unsaturated hydrocarbons is determined by the sulphuric acid or wash test, which depends on the reaction of unsaturated hydrocarbons with sulphuric acid to form compounds of pronounced colour. The sample is agitated with concentrated sulphuric acid, allowed to stand for several hours, and the coloration produced measured against standards.

Turpentines — The B.S.I. standard method for this is :-

" Five c.c. of the turpentine shall be slowly added, drop by drop, to 20 c.c. of 98.5 percent sulphuric acid contained in a *Leffman-Beam* or Babcock Milk-Fat flask, immersed in iced water. The flask shall be frequently shaken, and care shall be taken to prevent the temperature rising above 60°C.(140°F). When the mixture no longer warms up on shaking, the whole shall be throughly agitated and the flask placed in a water bath and heated to between 60° and 65°. (140° to 149°F). for ten minutes, the contents being throughly mixed by shaking vigrously five or six times during this period.

The flask be cooled to room temperature and sifficient concentrated sulphuric acid shall be added to bring the level of the liquid into the neck of the flask near the zero of the graduated scale. The flask shall be allowed to stand overnight (or it may be centrifuged) and the volume of the unpolymerised residue shall be read off."

Alcohols :- *Verley and Bolsing Method* — One to 2 gms. of the liquid is weighed into a 200 c.c. flask, and to this is added 25 c.c. of the following mixture :-

Pure acetic anhydride,	12%
Pure pyridine	88%

The flask is then fitted with a reflux condenser and digested over the water bath for 15 to 30 minutes. It is then cooled, 25 c.c. distilled water are added, and titrated with N/2-caustic soda, using phenol phthalein as an indicator. The amount of the alcohol is calculated from the amount of acetic acid found, according to its molecular weight, one molecule reacting to form one molecule of acetic acid.

Ketones — *Messanger's Method* — This depends on the reaction of ketones with iodine to form idoform; in the case of acetone this takes place according to the equation :-

$$(CH_3)_2CO + 3I_2 + 4NaOH = CHI_3 + CH_3COONa + 3NaI + 3H_2O$$

Acetone — Idoform — Sodium Acetate

The sample is treated with excess of standard caustic soda solution, excess of iodine solution added, and the amount of iodine absorbed by the reaction determined by titration; as the excess of iodine reacts with the excess of caustic soda to form iodate, this is decomposed by acidfying with sulphuric acid before titration, to ensure that all the iodine is in the free condition. The excess of iodine is then titrated with sodium thiosulphate, using starch as an indicator.

Hydroxylamine Method

The addition of a ketone to a neutral solution of pure hydroxylamine hydrochloride liberates acid according to the reaction :-

$$(CH_3)_2CO + NH_2\ OH\ HCI = (CH_3)_2\ CNOH + HCI + H_2O$$

By titrating the acid thus set free with standard alkali the amount of ketone is determined.

The method of conducting the test recommended in the B.S.I. specification is :-

25 c.c. of N/5 hydroxylamine hydrochloride , previously made neutral to phenolphthalein with N/5 caustic soda and then just acidified, shall be placed in a 100 c.c. stoppered bottle. About 0.1 to 0.2 grams of the material, previously dried over anhydrous sodium sulphate, shall then be weighed out in a small scaled thin glass bulb and the bulb transferred to the bottle.

A short piece of stout glass rod shall then be placed in the bottle and the stopper wired down. The bottle shall now be shaken to break the bulb and then placed in a cold water-bath, which shall then be heated to boiling and kept at that temperature for one hour. the bottle shall then be cooled and the contents titrated with N/10 sulphuric acid, using methyl orange as indicator and a diluted methyl orange as a colour standard for comparison. A blank experiment shall be run at the same time and titrated to the same colour standard.

Esters

About 1 gram of the material is weighed into a small tared tube and its contents are immediately transferred to a flask containing 25 c.c. of approximately N/2 alcoholic caustic soda solution. A water cooled reflux is fitted to the flask, and the latter heated for one hour on a water-bath at 100°C., at the end of which period the condenser is rinsed with neutral distilled water. After cooling, the flask is removed and the contents are titrated with N/2 hydrochloric acid, using phenolphthalein as indicator. A blank determination is made with the alcoholic soda solution at the same time.

Table -- Properties of Solvents

* **FLASH POINTS** are given in both Fahrenheit and Centigrade degree for convenience.

L indicates that the substance flashes below 40°F.

H signifies that the flash point is so high that the substance may be regarded as non inflammable

Flash points in brackets are abnormal in not indicating inflammability

Substance	Formula	Molecular weight	Boiling Range °C	Flash Point °F	Flash Point °C	Specific Gravity at 15°C	Refractive Index at 20°C
Turpentines—							
Turpentine, American,	$C_{10}H_{16}$	136	150-180	90-95	32-35	0.860-0.880	1.466-1.478
Turpentine French,	$C_{10}H_{16}$	136	155-170	86-90	30-32	0.857-0.872	1.466-1.478
Turpentine Indian	$C_{10}H_{16}$	136	155-190	99	37	0.865-0.880	——
Wood turpentine, American,	$C_{10}H_{16}$	136	150-170	93-97	34-36	0.860-0.863	1.467-1.469
Wood Turpentine, Russian,	Indefinite	——	160-180	95-100	35-38	0.862-0.875	1.476
Tar spirit	Indefinite	——	160-270	——	——	0.9-1.0	1.481

Pine Oil	Indefinite	——	190-218	——	——	0.93-0.95	1.480-1.483
Rosin spirit	Indefinite	——	115-120	97-102	36-39	0.856-0.883	——
Petroleum Hydrocarbons							
Petroleum Ether,	Indefinite	——	40-60	L	——	0.670	1.37-1.39
Petrol,	Indefinite	——	70-175	L	——	0.720-0.750	1.37-1.45
Petroleum Spirit,	Indefinite	——	60-100	L	——	0.670-0.700	1.38-1.44
Benzine,	Indefinite	——	60-120	L	——	0.650-0.730	1.38-1.44
White spirit,	Indefinite	——	140-220	75-100	24-38	0.760-0.810	1.38-1.41
Shale spirit,	Indefinite	——	65-100	60-70	15-21	0.718-0.730	——
Coal-Tar Hydrocarbons:-							
Coal-tar naphtha,	Indefinite	——	80-170	L	——	0.9	Variable
Benzol	Indefinite	——	70-130	L	——	0.865-0.900	1.5
Solvent naphtha, light,	Indefinite	——	130-170	70-73	21-23	0.865-0.875	1.5
Solvent naphtha, heavy,	Indefinite	——	160-190	75-100	24-28	0.880-0.910	1.496
Benzene,	C_6H_6	78	80	L	-8	0.884	1.501
Toluene,	$C_6H_5 . CH_3$	92	111	45	7	0.881	1.496
Xylene (meta)	$C_6H_4 . (CH_3)_2$	106	139	70	21	0.868	1.499
Xylol,	Indefinite	——	135-140	86	30	0.865	1.499
Cyclohexane,	C_6H_{12}	84	81	L	——	0.790	1.426-1.429
Tetralin,	$C_{10}H_{12}$	132	205	172	78	0.980	1.540

Dekalin,	$C_{10}H_{18}$	138	190	135	57	0.890	1.467
Alcohols :-							
Methyl alcohol,	CH_3. OH	32	66	59	15	0.796	1.332
Absolute alcohol,	C_2H_5. OH	46	78	53	12	0.79	1.367
Industrial spirit,	Impure	——	76-79	64	18	0.815-0.820	1.362
Propyl alcohol,normal,	C_3H_7. OH	60	97	——	——	0.804	1.386
Propyl alcohol iso,	C_3H_7. OH	60	79-81	——	36	0.790	1.381
Butyl alcohol,	C_4H_9. OH	74	110-118	97	36	0.810	1.396
Amyl alcohol,	C_5H_{11}. OH	88	126-131	111	——	0.825	1.408
Di-acetone alcohol,	C_2H_5. CO. $(CH_3)_2$. COH	116	90-166	L	——	0.910-0.930	——
Benzyl alcohol,	C_6H_5.CH_2. OH	108	206	——	——	1.051	——
Cyclohexanol,	C_6H_{11}. OH	100	160	154	68	0.945	1.468
Methyl-cyclohexanol,	C_6H_{10}. CH_3. OH	114	170-180	154	68	0.930	1.463
Ketones and Ethers :-							
Acetone,	$(CH_3)_2$. CO	58	56	L	——	0.792-0.799	1.358
Methyl ethyl ketone,	CH_3. CO. C_2H_5	72	70-82	L	——	0.808	1.379

Methyl acetone,	Indefinite	——	50-70	L	——	0.840-0.850	1.35-1.36
Ethyl ether,	$(C_2H_5)_2O$	74	35	L	——	0.719-0.735	1.356
Esters:-							
Methyl acetate,	CH_3. COO. CH_3	74	53-59	L	-6	0.923-0.930	1.361
Ethyl acetate,	CH_3. COO. C_2H_5	88	70-85	L	-3	0.893-0.895	1.373
Butyl acetate,	CH_3. $COOC_4H_9$	116	117-135	76-83	24	0.870-0.875	——
Amyl acetate,	CH_3. COO. C_5H_{11}	130	125-150	77	25	0.870-0.875	1.404
Cyclohexanol acetate,	CH_3. COO. C_6H_{10}. OH	158	165-180	147	64	0.965-0.970	1.438
Ethyl lactate,	CH_3. CHOH. COO. C_2H_5	118	145-159	117	47	1.038	——
Chlorine Derivatives:-							
Methylene Chloride,	CH_2Cl_2	85	42	(100)	——	1.328	——
Chloroform,	$CHCl_3$	119.5	61	H	——	1.48-1.49	1.449
Carbon Tetrachloride,	CCl_4	156	77	H	——	1.629	1.461
Dichlorethylene,	$C_2H_2Cl_2$	97	48-60	(36)	——	1.278	——

Trichlorethylene,	C_2HCl_3	131.5	87	H	——	1.471	1.479
Perchlorethane,	$C_2 . Cl_4$	166	121	H	——	1.624	1.505
Tetrachlorethane,	$C_2 H_2 Cl_4$	168	147	H	——	1.601	1.501
Pentachlorethane,	C_2HCL_5	202.5	159	H	——	1.685	1.502
Monochlorbenzene,	$C_6 H_5 .Cl$	112.5	132	56	13	1.11	1.527
Dichlorbenzene	$C_6 H_4 . Cl_2$	147	172	62	17	1.35	——
Dichlorhydrin,	$CH_2Cl. CH$						
	$OH .CH_2Cl$	129	178	H	——	1.37	——
Epichlorhydrin,	$CH_2Cl .$						
	$CH . CH_2$	76.5	117	H	——	1.194	——
Carbon bisulphide,	CS_2	76	46	L	-20	1.268-1.293	1.620

Table - Oils and Solvents

SPECIFIC GRAVITY AND GALLONAGE PER HUNDRED WEIGHT AND TON.

English imperial gallon = 277.27 cu-inches

American Gallon = 231 cu-inches

Lbs. of water = 4.544 Litres

Lbs. of water = 3.785 Litres

Specific Gravity	English Gallons		American Gallons		Specific Gravity	English Gallons		American Gallons	
	Cwt.	Ton.	Cwt.	Ton.		Cwt.	Ton.	Cwt.	Ton.
0.700	16.0	320	19.2	384	1.000	11.2	224	13.4	269
0.710	15.8	316	18.9	379	1.025	10.9	219	13.1	262
0.720	15.6	312	18.7	373	1.050	10.7	213	12.8	256
0.730	15.4	307	18.4	368	1.075	10.4	208	12.5	250
0.740	15.2	303	18.2	363	1.100	10.2	204	12.2	244
0.750	15.0	299	17.9	359	1.125	10.0	199	12.0	239
0.760	14.8	296	17.7	354	1.150	9.7	195	11.7	234
0.770	14.6	292	17.5	349	1.175	9.5	191	11.4	229
0.780	14.4	288	17.2	345	1.200	9.3	187	11.2	224
0.790	14.2	284	17.0	340	1.225	9.1	183	11.0	219
0.800	14.0	280	16.8	336	1.250	8.9	179	10.8	215
0.810	13.8	276	16.6	332	1.275	8.8	176	10.6	211
0.820	13.7	273	16.4	328	1.300	8.6	172	10.3	207
0.830	13.5	270	16.2	324	1.325	8.5	169	10.2	203
0.840	13.3	267	16.0	320	1.350	8.3	166	10.0	200
0.850	13.2	263	15.8	316	1.375	8.1	163	9.8	196
0.860	13.0	260	15.6	312	1.400	8.0	160	9.6	193
0.870	12.9	257	15.5	309	1.425	7.8	157	9.4	189
0.880	12.7	254	15.3	306	1.450	7.7	154	9.3	185
0.890	12.6	252	15.1	302	1.475	7.6	152	9.1	182
0.900	12.4	249	14.9	299	1.500	7.5	149	9.0	179
0.910	12.3	246	14.8	295	1.525	7.4	147	8.8	176
0.920	12.2	244	14.6	292	1.550	7.2	145	8.7	173
0.930	12.0	241	14.5	289	1.575	7.1	142	8.5	171
0.940	11.9	238	14.3	286	1.600	7.0	140	8.4	168
0.950	11.8	236	14.2	283	1.625	6.9	138	8.3	165
0.960	11.7	233	14.0	280	1.650	6.8	136	8.1	163
0.970	11.5	230	13.9	277	1.675	6.7	134	8.0	160
0.980	11.4	228	13.7	274	1.700	6.6	132	7.9	158
0.990	11.3	226	13.6	272	1.725	6.5	130	7.8	156
1.000	11.2	224	13.4	269	1.750	6.4	128	7.7	154

4

THINNERS

Introduction

In order to reduce the cost of the product, the solvent is often diluted with one of the cheap volatile liquids, which is not in itself a solvent for nitro-cellulose, the products of this type available being the petroleum and coal-tar distillates. Owing to the fact that these are non-solvents, it is essential that they should be chosen so that they evaporate substantially at the same rate as the true solvent; if too high a distillate is used, the result will be that it remains after the solvent has evaporated and prevents the formation of a proper film. The same principle holds true of the active solvents — their range of evaporation should overlap; if two solvents are used of widely different rates of evaporation. such as acetone and amyl acetate, there is danger of pinholing of the film being caused by the volatile ingredient coming off rapidly during the drying.

The purity of the solvent used is another important consideration, as solvents, like most other substances, cannot be obtained industrially in a state of absolute purity. As a general rule, the impurities in commercial solvents are not harmful, and very often consist of substances which are also used in the formula, so that the impure article is really more efficient than a pure product — residual butanol in butyl acetate, and acetone in di-acetone alcohol are examples. It is, however, desirable to know the proportion of such impurities present, so that the formula can be accurately adjusted. these statements do not apply to certain impurities which are highly objectionable, and should be carefully eliminated — the most common of these may be briefly indicated as acidity, moisture, sulphur compounds, and dissolved solids. As in the case of the nitro-cellulose, a specification should be estiblashed for all solvents used, and supplies regularly tested for conformity.

A useful indication of the efficiency of a solvent is afforded by determining the stability of the solution formed with it. For this purpose a solution of a standard nitro-cellulose in the solvent is diluted with a thinner or non-solvent until the nitrocellulose is precipitated. The volume of thinner added, divided by the volume of solvent used, gives the *"dilution ratio"*. The following ratios are given : 2 gms. of nitro-cellulose being dissolved in 20 c.c. of solvent, the dilution ratio being found adding diluent to this solution until precipitation occurs, and dividing the volume required by 20.

Solvent	Dilution Ratio		
	Toluene	Petroleum Spirit	Water
Ethylene glycol mono-ethyl ether,	6.25	1.50	0.35
Ethyl lactate,	5.25	0.75	0.27
Di-acetone alcohol,	3.25	0.50	0.22
Butyl acetate,	2.75	1.00	0.00
Secondary amyl acetate,	2.00	1.00	0.00

The various solvents and thinners available may be usefully grouped according to their distillation range, which indicates approximately their evaporation rate, as in the following table :-

Below 100°C	**100-125°C**	**125-150°C**	**150-200°C**	**Over 200°C**
Petroleum ether,	Petroleum Spirit	Benzine	White spirit	Tetralin
Benzol,	Toluene	Light solvent naphtha	Heavy solvent naphtha	Benzyl alcohol
Industrial spirit,	Butanol	Xylol	Dekalin	
Absolute alcohol,	Butyl acetate	Amyl alcohol	Diacetone alcohol	
Isopropyl alcohol,	Ethyl carbonate	Amyl acetate	Cyclohexanol	
Acetone,	Light acetone oil	Tetrachlo- -rethane	Cyclohexane	
Methyl-ethyl ketone,	------	------	Cyclo-hexanol acetate	
Methyl acetone,	------	------	Ethyl lactate	-----
Methyl acetate,	------	-------	Ethyl oxalate	-----
Ethyl acetate,	------	------	Heavy acetone oil	
Ethyl propionate,	-----	------	------	------
Methylene chloride,	------	------	------	------

The following are some typical examples of solvent mixtures used in the preparation of lacquers :-

	1 %	2 %	3 %	4 %	5 %	6 %
Industrial spirit	15	-----	15	20	2	-----
Butyl alcohol	15	20	5	-----	------	10
Ethyl acetate	15	15	20	20	------	25
Butyl acetate or amyl acetate	10	15	5	-----	68	15
Methyl acetone,	10	10	10	-----	-----	-----
Benzol,	20	20	20	60	30	-----
Toluol,	25	20	15	-----	-----	25
Xylol,	-----	-----	10	-----	-----	25

1. Medium grade lacquer for wood
2. High-grade lacquer for wood
3. Cheap wood lacquer
4. Artificial leather
5. Bronzing medium
6. Enamel medium

POWDER COATING PRODUCTION

Introduction

In contrast to the powder applicator who is bombarded with alternative suppliers of equipment, the powder manufacturer has a limited choice in manufacturing equipment. It should also be noted that the basic operating principles of this equipment have remained fairly constant for the last 25 years.

Considering the overall process of taking the resins, pigments and additives through to the finished powder, each stage can be clearly identified as shown in the process flow sheet.

1. Pre-mix of raw materials
2. Compounding
3. Cooling and flaking molten extrudate.
4. Grinding.

Taking each stage in turn :

Pre-mixing

This stage in the process is necessary to create a uniform mix of raw materials to present to the compounder, and carry out some of the distributive mixing required. It could make economic sense to remove this stage of the process and carry out all of the mixing required in the compounder.

However as a typical formulation contains up to 10 different ingredients, some in a very small percentage, the difficulties of feeding such a number with sufficient accuracy and with multiple feed streams would be probably too expensive.

Hence the most economic and reliable method is to accurately weigh the ingredients into a pre-mixer.

Early pre-mixers were of the drum roller type and this type of mixer is still in use, it is a basic reliable unit with low capital outlay costs, its main drawback being the long mixing cycle, and stagnant zones in the corners of the drum. Subsequently slow mixing static machines such as ribbon or Z blade mixers were used. The main problem with this type of mixer being the long mixing times of 1 to 2 hours meant that any adjustment could cause unacceptable processing delays in production. The more reliable method uses a high speed fixed bow 1 mixer, *e.g.* the APV Dry disperser and the high speed change bowl mixer *e.g.* Mixaco. The operating principle is the same, i.e. a high speed intense mixing action using a blade rotating at fixed speed. Both units have very short mixing cycles. The main difference being the ability to change the actual mixing bowl/vessel on the change bowl unit, this does not have advantages regarding colour change/cleaning but by its more complex nature involves higher capital outlay.

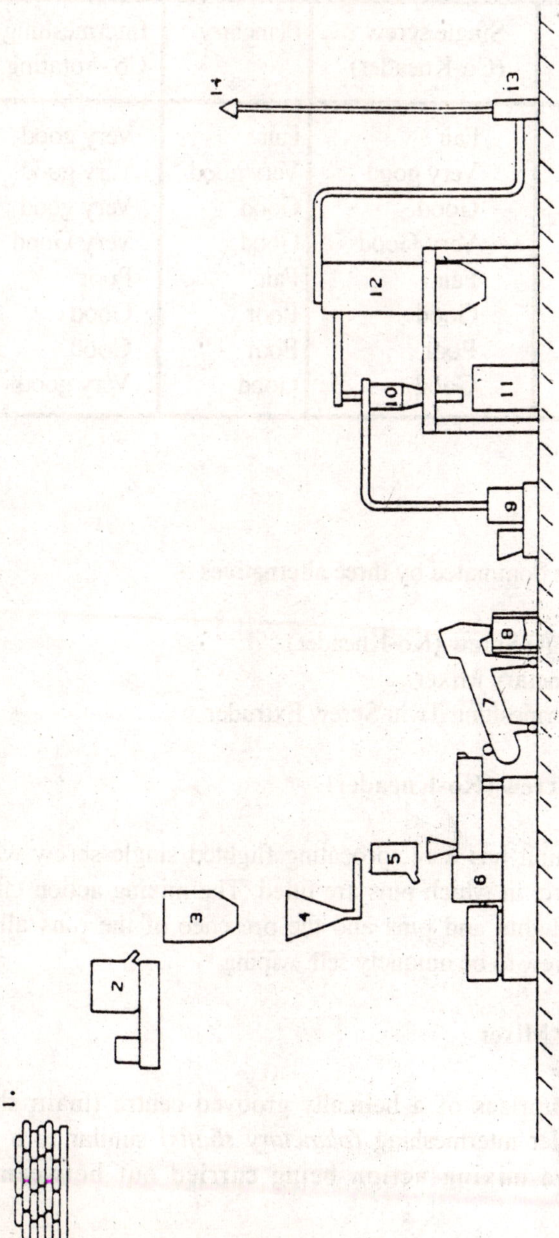

1. Raw materials stored in bags 2. High speed mixer 3. Pre-mix storage hopper 4. Single screw volumetric feeder
5. Metal detector 6. Twin screw extruder 7. Cooling conveyor with integral kibbler
8. Chip storage bins 9. Grinder 10. Cyclone
11. Finished product bagging and boxing unit 12. Dust collector 13. Fan unit 14. Atmospheric vent

Fig. 1: Process flow sheet (Powder coatings plant)

Figure 2

Characteristics	Single screw (Co-Kneader)	Planetary	Intermeshing Co - rotating
Free volume	Fair	Fair	Very good
Distributive mixing	Very good	Very good	Very good
Dispersive mixing	Good	Good	Very good
Kneading	Very Good	Good	Very Good
Heat transfer	Fair	Fair	Poor
Cleanability	Good	Poor	Good
Flexibilty	Poor	Poor	Good
Temp control	Good	Good	Very good

Compounding

The industry is dominated by three alternatives :-

A The Single Screw (Ko-Kneader)
B The Planetary Mixer
C The Intermeshing Twin Screw Extruder

A. The Single Screw (Ko-Kneader)

This type of unit has a reciprocating flighted single screw which moves within a barrel in which pins are fitted. The mixing action taking place between the flights and pins and the presence of the pins allows this type of single screw to be uniquely self wiping.

B. The Planetary Mixer

This unit comprises of a helically grooved centre (main shaft) surrounded by smaller intermeshing *(planetary shafts)* similar to a gear box in design. The mixing action being carried out between the intermeshing faces.

C. The Intermeshing Co-Rotating Twin Screw Extruder

In this type of extruder two shafts are set at specific centre distance ratios to give the intermesh. The shafts are co-rotating, the mixing action being carried out between the mixing elements fitted to the shafts.

Looking at the basic mechanics of the three methods of extrusion above, two key areas relevant to the process should be highlighted.

(I) Heating Method

Three methods in use, electricity, super heated water and oil. With electricity *(only available on twin screw extruders)* there are some obvious advantages to the user, these being, larger temperature range available, the electrical systems are designed to be intrinsically safe, faster response, cheaper to operate and cleaner to use. With the alternative method of superheated water and oil the same flexibility is not afforded to the user.

(II) Ease of Cleaning & Maintenance

Where plant operation demands frequent colour change with vastly differing colours, the ability to open and close the barrel on a Twin screw gives an abvious major advantage to the user. The opening barrel also allows easier maintenance and inspection.

If we take a general overview of the above mentioned compounding methods each has merit.

If we rate the terms used in figure 2 ranging from 1 to 4, poor =1. Fair = 2, Good = 3, Very Good = 4, we can obtain a comparitive rating. Figure 3. Although both the terms and rating may be arguable, we feel they give a fair representation of current compounders.

Cooling and flaking molten extrudate

Two main types of units exist, these being the chill roll type units as originally manufactured by Richard Simon *(currently available from several alternative suppliers)* and the cooled band as made by Sandvik or SBS. In both units, the extrudate is squeezed between two chilled rollers to form a thin sheet.

This sheet is then either :-

A. In the case of a chill roll, held in intimate contact with a large cored roller which is cooled with chilled water to stiffen the sheet prior to its being fed into a kibbler unit.

B. In the case of a conveyor, fed along a belt *(usually stainless steel)* which has its underside cooled by cold water spray, prior to feeding into a kibbler unit usually mounted on the end of the band. This can be supplemented by cooled air blown on the upper surface.

By comparison the chill roll has the advantage of being compact and usually less expensive. But, because of its design has a very low discharge height.

Grinding

The basic principle of the grinding process have remained unchanged and until recent years the choice of suppliers has been very restricted with one manufacturer having a virtual monopoly. The basic principle is that the chip is fed either by gravity, screw feeder, or drawn in by the air flow and controlled by a rotary valve, into a grinding chamber which grinds product using a disc fitted with a series of pins or hammers. The powder is then classifed by a vaned disc driven at a variable speed within the mill and finally the powder is separated from the airstream using a cyclone, and fed off to a boxing unit.

Figure - 3

Characterics	Single Screw	Planetary	Intermeshing Co-rotating
Free volume	2	2	4
Distributive mixing	4	4	4
Dispersive mixing	3	3	4
Kneading	4	3	4
Heat transfer	2	2	1
Cleanability	3	1	3
Flexibilty	1	1	3
Temp control	3	3	4
Total	**22**	**19**	**27**

Process Developments

Having looked at the mechanics of the process, we must look at the process in itself. Powder is billed as the environmentally friendly solution to solvent based paints and that to a certain extent is true. We must not however become complacent about this statement. Any process that handles very fine powder can be inherently dangerous. There is always the risk that with the wrong combination of powder and air in the presence of an ignition source, there can be an explosion. This is leading to legislation in certain countries and a move towards 10 bar overpressure systems for the grinding.

It is true that powder by comparison to solvent based paints is environmentally friendly and with pressure from the environmentalist groups the move from solvents will continue. Growth projections for powder range from 5 to 15% per annum dependant on the country and the body or agency you talk to. Obvoiusly this growth will also be effected by world economy and recession, but in general terms in a good economy, growth in developing areas/markets of 10% per annum would not be unusal. There is then the question of some of the additives used and their long term health effects with continuous exposure. The manufacturer is constantly facing new governmental legislation, for example the new C.O.S.H.H. regulation *(control of substances hazardous to health)* in *England* places the responsibility on the employer to monitor long term exposure to such potentially dangerous additives and we therefore see a move towards the *T.G.I.C.* free range of products.

Demands of the end users/applicators also place heavy demands on the powder manufacturer and hence the extruder supplier. It should also be noted however that the technology of the extruder has moved on considerably to keep pace with both the manufacturers requirements, and state-of-the-art *Engineering Practices*. These changes have led to improvements in machine thruputs, control systems and their accuracy, materials of construction, ease of equipment operation, and far more ergonomically designed machines. All of these features pass on very obvious benefits to the user. It is critical for the powder manufacturer to be able to produce consistent *"bit free"* powder with the correct degree of gloss, dispersion etc, to suit the requirements of his customer, and advances in compounder technology as mentioned above clearly help him to achieve this aim.

New markets for the use of powders are always being sought which may require the coating to have different characteristics from currently available powder *e.g.*, flow etc. One of the *"Golden Chalices"* of the industry being automotive finishes market where the powder must have the ability to resist chipping, retain colour and gloss and have a low enough cure temperature so as not to cause distortion of body shells, during curi... his requires low temperature extrusion with perfect dispersion which is not easy to achieve.

An integral part of this new formulation technology is the agitator configuration used in the compounder. With the flexibility of the slip on agitator component method which allows the intensity of the work being put into the pre-mix to be varied and also allows where necessary the development of specialist agitator components the extruder manufacture can help the resin chemist to achieve necessary product quality. Fines and their disposal are an industry wide problem, this type of interchangeable screw allows configuration to be designed and set for the re-working of fines, to put them into a re-usable form, thus helping to solve the problem of disposal of finess. This is a major advantage of the twin screw over the ko-kneader and planetary type mixer where changes in the mixing tool configuration are extremely dificult or not possible.

It is critical to the future of the industry that the development of the extruder goes hand in hand with the formulation development and to this, end both powder and extruder manufacturers must work closely together

Formulation of Powder Coatings

Powder coatings are 100% solid containing a reactive binder group, a resin and a crosslinking agent and formulated with pigments fillers as well as flow agent and often accelerators are dispersed in the extruder below the reaction temperature, ground and cooling and sieved to a particle size below 100 μm.

The crosslinking temperature of powdercoating is that temperature at which the cross linking of the powder film to a coating take place *i.e.* between 140° to 200°C.

Epoxy powder coatings consists of epoxy resin which cross link with modified dicyanodiamides, pyromellitic dianhydride etc. The polyurethane powder coatings consists of saturated polyesters containing hydroxyl groups and blocked aliphatic isophorone desocyanate adducts. During cross linking a deblocking takes in isocyanate adduct and the free isoyanate group reacts with OH groups of polyesters and forms an urethane.

The hybrid system in which epoxide systems which cross link with saturated polyesters containing carboxylic groups. Apart from this binder components, the influence of powder coating formulation on the film properties are well defined. The formulation defines its limit, on which substrate it is to be used *(nature of substrate)*, to which environment it is to be exposed, and any special requirement as described, these perfections can be achieved only by careful selection of binder, pigments, fillers, selection of binder, pigments, fillers, flow agent and more often accleraters. The basic recipes of these formulations are more or less similar.

Epoxy System :-

Binder	[Epoxy resin 54-55% + Cross linking agent (Ratio 1:1 - 1:1.2)	[Epoxy resin 64-65% + Cross linking (1:1 - 1:1-2)
Pigments	[Pigment and 44-45% filler	[Pigment and 34-35% filler
Flow agents	0.5%	0.5%

Dry-blending process

Epoxy Polyester System :-

	A	B
Binder	[Expoxy polyester + (54-55%) Cross linking (1.1 - 0.7.0.3)	[Epoxy polyester + (64-65%) Cross linking
Pigment	[Pigment + (54-55%) filler	[Pigment + (34-35%) filler
Flow agent	0.5%	

Polyurethane System :-

Binder	Polyurethane + (54-55%) Cross linking agent (0.9:1.1-1.1:0.9)	Polyurethane + (64-65%) Cross linking agent (0.9:1.1:1.1:0.9)

Pigment	Pigments + (44-45%) Filler	Pigments + (34-35%) Filler
Flow agent	0.5%	
Benzoine	0.5%	

Epoxide powder have the advantage of lowest curing temperature and the shortest curing temperatures.

Polyurethanes have prolonged curing period at relatively higher temperature the curing reactions can be accelerated by adding suitable additives.

(The above formulations of powder coatings are mainly suitabe for matt surface finishes and weathering resistant coatings).

6

BITUMINOUS PAINTS

Introduction

Bituminous coatings include both petroleum and natural asphalts and coal tar or pitch products and their combinations or blends with resins or bi or polyfunctional reagents, such as chlorinated rubber, acrylonitrile polymers, epoxy resins, polyesters, isocyanates, polysulfides and vinyl resins. All types have been formulated and applied in both the molten form and from solvent solutions.

Gilsonite is a natural asphalt. It has a very high softening point and may be blended with softer asphalts, and it is also cooked with linseed and fish oils to produce asphaltic varnishes and *"Japans"*. The tar produced from thermal decomposition of coal is only tar or pitch which is widely used in paints. Bituminous coatings are widely used for the protection of steel, concrete, and wood because of their relatively low cost, excellent resistance to water, chemical inertness, adhesion, and high electrical resistivity. With the exception of the chemically-cured and mineral-filled emulsion types, they are thermoplastic and tend to cold flow even at moderate temperatures. The thermoplastic types are degraded by sunlight, which produce the familiar crazing or alligatoring in exterior coatings. In general, thermoplastic coal tar coatings alligator more than those based on asphalt. Alligatoring is the result of the surface becoming hardened either from oxidation or evaporation of plasticizing oils and subsequently cracking from cold flow movement of the subsurface. This process is repeated until the cracks become quite wide resembling the skin of an alligator.

Two major bituminous substances degrade or weather by different mechanisms. In general, coal tar pitch weathers by surface hardening through loss of plasticizing oils by evaporation and sublimation, whereas asphalt weathers through osidation to-water soluble acids. The chemically-cured and mineral-filled emulsion type bituminous coatings are apparently free of these types of degradation and weather by the familiar chalking. Bituminous coatings are produced in five general types.

1. Solutions of bitumens in solvents without fillers referred to as cutbacks and applied cold.
2. Heavy compositions of bitumens and fillers without solvent and applied hot after referred to as *"enamels"*.
3. Aqueous emulsions of bitumens with or without fillers or polymeric resins.
4. Heavy compositions of bitumens and fillers known as mastics, applied by trowelling or pressure spraying.
5. Two-component compositions; one which contains the bitumen and filler and curing agent, the other which contains a reactive resin. When combined, they form a heavy mastic heavy mastic having a limited pot life but which cures on application to a thermo-setting bituminous coating.

Bitumens are black or dark brown in colour. Therefore, they are used to a limited extent in coloured paints. However, the addition of aluminium pigment produces a bright metallic appearance of the leafing characteristics of flake aluminium. The addition of aluminium to roof coatings reduces cold flow and alligatoring and also lowers the temperature in the building because of the heat reflecting property of aluminium. Leafing power of the vehicles in asphalt roofing paints is affected by their viscosity and specific gravity and solvent power of the solvent. Better leafing is obtained with strong solvents such as xylene or high flash naphtha than with mineral spirits.

The hot-applied bitumens commonly called *"enamels"* are produced and consumed in the largest volume. Hot-applied enamels are used extensively on the exterior of underground oil and gas pipelines and on the interior and exterior of water lines where coal tar products are the only type permitted. For these types of applications it is customary to apply a fluid cutback coating as a primer. Usually this is a special bituminous cutback; however a recent development is fast-drying primers based on chlorinated rubber. These primers have eliminated the former difficulty of obtaining enamel bond at low temperatures and high humidities. The primer application is followed in oil and gas pipelines with a coat of molten enamel about 1/16 or 3/32 in and a wrap of asphalt or coal tar saturated felt or glass fiber.

Bitumens may be emulsified in water with soap or chemical emulsifiers or with mineral emulsifiers such as bentonite. A formulation for the preparation of asphalt emulsion which contains bentonite or colloidal clay is given below

Ingredients	*% by weight*
Asphalt	55-60
Water	36-46
Colloidal clay	1.75-3.0

The clay should be thoroughly dispersed in the water and the melted asphalt added slowly with constant agitation. Acid treatment of the bentonite slurry is necessary for adequate dispersion or emulsification.

Asphalt emulsions are thixotropic, which permits application of heavy coats without subsequent flow or sagging. In addition, it appears that a clay structure remains in the coating after drying which eliminates the troublesome cold flow characteristics of cutbacks and hot-applied coatings. However, coatings from asphalts emulsions are fairly sensitive to moisture, and in some cases they may be re-emulsified after application and normal drying. For this reason, they should be used with caution on surfaces which will be submerged or subjected to condensation of moisture.

Coal tar water emulsions, in contrast to asphalt emulsions, are invariable emulsified in the presence of a mineral filler and stabilized with a colloidal clay.

A typical formulation is as follows :

Ingredients	*% by weight*
Coal tar pitch	30-40
Mineral filler	20-30
Water	40-50
Bentonite	1-2

It has been found that prolonged aging of the clay slurry is essential before emulsification to obtain optimum performance. Coal tar emulsion coatings are completely resistant to re-emulsification after drying, exihibit low vapour absorption, low moisture vapour transmission *(usually less than 0.8 perms)*, and in some forms are quite resistant to jet fuel and gasoline attack. These emulsion coatings may be used on moist concrete without danger of blistering which amy occur with cutback or hot applied coatings. Emulsion coatings eliminate the fire hazard of cutbacks and the problem of providing heating equipment for hot applied materials.

The filled type of bituminous paints contain materials such as asbestos, cork, mica, sand and finely powdered inorganic materials. Cost and end use requirements determine the type of filler used, but all fillers tend to reduce cold flow, alligatoring and flammability.

Bituminous mastics containing short fiber asbestos and other mineral fillers are heavily bodied, thixotropic compositions which may be applied by trowelling, brushing, or spraying. A typical example is the cold applied asphalt mastic which has following requirements :

Composition	***% by weight***
Filler	40%
Vehicle	60%

Filler :

Inorganic, containing short fiber asbestos and fine inert materials	100%

Vehicle :

Asphalts	55% ± 10%
Petroleum solvents	45% ± 10%

The fine inert materials are mica, silica or slate floor.

Bituminous coatings give excellent service for many years on ships and docks, steel structures, and underground tanks and pipelines.

Use of coal tar the protection of steel plants are described below :

1. 400 sq. ft. per gallon per coat for mild conditions using a fluid cutback coating.
2. 100-150 sq. ft. per gallon per coat for more severe conditions, using a viscous cutback coating.
3. 35-70 sq. ft. per gallon per coat for very severe conditions using a filled high-consistency thixotropic cutback type composition.
4. 50 sq. ft. per gallon per coat for corrosive atmospheres using an aqueous dispersion of coal tar pitch and filler. A primer is recommended.
5. 400 sq. ft. gallon per coat for water lines and tanks handling potable water and air-conditioning equipnment using a cutback of selected pitches in solvents which do not contribute taste or odour.

For adequate protection, at least two coats of a fore-mentioned material should be applied, and frequently three coats are specified.

The coal tar emulsion type coatings have been modified through incorporation of acrylonitrile polymers to obtain products which not only markedly reduced water absorption, lowered moisture vapour transmission, and improved oil resistance, but also have the ability to bond firmly and protect steel and other metals having imperfectly prepared surfaces.Their bonding properties and chemical resistances are so great that they are employed for chimney linings, chemical resistant mortars for insulation and the adhesion of semi-resilient flooring. They exihibit no flow over a wide range of temperature. The dried film slowly cokes to a hard imprevious carbonaceous structure at temperature approximating 400°F.

The more radical change in the field of bituminous coatings has come about through the incorporation of diepoxy and polyepoxy resins and isicyanates into the bituminous material. The resultant product is modified with solvents and pigments to make two component systems, one of which contains the curing agent which is added just prior to application.

The pot life varies from 1/2 to 8 hours over the temperature range 40-120°F. It is reported that the coal does not behave as a diluent but actually enters into the curing reaction in some fashion. The tar-resin reaction products have improved resistance to water, chemicals and weathering, and better adhesion than the resins alone.

A typical formulation is :

Composition	*% by weight*
Reactive resin	25
Coal tar	25
Solvent	20
Pigment	25
Curing agent	5

Bitumen Varnishes

	Ingredients	*Parts by weight*
(a)	Petroleum bitumen (m.p.80-90°C)	55.0
	High flash solvent naphtha	10.0
	White spirit	35.0

Heat the bitumen to 200°C, cool to 170°C, and stir in thinners.

(b)	Natural bitumen (gilsonite)	28.0
	Tung oil	28.0
	Litharge	2.0
	White spirit	41.0
	Coablt-naphtha (6% metal)	1.0

Mix the bitumen and tung oil and heat to 250°C. Sprinkle litharge and raise the temperature to 280°C, with stirring. Cool to 180°C, thin and add drier solution.

Bitumen Emulsion

An emulsion for road making contains spramex bitumen 48, water 49.5, oleic acid 2 and calcined Na_2Co_3 0.5 %. The bitumen is warmed at 95°-98°C, and the oleic acid added. The water is heated separately with the Na_2Co_3, and the two liquids are introduced into the emulsifier. Another emulsion contains sparmex bitumen 50, mineral oil 2-2.5, resin soap 1.5 - 2, KoH 1, and water 45 %. The bitumen is melted and the mineral oil added during agitation. The water is heated to boiling, and in it are dissolved the soap and KoH. The liquids are mixed at 95°. With more bitumen there must be added 1-2% of glue, starch, gelatin or Na silicate, during or after emulsification.

Bituminous Coating

A composition suitable for coating or surfacing purposes or incorporating in road making materials comprises low temperature tar with a fatty pitch dispersed therein and an addition of CaO or other alkaline compound adapted to accelerate hardening. In an example 2 parts stearin pitch is heated with 5 parts shale oil at not over 60 lb. per sq. inch to 150° for 4 hour to give a solution which is diluted with 40 parts shale oil and stirred into 250 parts tar warmed to 50°C. The cooled product may be mixed with gravel and shaked CaO.

Bituminous Enamel

	Pounds
Paving Asphalt	52
Trinidad Asphalt	15
Rock Asphalt	15
Rosin *(Dark Grade)*	1
Portland Cement	17
Slaked Lime	2-1/2

This product must be heated before applying.

Asphalt or Bitumen Emulsion

Rosin	100 lb.
Slaked lime	3-3/4 lb.
Heat at 149°C and mix until uniform.	
Add while mixing. Fuel oil	103 lb.

Take 4 lbs. of above mixture and add to 100 lbs. melted bitumen or asphalt and then disperse mixture in 0.05 N potassium rosinate solution to give a 57 % bitumen content.

7

SYNTHETIC ENAMEL PAINTS

Introduction

By definition an enamel is a paint which has a smooth high-gloss finish. The term *enamel* is borrowed from ceramic industry to describe paints which appear like appear like glazed porcelain. Most synthetic enamels contain alkyd varnish vehicles or use vehicles that have good or levelling properties; pigments that have fine particle size and good ready dispersibility and generally have low pigment volume concentration.

Vehicles for low cost interior enamels are either coldent blends of bodied oils and resin solutions or regular heat-processed varnishes. Vehicles for high-grade enamels are chiefly oil-modified with pentacrythritol is widely used for this purpose. The phthalic anhydride content ranges from 23-30%, with the majority at about 25%.

For white enamels of highest gloss, pure titanium dioxide is the best pigment but reasonably good gloss results from the extended pigments at higher pigment volume concentration because of the fine particle size and good flow properties of the extenders. Most white enamels are *"blued"* or *"bleached"* by addition of a small percentage of ultramarine blue or a combination of blue and a permanent violet toner. The use of zinc oxide in white enamels is controversial because it imparts both desirable and undesirable properties. The desirable properties include after yellowing, absorption of ultra-voilet rays, improved drying and hardening of the coating. The undesirable property is its tendency of becoming brittle and haze or fog on prolonged aging shortly after drying in hot humid weather.

Normal amounts of lead and cobalt drier are added to both interior and exterior white enamels. Manganese drier should not be used because it accelerates after yellowing. Leaded cobalt drier should be used together. Cobalt drier when used alone will dry more slowly if titanium di-oxide is used since it absorbs cobalt during aging of the enamel in the container and the enamel will dry more slowly after aging unless steps are taken to prevent the absorption. This may be done by grinding a small percentage of litharge with the pigment during manufacture of the enamel.

A number of additives are used to improve dispersion of the pigment and thereby to obtain higher gloss and better hiding or to control the consistency and leveling properties. They must be selected carefully and used in specific proportions depending on type of vehicle and pigment.

The principal vehicles for interior enamels are the modified phenolic resin varnishes. Such vehicles have good stability with colour pigments and they are fast drying and have good gloss. For exterior applications such varnishes do not have the disability of alkyd resins. Exterior enamels may be used on wood and metal furniture and also on the train around windows and doors; harder drying finishes are required on furniture; therefore the enamels are based on medium oil length alkyds, Trim enamels require alkyds of longer oil length either or with addition of linseed oil.

Enamels based on iron blue and chrome green frequently are brightened by addition of white or chrome yellow, and in such case pigment ratio would be higher.

Formulations of Synthetic Enamel Paints

1. Crimson Enamel

	Kg.
Rubine toner	1.50
Resin, pentacite 405 *(solid)*	12.0
Cobalt naphthenate	0.25
White spirit	6.0
Lead naphthenate	0.500

2. Orange Enamel

	Kg.
Orange dye	4.0
Phenolic resin	1.0
Resin, Becasol PLL 60	12.0
White spirit	6.0
Lead naphthenate	0.15
Cobalt naphthenate	0.075

3. Smoke-Gray Enamel

	Kg.
Titanium dioxide (Rutile)	4.0
Middle chrome	0.009
Red oxide	0.50
Ultramarine blue	0.30
Prussian blue	0.095
Black Fe_2O_3	0.002
Resin Becasol PLL 60	15.00
White spirit	4.0
Cobalt naphthenate	0.250
Lead naphthenate	0.500

4. All India Gray Enamel

	Parts
Lithopone	15.0
Chalk	10.0
Barytes	45.0
Carbon black	0.1
Yellow ochre	5.0
Double-boiled oil	22.0
White spirit	3.0
Naphthenate drier	0.5

5. White Enamel

	Parts
(a) Titanium dioxide	26
Antimony white	3
Refined linseed oil	20
After through grinding add,	
refined oil	50
Alkyd resin	1
(b) Titanium dioxide	25
Refined linseed oil	6
After through grinding add,	
varnish	60
White spirit	7
Linseed oil	4

6. Sea-Green Enamel

	Parts
White zinc oxide	32.0
Deep chrome-green	3.0
Light chrome-green	5.0
Varnish	60.0

7. Green Egg-Shell Finish

	Parts
Prussian blue	0.5
Titanium Dioxide	15.0
Zinc oxide	2.0
Alkyd resin	0.5
Lemon chrome	7.5
Aluminium stearate	1.0
Slate powder	15.0
Copal varnish	30.0
Grind well the above ingredients in a uniroll mill and copal varnish	30.0
White spirit	8
Driers	1

8. Stoving Black Enamel

	Parts
(a) Barytes	3
Carbon black	5
Silica	9
Varnish	30
China clay	15
White spirit	20
Driers	1

	Parts
(b) Gilsonite	112
Cashew nut shell oil	47
Cobalt-maganese drier	45
Double-boiled oil	40
Solvents	200

First if all dilute the Gilsonite and add cashew-nut oil gradually in it and then heat it to 315°F. Heat it at this temperature for 1/2 hr. then lower the temperature to 280°F and heat it at this temperature for 1/2 hr. Now cool it to 230°F and add drier to it. Gradually cool it to 180°F and then add solvent. Solvent is 10% pine oil, 5% white spirit.

9. White Synthetic Stoving Enamel

Ingredients	*Parts by weight*
(a) Rutile titanium dioxide	24.0
Linseed/glycerol alkyd *(as above)*	40.0
(44% fatty acid, 55% solution in xylol)	
xylol/butanol (4/1)	6.5
Grind the above in ball mill for 18 hours	
and add Alkyd as above	19.0
Thinner as above	5.0
melamine-formaldehyde resin	
(60% in butanol)	5.5
(b) Rutile titanium dioxide	24.0
Linseed/glycerol alkyd *(as above)*	41.9
Urea-formaldehyde resin	
(60% in xylol/butanol)	25.6
Thinners as above	8.5

10. Stoving Enamels for Refrigerators

	%
Titanium dioxide	18
Castor alkyd solution	37
Urea formaldehyde resin	30
Xylol	12
Butanol	3

11. Wood Flour Enamels

New wood is treated with a sealer of the following composition.

	% by weight
Glyptal solution	66.0
Xylol	3.0
Petroleum spirits	30.5
Cobalt naphthenate (6%)	0.5

Gray Flour Enamel

	Pounds
Lithopone	170.0
Rutile titanium-calcium pigment	82.0
Lead titanate	62.0
Modified phenolic linseed dehydrated castor oil varnish (80% castor oil, 25% linseed oil of 25 gallon-length)	*gals.* 89.0
Lead naphthenate (8%)	1.5
Manganese naphthenate (2%)	1.5
Cobalt naphthenate (2%)	1.5

Non-Yellowing Utility Enamel

	Pounds
Titanium dioxide *(Colour Retentive)*	288
Zinc oxide, fine particle size reactive	48
Soya type modified alkyd (32% phthalic anhydride), 65% mineral-spirits solution	226
Lead naphthenate 24%	8
Grind on 3 roller mill and reduce paste with	
Soya type midified alkyd (32% phthalic anhydride), 65% mineral spirit solution	340
Mineral spirits	114
Cobalt naphthenate	1.25

Non- Yellowing Super White Architectural
(Easy Lapping and Non-Saffing)

	Pounds
Titanium dioxide, *(Colour retentive)*	288
Zinc palmitate	4
Zinc oxide, *fine particle size reactive*	32
Soya type alkyd *(29% phthalic anhydride),* 85% mineral spirits solution	288
Lead naphthenate (24%)	3
Mix, grind and Thin paste as follows	
Soya type alkyd (35% phthalic anhydride), 50% mineral spirits solution	147
Soya type alkyd *(29% phthalic anhydride)* 85% mineral spirits solution	75
Mineral spirits	159
Cobalt naphthenate (6%)	3
Lead naphthenate (24%)	6
Tint as required	

Low Cost Synthetic White Enamel

	Pounds
Titanium dioxide *(calcium base)*	800
Surfex	200
Ester Gum Modified Alkyd (15% Phthalic Anhydride), 80% Mineral Spirits Solution	635
Mineral Spirits	175
Cobalt Naphthenate (6%)	4
Lead Naphthenate (24%)	9

Bobbin Enamel

	Pounds
Shellac	120
Alcohol	180
Mix until dissolved and then add Castor oil	1
Pigment	20
Toluol	2

Olive Green Dipping Enamel

Carbon black	10
Chrome green (25%)	192
Boiled linseed oil	63
Varnish	15
Benzine	13

White Enamel Paint Indoor

Zinc white	80
Titanium white	20
Varnish	120

Grind together throughly and thin to brush consistency.

Enamel Coating for Cans

Varnish	1 gal
Mica	5 lb

Porch and Deck Enamel (Gray)

	Ox.
Lithopone, high strength	63
Aluminium Stearate	1
Blue tone lamp black	1
25-Gallon length, hard, through drying spar varnish	35

Grind above paste in roller mill and thin with twice its weight of varnish which should give the optimum consistency.

8

EMULSION PAINTS

Introduction

Emulsion paints are becoming increasingly popular these days. This may be attributed to the fact that production methods used in the making of latices and emulsions involve relatively simple equipment, much less complex than that used in the making of alkyd resins.

The early paints based on synthetic rubber latex did not hae sufficient cohesive property and water proofness after drying and their brushability had to be improved by the addition of casein. The waterproofness and adhesion of such paints was upgraded by the addition of emulsifying agents. One of the major drawbacks of these paints was the long time taken by the drying oil or alkyds to dry. Polyvinyl acetate emulsion paints have certain advantages as well as disadvantages over rubber latex finishes. PVA emulsion paints are relatively unaffected by sunlight or oxidation and form good outside finishes particularly over masonry. Polyvinyl acetate resin is water receptive and films made from it breathe and allow the passage of moisture but on exterior walls it reduces washability and in this regard these emulsions are not generally as good latex coating. But the processing methods required for making polyvinyl acetate emulsions are simpler than the styrene butadiene types because pressure equipment needed to liquefy and store butadiene is not required.

The acrylic emulsions contain polymers of acrylic esters and have a number of outstanding properties. They are very stable, resistant two freezing and less permeable to moisture than polyvinyl acetate. When made into paints they have very good chemical resistance, adhesion, flexibility. and durability. Their outstanding adhesion and flexibility properties are afforded by the successful use of acrylic emulsions on exterior woodwork over lead based primers.

Acrylic emulsion are coming into extensive use for alkaline plasters and for external painting over new stucco and cement.

Emulsion paints can be grouped into oleoresinous emulsions paints and latex emulsion paints. latex is a family of paints made by mixing or emulsifying various chemicals into a number of formulate with water, instead of dissolving them in solvents such as mineral spirits or turpentine. The methods of preparation, however, differ from those for distemper emulsions. Since the substances used in making latex paints are plastics, these paints are sometimes also called plastic emulsion paints. These paints are very popular in India and their production is still on the upward trend.

Oleoresinous Emulsion Paints

The three classes of emulsion paints depending upon the type of emulsion to which the vehicle belongs are :

(i) Emulsion paints of the oil/water (oils in water) type.
(ii) Emulsion paints of the water/oil (water in oil) type.
(iii) Emulsifiable paints.

Emulsion Paints of the oil/water type

In these paints the vehicle is an oil in water emulsion in which oils, resins, and other hydrophobic substances form the dispersed phase and water of aqueous solution the continuous phase. This type of paint can be thinned with water, produces hydrophobic coatings after drying and is most important type of emulsion paint.

A typical formulation of oil-water type emulsion paint will have the following necessary and optional ingredients :

(a) Necessary Ingredients

(i) Water emulsifying agents
(ii) Bodying agents
(iii) Preservatives
(iv) Oils and resins or combination of the two
(v) Driers
(vi) Hiding Pigments.

(b) Optional Ingredients

(i) Anti-foaming agents, salts and alkalies, etc.
(ii) Organic solvents
(iii) Extenders

The selection and quality of emulsifying agent to be used is one of the most difficult tasks of the formulator. Usually two or more agents are combined. A sound combination consisting of soaps and casein is cheap and efficient. It can be further improved by the addition of an agent of the ester type and a small amount of sulphated or sulphonated substance.

Bodying agents also help in increasing the emulsifying properties of the system. They raise the viscosity of the system when added even in relatively small concentration. They are used in paints to improve the stability by raising the viscosity of the continuous phase and to act as protective agent for dispersed phase. Most commonly employed bodying agents are alginates, gum tragacenth, and methyl cellulose. Their presence to the extent of fractions of one percent wil give the desired results.Use of preservative is essential to prevent natural agents like casein from deteriorating by the action of bacteria. An excellent preservative is mercuric chloride, but its use is dangerous because it is extremely poisonous. Phenol and its derivatives are widely empoloyed, e.g., sodium orthophenyl-phenate, para-chloro metaeresol and phenyl mercuric acetate.

Besides operating at elevated temperature, reducing the speed of agitation and avoiding any unnecessary sunction of air into the batch, some efficient anti-foam agents may also be employed during emulsification to reduce the foaming to a minimum. Pine oil is a cheap anti-foaming agent which is not detrimental to emulsion, even if employed in rather large doses (1-2% of the vehicle). Similar to pine oil is the octyl alcohol. Other synthetic anti-foaming agents like methyl-stearate of high efficiency must be used in smaller amounts. Salts, alkalies are sometimes necessary in formulations, e.g. to bring the castor or soya protein in solution, or to balance the pH of the emulsions. The alkali is best supplied in the form of ammonia or a buffered alkali soft like borax, tri-sodium phosphate, and tetra sodium dyprophosphate.. The amount of alkali sholud be kept as low as posible. Most common emulsions are on the alkaline hideee with pH around 8.

Manufacture of this kind of paints is carried out in different steps as indicated below.

(a) Preparation of the Aqueous phase

The first step is to bring the solid constitunt in solution. Casein and other proteins are sokd in pure water to form a pulp. The alkali previously dissolved in water is added under agitation to the pulp. heating helps on fast carrying out the operation. Other ingredients like alginates, bentonite, and water soluble gum etc. can be dissolved seperately in cold water or added directly to the casein solution. Finally the emulsifiers, the anti-foaming agents and the mixture are homogenised by the continuous agitation. If the batch is uniform and free from dissolved particles, it is ready to take the seperated oil phase.

Water phase (external phase) is responsible for the formation of paint stability, thinning, brushing properties, and initial drying. It is the main constituent upto 80% by volume. Pure and clean water may be used but soft water is more desirable.

(b) Preparation of the Oil phase

The oil phase determines the properties of the ultimate film with respect to its through drying, hardness, elasticity, outdoor resistance etc. The selection of the ingredients of the oil phase follow the same lines as the formulation of the aqueous phase, depending upon the end use of the paint. Exterior paint will be formulated on high grade oleoresinous base combinations with long-oil alkyd resin. For interior formulations, shorter oil length or lower grade resins will be emploued. Vehicle for white or light shadeswill be extra pale resins or oils etc.

Oil, Resins & their Combinations

As a general rule, any combination of oils and resins can be emulsified, but metal resinates as limed rosins or zinc resinate should be avoided. The use of blown oils or magnesia-treated oil should also be avoided. The driers should be throughly mixed with the oil phase before emulsification. The amount of driers used in these paints is alittle higher than in solvent type vehicles.

Solvents and thinners play an important role in oil-water type emulsion paints. Any ordinary paint and varnish thinner can be employed in emulsion formulas, with the exception of some water-soluble solvents like acetone or methyl alcohol which are frequently used in solvent type lacquers; solvents are used only to reduce the cost or decrease the consistency of an oil phase but in case solid resins are to be emulsified, the addition of suitable solvents becomes indispensable.

Vehicle

Two different principles of formulating emulsion paint vehicle are practised.

(i) In the first case, concentrated emulsiona with 50-60% non-volatile are produced and kept in stock for later use. They are reduced with some additional water or blended with some casein solutions etc. just before the pigments are introduced. This type of procedure is quite advantageous since by blending the concentrate with several ingredients in varying proportions, different products may be obtained, e.g. exterior, interior and low-cost types.

(ii) In the second case, vehicles ready for use with 25-40% non-volatile, are prepared and worked up without being stored for any length of time, sometimes in one single operation with the pigmentation.

Pigmentation of Emulsion Paints

Certain restrictions are made in selecting the pigments and extenders for oil-type emulsion paints. Pigments and extenders to be avoided are those which are sensitive to alkali or water-soluble reaction. The use of large amounts of carbon pigments is also avoided. The use of following pigments in this type of paints is generally recommended.

White

Titanium dioxide; zinc sulphide and barium sulphide extender types as lithopone, titanated lithone; and titanium0barium pigments.

Yellow

Yellow iron oxide (precipitated or natural), cadmium yellow, organic yellow (Hansa yellow).

Green

Chromium oxide green, chromium hydrate green, phthalocyanine green.

Blue

Ultramine, phthalocyanine blue.

Red

Iron oxide red (precipitated or natural), organic pigments.

Black

Iron oxide black, certain water dispersable blacks.

Extenders

China clay, mica, magnesium silicate, barium-sulphate.

Proportion of Pigment to Vehicle

Most of the emulsion paints are manufactured as paste or semi-paste to be reduced with water before using. The proportion of pigment to vehicle varies with type of pigments and end use. For exterior paints of high grade, non-chalking pigments are used with the pigment volume rather low; for interior use, especially if dull fastness is desired, extended pigments may also be used and the pigment volume may be kept rather high.

The following formulas may serve as a guide.

Exterior Paste Paint

Water	0 to 20%
Pigments	40 to 50%

Interior Paste Paint

Vehicle (25-30% non-volatile)	40 to 50%
Pigments and Extenders	50 to 60%

Manufacture of Paste Paints

There are different ways of introducing the pigments into an emulsion vehicle. The simplest and probably the most commonly employed method is to add the pigments to the ready prepared vehicle. Some other procedures have also been prepared vehicle. Some other procedured have also been suggested e.g. to grind the pigment in the water phase or the oil phase before emulsification.

The mixing can be excuted in any type od mixer for heavy paste. The vehicle, or the emulsion and the solutions to be blended, are put in the machine and the pigments are gradually added under continuous agitation. In many cases through mixing will be sufficient to produce smooth and lump-free pastes, especially if water-dispersible pigments are used. For colours and pigments of less good dispersion it wil be necessary to mill the paint by passing over a stone or a roller mill at loose seting. If high-speed mixers equipped with a heating device are available, the pigmentation can be executed successfully at elevated temperatures. Under these conditions the vehicle becomes thinner, allows swift agitation and shows excelent wetting properties. Most emulsion paints are supplied as a soft paste to be reduced to brushing consistency with water before use. This saves not only shipping weight and volume but is also the safest form for storage over long periods from the stand point of stability. The reduction with water must be easy to perform by mixing with a paddle. The amount of water to be added depends upon the formulation and the intended use. The water should be added in several small portions undr continuous agitation; adding too fast may produce lumps. The paint after thinning must look smooth and uniform.

Exterior emulsion paints containing a higher ratio of vehicle take more water to be reduced to brushing consistency, e.g. 3-4 quarts to the gallon, whereas the average interior paint requires 2-3 quarts to the gallon.

Oil Water Type (Alkyd) Emulsion Paints

Alkyd emulsion paints are suspensions of pigments in an aqueous emulsion of an alkyd resin. After drying, the films of such paints are insoluble in water and posses the characteristics of the alkyd resin employed.

In this case, emulsions are heterogenous dynamic systems. As such, they differ in physical characteristics from oil or varnish vehicles and from the common casein aqueous glue bases. Broadly speaking, they may be divided into two components — the dispersed phase and the continuous phase. In the emulsified alkyds, these terms are synonymous with the resin phase and the aqueous phase respectively. The interfacial film differs from either component in actual composition, but usually differs from the continuous phase only in percentage composition, and may be considered as part of the continuous phase.

The Resin Phase

Properties like colour, viscosity, and hardness of the resin may vary over a wide range without producing noticeable change in the emulsion. In the dried film, of course, such variation becomes readily apparent. Solubility of alkyds has a decided effect on the emulsion produced. Long-tail alkyds show the least reactivity; short-oil alkyds show marked salt-forming tendencies, and present difficulties in preparing stable emulsions. Well-dispersed alkyd resin emulsions are milk-white in colour, regardless of whether the alkyd itself is relatively good or poor in colour. Discolouration in the emulsion develops as the particles increase in size through asslomeration; or when films of dehydrated emulsion deposit on the surface. Partially dried, opaque films are likely to appear darker to theeye against the white background of emulsion than dried transparent films of the resin.

The average particle size of the dispersed alkyd is between 0.5-1.0 micron in diameter. In a good alkyd emulsion, all particles should be below 1 micron and at least 25% of the particles should be less than 0.5 micron in diameter. Liquid driers are conveniently added to the resin before emulsification and constitute a part of the resin phase.

The Aqueous Phase

The ingredients and general properties of the aqueous phase determine, to large extent, the properties and behaviour of the emulsion. The viscosity of the aqueous phase is determined by the nature and concentration of emulsifying agents, stablizer, and wetting agents present. The viscosity is also present. The viscosity is also affected by the pH of the solution, salts present, and changes in molecule size in some of the ingredients. In order to obtain the most stable and finely dispersed emulsions, it has been found desirable to emulsify alkyds in slightly basic solutions. For this purpose, ammonia or morpholine is used.

To facilitate the mechanical operation of emulsification and to stabilize the emulsion against mechanical and thermal shock, certain emulsifying agents in relatively very low concentartion agents in relatively very low concentration are used. Casein is one of the most effective agents if it is used in a suitable form.

When the emulsion is spread upon a surface in a thin film , water evaporates, the emulsion breaks, and the resin particles coalesce to form a continuous, homogenous, clear film.

Manufacture

Emulsified alkyds have been successfully developed and used commercially in the production of paints which have outstanding properties. It is not possible to make broad statements regarding the use of alkyd emulsion in general. The emulsion is a very complex system, especially a pigmented emulsion, and there is a wide variation in behaviour. Such properties as brushability, rate of drying, water-proofness, and durability vary widely with emulsions of alkyd resins. A very caretul control of all the factors involved is necessary if satisfactory results are to be obtained.

Alkyd emulsions usually contain 40-50% solids. Drying oil modified alkyd resins which possess good durability and clour retention should be used. Emulsified alkyds give films of satisfactory durability, and may be used in formulating either interior or exterior paints. Compared with oil paints, this type of finish is easier to apply and gives cleaner shades. It may be applied to wet surfaces.

Properly made emulsions possess good wetting properties and may be used with a good variety of pigments; water-disposable pigments which are resistant to lime and cement should be used. Such pigments include titanium-dioxide, barium-titanium pigment, lithopone, chine clay, silica, and mica. Use of such pigments as zinc oxide, white lead, iron blue, whiting and asbestine should be avoided.

The aqueous emulsion and the pigments are mixed in the usual way. The paste is then passed through a stone or roler mill. In many cases, only one mixing is necessary. The mill should be loosely set so that the stones or rolls are not overhead while dispersing the resin. It is more desirable to supply these paints in the form of heavy pastes, employing only enough water to ensure good handling. Such pastes are readily reduced with water before application.

During the manufacture of emulsion preservatives like phenol, cresylic acid, borax etc. are added in sufficient quantity. The employment of very high ratio pigments requires the use of additional quantities of preservatives if they are not used in reasonable lengths of time. The correct reduction to secure proper application must be determined for each formulation. The ratio of binder to pigment depends on the purpose for which the paint will be wmployed. Dyrable exterior white paints should contain approximately one part by weight of binder to one part of pigment. A good interior paint would contain five or six parts by weight of pigment to one part of binder.

A typical formulation of an exterior and an interior white alkyd emulsion paint is given below :

Exterior White Paint Interior White Paint

Titanium dioxide (Water-dispersable)	100 lbs.	Titanium dioxide	200 lbs.
Barium-titanium pigment (extra-strength)	100 lbs.	Barium-titanium pigment 200 lbs.	
		Collodial silica	150 lbs.
Flake mica	25 lbs.	Flake mica	25 lbs.
Silica (50% solids)	25 lbs.	Alkyd emulsion	400 lbs.
Alkyd emulsion (50% solids)	400 lbs.	Water	450 lbs.

Uses and Application

Alkyd emulsion paints dry quite rapidly and in good drying weather two coats may be applied the same day. The speed of drying, freedom from odours and the washability make them especially suitable for use in apartment houses, hotel rooms and offices. This type of finish is especially suited for porous surfaces of all kinds including concrete, stucco, plaster, brick and fibreboard. By varying the ratio of pigment to non-volatile binder, paint suitable for a wide variety of uses may be formulated. In cases of wood or metal surface, an oil type primer should be employed. This type of paint has also been successfully over fresh plaster.

Water-oil Type Emulsion Paints

In this type of paints the vehicle is an emulsion of water in oil type. A small amount of water or aqueous solution of soap, alkali or sodium silicate is added to regulate the consistency and the price. Emulsifying agents like aluminium stearate or calcium linoleate present in the batch.

In attempting to formulate water-oil emulsion paint of brushing consistency with large doses of dispersed aqueous phase, the viscosity of the continuous oil-phase must be kept very low in order to obtain finished products of workable consistency. This must be done by using low viscosity binder, e.g. raw oil or if bodied oils or oleoresinous binders of high viscosity are employed, the body of volatile thinners.

The water-oil emulsion paints are, as a rule, low in volatile binders. Some improvements over this shortcoming is to be excepted by the use of efficient emulsifying agents (of the hydrophobic type), which will produce water-oil emulsions of finer particle size and lower viscosity. Durability conditions of the film produced from water-oil type emulsion paint, on the whole, are more favourable than with oil-water type.

Emulsifiable paint, in itself, is not an emulsion, but produces an emulsion on addition of water. The main reason for developing this type of paint seems to be endeavour to some shipping weight and space, since the paint can be extended with its own volume of water to yield paint of brushing consistency and with still higher proportions of water to be used as spraying or dipping paint. It can be thinned down with petroleum thinners as well, there by producing a normal solvent type coating.

Application of Emulsion Paint

Emulsion paint is usually applied with the brush, although it can also the applied by spray gun or by dipping. Recently, the application with the "roller-coater" has been much advocated as especially fitted for emulsion paint on large and plain surfaces.

For cleaning the brush, water; warm soap water with the addition of some ammonia; or mineral spirit may be used. Emulsion paint can be employed on almost any surface, e.g. raw plaster, brick, stucco, wall-board, wood, and old painted surfaces. It is particularly suited to moist surfaces. Two coats produce excellent results, the first acting efficiently as a primer-sealer for porous surfaces.

These paints cannot be used over old water-paint coatings which would be dissolved by the aqueous phase. It should not be applied on unpainted metallic surfaces. Nail heads etc. should be prevoiusly touched up with some rust preventing oil paint.

Merits and Demerits of Emulsion Paints

Merits

(1) Water is cheap and readily available.
(2) No intoxicating vapours or strong odours on drying.
(3) No fire hazards involved
(4) Easy brushing
(5) Fast drying (two coats can be applied on the same day.)
(6) Application on moist surfaces is practicable.
(7) Flat coatings of high light reflectance are formed.
(8) Better hiding at lower cost.

Demerits

(1) Use of emulsifying and stabilizing agents is indispensable.
(2) Formulation and manufacture more complicated
(3) Slightly inferior in storage stability.
(4) Sensitive against heat and frost.
(5) More porous films are formed
(6) No gloss or semi-gloss finishes are practicable.

(7) Slightly inferior in washability and weather resistance.

Latex Emulsion Paints

Latex emulsion paints have been developed during the last twenty years. Of the great number of synthetic latices known, economic considerations have allowed only polyvinyl acetate, polystyrene, styrene butadiene and polyacrylic ester latices to achieve importance as water paint media.

Latex emulsion paints or emulsion polymerized paints are those paints in which the film forming vehicle is a thermoplastic polymer, formed by polymerization together with plasticisers, pigments and additives.

A dispersion of an organic polymer in water can be prepared by two distinct methods. A pre-formed polymer can be emulsified in water; alternatively the polymer can be prepared by polymerization of an aqueous emulsion of the monomer. The method chosen to prepare an emulsion of a particular system will depend upon the type of polymer and on second-order transition temperature of the polymer. For example. the vinyl and acrylic polymer emulsions are prepared by emulsion polymerization of the monomer. Emulsion polymerization is a process which is widely used for all types of monomers. The monomer is added to water in a vessel fitted with agitators for vigorous agitation and is emulsified by the addition of soaps or the other surfece active agents, protective çolloids etc. A catallyse is then added and on heating the emulsion, usually in the temperature range of 40-100°C, polymerization of the monomer results and the polymer is obtained in the form of a stable colloidal dispersion in the water.

Variations of the above process are in use; for example, the monomer may be added gradually as the polymerization proceeds. In some cases the dispersions during manufacture are allowed to reflux; in other cases, for example, with vinyl chloride, the polymerization is carried out in sealed vessels under pressure.

An important technical advantage of this process is that water which is present as an inert diluent provides better heat transfer. The refluxing of the reaction mixture can also be employed as a means of removing exothermic heat from the system. The final aqueous dispersions are commonly used in that form in many surface-coating applications, for example, vinyl acetate polymer and copolymer dispersions are widely used in the so-called emulsion paints.

The latex is prepared by emulsifying the liquid monomer (or monomers) in water with the aid of an anionic emulsifying agent, and then inducing polymerization by heating in the presence of a peroxide catalyst to give a colloidal dispersion of soild or semi-solid polymer particles. Applied films are dry as soon as the water has evaporated, but with polyvinyl acetate and polystyrene they are extremely friable or powdery unless a plasticiser has been incorporated. Plasticised particles have sufficient fluidity to allow the surface tension, brought into play in the minute voids between them when they come together as the water evaporates, to cause the spheres to fuse together to produce a cohesive film.

In a paint made from such a latex, the pigment particles, originally in the aqueous phase are embedded in the coalescing spheres of plasticized polymer as the water is lost. It would seem that such paint coatings fall considerably short of a continuous film of binder with pigment uniformly dispersed in it. THeir heterogeneous structure may partly explain their permeability to moisture even when only lightly pigmented, which in turn, and in conjuction with their alkali resistance, allows them to be applied to new plaster, etc.

Advantages

Latex paints have a number of advantages over oil-bound water paints. They are virtually odourless and can be recoated after about 4 hours. They possess excellent sealing power, and consequently with correct handling, allow a uniform finish to be obtained over surfaces, exhibiting considerable and varying suction. The finish becomes extremely washable, even scrubbable, in the course of a few days or weeks, and this in conjuction with their course of a few days or weeks, and this in conjuction with their stain resistance, due to the smooth, non-absorbent character of the finish, makes them particularly well-suited for locations where the decoration is likely to be soiled and may therefore need frequent washing.

Disadvantages

The disadvantges are few, but serious, because they concern the very important properties, adhesion and flexibility, on which the performance of a paint is built. Absorption surfaces, such as plaster, cement, brickwork, wall-boards and probably old water paint, cement. brickwork, wall-boards and probably old water paint, present no adhesion problem if perfectly clean and firm , because they provide the necessary mechenical key, a microscopically rough texture. On the other hand, with smooth non-absorbent surfaces, presented for example, by oil paint and enamel paint decorations, attempt has to be made to provide a mechanical key, a microscopically rough texture. On the other hand, with smooth non-absorbent surfaces, presented for example, by oil paint and enamel paint decorations attempt has to be amde to provide a mechanical key by thorough scouring, and whether any real adhesion is obtained on such surfaces largely depends on how efficiently this is done. Moreover, if a surface carries a film of grease, or any suspension of loose, powdery material, adhesion is obtained on such surfaces largely depends on how efficiently this is done. moreover, if a surface carries a film of grease, or any suspension of loose, powdery material, adhesion, failure manifested by peeling and flacking is almost sure to occur. A finishing paint, of course, would not normally be applied direct to such surfaces; loose, powdery surfaces would be applied direct to such surfaces; loose, powdery surfaces would be first bound down with a primewr, and dirty or greasy surfaces would be washed down. These are perfectly satisfactory preparations for all paints except plastic emulsion paint, which can be relied upon to adhere firmly preparations for all paints emulsion paint, which acan be relied upon to adhere firmly to the smooth surface of a primer or of any oil or enamel painteven after washing down unless or of any oil or enamel paint even after washing down unless it is first throughly scoured. Adhesion defects are particularly likely to occur when the paint is exposed to condensation or very high humidity, e.g. in kitchens and bathrooms, and may become strikingly evident when the finish is washed.

It is however, not our purpose to over-emphasize these shortcomings because latex paints, when used with discretion, have proved to be a valuable addition to the range of decorative materials. Their practical significance, however, must be recognizsed, because not only this adhesion failure or embrittlement manifest itself only after some subsequent re-decoration, but it is most difficult to deal with. Such failures are less likely to occur with oil-bound water paints, and moreover, with water paints, they can abe prevented by priming between decorations, or if flacking has occured it can be usually rectified by treatment with a suitable primer. Both these practices, however, are ineffective with latex paints.

Loss of adhesion can be obviated and improved water resistance and washability obtained by modifying latex paints with alkyd or oleoresinous varnish emulsions, but a fairly highproportion is nedded to be really effective. At the same time, it allows higher pigmentation levels to be used and imparts greater resistance to film-embrittlement. however, it complicates formulation, especially pigmentation reduces the alkali resistance even to a paint can be no longer applied direct to new plaster. It tends to make brushing and cleaning morte difficult and renders the paints no longer truly odourless.

Equipment used for emulsion making

The choice of emulsification equipment is usually dictated by the application of the resulting emulsions. The major factors affecting the choice of emulsifying equipment are the apparent viscosity in all stages of amnufacture, the amount of mecahnical energy input required, and heat exchanger demands. Various equipments used for emulsion making are described below :

(1) Hand stirring

Hand stirring is the simplest form of agitation. Depending upon the selection of emulsifiers and the ingredients to be emulsified, either stable or semi-stable, large or small particle size emulsions may be prepared. For hand-stirring a formulation having a maximum ease of dispersibility is, of course, required. Good cases of dispersibility is not related to good stability.

(2) Slow-speed mechanical stirring

For many viscous amulsions containing high solids, soapgels, resinous materials etc., a mechanically rotated paddle or anchor-type agitator is best.

(3) The Kaddy mill

It consists basicaly of a high-speed rotor mounted at the end of a shaft which revovlves in a closely fitting stator. Both rotor and stator are slotted so that material undergoing dispersion is drawn into the rotor and then ejected through the stator slots at high speed. Kaddy mills are made in a range of sizes and are used for the dispersion of "soft" pigments in both aqueous and non-aqueous paints.

(4) Silverson mixer

It is also based on the rotor/stator principle. The rotor consists of a propeller around which is fitted a circular wire-mesh ring. The action of the propeller is to draw in the material and then effect it at high speed through the gauze. Dispersion is by impact, shear, and attrition. Both these pre-mixing devices of Silverson and Kaddy type are followed by the use of colloid mill and pebble mills.

(5) Colloid mill

Colloid mill may be considered as a modification of a turbine. In this case, the clearence between the rotor and stator is of the order of a few thousandths of an inch which results in an extremely high shearing action. The product from a colloid mill usually has a uniform particle size. Owing to the tremendous shearing forces applied to the emulsion, a significant temperatures rise occurs must be employed. Milling may be done on fluids and pastes. Rate of throughput in this well varies inversely with the viscosity.

Pebble and Ball Mills

Pebble and ball mills may also be used to make some emulsions and more extensively in pigment suspension. They represent a class of relatively slow-speed equipment for emulsification.

Besides these other equipments like propellers, turbines, homogenizers or a combination of these may also be employed for the manufacture of emulsion.

Equipment used for polymerization

Different types of equipments are used for polymerization. A brief account of such equipments is presented below :

(i) Stirred-Reactors in glass

For batches larger than one litre, stirred-reactor is employed. In the case of monomers of not too low boiling points, this may be arranged from standard glassware with a reflux condenser.

If low boiling monomers are being polymerized, a Sutherland glass reactor or a reactor constructed from a section of industrial glass is more desirable.

(ii) Pilot Plant and Plant Techniques

Most units of pilot-plant size for emulsion polymerization (5-500 gal. reactors) and many full scale commercial plants use single-batch reactors. The general arrangement of such units is shown in the diagram.

It is seen that in addition tot the stirred reactor, stock solution tanks, blow-down tank, flash-tank and strippping column are also nedded. The field of emulsion media is expanding so rapidly that it would be beyond the scope of this book to mention more than a few of those in actual use or under development. The discussion of specific materials will, therefore, be limited to those which have already found widespread application in emulsion paints.

Poly Vinyl Acetate

Poly vinyl acetate (PVA) emulsion were the first synthetic high polymer emulsions ever to be used on a large scale in the manufacture of paints. In Europe, by far the greatest volume of emulsion paints is based on PVA, and in the U.S.A. and India, the popularity of PVA emulsion is growing steadily.

In recent years the performance of PVA emulsion paints has been markedly improved by the introduction of vinyl acetate copolymer emulsions . In these, permanently flexible resins are obtained by the copolymerization of vinyl acetate with other ethylenically saturated compounds . The most widely used co-monomersw are the C^2 to C^{10} alkyl esters of acrylic, maleic and fumaric acids and the higher vinyl esters, especially vinyl propionate, corporate and sterate.

Copolymer emulsions owe their better performance to several factors, the most important of which is of course the absence of volatile or migrating plasticizers. Contributing factors are the better bleed resistance and tolerance for organic pigments , finer particle size with lower water absorption of the copolymer resin. A fairly wide compatibility with oleoresinous materials not only enhances "wet" adhesion to oil paints but also facilitates the compounding with alkyds, tung oil or polymerized dehydrated castor oil, and thus helps to obtain a good key on chalky surfaces and gloss paints.

It should be mentioned, however, that the copolymerization is not always so simple a process that one has merely to use a performed mixture of the monomers in the appropriate proportion. It seldom happens that monomers polymerize at approximately the same rate and, unless some precautions are taken , the copolymers formed at the beginning of a polymerization would contain a high percentage of the faster polymerizing monomer. A more uniform copolymer may be prepared in such a case by gradual addition of the more active monomer during polymerization.

Properties and Uses of Vinyl Emulsions

Plasticizer loss leading to embrittlement has resulted in homopolymer types being replaced by copolymers. The latter are also more resistant to repeated freezing and thawing. Copolymers show greater adhesion with the result that they can be applied in conditions where the homopolymers are unsuitable, *e.g.* in kitchens , bathrooms and over old paint work. They are used on both interior and exterior wall surfaces. On the latter the durability is good but not quite as good as that of acrylic emulsions. They are, however, a little less costly. Co-polymer emulsion paints are textured with sand to produce imitation stone paints for exterior use. Other uses are as primers for a number of porous surfaces such as hardboard and various types of building boards.

The most widely used emulsion paint is the general purpose eggshell finish and the following formulation illustrate the proportions of the major ingredients.

(1) Eggshell finish (Homopolymer)

	% by weight
Rutile titanium dioxide	30.0
Paris white	6.0
Carboxymethyl cellulose (5% solution)	7.0
Preservatives	0.1
Calgon 5% solution	1.0
Water	15.7
PVA emulsion	40.2

{14% plasticizers
55% solids; P/B = 1.6/1}

(2) Eggshell finish (Co-polymer)

	% by weight
Rutile titanium dioxide	30.0
Paris white	7.0
Carboxy methyl cellulose (5% solution)	7.0
Preservatives	0.1
Calgon 5% solution	1.2
Water	21.1
Copolymer emulsion (55% solids) (P/B=2/1)	33.6

Polyvinyl Chloride Emulsions

Today the bulk of the so-called vinyl coating resins are copolymers of vinyl chloride with vinyl acetate or less frequently with vinylidine chloride. By adjusting the nature and properties of the co-monomers the properties of the copolymer resins may be varied over a wide range.

The vinyl chloride-vinyl acetate co-polymers not only are more soluble, but they also leave better compatibility with plasticizers and other synthetic resins. Some effect of the progressive replacement of vinyl chloride by vinyl acetate may be considered. The higher figure given in the following preparations refer to vinyl chloride content. A 99.5% copolymer for example, shows some solubility in cyclic ketones at room temperature. By increasing the vinyl acetate to a 90:10 ratio the copolymer can be dissolved in aliphatic ketones. At 87:13 ratio the copolymer is soluble in ketones and the solution tolerates addition of aromatic hydrocarbons; such a polymer can be used in solutions as highly concentrated as 35% solid content. A 62:38 co-polymer is soluble in ketones and esters and such solutions tolerate additions of hydrocarbons and alcohols. A typical commercial product can be employed at a concentration of 40 percent; it is compatible with nitrocellulose and many other resinous materials. Another typical commercial product containing

91% vinyl chloride 3% vinyl acetate and 6% Vinyl alcohol, is soluble in a wide range of solvents such as ketones, esters, and tolerates hydrocarbons and alcohols.

Vinyl co-polymer emulsions are used on both exterior and interior wall surfaces. These are also suitable for use in kitchens, bathrooms and over old paint works. These are less costly than acrylic emulsion paints and are textured with sand to produce imitation stone paints for exterior use.

Acrylic Emulsion Paints

Acrylic emulsion paints contain polymers of acrylic esters and have shown a number of outstanding properties. They are very stable, resistant to freezing and less permeable to moisture than polyvinyl acetate. When made into paints they show very good chemical resistance, adhesion, flexibility and durability. An example of their adhesion and flexibility is afforded by the successful use of acrylic emulsion on exterior woodwork lead-based primers. Acrylic emulsions are coming into extensive use for alkaline plasters and for external painting over new stucco an cement. A recent development in exterior paints is a vinyl-acrylic resin that is compatible with zinc oxide and leaded-zinc oxide pigments. It is expected that exterior formulations will benefit from the desirable properties of zinc-good opacity to ultra voilet light, good cleaning and colour retention properties and resistance to mildew. In the industrial field, there is a new thermosetting acrylic emulsion which shows hardness, impact resistance, adhesion, gloss and resistance to water and chemicals. Acrylic emulsion paints have also been used chiefly for interior work. It dries faster and keeps its colour better than any type of paint. The only drawback is that it is little more costly.

Owing to the high price of monomeric acrylic esters the commercial exploitation of acrylic emulsions was slow to develop, except perhaps in Germany where the early realization of the direct synthesis of acrylates from acetylene reduced their production costs to acceptable levels. The old route for the production of acrylic esters from acetaldehyde cyanohydrin is now being replaced by more modern processed, *e.g.*, the reaction of ketone with formaldehyde which leads to acrylic acid with formation of Beta-propiolactane as an intermediate. In future, the oxidation of propylene to acrolin and acrylic acid, or perhaps other petro-chemical routes, may be found even more economical.

The other commercial type of acrylic esters is methacrylates which are esters of methacrylic acid. Methacrylates are still chiefly produced from acetone, hydrocyanic acid and alcohol via acitone cyanhydrin.

When the price of acrylic monomers begins to approach that of less expensive monomers used for the production of paints and surface coating media, notably vinyl acetates, styrene and butadiene, a rapid expansion of the commercial uses of acrylic esters themselves, other acrylic monomers like acrylonitrile, acrylamide, acrylic acid, and last not the least, methyl methacrylate may be used in such materials.

The four principal acrylic acid derivatives and seven methacrylic acid derivatives available commercially as monomers are the following :

(1) Acrylic acid
(2) Methyl acrylate
(3) Ethyl acrylate
(4) n-butyl acrylate
(5) Methacrylic acid
(6) Methyl methacrylate
(7) Ethyl methacrylate
(8) n-butyl methacrylate
(9) n-hexyl methacrylate
(10) n-octyl methacrylate
(11) n-lauryl methacrylate

The main difference between the polymers of the two series is that the polymers of the lower esters of methacrylic acid are considerably harder than the polymers of the corresponding esters of acrylic acid. Methyl methacrylate polymer is widely used in plastic industry, where as acrylic and methacrylic and ester polymers are widely used in the form of their aqueous dispersions in textile treatment and in the coating of leather. They are used widely in the so-called emulsion paints instead of polyvinyl acetate or styrene-butadiene co-polymer.

Bulk of the acrylic are produced by the emulsion polymerization which is the most useful process for polymerizing the acrylate esters, producing stable dispersions with excellent film-forming properties for use in paint industry. Emulsion polymerization by a batch process is illustrated by the flow diagram.

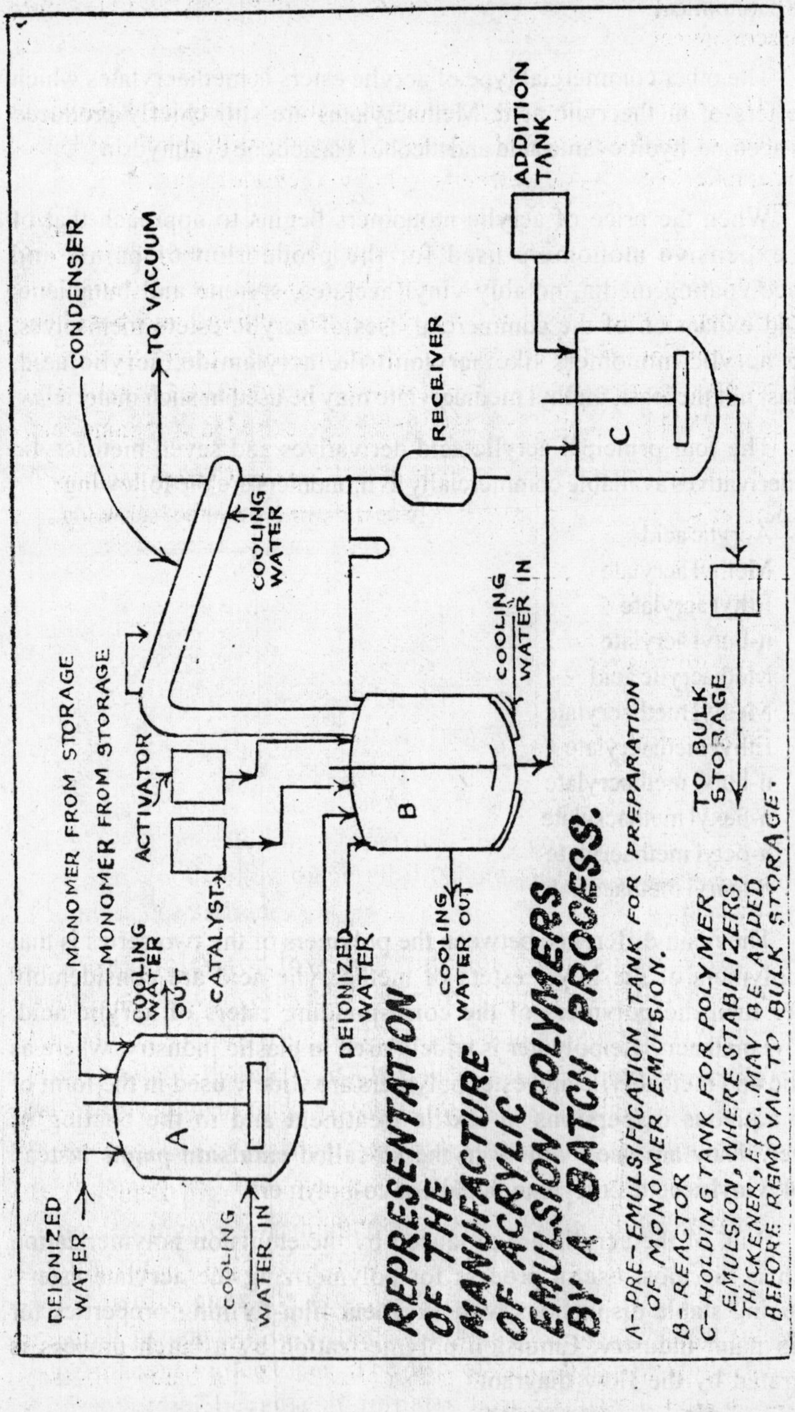

REPRESENTATION OF THE MANUFACTURE OF ACRYLIC EMULSION POLYMERS BY A BATCH PROCESS.

A - PRE-EMULSIFICATION TANK FOR PREPARATION OF MONOMER EMULSION.
B - REACTOR
C - HOLDING TANK FOR POLYMER EMULSION, WHERE STABILIZERS, THICKENER, ETC. MAY BE ADDED BEFORE REMOVAL TO BULK STORAGE.

A process for carrying out what is essentially a batch reaction in a continuous fashion utilizes a series of reactors. This process should not be confused with a steady-state reaction in which the conversion changes with time; in the continuous methos using a series od ten reactors the conversion changes with position. For example in a series of the reactors the conversion in the eighth reactor is higher than in the sixth. Each separate reactor in the series is itself in a steady-state condition, however, the concentration of reactants in a particular reactor remains constant. One might consider carrying out an emulsion polymerization continuously under steady-state conditions in a single reactor. Since the concentration of initiator, monomer, emulsifier, and modifier are constant. This would be expected to lead to a more homogeneous polymer compared with a batch reaction where the concentrations are constantly diminishing. This is not necessarily found, however, since residence time in a single-stage reactor under ideal stirring conditions is only an average. Some latex particles will be in the reactor for much less than average residence time and others for a much longer period. Among the advantages of the continuous reactor type over the batch process are :

(a) the uniformity of the reaction,
(b) the operational control, and
(c) the fact that no time is lost in filling and emptying the reactors.

The techniques employed in emulsion polymerization of acrylic monomers usually follow conventional lines. Emulsion stabilizers may be non-ionic surfactants like the polyethylene glycol ethers of alkyl phenol, the alkali metal sulphonates of alkylated aromatic hydrocarbons, long chain alkyl sulphates, fatty acid soaps and similar surface tension depressant with micelle-forming ability. In addition, hydrophilic colloids are sometimes employed, especially synthetic materials such as the alkali metal or ammonium salts of polyacrylic and polymethacrylic acid. The most commonly employed polymerization initiators are the alkali metal or ammonium salts of peroxydisulphuric acid, often in conjunction with organic peroxides such as tertiary butyl hydroperoxide, and the redox activators such as sulphoxylates, hydrosulphites, bisulphites or ferrous salts. Acrylic emulsions normally have rather fine particles with diameter of the order 0.005 to 0.3 microns. Then dry to clear, glossy, colourless water-resistant films. The excellent light resistance combined with oil and tar resistance has contributed to the recent developments in U.S.A. automobiles finishes containing methacrylic acid ester polymers.

Occasionally, the acid value of these products is deliberately raised by copolymerizing the acrylic or methacrylic acid ester with a small proportion of acrylic methacrylic acid itself.

The case with which acrylic monomers can be copolymerized with each other and with vinyl or other unsaturated compounds makes these very versatile starting materials for surface coating media, and commercial acrylic ester resins are generally copolymers combined to produce the optimum drying and film properties. The composition of commercial resin is generally not available. So far, only relatively few of the many possible acrylic copolymers have been studied on a commercial scale. The paints media which have undergone the most extensive field trials are emulsions of acrylate-methyl methacrylic copolymers containing as a third component a minor proportion of acrylic or methacrylic acid. Much of the information published to-date on decorative acrylic emulsion paints refer to this system or to similar systems containing ethyl acrylate as the major constituent. Any generalisation on the behaviour of acrylic media would at this stage appear a little premature. A great deal remains yet to be discovered and no doubt the recent substantial reduction in manufacturing costs of the higher alkyl esters will stimulate extensive trials with acrylic media in the near future.

Formulations of Emulsion Paints

High Thixotropic Emulsions

A number of commercial paints of a more highly thixotropic character than usual have been announced in recent years. They have special utility on application to ceilings, and may make it possible to give adequate coverage to some vertical surfaces with only one application. Folowing table gives some typical formulations of thixotropic paints. These paints set to firm gels within 24 hours of adding the sodium silicate solution. It is considered that these formulations should be stable for at least six months at normal storage temperatures, although a little syncresis can occur. This can be prevented by the addition of about 0.2 percent of a bentonite clay to the paint.

Thixtropic Paint Emulsions

Ingredients	Parts by weight		
	1	2	3
1. Rutile Titanium Dioxide	25.8	25.8	25.8
2. China clay	5.3	5.3	5.3
3. Ethyl-hydroxy cellulose (2% aq.)	12.9	—	—
4. Sodium carboxy methyl cellulose (4% aq.)	—	12.9	—
5. Methyl cellulose(4% aq.)	—	—	6.5
6. Sodium Hexametaphosphate (4% aq.)	0.9	1.4	0.9
7. Sodium benzoate (10% aq.)	3.5	3.5	3.5
8. Polyvinyl acetate copolymer emulsion (55% aq.)	34.6	34.6	34.6
9. Sodium silicate (10% aq.)	4.3	4.3	4.3
Water net	12.7	12.2	19.1

Thixotropic Paint

The following are dispersed in a kinetic dispersion mill for 10 mins.

Ingredients	Paint by weight
Water	1,000
Ammonium polyacrylate	10.5
Ammonia (10% aq.)	10.5
Sodium hexameta phosphate	3.5
Rutile titanium dioxide	1,400
Micronised asbestine	210
Whiting	7.5
Then Add	
Hydroxyethyl cellulose, medium viscosity	
Water	16 proir }
Vinyl acetate-n-butyl acrylate copolymer	475 solution }
emulsion (54% soild)	1700
Water (to wash mill)	50

To the abov(.iny of the following may be added to produce a thixotropic paint.

Ingredient	*Parts by weight*		
	1	2	3
Triethanolamine zinconate in n-butanol (80% aq.)	40	—	—
Potassium titanium oxalate (20% Ti O_2)	—	60	—
Potassium aluminium sulphate (potash alum)	—	—	80

Among the most interesting of modern of obtaining thixotropy, the use of water-based chelates of titanium may be mentioned. In general, in order that titanium chelates should be most effective, the emulsion should include a hydroxy group containing stabilizer such as hydroxyethyl cellulose, a starch or polyvinyl alcohol. The titanium chelate is added in a proportion of 0.25-5% by weight of the emulsion, and there is no restriction on the nature of the polymer. It is claimed that among other advantages these products have less tendency to syncresis and the final dried films show improved scrub resistance compared to films without the titanium additive. Under comparable conditions diethanolamine titanate produces rather more powerful gels than triethanolamine titanate, and this gel strength increase with time *(up to 5 times the original strength within 40 days after preparation)*.

Following table gives some typical formulations.

Ingredients	*Parts by weight*		
	1	2	3
Rutile titanium dioxide	250	296	168
Talc	36	47	—
Whiting	—	47	—
Sodium hexameta phosphate (4% aq.)	12	14	9
Sodium carboxymethyl cellulose (4% aq.)	84	63	100
Water	110	100	70
Sodium carboxymethyl starch (5% aq.)	—	51	—
Nos. 1 and 3 are ground in a colloid mill, No 2, in an edge runner: then add			
Vinyl acetate — 20% Vinyl caprate copolymer (56% aq.)	360	—	—
Acrylic ester copolymer	—	254	—
Copolymer-Emulsion copolymer of styrene, acrylonitrile, ethyl-acrylate, methacrylic acid (47% aq.)	—	—	200
Iragalite Yellow (Pigment dispersion)	—	10	—
Water, net	140	100	70
Di-isopropoxy-bis-(beta-di-ethanolamine ethoxy) titanate (82% aq.)	10	13	7.7

It is possible to use complexes of zirconium rather than titanium to attain thixotropy. Examples of suitable complexes are shown in the following table.

Zirconium Complexes

Ingredients	*Proportions by mols.*		
	1	2	3
Zirconyl carbonate	4	4	1
Acetic acid	16	16	3
Coconut oil fatty acid	2	1	—
Methacrylic acid	—	—	1
Isopropyl alcohol	As required		

Like the complexes of titanium, the zirconium complex seems to function by further complexing with the coloid, and it is stirred slowly into the paint after all other components are added; the recommended addition being 1/2 to 10 times the weight of colloid. Gel formations may develop immediately or after a few hours.

An alternative type of zirconium compound used to impart thixotropy is an aminoalkyl zirconate, or other organic zirconium compounds. Examples of both with zirconium compounds are shown in the following table.

Thixotropic Emulsion Paints

	Parts by weight	
	1	2
Rutile titanium dioxide	282	290
Micronised talc	—	40
Blanc fixe	206	52
China clay	21	—
Sodium carboxymethyl cellulose (5% aq.)	64	90
Hydroxylpropyl methyl cellulose	7.3	—
Sodium hexameta phosphate	0.55	—
Water	500	50

The above is ground into a paste, then the following is added.

Vinyl acetate-vinyl caprate copolymer (55% aq.)	382	—
Vinyl acetate-iso-octyl acrylate copolymer	—	255
Hexylene glycol	11	—
Water (with emulsion)	—	180
Zirconium complex (as prepared in last table)	18.5	—
Reaction product 1 mol zirconium tetra-n-butoxide; 3 mols 2-amino-2ethyl propane-1, 3diol.	—	30

Anti-Efflorescent For Roofing Tiles

If it is desired to coat cement roofing tiles so that efforescence is avoided a pigmented paint based on styrene : butadiene, at, optionally, a ratio of 60:40, may be used with advantage. Mica is a desirable constituent, and PVC should be between 20 and 30 percent.

Paint For Cement Roofing Tiles (Anti-Efflorescent)

Ingredient	*Parts by weight*
Water	13.3
Pigment dispersant	0.1
Potassium pyrophosphate	0.1
To solution of above add:	
Iron oxide	8.0
Barium sulphate	2.85
Talc	2.0
Micro-mica, 20 h	1.65
Quartz flour	3.0
After stirring for 30 min. add, avoiding foam	
Methyl cellulose, or hydroxyethyl cellulose (2% viscous solution)	16.0
Styrene-butadiene copolymer emulsion (60:40) 48%	33.0
Water	20.0

300 g of the above paint per m^2 the surface may be used.

Whilst efflorescence is particularly noticeable on plaster, it may be overcome in any one type of system by the complete or partial replacement of sodium salt by potassium salt in the emulsifiers, polyelectrolytes, and if necessary, in the initiators. The use of acrylic emulsions of all types, or of a styrene butadiene copolymer can also avoid lime staining; in the latter cases, however, exterior durability is generally rather unsatisfactory.

Gloss Paints

A number of specific methods have been claimed for the production of emulsion gloss paints. It is claimed that suitable emulsions can be produced if a monomer which is film forming, *e.g.*, a higher acrylate ester, is polymerised to a degree of at least 70% followed by addition of a non-film forming monomer, *e.g.* styrene together with 0.5-5% of polymerizable acid. There is some flexibility in formulation. This type of polymerization, sometimes referred to as a *'core'* polymer can be considered as a very soft polymer *(giving good flow characteristics)*, in which is embedded a harder polymer. A typical example of an emulsion is given in the following table.

"Core" latex Emulsions

Ingredients	*Parts by weight*
Initiator-emulsifier Premix	
Potassium persulphate	0.4
Sodium lauryl ether sulphate (25% aq.)	6.0
Sodium salt; polymeric carboxylic acid (25% aq.)	4.0
Water	91.7
Filming monomer Premix	
Ether acrylate	59.7
Styrene	19.9
Methacrylic acid	1.5

Non-filming Monomer Premix	
Styrene	15.9
Methacrylic acid	3.0
Second Initiator	
Tert-butyl hydroperoxide (60% aq.)	0.04
Promotor	
Ascorbic acid (0.01% aq.)	4.0

Procedure

The filming monomer premix is added to the initiator-emulsifier solution over 90 minutes at 75-82°. When this reaction is substantially complete, the total non-filming monomer is added at 77°, followed by the second initiator. The promoter solution is gradually added, temperature rising to 87°.

The product at 50% solids, and viscosity 500 cp, is neutralised with ammonia to pH 8.8 with a viscosity of about 2,000 cp. Particle size is 0.1 h; minimum film-forming temperature is 82-84°c.

Gloss Paint Formulation

Ingredients	*Parts by weight*
Pigment Grind in Water	100
sodium salt, olymeric carboxylic acid (25% aq.)	2
water-dispersable lecithin	2
Antifoam (50% aq.)	5
Tributoxyethyl phosphate	14
Phenylmercuric preservative	0.25
Casein (15% aq.)	65
Titanium dioxide	200

Paint preparation	
To pigment grind add	
Emulsion as in last table, pH 9.0-9.5	198
Water	62
Antifoam (50% aq.)	5

The resulatant paint, with the high pigment binder ratio of 2:1 PVC *(about 33%)*, produce a film with a range of 70-80 on the Gardener Gloss Water.

The use of a ketone aldehyde resin, dissolved in a coalescing solvent, added to a polyvinyl-acetate emulsion prepared with the aid of a block copolymer of ethylene oxide-propylene oxide as a stabilised, is stated to be a useful basis for an emulsion gloss paint. An example is illustrated in the following table.

Gloss Paint Containing Ketone-Aldehyde Resin

Ingredients	*Parts by weight*
Paint medium	
Polyvinyl acetate emulsion (55% solids)	48.1
Ketone-aldehyde resin	28.4
Ethylene glycol monoethyl ether	13.4
Water	10.1
	100.0

The resin is dissolved in the solvent, stirred into the emulsion, and solids adjusted to 55% by adding water as shown. Light reflectance of dried films is 95-100%, as against 85-90% for unmodified emulsion, and Sward hardness 54%, against the normal 20%.

Pigment Grid

Ingredients	*Parts by weight*
Water	135.5
Sodium salt, carboxylated electrolyte (25% aq.)	3.4
Rutile Titanium dioxide	124.5
Clay	4.7
Calcium carbonate	4.7
Sodium carboxymethyl cellulose (2%aq.)	87.0
Octyl alcohol (defoamer)	0.3

Paint

Paint medium (above)	577.0
Dibutyl phthalate (D.B.P)	16.6
Ethylene glycol monoethyl ether	25.0
	987.7

Pigments, are ground to Hegman grind of 6-7. Defoamer is added last, then plasticized paint medium is added.

The final paint will have pH 7.0, PVC 10.5% and solids content 48.0%. It has very good brushing and levelling properties. Films have 60° gloss of 90% and contrast ratio of 95%. Its resistance to detergents is good.

Technical Acrylic Emulsions

Some technical acrylic latices are claimed to be suitable directly for forming compositions with reasonable gloss of pigment volume concentration up to 23.5%.

Acrylic Type Gloss And Semi-Gloss Emulsion Paints

Ingredients	*Pounds weight*	
Pigment Grind	***Gloss***	***Semi-gloss***
Rutile titanium dioxide	275.0	257.6
Sodium salt, di-isobutylene-maleic-anhydride co-polymer (25% aq.)	11.0	10.3
Antifoam	2.0	1.87
Propylene glycol	67.0	62.75
Barytes	——	46.8
Paint		
To above add		
Propylene glycol	85.5	105.8
Acrylic emulsion	590.5	492.5
Antifoam	4.0	1.87
Preservative (10% mercury) } Premix	1.0	0.93
Water } Premix	20.0	22.8
Butoxyethanol } Premix	27.5	22.8
Dioctyl sodium sulphosuccinate	2.0	1.87
Hydroxy ethyl cellulose (2.5 % aq.)	42.4	43.6
Total solids (%)	48.47	48.2
Pigment-volume concentration	22.0	25.6
Photovolt gloss, 60°	82	45

An emulsion, prepared, using a phosphate type surfactant and an ethylene-maleic anhydride salt as colloid, which is recommended for use in corrosion resistant emulsion paints, is also considered suitable for the preparation of gloss paints.

Acrylic Type Gloss Emulsion Paint

Ingredients	*Parts by Weight*
Pigment Grind Rutile titanium dioxide	187.0
Sodium hexameta phosphate (10 % aq.)	5.2
Hydroxy ethyl cellulose (2% aq.)	9.4
Defoamer	1.0
Hexylene glycol	12.3
Ethylene glycol	12.3
Water	22.0
Emulsion	
Acrylic emulsion	597.0
Water	91.8
Add to the mix of above two	
Hexylene glycol	28.5
Ethylene glycol	28.5
Silicon additive	5.0
	1,000.0
Total solids content (%)	50.0
Pigment: binder ratio	0.6-1.0
Pigment-volume concentration (%)	150.0

For the best results, it is recommended that the paint be applied at 50-60 square yards per UK gallon. For most substrates a primer undercoat system should be applied first, followed by two coats of gloss paint. There should be a drying time of 1-2 hours between each coat, although maximum water-resistance is not attained for about 24 hours applications.

Addition of alkali Soluble Resin

Another practical way to prepare a good gloss emulsion paint is to utilise an alkali soluble polymer. An emulsion in which the alkali-soluble resin is polymerised on to a "*seed*" later is particularly useful as it enables a very high degree of water resistance to be attained, inspite of the comparitively hydrophilic nature of the resin. Up to about 30% of the resin weight may consist of an alkali-soluble resin. The remainder may be any suitable copolymer capable of giving a good *"egg-shell finish"* in its own weight. The imortance of good grinding of the pigment in the alkali-soluble resin, must however he emphasised.

Gloss Emulsion Paint, Vinyl Co-polymer Emulsion With Alkali-Soluble Acrylic

Ingredients	*Parts by weight*	
	1	2
Pigment Grind		
Rutile titanium dioxide	2030	2650
Alkali-soluble acrylic emulsion (pH-9.0)	1220	1590
Tributyl phosphate	200	130
Butoxyethoxyethylene glycol	—	130
Water, net	—	200
Polymer addition		
Alkali - soluble acrylic emulsion (pH 9.0)	1830	850
Vinyl acetate-acrylic ester copolymer, 55% solids, pH 9.0	—	3760
Silicone	100	130
CVP defoamer (10% dispersion)	—	210
Butoxyethylene glycol	—	200
Water, Net	—	150
	10,000	10,000
Pigment : binder ratio	0.62:1	1.0 : 10
Pigment volume concentration	155	230
Solids (%)	53.5	53.5
Paint viscosity approx. (pioses)	10	10

Alkali-soluble acrylic polymers may also be used in gloss formulations based on polyvinylidene chloride copolymer emulsions.

Gloss Emulsion Paint Based On Vinylidine Chloride Co-polymer

Ingredients	*Parts by weight*
Part 1	
Rutile titanium dioxide (Chloride process pigment optimum)	197.0
Alkali-Soluble acrylic copolymer (40% solids)	80.0
Hexylene glycol	26.5
Ammonia	2.6
Part 2	
Propylene glycol	100.0
Water	26.0
Part 3	
Vinylidene chloride co-polymer (55% solids)	53.0
Ammonium polyacrylate (40% solids)	7.0
Ammonia (0.88)	8.0
	977.1

Properties (Paint)

Solids content (%)	53.5
Pigment volume concentration	16.5
Pigment : binder ratio	0.6:1

Properties (film)

Gloss at 45° = 95-100%

Undercoats and Primer Sealers

The term *"undercoat"* is intended to include all pigmented base coatings for decorating finishes which dry under normal ambient temperatures. It may include different substrates of varying porosity, such as wood, plaster board, concrete, etc. When porosity is not excessive, and a two coat system is sufficient for a complete finish, a fundamental property of an undercoat is to have perfect flow properties when brushed out, so that a perfectly smooth coating will be presented for the top coat. An emulsion paint may be used as an undercoat for either an alkyd or another emulsion paint top coat.

It is often advantageous to seal every porous surface with a coating of neat emulsion, normally diluted somewhat, preferably of moderate particle size of 1μ without excessive surfactants to avoid excessive penetration.

Vinyl Acetate Polymers

Polyvinyl acetate emulsions have been recommended for undercoats. Major advantages are the excellent adhesion on a wide variety of surfaces, the rapid drying which makes it possible to apply to a top coat within 60 minutes of application of the primer sealer, and the extremely good sealing properties due to the rather large particle size, which mitigates against excessive penetration of the substrate.

Due to the lack of compatibility of polyvinyl acetate homopolymers with drying oil based coatings, there is little softening of the surface during the top coat application. A particular advantage is the coating of asphalt, for which polyvinyl acetate acts as complete seal, preventing undesirable *"bleeding"*.

Primer-Sealer formulations

Ingredients	*Parts by weight* 1	2
Pigment grind		
Water	112	25
Methyl cellulose, high viscosity (2% aq.)	—	75
Sodium salt of di-isobutylinemaleic anhydride co-polymer	8	20
Non-ionic *(polyoxethylene)* dispersant	4	3
Ethylene glycol	—	20
Diethylene glycol monoethyl ether	50	—
Antifoam (proprietary)	4	2
Rutile titanium dioxide	—	75
Calcium carbonate	100	—
Clay	—	100
Talc	—	100
Reduction		
Methyl cellulose, high viscosity (2% aq.)	200	75
Water	150	185
Orthophenyl phenol, sodium salt (20% aq.)	10	—
Phenylmercuric acetate	—	0.3
Diethyleneglycol monoethyl ether acetate	—	8
Vinyl acetate co-polymer 55% solids, particle size less than 0.5 M : borax stable; emulsion viscosity 9-15 poise	600	—
Vinyl acetate-maleic ester co-polymer emulsion, 56% solids, particle 0.24-0.30 M emulsion viscosity 7-14 poise	—	360
Solids content (%)	48.2	48.8
Pigment-volume concentration (%)	31.0	34.4

Alkali Soluble Acrylic Polymer

Another method of obtaining a satisfactory water-based under coat is to use an alkali soluble resin as part of the medium. The same type of alkali soluble acrylic polymer as used in gloss paints is particularly suitable. The illustrations are undermentioned for some typical formulations for undercoats. Primers for wood may have the lower range range of pigment of binder ratio (1.7:1 to 2.0:1)

Undercoat Formulations ***(Including Alkali-soluble Acrylic Polymer)***

Ingredients	*Parts by weight*		
	1	2	3
Pigment grind			
Rutile titanium dioxide	219	220	210
Barytes *(micronised)*	37	40	44.5
Calcium carbonate *(whiting)*	68	100	89
Fine silica	40	—	—
Laponite "S"—a water swellable clay	1	—	—
Macaloid - a synthetic, water-swellable clay	—	4	3.5
Tributyl phosphate	6	6.3	6.5
Alkali soluble acrylic emulsion *(pH 9.0)*	212	113	157
To above add			

Paint Blend

An emulsion co-polymer of 75-parts vinyl acetate and 25 parts Veova 10 at 55% solids, ph 8.0	283	278.5	295
Butoxyethyoxyethyl acetate	10	8.3	10
CVP defoamer *(10% dispersion)*	10	7.4	10
Water	—	177.2	112.5
Solids	55	53	55
Pigment : binder ratio	2.0:1.0	2.0:1.0	1.7:1.0
Pigment-volume concentration *(%)*	40	38	36
Ratio emulsion polymer : alkali soluble polymer	3.0:1.0	5.6:1.0	4.4:1.0

A primer-sealer may be applied to new plaster, which often develops hair-line cracks. Some of the polyvinyl alcohol based emulsions may be used with advantage here, as the rather larger particle size, 1ñ, tends both to reduce excessive penetration, and to bridge the cracks.

Coating of Old Oil Paint

The principle trouble in the coating of old oil paints is one of adhesion. Thus the old coating should be degreased if necessary, and roughened mechanically to give a god *"key"*. Vinyl acetate co-polymers mill in general give better adhesion than homopolymers. Acrylic paints would in most cases give satisfactory adhesion under these conditions, particularly where an acid has been co-polymerised with the monomers.

Another method by which adhesion to old oil paint can be improved is the addition of an abietic acid or other rosin derivative to the paint mixture. An example is given below.

Emulsion With Added Keying-Agent

Ingredients	*Parts by weight*
Pigment grind	
Titanium dioxide	275
Water-ground mica (325 mesh)	30
Micronised mica	30
China clay	30
Diatomaceous earth	35
Di-n-octyl sodium sulphonate	1
Polyethylene oxide oleic acid condensate	1
Water	395

To the above add the following as a whole.

Paint	
Polyvinyl acetate emulsion (50% solids)	500
Di-n-octyl sodium sulphosuccinate	1
Polyethylene oxide oleic acid condensate	1
Water	18

To the above the following is added slowly after heating:

Ethyl acetate	60
Di-n-butyl phthalate	25
Pentaerythritol abietate	25
Water (dispersed)	5

Emulsion Paint for Exterior Use

The requirements of paint intended for exterior use are quite stringent, involving many specific problems in formulation. Thus the paint, apart from having suitable application properties, must have good resistance to exposure. Most types of polymer are suitable for exterior application provided that both emulsions and paints have been properly formulated. The optimum pigment-volume concentration for exterior paints is 30-35%.

Acrylic and Vinyl Acetate Co-polymers

Vinyl acetate homopolymers which have been externally plasticised are, on the whole, less suitable than co-polymers for exterior use, but this depends to some extent on the alkalinity of the substrate and some polyvinyl acetate emulsion paints have been known to withstand many years of exterior exposure, even strongly acid conditions.

The olefin copolymers of vinyl acetate should also be very suitable for exterior applications, particularly under alkaline conditions. Following table illustrates the formulation of an exterior sand paint containing an olefin graft co-polymer. This type of finish includes a relatively large size filler and has become quite popular but may require a conventional type of undercoat.

Exterior Sand Paint

Ingredient	*Parts by weight*
Mill Base	
Rutile titanium dioxide	100
Blended cellulose thickners *(2% aq.)*	40
Potassium polymethacrylate *(5% aq.)*	20
Diethylene glycol monobutyl ether acetate	10
Non-ionic wetting agent	1

Preservative proprietary	3
Water	18
Then add with slow stirring 50% solid olefin grafted polymer	257
Industrial sand	551
	1000
Pigment-binder ratio	5:1
Solids content (%)	78

Exterior Paint, Acrylic and Acrylic-styrene Polymer Based

For exterior work, styrene-acrylic co-polymers, which are less susceptible to chalking at the higher PVC levels, should be suitable.

Ingredients	*Parts by weight*		
	1	2	3
Mill base			
Rutile titanium dioxide, chalk resistant	220	162	162
China clay	___	73	122
Calcium carbonate	38	72	122
Talc	82	___	___
Carboxymethyl cellulose, Na salt (5% aq.)	___	61	81
Ethyl hydroxyethyl cellulose (2-1/2% aq.)	100	___	___
Sodium hexametaphosphate (5% aq.)			

Emulsion Paints for Interior Use

The formulations of emulsion paints for interior use are generally less stringent than those required for exterior application. The specific requirements for high quality interior paints include high opacity, good flow, and superior scrub resistance. Because of the high binding power for pigments of all acrylic and acrylicstyrene co-polymers, they may prove more economic in cost than a vinyl acetate co-polymer type. A 76% PVC is considered to be of very good opacity, with high water resistance, and is suitable for conditions of severe condensation.

Interior Emulsion Paint *(Styrene-Acrylic Emulsion)*

Ingredients	*Parts by weight*	
	1	2
Mill base		
Rutile tutanium dioxide	70	175
Calcium silicate	20	20
Calcium carbonate	358	296
Hydroxy propylmethyl cellulose (2% aq.) (No. 1 high viscosity, No 2 extra-high viscosity)	315	200
Sodium hexametaphosphate	15	30
Paint		
To above add in order shown :		
Di-ethylene glycol butyl ether	15	20
Formaldehyde (40% aq.)	3	—
Water	160	138.6
Ammonia (0.88)	—	2
Preservative, proprietary	—	0.4
Vinacryl (a styrene-acrylic co-polymers, 50% solids)	44	118
	1,000	1,000
PVC (%)	90	76
Pigment-binder ratio	20.4:1	8.3:1
overall solids (%)	47	56
Viscosity, poises (25°C)	9.5	7.75

Polyvinyl acetate and its copolymers have the advantage of a fairly high moisture vapour transmission-rate, which in interior as well as exterior conditions amy tend to avoid blistering under conditions where external and internal humidity varies widely. The emulsions also have the advantage of inparting strong grease resistance and various stains such as kitchen grease and wax crayons can easily be removed by soap and water.

Interior Emulsion Paints *(Vinyl Acetate Co-polymer Emulsions)*

Ingredients	High opacity	Tint base	Structured	General
Rutile titanium dioxide	250	100	290	120
China clay	191	—	60	—
Chinese fale	—	—	—	50
Calcium carbonate	—	332	—	249
Microtal ET	—	—	—	10
Potassium polymethacrylate(5% aq.)	35	29	—	5
Hydroxyethyl cellulose, medium viscosity, solid	—	—	4	—
Hydroxypropyl methyl cellulose, high viscosity (2% aq.)	—	—	—	200
Sodium hexmetaphosphate (5% aq.)	—	—	20	10
Potassium hydroxide (50% aq.)	—	—	—	2
Ethyl hydroxyethycellulose (high viscosity, 4% aq.)	65	120	—	—
Antifoam, proprietary	1	1	—	—
Phenyl mercury salt, organic acid (preservative or other preservative)	3	3	0.4	—
(continued)	2	2	—	—
Ammonia (0.88)				
Coalescing solvent, ester (water-insoluble)	—	—	—	10
Diethylene glycol monoethyl ether acetate	—	—	10	—
Formaldehyde (40% aq.)	—	—	—	2

Vinyl acetate polymer (52% solid emulsion)	208	226	—	—
Vinyl acrylic polymer emulsion	—	—	270	142
(50%) Solids Water	210	152	303.6	142
Hexylene glycol	15	15	—	—
Propylene glycol	20	20	—	—
	1,000	1,000	1,000	1,000
PVC (%)	60	60	42	70
Pigment; binder ratio	4.1:1	3.7:1	2.6:1	6:1
Solid content(%)	55	55	48	50
Viscosity, poises (25°C)	3.5	4.5	3.5	4

9

DISTEMPERS

Introduction

Distemper is composed chiefly of whiting and a solution of size which is used as the binder. It is often made up according to specific requirements, the size being dissolved in hot water and the whiting stirred into the solution; a small proportion of coloured pigment may be added to produce and desired tint. They are produced in washable and non-washable types and are available in two forms — dry powders and pastes.

Dry distemper

Dry distemper is a mixture of pigment and binder in powder form, which when dispersed in water gives the required water paint.

Paste Distemper

Paste distemper is prepared by mixing dry distemper with some boiled oil and is obtained in the form of emulsion with water. The paste is stirred up with water before application.

Distemper are generally formulated with a protein binder, usually casein or soyabean protein or glue.

Glue

Glues are complex nitrogenous substances known as protein and are obtained from animal sources — *i.e.*, from skin and bones of the animals. The finest quality of glue *i.e.*, gelatine is prepared from the hides and bones of calves and are generally finished in the form of thin sheets about 8" x 3" which are transparent and colourless, flexible and tough.

It does not dissolve in cold water, but adsorbs water and swells into a jelly; in hot water it dissolves into viscous solution which on cooling sets into a jelly with strong adhesive properties. If this solution is applied to a surface, it forms a lustrous coating which is not water-proof and swells and loses its adhesion power on exposure to moisture. The addition of a small proportion of sodium bicarbonate or formaldehyde renders the film substantially insoluble and water-proof after exposure to light.

Casein

This substance is a protein contained to the extent of about 3 percent in milk. casein is prepared on a large scale by warming the milk in steam-jacketed pans and adding hydrochloric acid when it is precipitated as a granular powder. A less carefully prepared variety of casein is used as a binder in washable distempers while the pure casein is used in food processing industry.

Casein is insoluble in water, but soluble in alkaline solution, as it is an acid substance and combines with alkalies to form soluble salts. A solution can then be prepared by treating it with either potash, soda or ammonia. If casein powder is intimately mixed with slaked lime, the mixture is soluble in water, but if this solution is exposed to the air it gradually becomes insoluble on drying, owing to the conversion of the calcium hydroxide into carbonate the casein being set free into original form. This reaction is utilisede in the preparation of washable distempers supplied in powder form.

Distempers are manufactured in a wide range of bright colours and find extensive use as wall-coatings on cemented surfaces just like white-wash. Distempers have replaced white-wash and calcimine. This is mainly due to their superior retention power, durability, and light fastness on exposure to exterior conditions.

Calcimine in a distemper in which animal glue or dextrin is used as non-volatile vehicle and whiting as the principal pigment. It is sold in the form of dry powder to be mixed with water by the painter and is intended primarily for the decoration of plastered interior walls. Calcimine represent the least exensive decorative coatings available above the crude level of white-wash or lime-wash. It makes flat coatings with clear, soft colours that do not fade and do not turn yellow in subdued light.

Washable calcimine can be made in a number of ways with a combination of glue and paraformaldehyde, with sodium silicate, and starch with albumin and an aldehyde but the simplest and most economical way is by substituting casein and lime for the animal glue.

Distempers amy be calssified as

(i) Oil-free distempers
(ii) Oil-bound distempers.

Oil-free Distempers

Oil-free distempers may again be divided into soft distempers and oil-free *"washable"* distempers.

Soft distempers or ceiling is a dispersion of whiting in glue solution in the following proportion by weight : whiting 83, water 35, spin glue 2. In addition 0.1 percent of preservative such as para chlorometacresol and a trace of nitrobenzene are added. The latter gives ceiling white its characteristic almond-like odour.

Ceiling white is supplied in paste form and is thinned to a thin creamy consistency before use. The film remains water-soluble but resists dry rubbing.

Oil-free washable distempers are prepared by mixing casein, lime and borax, with Paris white and barytes, or a similar blend of other extenders. The ingredients being ground together to a fine powder in any edge-runner to form a white distemper.. to produce any required tint, a small proportion stainers are added. The pigments used for required tints must be stable towards the alkaline reaction of lime and borax. Prussian blue and lead chromes should not be used, as the tints obtained by their use are liable to alter considerably when the powder is mixed with water and to suffer degradation after application owing to the alkalinity of the binding medium.

A typical washable distemper-white can be formulated as follows :

Paris white	55 percent
Barytes	25
Casein	10
Lime	6
Borax	4

During application, powder is made into a thin paste with water, when the casein reacts with lime and borax to form the binding medium. It is preferable to mix it throughly with hot water and then allow it to stand for an hour or so before application, in order to anable all air entangled in the powder to escape; if used immediately, *"pinholing"* is liable to occur.

Casein distempers are readily washed from the surface immediately after they have dried off, but as the lime becomes carbonated and the casein returns to the insoluble condition, they gradually harden and then stand a considerable degree of washing.

Oil-bound Distempers

These are also known as washable distempers. They are made by dispersing a mixture of lithopone and whiting in a distemper emulsion. The binder of oil-bound distemper generally consists of an emulsion of a process drying oil or an oleoresinous varnish in water using a soap as emulsifying agent, glue or casein or their mixture using a soap as the protective colloid. The process of emulsification consist of stirring the binder into the colloid solution in the presence of an emulsifying agent.

For maximum stability of emulsion the dispersed droplet of binder should be as small as possible. So after oil is stirred into the colloidal solution, the dispersed pigment is mixed with emulsion and is passed through a colloid mill. This mill consists of concentric corborundum or steel disc closed together, one of which rotates at high dispersion speed, the other being stationary. The dispersion is fed into the centre of the stationary disc and is carried outwards between them by centrifugal force. At the end, a preservative must be added since glùe or casein are readily attacked by bacteria and fungi.

An emulsion based on glue and linseed stand oil can be produced on the following basis :

Part A

Skin-glue	7.0 Kg
Water	70.0 Kg
p-Chloro-m-cresol	80 Gms
Triethanolamine	0.5 Kg

Part B

Linseed stand oil	30.0 Kg
Oleic acid	2.0 Kg
Cobalt drier	0.3 Kg

Part A is prepared by soaking the mixture overnight, followed by warming to 60°C maximum to dissolve. Part B is then added to part A while stirring and the emulsifier is then added. This gives a high quality emulsion containing about 28 percent oil.

Pigmentation is carried out in an edge-runner or in pugmixer followed by grinding in a triple roller mill. The oil-bound distempers are usually supplied in paste form in tin containers. It is thinned with water to a creamy consistency before use.

Process of Manufacture of Oil-Free Distempers

(A) Casein-based Distempers

Because casein paints employ water as the solvent for the binder and they require some period of hardening before they show any resistance to weathering, they have not been used widely for exterior paints or paints which would be subjected to severe washing or abrasion. The decorative values of casein-bound paints have been appreciated in recent years and their popularity has increased despite their lack of durability. In addition, recent developments have improved the durability of casein paints, particularly the *"oleocasein"* type, without materially lowering their decorative values, so that now more durable casein paints are appearing in the market.

Casein paints generally sold at lower price than oleoresinous paints have acquired the name of *"cheap paints"*. new uses for casein have been found that may tend to maintain its cost at a higher level. Therefore, in comparing casein paints with oleoresinous paints from the point of view of cost, it can be said that on the basis of decorative value or hiding power, casein paints are cheaper, and on the basis of durability, oleoresinous paints are cheaper. With the rapid strides that are being made in the casein paint technology, with these conditions may not exist for long.

Raw Materials for Casein Paints

Various raw materials used in the manufacture of casein paints are discussed below:

1. Opaque White Pigments

Zinc sulphide pigments and the titanium pigments being lighter in weight and cheaper are in common use in casein paints. These are available in grades different from those used for oil paints.

The principal zinc sulphide pigments are :-

(i) Regular Lithopone, containing 28% zinc sulphide and 72% barium sulphate.

(ii) Double strengths lithopone, contains enough zinc sulphide to make up 50% of the pigment.

(iii) Zinc sulphide magnesium pigments, a mechanical mixture of zinc sulphide and magnesium silicate in which the zinc sulphide amounts to 50 percent.

The principle titanium pigments are the following:

(i) Titanium Barium pigments. They are available in two grades -

- one containing 25 percent and the other 30 percent titanium dioxide precipitated in the presence of freshly prcipitated barium sulphate, and the mixture calcined.

(ii) Titanium — calcium pigment contaning 30% titanium dioxide and 70% calcium sulphate.

(iii) Titanium — Magnesium pigment — a mechanical mixture of 30% titanium dioxide and 70% magnesium silicate.

2. Pigments of Low Opacity

These pigments are used in part to lower the cost of the finished product which may be more if the opaque pigments alone are used. The principle pigment of low opacity used in casein paints are whiting *(calcium carbonate)* and Kaoline *(china clay)*, Paris white is so finely ground that 99 percent of it passes through a 300 mesh sieve. Dry ground limestone and precipitated whiting are also used to some extent.

Other pigments of low opacity used in casein pants include magnesium silicate *(fibrous talc)*, barium sulphate, silica, diatomaceous earth, and calcium silicate.

3. Coloured Pigments

The coloured pigments for casein paints be line-proof, that is, non-reactive with alkalies. Following coloured pigments are commonly employed in casein paints :

Red Pigments

Natural and artificial iron oxide pigments, lithol red, paratoluidine red and para-nitraniline red are generally used. Cadmium reds are also suitable.

Yellow Pigments

Iron oxide yellows, zinc chromate, lead antimonate, cadmium sulphide, cadmium lithopone and hansa yellow are the most commonly used yellow pigments in casein paints. The earth colours, and raw sienna are also widely used. Orange chrome may also be used safely in casein paints.

Green Pigments

The chromium oxide and malachite green are the most commonly used green pigments. The chrome greens and zinc greens and zinc greens are unsuitable.

Blue pigments

Ultramarime and lime blues are widely used. Lime blue means ultramarine mixed with calcium sulphate or an organic lake colour such as methtylene blue lake. The new copper phthalocyanine lake pigments are also widely employed.

Black pigments

Various carbon blacks, black oxide of iron, and maganese dioxide are suitable in distempers.

4. Casein

Sulphuric-acid or hydrochloric-acid casein is often found more satisfactory than lactic-acid or grain-cured casein. It is convenient to specify that the viscosity of a 10 percent solution of the casein in 15 percent aqueous borax should agree with that of a similar solution of a control sample of casein. Casein for use in powder paints must be finely ground and bolted. Most of it should pass through a 100-mesh sieve. Casein for use in paste paints is more conveniently purchased in granular form. The casein should be clean, free from rancid or sour odour, with a moisture content less than 9.0 percent; ash should not exceed 4.0 percent, and fat should be less than 1.0 percent.

5. Chemical Reagents

The hydrated lime for use particularly in casein powder paints should be purchased under specifications to ensure uniformity in character. A hydrated lime of the following typical analysis is acceptable :

Total lime	CaO	70.44	Percent
Magnesia	Mgo	1.50	Percent
Silica, iron oxide & alumina	SiO_2, Fe_2O_3 Al_2O_3	2.40	Percent
Carbon dioxide	CO_2	1.40	Percent
Combined water	H_2O	24.09	Percent

Besides lime, other chemical reagents used in casein-paints include borax, sodium-fluoride, ammonium fluoride, trisodium phosphate, ammonium hydroxide, sodium hydroxide, sodium carbonate, sodium abietate or oleate and sodium silicate.

Other reagents included are ammonium and alkali metal meta phospahtes and pyrophosphates, sodium fluoborate, sodium tungstate, calcium aluminate, ammonium or sodium thiocyanate and organic bases such as urea, triethanolamine, ethylamine, piperidine and piperazine.

6. Other Ingredients of the Non-Volatile Vehicle

In many of the powder paints, a part of casein is replaced by dextrin in order to increase the viscosity and improve the consistency. Dextrin also plasticizes the casein. Other plasticizers used include gly-cerol glucose, sorbitol, castor oil, and sulphonated castor oil. Rubber latex and rubber derivatives are employed in larger proportion to make exceedingly flexible paints.

Other non-volatile vehicles added may be classified as paraffin wax vegetable wax, bees wax, gum arabic, gum tragacanth, rosin, natural resins, oleoresins, shellac, phenolic resins, alkyd resins, soaps, aligin and water soluble cellulose compounds.

7. Anti-Foaming Agents preservatives and Volatile Thinners

Pine oil to the extent of 1 to 2 percent is often used to prevent foaming. Octyl alcohol is somewhat less effective than pine oil but is less odorous and irritating. Diethyl phthalate (D.E.P) in the proportion of 1/2 to 2 percent of the powder or paste, and liquid tertiary amines are also effective.

Zinc sulphate in amounts less than 0.25 percent of the casein sodium fluoride 1 percent of casein, alumino-fluosilicid acid as 25% aqueous solution and sodium silico fluoride are the effective preservatives. Organic preservatives generally preferred are beta naphthol, sodium salicylate *(1% of casein)*, thymol, sodium orthophenyl phenate *(0.25% of casein)*, phenol, cresol. chlorinated phenols, pine oil *(1 to 2%)*, phenolic resins, chlorinated naphthalene, lead naphthalate, boro-salicylic acid, and mineral oils containing sulphur. Camphor may be employed as an insect repellant.

The volatile vehicle in casein paints is nearly always water. Other volatile liquids such as ethyl alcohol may also be used in making casein paints for special purposes. Mixtures of organic liquids and water may be used as solvents for reducing viscosity. Acetone and ethylene glycol butyl ether are particularly suitable for this purpose.

Manufacture

Dry powder paint manufacture consists of a thorough mixing of the dry components of the paint. Casein should be very finely ground. The paint manufacturer usually grinds or regrinds the casein and sifts it, returning the tails to the pulverizer. The reagents, pigments, plasticizing materials, and preservatives are then added in correct proportions and incorporated thoroughly in a dry mixer. The mixer has a set of revolved curved blades and is similar to the dry mixers sometimes used for blending pigments in the manufacture of oil paints. After mixing, the batch is passed through a stone mill or high speed pulverizer. It is then sifted again and sent back to the pulverizer until the whole batch has been reduced to a satisfactory degree of fineness. After this, it is again mixed and packed, usually in 5 pounds cartons lined with moisture-proof paper of which either 10 or 20 are put in a case. Large quantities are packed in boxes, or drums containing 25, 50 or 100 pounds.

The casein may be brought to moisture content of 25 or 32 percent, mixed with sufficient readily hydrolyzable salt of an alkali metal to a soluble casein, the mixture warmed and extruded in an apparatus similar to that used in casein plastics, and then dried and ground before making powder paints in the customary way.

Another procedure is to dissolve the casein in a nearly neutral solution and spray it on the pigment, mix during mixing. Finally the mix is dried, ground and bolted.

For a white distemper a suggested formulation is as follows :

Paris white	55 lbs
Casein	10 lbs
Barytes	25 lbs
Lime	6 lbs
Borax	4 lbs
	100 lbs

The ingredients are brought in powder form or ground into a powder and then mixed in an Edge Runner or any other suitable mixer.

In the manufacture of paste paints casein is first dissolved in water to form a solution of reasonable constant viscosity. The pigments are then dispersed in the solution by wet grinding on a roller mill or any other suitable mill just as pigments are ground in oil or varnish in making oil paints or enamels.

The method commonly followed is to heat the casein in the warm aqueous solutions of suitable salts until it is greatly swollen and softened and add sufficient weak alkali or alkaline salt to effect solution at a pH between 6 and 7. According to a typical example in a patent, 55 pounds of casein is soaked in a 30 gallons of water at 150 to 160°F, 5 pounds of sodium fluoride and 2 pound of ammonium chloride are added and the temperature maintained until the casein is greatly swollen, after which 6 pounds of borax is added and the batch agitated throughly until complete dissolution is effected. Amorphous silica, particularly diatomaceous earth, facilitates the formation of a smoooth solution.

The preparation of casein solution is usually carried out in open tanks fitted with agitators. They are preferably of such shape that the solution may be drawn off rapidly and completely. The formerly the heating was done by blowing direct steam into the cooker, but the more modern method is to do cooking in steam-jacketed tanks. After the casein is dissolved, additional ingredients such as preservatives, anti-foaming agents, plasticizers, and modifying vehicles such as drying oils and resin may be added. The pigments are then mixed with the vehicle usually in a change can mixer. Finally the batch is ground on a paint mill the vehicle usually in a change can mixer. Finally the batch is ground on a paint mill to incorporate the pigments with the vehicle throughly. For white and tinted paints a three-roller grinding mill is commonly used. Stone mills are some-times used particularly when particularly when the pigments are difficult to wet and disperse throughly in the vehicle, as is the case with some of the coloured pigments.

After grinding casein paste paint the mills should be cleaned promptly and thoroughly and the iron-rolls, scraper knife, and discharge chute greased to protect them from corrosion. The metal cans in which casein paste paints are packed must be made resistant to corrosion.

(b) Glue-based distempers

Like other surface coatings, these distempers are also formulated in a similar manner. A typical example of large scale manufacture of one of the different shades of distempers is given below.

Dry Distemper (Light-Yellow or Prime-rose colour)

Material	*% by weight*
Calcium carbonate	300.00
Titanium dioxide	4.0
Sulphonate castor oil	4.0
Glue powder	20.0
Ochre *(mid stone)*	900.00
Hansa yellow *(dye)*	5.0

All the ingredients are put in the ball or pebble-mill and the same is filled to about 55% of its capacity. However, glue powder and cresylic acid are mixed together and then added to the ball mill. The mill is allowed to run for 6-8 hours to facilitate through mixing and grinding of the raw materials. To ensure the process of mixing and grinding sample may be withdrawn and tested at intervals. After grinding for the desired results, the distemper is taken out of the mill. For economy, pebble mills are more favoured.

Oil-bound Distempers

Oil-bound distempers are used as interior wall coatings on both new and old work. When the film dries through water evaporation, the oil droplets in the distemper are dispersed in a mass of pigment particles which are probably coated with colloid. They lose their charge and this results in a tendency of oil droplets to coalesce and become associated with the pigment. The degree to which this phenomenon takes place depends on the concentration of oil droplets, *i.e.* the oil content of the emulsion, and will determine the water resistance or washability of the film. Even with high oil contents, the films produced from oil-bound distempers are more porous than those from oil paints and they are useful therefore as a first coating on new walls may not have dried out thoroughly.

These are not well-suited for the decoration of bath rooms, kitchens, or other places where it will be exposed to steam and condensation, because continued wetting and drying of the paint film tends to induce peeling and flaking. In all other locations, it gives excellent service and provides a sound foundation for any type of decoration — a very important consideration.

For the painting of the exterior faces of building, there is no better material than an exterior quality water paint. Besides retaining a good appearance throughout its life, it has the outstanding merit of weathering elegantly; the finish, when properly formulated, does not crack or peal, but slowly erodes away, thus ensuring that re-decoration involves no problem.

(a) Casein or Glue-based Distempers

Oil-bound distempers have greater washability and durability. The binder generally consists of an emulsion of a processed drying oil *(boiled oil, stand oil, blown oil etc.)* or of a varnish *(oleoresinous or synthetic)* in an aqueous solution of glue or casein. The emulsion is generally prepared in a *"High Speed Mixer"* or in a colloid mill. The pigment dispersion is accomplished in Edge Runners or pug-mills followed by granite tripple roller. However, it has been claimed that the entire process of emulsification and pigment dispersion may be accompolished in a single stage using *"High Speed Carburundum Mill"*. Oil-bound distempers are usually supplied in paste form to be thinned with water before application. Casein or glue may be added as protective colloids. Most of the manufacturers supply a thin emulsion of some processed drying oil or water called *"petrifying liquid"* which is used as a thinner instead of water. It increases the proportion of oil in the distemper. Films made by this liquid as thinner are more water resistant and more durable, being most suitable for surfaces exposed to outside conditions. They are more expensive than ordinary distempers. Conditions of storage of oil-bound distempers are important and extremes of temperatures should be avoided.

(b) Soyabean Protein-based Distempers

Soyabean proteins are most widely used in water paints or distempers. Their composition in general is as follows :

Protein	35 - 40%
Oil	18 - 40%
Moisture	10 - 11%
Carbohydrate, Fibre, Etc.	25 - 30%

Alpha and gamma proteins present in the soyabean are the main products of utility to the surface coating industry.

Alpha Protein :

The process of extracting alpha protein from soyabean consists of

(i) Preparation of meal or flakes,

(ii) Extraction of the protein.

Meal should be free from oil and should be subjected to as low temperature as possible in its manufacture from raw beans. The process employed in securing proper meal play an important part in the subsequent steps of the operation. Best meal can be obtained by solvent estraction with a mineral oil solvent like hexane *(b.p. 155-158°F)*. The meal obtained from the solvent extraction process will generally contain :

Protein	44.0%
Fat	0.5-1%
Fibre	7.0%
N.F.E. *(carbohydrate)*	29.0%

The remainder of the product consists of extraneous matter such as cellulose etc. Following three steps are involved in extracting the protein :

(i) Protein is separated from extraneous matter, such as cellulose by dissolving in a suitable electrolyte such as sodium chloride, sodium sulphite, sodium hydroxide, suphuric acid and hydrochloric acid etc.

(ii) Removal of carbohydrate is accomplished by the re-precipitation of the protein and removal of the soluble sugars, pentosans etc. by subsequent filtration

(iii) Hydrolysis is carried out in such a manner so as to control the physical properties of the resulting products. Temperature, pH control and other factors are very vital in this step.

The dried commercial product will contain :

Protein	96.97%
Ash	0.5% (maximum)
Crude Fibre	0.5% (maximum)
Carbohydrate	2.0% (maximum)

Alpha protein is now being used as the adhesive, film-forming and water-proffing agent in cold water paste paints or distempers.

A typical formulation is prepared by using following ingredients.

1.	Alpha Protein	100 lbs
	Water	400 lbs
2.	Borax	15 lbs
	Water	110 lbs
3.	Phenol	6 lbs
	Water	50 lbs
4.	Diglycol Laurate	5 lbs

5.	Linseed oil containing 0.02% cobalt	35 lbs
6.	Pine Oil	7 lbs
7.	Phenol	2 oz
	Locust Beam Gum	2.5 lbs
	Water	50 lbs

Soak No. 1 for 10 minutes, start heating with either live steam or in steam-heated jacketed kettle under agitation.

Add No. 2 Allow the temperature to rise to 160°C and hold it between 160 - 170 °C until the protein is throughly cut. Add solutions 3,4,5,6 and 7 in order, allowing approximately 5 minutes between each step and maintaining the temperature between 140-160°C. Agitate the solution for approximately 20 minutes and pass through colloid mill, if possible. Add one-half the total protein solution in a change can mixer and then add the following pigments in indicated amounts.

Lithopone	825 lbs
Whiting	110 lbs
Titanium Dioxide	75 lbs

This will form a very heavy paste. Continue agitation until a through mix is obtained. Add remainder of the protein solution and continue agitation until pigments are properly dispersed. Grind in roller mill, with loose setting.

Gamma Protein

Gamma Protein is derived from soyabean meal by mechanical means. A typical analysis of extracted gamma protein is as follows.

Moisture	6.07%
Protein	54.00%
Fat	0.70%
Fibre	2.19%

In the manufacture of gamma protein special equipment is required to ensure a very fine texture, 97.5- 98% passing through 300 mesh. Being relatively cheaper; it is finding wide application in the coating work.

Gamma protein is also used in satisfactory paste paint. The following is a typical formulation.

1.	Gamma Protein	100 lbs
	Karaya gum	1.5 lbs
2.	Water	550 lbs
3.	Lithopone	400 lbs
	Asbestine pulp	100 lbs
4.	Sodium hydroxide	2 lbs
	Water	50 lbs
5.	Raw linseed oil containing	
	0.02 % Cobalt	50 lbs
6.	Pine Oil	5 lbs
7.	Phenol	6 lbs
8.	Lithopone	400 lbs

Mix No. 1, dry and soak with No.2 for 15 minutes. Add 3 and agitate at room temperature for 20 minutes.

Add No. 4 and bring temperature to 160 - 170°C and hold for 15 minutes. The mixture should be agitated throughout the operation. Add No. 5 and agitate for 20 minutes at a temperature between 140-160°C. Then add 6,7,8 in order. In case diglycol laurate is available, 5 lbs. of it should be added at the end of step 4.

Some more formulations of distempers are as follows :

Glue solution	25 parts
Casein solution	25 parts
Latex	30 parts
Lithopone	100 parts

Drying oil can, if desired, be incorporated with the above; they have some advantages also but tend to discolour the paint more rapidly.

1. **Dry Distemper *(White)***

Titanium dioxide	15.0%
Mineral filler	19.0%
Special velvet filler	39.8%
Casein	12.0%
Mica	5.0%
Borax glass	1.1%
Sodium fluoride	1.0%
Gelling agent *(Pectin or agar-agar)*	0.1%
Lime	7.0%

Ten to thirteen gallons of water are required for 100 pounds of dry powder to make a paint ready for use.

2. **White Distemper *(White)***

Casein	1,000 parts
Urea	340 parts
Hexamethylene Tetramine	210 parts
Lithopone	6,950 parts
Zinc oxide	1,000 parts
Lime	500 parts

3. **Dry Distemper *(Bright colour)***

An example of bright coloured distemper for interior as well as exterior use is as follows :

Pigments and Fillers	74.4%
Mica	10.0%
Casein	12.0%
Borax glass	1.1 %
Sodium flouride	1.0%
Pottasium dichromate	1.5%

Water is added to the above powdered mixture in the proportion of 10 to 18 gallons of water per 100 pounds of dry powder. Drying oil may also be added to the paint water mixture.

Distemper can also be satisfactorily prepared by using a rubber solution. The solution readily emulsifies in a glue solution, to which the pigments can be incorporated. The following is an example of this type of distemper.

Glue solution	20 parts
Rubber solution	16.2 parts
Water	25 parts
Lithopone	100 parts

The rubber solution consists of milled crop, 8 parts, cobalt limolate, 0.2 part, and cobalt spirit, 8 parts.

Casein-bound Distempers

1.	Water	78.5 lbs
	Collodial clay	3.0 lbs
	Casein	16.0 lbs
	Caustic soda	2.5 lbs
	Zinc oxide	120-140 lbs
2.	Dehydrated Castor oil	33.41 lbs
	Lithopone	39.81 lbs
	Casein	3.31 lbs
	Phenol	0.06 lbs
	Ammonium Hydroxido	23.41 lbs

Mix well until uniform and dilute before using.

3.	Casein	5 kgs
	Hydrated Lime	5 kgs
	Whiting	40 kgs
	Borax	50 kgs
	Ultramarine	100 kgs
	Casein	1 kg
	Calcium oxide or hydroxide	1 kg
	Pigment colour	5-8 kgs

This mixture should be stored dry and made up with water to the desired consistency just before application. The pigment may be added immediately or later, if so desired.

Plastic Wall Distemper

1.	Casein	12.50 kgs
	Plaster	30.00 kgs
	Lime	12.50 kgs
	Lithopone	13.75 kgs
	Asbestos	21.75 kgs
	Glue, strong	10.00 kgs

Make it a creamy paste water directly before use.

2.	Titanium dioxide	4.25 lbs
	Lithopone	15.45 lbs
	Barytes	5.50 lbs
	Whiting	2.60 lbs
	Magnesium silicate	3.25 lbs
	China clay	2.40 lbs
	Mica, silver	2.15 lbs
	Casein	8.15 lbs
	Talc	3.0 lbs
	Borax	1.3 lbs
	Sodium Fluoride	1.4 lbs
	O-Phenyl Phenate	1.3 lbs

10

NITROCELLULOSE LACQUERS

Introduction

Lacquer is a clear or pigmented coating that dries completely by evaporation of the solvents. it is the fastest drying finish available. It produces a tough and durable coat that is easy to sand, rub or patch. Its surface is resistant to heat and alcohols and does not scratch easily, giving it an advantage over varnish and shellac. However, it is low in solid contents and it needs several coats to produce film thickness equivalent to a varnish or enamel coat. Alcohol-wet nitrocellulose or other celluloic ester-cellulose acetate, bitryrate, or similar material are cut mechanically in a suitable solvent such as ketone, alcohol, or ester solvents. Resin solutions, the choice of which depends upon the properties desired, and plasticizers, the choice of which depends on the end use of the lacquers, are added under agitation. The solutions of solid materials are then let down with carefully balanced thinners or solvent combinations made up of alcohols, esters, ketones, naphthas etc., to give the correct evaporation rate, solubility, viscosity and application performance.

Pigmented lacquers and lacquer enamels are processed by procedures similar to those used in the manufacture of paint enamels—by grinding in ball mills.

Although so many products first named were formerly known as lacquers, the present-day lacquers are primarily nitrocellulose *(pyroxylin)* coatings, which may be either clear or pigmented.

Nitrocellulose lacquers have the following advantages over the oleoresinous coatings

(i) Then dry evaporation, a fast process as compared with the relatively slow process of oxidation by which the oleoresinous finishes dry.

(ii) Owing to the better control of chemically pure raw materials, such as nitrocellulose, solvents, resins, and plasticizers, products of more uniform characteristics are obtained.

(iii) Owing to speed of application, drying, and ease of handling, there is less necessity for expensive production equipment, small floor space is required, and there are fewer rejects.

(iv) They have remarkable durability, water-resistance mar and abrasion resistance, hardness, colour retention, chemical resistance, flexibility and toughness, all of which place nitrocellulose lacquers among the highest quality protective coatings.

(v) The manufacture and control of nitrocellulose lacquers is more of a chemical and technical problem than the making of varnishes and paints, because of the chemical nature of the ingredients used, chief of which is nitrocellulose.

Raw Material Used

1. Nitrocellulose

Several types of nitrocellulose are commercially available. The prominent among them include :

(a) Regular Soluble (R.S.) Nitrocellulose

It has a nitrogen content of 11.80 to 12.20 percent by weight and is supplied in viscosities of 1/10 second, 1/4 second, 1/2 second, 5-6 seconds, 8-10 seconds, 15-20 seconds, 30-40 seconds, 60-80 seconds, 125-

175 seconds, 250-400 seconds, and 900-1,300 seconds. It is soluble in the ester solvents, ketones, and in alcohols with ester or ketones.

One-tenth second is an exceedingly law-viscosity grade and is used in lacquers where an unusually high solid content is desired. One 1/2 second type is most widely used in automobile, furniture, and other lacquers of good durability. The 5-7 seconds viscosity nitro-cellulose is used extensively in all types of industrial lacquers. The higher viscosity type, 8-10 seconds are used in lacquers, coated fabrics, artificial leather, window shades airplane dopes, leather cement, photographic film, and various other special applications.

(b) Alcohol-Soluble (A.S.) nitrocellulose

It has a nitrogen content of 11.40 to 11.70 percent by weight. It is made in viscosities of 1/2 second, 30-40 seconds, and 300-500 seconds, This type will stand a higher dilution with alcohol before precipitation as compared with the R.S. type, which will tape a higher toluol dilution. It is of importance in certain formulations where alcohol-soluble resins are used, or where the use of coal tar diluents is in advisable.

(c) Spirit-Soluble (S.S.) nitrocellulose

It is made with a nitrogen content of 10.80 to 11.00 percent and is available in several viscosities, as 1/4 second and 5-6 seconds. Best solvent for this type consists of alcohol, toluol, and ethyl acetate. It finds use in odourless lacquers, wood sealers, and lacquers containing alcohol-soluble resins, such as shellac.

(d) Bronzing nitrocellulose

It has a nitrogen content of 11.80 to 12.40 percent by weight and is available in viscosities of 35-40 seconds and 60-80 seconds. This type is specially prepared to hold bronze powders in solution with the minimum gelling tendency. The esters and ketones are employed as solvents in bronzing lacquers.

(e) Silver Lacquer nitrocellulose

It is made in viscosities of 20-30 seconds. It is used where palest colour is required. It gives a clear water white solution without any haze. It is used in the manufacture of clear silver lacquers such as are applied on silver articles and other highly polished surfaces where a thin film is desired to prevent tarnishing.

Viscosity plays an important role in nitrocellulose technology. The main consideration for having lacquers of various viccosity is to obtain nitro-cellulose films of varying thickness. The viscosity of nitrocellulose is an important factor to assure the user that when he uses similar lots recieved from time to time he will obtain the same results. Therefore, it is very important that this property be uniform in different lots used day to day.

It is essential to decide upon a detailed specification to suit the type of article to be manufactured, as the requirements for different types of product vary considerably more especially as regards viscosity.

The use pattern of lacquers according to viscosity is as shown below:

Type of Product	*Viscosity required*
Metal lacquers	60-80 seconds
Bronze paints	40-60 seconds
Leather finishes	30-40 seconds
Imitation leather	20 seconds
Lacquers for toys etc.	10 to 15 seconds
Cheap enamel	4 to 8 seconds

High-class motor and furniture finishes 1/8 to 1/4 seconds. An ester of low viscosity is essential to the production of high-grade finishes for spraying and brushing, in order to obtain sufficient concentration to produce a reasonably thick film on drying without imparting the working consistency.

In addition to the viscosity, the specification should define the limits required as regards stability, solubility, acidity, colour, freedom from impurities etc. In this connection it will be readily understood that it is impossible to control the manufacture on an industrial scale with such nicety that every batch is of uniform composition and properties. Every delivery should, therefore, be carefully checked and slight variations allowed for by adjustemnt of the formula, or by blending different batches on situation to ensure a uniform standard.

For all high-class products it is essential to use specially prepared cellulose esters. The temptation to use cheap sources of supply, such as film scrap, smokeless powder residues, and similar products, has been a frequent cause of failure in the past. Such types of esters are only admissible for the cheaper class of materials where durability is of little importance.

Ethyl cellulose is compatible with nitrocellulose in all proportions and is used in combination with it to reduce the inflammability and increase the flexibility of the film. It is also used as the main constituent of special lacquers where exceptional flexibility is required, such as coatings for cables and lacquers for metals.

A film of nitrocellulose alone, is not satisfactory for most uses, as it lacks adhesion, is stiff and brittle, lacks flexibility and elasticity; as a result of this, it will split or peel off the surface. Nitrocellulose has a high viscosity, and a lacquer solution will not contain as much solids for the coatings as a paint or varnish of like viscosity.

2. Resins

Resins are important constituent of modern nitrocellulose lacquers. They perform various functions some of which are :

1. To increase adhesion.
2. To increase body, depth and solid or non-volatile content without unduly raising the cost and without changing the viscosity appreciably.
3. To increase gloss, lustre and brilliance.
4. To improve outdoor durability by the use of certain alkyd resins particularly in clear finishing lacquers.
5. To improve water resistance, chemical resistance etc., such as necessary under special conditions.

The most suitable resins are those which are soluble in mixtures of ester, alcohols, and hydrocarbons and give a clear, transparent film, with good permanent gloss. Resins most commonly employed include natural resins as shellac, dammar and gum elemi; and synthetic resins as ester gum, alkyd resins, phenolic resins, urea-formaldehyde resins, vinylite resins, and ancryloid resins, etc.

Adhesion of the film is increased by the use of proper resins or resins and plasticizer combinations. A single resin will not always give the desired results so that the lacquer chemist must find out by experimentation what combination of resins, with plasticizers and nitrocellulose, will produce a film that will meet service requirements. For example, for adhesion to bare metal, a different type of formulation is required than for use over a baked or airdried oil primer.

The quantity of the resin used in ratio to the nitrocellulose depends upon the film desired. However, the tendency is to use as high percentage of resin as possible, because of the relatively low cost of the resin and also bacause of the increased fullness of film, depth of finish, and increased lustre which is obtained with a high resin content. It is also important that the lacquer in whicha resin is used remain clear on ageing.

The proper selection of solvents is particularly important in high-resin lacquers so that there will be no precipitation of either resin or cotton during the evaporation of the solvents, as this would ruin the film. The thinner which is used to reduce the lacquer to the required consistency for application *(spraying, dipping, brushing, and other methods)* must be formulated so as to blend perfectly and hold all the lacquer ingredients in a clear solution.

3. Plasticizers

The addition of a plasticizer is essential with cellulose lacquers, particularly for application to metals. It is characteristic of cellulose esters that they swell considerably on the addition of the solvents before actual dispersion takes place, and on drying a reversal of this process occurs as the solvent evaporates, which results in a pronounced contraction of the film, which parts away from the surface to which it is attached. The function of the plasticizer is to overcome this film elasticity without destroying its hardness, which is one of its most valuable characteristics. The lower the viscosity of the cellulose derivative employed, the higher is the proportion of plasticizer required, the amount used is adjusted accordingly, taking care to avoid the excess, which impair the quality of the film.

The ideal plasticizer for high-class lacquers would be a material which is freely soluble in the cellulose solvent, form a stable dispersion with both the ester and the resin, and is perfectly non-volatile and chemically inert, so that the film retains its elasticity indefinitely. Plasticizers may be oils, such as castor oil, blown castor oil, blown rapeseed oil and lacquer linseed oil. A very important class is the high boiling esters which are solvents for the cotton and many times for the resins. In this class will be found, the ethyl, butyl and amyl esters of the phthalates, tricresyl phosphates, triphenyl phosphate etc. These plasticisers are non-volatile and remain in the film for a very long time. They tend to form solid solutions with the nitrocellulose. A very important class that is becoming popular is the resin-plasticisers. In this class will be found ethyl or methyl abeitate, beckolac 1308 as most popular today.

4. Solvents

By the term solvents, here, is meant those liquids that are used for dissolving the nitrocellulose. Solvents are classified as low-boilers and high boilers. Low boilers are used to carry the cotton into solution, provide volatility for the lacquer, and also give the initial set for the film. Usually the low boiler is a faster solvent than the higher-boiler. The most popular member of this class is ethyl acetate. The high-boilers provide smooth flow, prevent blush, and peel off and give homogeneity to the film. In this class are found butyl acetate, amyl acetate, butyl propoinate, ethyl lactate, butyl lactate, and cellosolves.

Latent solvents are compound or liquids that are not solvents for cotton by themselves. But they become so by the mere addition of a solvent. In this class are found the methyl, ethyl, butyl, propyl and amyl alcohols.

5. Diluents

In the making of a solvent mixture or thinner, for a lacquer, other liquids are used such as benzol, toluol, xylol solvent naphtha, and also special petroleum naphtha. These are called diluents as they are not solvent for nitrocellulose. They lower the solvent power of a solvent when used with it. They give bulk to the mixture, aid in keeping the resins in solution, help balance the formula and also lower the price.

It is essential that the diluents used should evaporate substantially at the same rate as the true solvent; if too high a distillate is used, the result will be that it remains after the solvent has evaporated and prevents the formation of a proper film. The same principle holds for the active solvents- their range of evaporation should overlap, if two solvents of widely differing rates of evaporation are used such as acetone and amyl acetate, there is danger of pinholing of the film being caused by the volatile ingredients coming off rapidly during the drying.

The proportion of diluent used is adjusted according to its compatibility with the active solvent, which is ascertained by determining the dilution ratio. It is usually determined by dissolving 1/2 second nitrocellulose in the solvent to form a 10 percent solution, and measuring the volume of toluene required to cause permanent precipitation of the nitrocellulose, the dilution ratio is the volume of toluene divided by the volume of solvent.

Manufacturing Process

Cellulose lacquers are definetly colloidal solutions — the pigments being in a state of colloidal suspension. Because cellulose lacquers are colloidal mixtures of many ingredients, it should be the responsibility of the chemists in the plant that his lacquers are as far as possible always given the same treatment in procedure and conditions of manufacture, after being assured by full laboratory control tests that the quality of the ingredients is constant and known.

In making the nitrocellulose lacquers the general practice is to

(i) Dissolve the resin in the diluent spirit in a slowly revolving churn or barrel in the cold to give some form of stock solutions and keep the same in upright aluminium containers.

(ii) Dissolve the nitrocellulose in the active solvents in a similar churn or whirl or *"dough mixer"* and keep the same in stock in this form.

(iii) Finely grind the pigments into paste in a pulverizer or in water-cooled roller mills or cone mills two or three times until impalpable.

(iv) Mix these stock together in required proportions in a mixer churn or ball mill uniform and add any more diluents and solvents if necessary. On storage, matter not perfectly dissolved in colloidal and resin solutions, either dissolves or settles out, and within reasonable time stored solutions are cleaner and better to use and to tolerate greater dilution with diluents than quickly made up solutions. This clarity and brightness may be hastened by filtering, of course, but this hardly necessary in most cases.

In mixing, the diluents are preferably added slowly and gradually because of the partial local precipitation which is apt to occur. As the diluents are usually much cheaper than the solvents, it is economical to use as much of the former as possible, especially in the cheaper lacquers made from scrap celluloid.

The mixers should not be more than two-thirds full and should contain an air-vent, and it should be borne in mind that a possibly explosive mixture may be present in the system and hence mixer should run slowly and are preferably stopped occasionally.

The clear lacquers should be stored in aluminium, earthenware or lead-lined iron tanks, and are brighter if stored for a while after making. Discolouration is apt to occur if it is stored in ordinary M.S. or Cast Iron (C.I) tanks.

Black Lacquer Enamels

Reaserch and development work on the dispersion of carbon black for use in nitrocellulose lacquers has resulted in the production of so called chip black pastes pigment-base, which provide the maximum fitness of black tone without the use of organic dyes. This is important in the production of automotive and other high-grade black lacquers where durability of colour exterior exposure is essential.

The chip blacks and pastes are dispersion of highly refined carbon blacks in mixtures of nitrocellulose and plasticizer, of which the following is a representative formula.

Carbon black	13.3%
Nitrocellulose	66.7%
Plasticizer	20.0

A black lacquer enamel is made by dissolving chips in lacquer solvent to which the desired amount of resins *(in the form of resin solution)* and plasticizers is added to produce the finished enamels. Sometimes, two or more hours of constant agitation is required to produce a satisfactory solution of chip blacks.

A black lacquer enamel is also made by preparing a solution of the nitrocellulose, resin, plasticizer, and solvents required in the formula, and, when these are thoroughly mixed, adding the black paste to the solution while continuing the agitation. After a uniform dispersion is secured, the lacquer should be centrifuged or filtered.

A representative black paste formula is

Ingredient	*% by weight*
Carbon black	6.7
1/2 Sec. nitrocellulose	33.3
Dibutyl phthalate	10.0
Ethyl acetate	18.75
Butyl alcohol	3.75
Butyl acetate	2.50
Toluol	25.00
Weight per gallon	8.7 lbs

It is made into a finish black lacquer enamel by using the following formula.

Dissolve 105 lbs of 1/2 second, wet nitrocellulose in solvent mixture composed of

Toluol	38.0 gal
Butyl acetate	14.0 gal
Butyl alcohol	4.0 gal

Then add

Resin solution (50% solids in toluol)	12.0 gal
Blown castor oil	2.5 gal
Dibutyl phthalali	1.0 gal

Mix all, then add 200 lbs. black paste.

Yield : 104 gallons.

Clear lacquers may be divided briefly into wood lacquers and metal lacquers. This classification may often overlap and further more may be divided into many subdivisions. Generally speaking, wood lacquers are characterized by comparatively high solid, metal lacquers, by their toughness and adhesion.

The introduction of low viscosity cotton revolutionized the finishing of furniture. Until 1922, all the transparent finishes were obtained by the use of shellac as a sealer and varnish as the finishing coat. Although shellac is still frequently used, owing to certain features of economy, varnish has been largely replaced by lacquers. The customary lacquer procedure in the finishing of furniture is the application first of a coat of lacquer sanding sealer, sanded within one hour with dry sand paper, then two coats of lacquer, with one to two hours between coats. The lacquer may be rubbed the following day, and then the finished articles are ready for packing and shipping.

Lacquer Sanding Sealer *(low viscosity type)*

1/2 second nitrocellulose wet with 35% ethyl alcohol	58 lbs
30% solid zinc stearate paste	62 lbs
Maleic resin (solid)	113 lbs
Blown castor oil	19 lbs
Ethyl acetate	12 gal
Butyl acetate	21 gal
Butyl alcohol	8 gal
Toluol	15 gal
Petroleum naphtha	15 gal
Yield	100 gal
Viscosity	26 seconds at 70°F
Total solids	27.0%

Zinc stearate paste *(30% solids)*

	% by weight
Zinc stearate	18
5-second R.S. cotton (dry)	6.5
Magnesium carbonate	3.0
Blown castor oil	2.5
Ethyl acetate	16.0
Butyl acetate	6.0
Ethyl alcohol	16.0
Petroleum naphtha	32.0

Lacquer Sanding sealer *(high viscosity type)*

5-7 second nitrocellulose wet with 35% ethyl alcohol	28 lbs
Zinc stearate paste (30% solids)	60 lbs
Maleic resin	60 lbs
Blown castor oil	10 lbs
Butyl acetate	24 gal
Ethyl acetate	15 gal
Toluol	18 gal
Petroleum naphtha	20 gal
Butyl alcohol	5 gal
Yield	100 gal
Viscosity	25 seconds at 70°F
Total solids	17.0%

Gloss Wood Lacquer *(low viscosity type)*

1/2 second nitrocellulose wet with 35% ethyl alcohol	57 lbs
Maleic resin	118 lbs
Non-oxidising long-oil alkyd { 60% solids, 40% toluol }	16 lbs
Ethyl acetate	21 gal
Butyl acetate	16 gal
Butyl alcohol	8 gal
Toluol	15 gal
Petroleum naphtha	16 gal
Yield	100 gal
Viscosity	25 seconds at 70 °F
Total solids	27 %

Gloss Wood Lacquer *(high viscosity type)*

5-7 second nitrocellulose wet with 35% ethyl alcohol	24 lbs
Maleic resin	146 lbs
Non-oxidising long-oil alkyd 60% solids, 40% toluol	20 lbs
Ethyl acetate	21 gal
Butyl acetate	14 gal
Butyl alcohol	7 gal
Toluol	18 gal
Petroleum naphtha	20 gal
Yield	100 gal
Viscosity	26 seconds at 70°F
Total solids	27.0%

Metal Lacquers

Clear Brass Lacquer

1/2 second nitrocellulose wet with 35% ethyl	150 lbs
Dibutyl phthalate	50 lbs
Ethyl acetate	19 gal
Butyl acetate	13 gal
Butyl alcohol	13 gal
Toluol	31 gal
4 lb. cut refined wax-free shellac in alcohol	8 lbs
Yield	100 gal
Toluol solids	27.0%

Silver Lacquer

30 second silver cotton wet with 35% ethyl alcohol	45 lbs
Dibutyl phthalate	7 lbs
Ethyl acetate	26 gal
Butyl acetate	13 gal
Butyl alcohol	7 gal
Toluol	45 gal
4 lb. cut gum elemi in toluol	3 gal
Yield	100 gal
Viscosity	45 seconds at 70°F
Total solids	10.0%

Airplane Dopes

	I	II
Ingredient	*% by weight*	*% by weight*
Cellulose nitrate (wet)	9.7	18.0
Glycol sebacate	1.5	2.4
Ethyl acetate	26.2	19.3
Butyl acetate	19.6	19.3
Butyl alcohol	6.6	7.6
Aromatic petroleum naphtha	36.4	33.4

Solids content is not less than 7.5% by weight in I, and not less than 14.0 by weight in II.

11

PIGMENTS AND EXTENDERS

Introduction

Pigments are finely divided solids of various shades used to give colour, hiding, consistency, build, durability and other properties to surface coatings. They are fine solid particles used in preparation of paint, and are substaintially insoluble in the vehicle. The vehicle is the entire liquid portion of a paint which includes the pigment binder or film-former, volatile solvent and anything that is dissolved in the liquid portion.

Pigments may be classified as natural and synthetic depending on their origin. Each of these two groups may be divided into

(i) Inorganic Pigments
(ii) Organic Pigments
(iii) Metallic or Luminous Pigments

Inorganic Pigments

Inorganic Pigments are known for the opacity and colour they impart to the paint film. They are, therefore, described under the different heads depending upon the colour they impart, such as white pigments, red pigments, blue pigments etc.

Pigments *(White)* :

The pigments of industrial importance included in this group are :

(a) White lead
(b) Zinc oxide
(c) Titanium dioxides and
(d) Antimony oxide

There are many other white pigments also like lithoponne, basic lead sulphide which are used to some extent in the manufacture of paints.

These types of pigments are generally used in white paints, enamels and lacquers and many types of industrial and architectural finishes.

Lead *(White)* :

It is also called basic carbonate of lead; it is probably a mixture of basic carbonates of lead with an average composition approximating to the formula 2 $PbCO_3.Pb(OH)_2$. The Proportion of $PbCO_3$ and $Pb(OH)_2$ varies in white lead and the limits of variation accepted in paint industry are

Lead carbonate	67 to 80 percent
Lead hydrate	20 to 33 percent

White lead is prepared by two main processes

- *stack process*
- *chamber process.*

The colour of white lead varies according to the method of manufacture. Stack lead is the least pure colour having a slightly pinkish or yellowish tone.

Texture

Stack lead is distinctly crystalline in structure, and the particles vary in size and shape, ranging from colloidal dimensions to 20 microns in diameter. The particles of chamber lead are smaller and more uniform in size.

Hiding Power

The high refractive index of white lead *(1.90)* gives it a high degree of hiding power and staining resistance. On account of its finer texture, chamber lead has rather greater hiding power than stack lead.

Oil Absorption

This varies with the type of white lead, the normal limit being 15-25.

Spreading Power

This is in general; rather low, owing to the high specific gravity and varies roughly in inverse proportion to the oil absorption.

Durability

White lead is perfectly stable i. pure air and is not affected by light. In impure air, however, it is permanent. It ia alkaline in nature and is rapidly attacked by even weak acids. It gradually changes colour on exposure to air containing sulfur gases, turning first yellow and finally dingy brown owing to the formation of lead sulphide. It is therefore inadmissible for water paints. Discolouration occurs sooner or later, however, even in oil paints.

Toxicity

The great defect of white lead is its poisonous nature, rendered more dangerous by its solubility in organic acids and consequent ready absorption into the system.

Basic Lead Sulphate

This pigment is sometimes known as sublimed white lead. It is less rective than white lead towards oils and varnishes and has been used to some extent in gloss paints and undercoats. The main use of basic lead sulphate is in certain types of primers for under water areas of ship's hulls.

Composition

Basic sulphate of lead not less than 94 percent. Zinc oxide, not more than 5 percent. Impurities, not more than 1 percent.

Properties

Coarse Particles	:	Not more than 0.1 percent retained on 240-mesh screen.
Oil Absorption	:	from 10 to 14.
Refractive Index	:	1.93 to 2.02
Hiding Power	:	13 to 16
Tinting Strength	:	120 to 150

Basic lead sulphate is a pigment of extremely fine texture and clean white colour. Although it is a fully saturated sulfur compound, the discolouration of the pigment iss almost as pronounced as white lead; it is, however, more resistant to the action of sulphur dioxide than white lead. Its toxic effect is not so marked as that of white lead.

On account of the fineness of its particles, basic lead sulphate works more smoothly than white lead, and paints made with it have a higher gloss. Its spreading power is also considerably greater. It is slightly soluble in distilled water and does not react with oil. It cannot, therefore, he converted into oil paste by wet pugging as white lead.

Lithopone

The best quality lithopone is clear white in colour, but lower grades have a decided yellowish cast, due to traces of iron, cadmium or other metals.

Lithopone posseses, considerable hiding and reducing power, exceeding that of zinc oxide or even white lead and surpassed only by titanium di-oxide. On exposure to air lithopone is prone to oxidation, forming polysulphides, and eventually soluble zinc sulphate. For that reason it is notoriously unsuitable for the preparation of paints for exterior use. It is used largely, however, in paints for interior use, and particlularly for the preparation of water paints.

Composition

Zinc sulphide	26 to 32 percent
Zinc oxide	2 percent
Barium sulphate	balance to make 99 percent minimum

Properties

Coarse particle	0.25 percent maximum
Oil absorption	12 to 20
Volatile matter	0.5 percent maximum
Matter soluble in water	0.5 percent maximum
Alkalinity	0.1 percent maximum

Zinc oxide

It is also known as *'chinese white'*. The composition of zinc oxide varies somewhat according to the method of production and in each process several grades are produced, varying slightly in purity and texture. The different grades are generally known as brands, the finest and purest as White seal and lower qualities as Green, Red, Blue and Yellow seal. A typical composition is

ZnO	95.77 percent
$PbSO_4$	4.03 percent
$ZnSO_4$	0.20 percent

Properties

Zinc oxide is remarkable for the brilliance of its colour. The finer grades, such as White seal and Green seal are pure white with a slightly bluish cast; the lower grades have a slight yellowish cast due to the presence of traces of iron or cadmium oxide. The hiding power and staining resistance of the pigment are slightly less than those of white lead when calculated on equal volume basis owing to the lower refractive index.

Although zinc oxide is rapidly attacked by sulphur gases with formation of zinc sulphide, this does not produce any discolouration of the pigment, as in the case of white lead, owing to the fact that the sulphide is also white. Zinc oxide presents an anomaly in that it is entirely free from toxic properties, although it is freely soluble in dilute acids and the soluble salts of zinc are actively poisonous.

When made up into paint, zinc oxide reacts with oil in an even more pronounced manner than white lead. owing to its basic character. Zinc oxide paints, therefore, tend to dry hard and are non-elastic, and are inclined to become brittle and crack on exposure to the weather.

Zinc oxide is especially suitable for the preparation of full gloss paints, as it does not interfere with the flow of the varnish medium, and produces a film of great smoothless, brilliance and hardness. It presents some difficulty owing to its pronounced basic character, as it reacts with highly acid varnishes, causing the finished paint to *'feed up'* and become unworkable owing to the formation of zinc soaps.

Titanium Dioxide

Titanium pigments are available as pure titanium dioxide and also as composite pigments. Pure titanium dioxide pigments are produced in two commercially important crystalline forms - rutile and anatase - the rutile type is most widely used because of its greater hiding power. The composite pigments are combinations of titanium dioxide and calcium sulphate in ratios of 30% titanium dioxide - 70% calcium sulphate, and 50% titanium dioxide - 50% calcium sulphate. The composite pigments contain the rutile type of titanium dioxide.

Properties

The colour of titanium dioxide is very brilliant and pure white. The texture is extremely fine. The outstanding feature of titanium dioxide is that it combines a low specific gravity from 3.7, with a high refractive index, which is 2.55. In consquences it has extremely high opacity and reducing power, considerably exceeding that of any other industrial white pigment. The oil absorption is also high, on account of the low specific gravity.

Titanium dioxide is the most stable compound of the metal and very resistant to chemical action. It is distinguished from all other white pigments, with the exception of silica and barytes, by being insoluble in all mineral acids. Like other insoluble substances, it is quite free from toxic properties. On account of this chemical stability, coupled with the fact that titanium is more acidic than basic in its properties, the titanium pigments are inert in character, and do not show any tendency to react when ground with acid vehicles as is the case with zinc oxide and lead pigments. This is in some ways a disadvantages in paint manufacture. Titanium di-oxide does not, for instance, combine with linseed oil, a characteristic of white lead, for accelerate the drying in any way. On the other hand, it has the great practical advantage that it can be mixed with all types of acid vehicles without any reaction resulting in *"feeding up"* which is often the case with zinc oxide under same conditions. This insolubility and inertness also renders it immune from attack by sulphur compounds; hydrogen sulphide, even in strong concentration does not react with it, neither does sulphur dioxide nor dilute sulphuric acid. Paints made with titanium white are, therefore, not subject to discolouration, and retain their colour to an exceptional degree on exposure to impure air. Owing to the inert character of the pigment the film produced by a paint containing titanium white alone shows excessive elasticity on drying. In this respect it is the opposite of zinc oxide, and a properly balanced combination of the two pigments is superior to either alone, producing a film which dries normally and wears well, showing neither excessive hardness nor excessive elasticity.

Antimony White

This pigment, essentially an oxide of antimony (Sb_2O_3) has been known and used on a minor extent for many years, but its usefulness is limited due to its indifferent colour and the gritty texture due to its pronounced crystalline structure.

Properties

The texture of antimony white is extremely fine, it rivals zinc oxide in this respect, the particle size being of the order of 1 micron. It is slightly heavier than zinc oxide, the specific gravity averaging 5.75, and has a lower oil absorption. The refractive index is 2.2 and the hiding power is greater than that of white lead and zinc oxide, but lower than that of titanium oxide.

Antimony oxide is slightly soluble in water, perticularly the lower grades and is distinctly acidic rather than basic in character. Its behaviour in paint is closely similar to titanium oxide on account of this acid character; it is inert to the oil, and does not react with acid vehicles in the manner of lead and zinc pigments. Like titanium di-oxide it does not accelerate the drying of the oil, tending to form an elastic film, and it works well in combination with zinc oxide. Unlike titanium dioxide, however, paints made with it are substantially free from the tendency to chalk on exposure, and it can be mixed with coloured pigments such as lakes without accelerating their fading to any noticeable extent, except in case of extremely pale tints. It is not readily soluble in dilute acids, and on this account does not show any pronounced toxicity inspite of the extremely poisonous nature of the soluble salts of antimony. It is soluble in strong hydrochloric acid, and is readily attacked by hydrogen sulphide with the formation of the orange-coloured antimony sulphide. Paints made with it are, therefore, liable to discolour on exposure to an urban atmosphere, but this tendency can be largely prevented by blending it with a proportion of zinc oxide, which absorbs the sulphur gases more readily than the antimony oxide, without any resulting discolouration.

Composition

Not less than 99 percent antimony oxide (Sb_2O_3)

Coarse particles	:	Not more than 0.25 percent retained on at 240-mesh screen
Oil absorption	:	from 10 to 15
Volatile matter	:	Not more than 0.5 percent
Matter soluble in water	:	Not more than 0.4 percent

Extenders

Extenders include all those colourless or white substances which are practically transparent in oil owing to their low refractive power. They are used largely in water paints, where they functions as white pigments, in many cases forming the bulk of the solid constituents. Their hiding power is negligible and they have little staining resistance. Extender pigments are much lower in price than prime pigments and are used in paints primarily to reduce cost. However, by careful selection of the particular type of extender for specific paints it is often possible to improve certain properties of the paint or the dry coating. In paints with high pigment concentration sufficient hiding may be obtained by replacing some of the opaque pigments with extender pigments. Since extenders are lower in price than opaque pigments, a reduction in material cost will also result.

The materials of this class are mostly of mineral origin and include:

(a) Barium compounds *e.g.* barytes, blanc fixe, witherite, and barium carbonate.
(b) Strontium as strontium white.
(c) Calcium as Paris white, Terra alba, satin white.
(d) Magnesium as magnesite.
(e) Aluminium as alumina white.
(f) Silicon as china clay, mica, asbestine, silica.

Barium Compounds

Barytes

This mineral *($BaSO_4$)* occurs extensively in many parts of the world but the colour and quality vary considerably. India possesses sufficient reserves of barytes, mainly in cuddapah, Khammam and Kurnool Districts in Andhra Pradesh and Alwar District in Rajasthan.

Physical Characteristics

The specific gravity of barytes is 4.5 and refractive index is 1.67 which is little higher than that of drying oils; it is consquently practically transparent in oil vehicles and has little hiding and reducing power. It is extremely stable and inert and insoluble in acids and alkalies with the exception of hot concentrated sulphuric acid. On account of this insolubility it is free from the toxic properties of the soluble barium salts.

It is widely used in oil paints ans water paints, Barytes may be used in chemical resistant paints because of its stability to acids and alkalies. Since barytes does not have a high pH it may be used with alkali-sensitive pigments such as iron blue and chrome green. It is frequently employed in combination with chrome green to impart greater density and compactness to fil: of green paints. The pH should be checked before using barytes in latex paints which require alkaline conditions.

Blanc fixe

The precipitated type of barium sulphate extender is known as blanc fixe. The principal difference between blanc fixe and barytes is in particle size. The smaller particle size of blanc fixe makes it suitable for gloss finishes and printing inks.

Although chemically of the same chemical composition as barytes, blanc fixe is not quite such a stable compound; it is more readily dissolved by sulphuric acid. It has a tendency to absorb gases and liquids, which limits its use to some extent in paint manufacture as it tends to reduce the gloss if used as an extender in full gloss paints. It has greater hiding power in aqueous vehicles owing ti its finer texture, and as it can be obtained practically free from impurities it is purer and more brilliant white. Blanc fixe is used as an extender in some types of oil paints and in high-class water paints.

Strontium White

The mineral *'celestite'*, which is found in beds of similar formation to barytes, consists almost entirely of crystalline strontium sulphate. It generally has a pinkish cast due to traces of iron oxide and other impurities. Physically, strontium white differs from barytes in its comparitive softness, which results in smaller and more uniform particle size. It is slightly lower in specific gravity which averages 3.9 and in refractive index which is 1.624; consquently it is even more transparent in oil than barytes and has less reducing power, a point which is an advantage for such uses as a base in the preparation of lake pigments.

Chemically, strontium white is less stable than barytes being readily soluble in strong alkalies. The soluble salts of strontium are practically non-poisonous and do not show the pronounced toxicity of barium salts.

Calcium Compounds

Paris White

It consists essestially of calcium carbonate *($CaCO_3$)*; the raw material is either chalk or white lime stone. Lime stone is widely distributed throughout the world. Chalk consists mainly of the calcareous shells of marine organisms.

A typical composition of Paris White is

$CaCO_3$ —98.20; $MgCO_3$—1.20; Al_2O_3 —0.12; Fe_2O_3 — 0.06; SiO_2 —0.45; MnO — 0.0035; Na_2CO_3—0.07; Moisture —0.20.

Paris white is rather dull broken white of fine texture, but the particles vary considerably in shape and size. Although insoluble in pure water, paris white is slowly dissolved by rain or tap water, as these usually contain carbon dioxide in solution which reacts with it to form the soluble bicarbonates. It is readily decomposed by dilute acids. It generally has a slight alkaline reaction, which is more pronounced if it is overheated in the drying process owing to partial decomposition to oxide. It is therefore liable to affect pigments sensitive to alkali *e.g.*, Prussian blue and chrome yellow. It is also somewhat hygroscopic and therefore chemically less stable or less inert, and consequently is not regarded as a really satisfactory extender for oil paints, its use being, in general restricted to under coats and finishing coats for interior use. It is used exensively in the preparation of water paints, being the main constituent of soft distempers.

Terra Alba or Mineral White

It is derived from the mineral gypsum, a natural crystalline calcium sulphate of the composition $CaSO_4 . 2H_2O$. It is a brilliant white powder, considerably brighter than Paris white. It is coarse and crystalline in texture and has a low specific gravity averaging 2.3. It is practically transparent in oil, and has less capacity in aqueous vehicles than Paris White. It is quite neutral in reaction and perfectly stable, but has the disadvantage of being slightly soluble in water. Terra alba is not suitable for use in oil paints on account of its texture, but it is largely used in water paints and distempers, and as a base for striking the cheaper qualities of lake pigments.

Magnesite

This mineral closely resembles calcite in appearance, but consists principally of magnesium carbonate *($MgCO_3$)*. It is occasionally ground and levigated for use as a pigment, which is closely similar to paris white but rather heavier, the specific gravity being 3.05. It is chiefly used in the preparation of paint required to dry with a dead flat finish instead of a gloss, especially mat stoving paints.

Alumina White

It is prepared by precipitating aluminium sulphate with an alkali. The most commonly used alkali is sodium carbonate as it reacts slowly.

Alumina white is a soft, fluffy powder of fine texture with a high oil absorption owing to its low specific gravity. The refractive index is so low that it is perfectely transparent in oil and has little opacity even in water medium it is not used extensively in paint manufacture, but is sometimes employed as a suspending agent in oil paints. Owing to its lightness and transparency it increases the viscosity of the medium and prevents the pigments from settling out. For similar reasons it is also used as an extender in the preparation of high-grade printing inks. Its main use in paint industry is as a base for the precipitation of high class lake pigments, for which its transparency and lightness render it eminently suitable.

Silicon compounds

China Clay

China clay is hydrated aluminium silicate with formula $Al_2O_3 . 2SiO_2 . 2H_2O$. It is widely distributed in India and throughout the world. In India, its ores are found in Rajmahal and Patharghatta hills in Bhagalpur (Bihar) and near Hatgamaria in Singhbhum, Bihar, Vailur in Trivandrum and Kundara in Kerala, Anantpur in Andhra Pradesh etc.

Physical Characteristics

It possesses the following physical characteristics.

Specific gravity	2.6
Refractive index	1.56
Oil absorption	30 to 35

Mean particle size range — 1 μ downward in finer grades.

Its composition is as follows :

Silica	46.6%
Alumina	39.5%
Water	13.9%

Clay is a perfectly stable and inert material. It is insoluble in dilute acids but is decomposed by strong mineral acids on heating. The texture is extremely fine and soft owing to the character of the particles, which are largely of the colloidal dimensions. Although china clay acts as a suspending agent to its low specific gravity, it is not used extensively as an extender in oil paints as it tends to give the paint unsatisfactory working qualities and produces a weak film. It is used to some extent in water paints. Its principal use in the paint industry is as base for the preparation of lakes.

Mica

The type of mica supplied to the paint industry is a hydrated potassium aluminium silicate, the composition of which is represented by the formula $K_2O.\ 2Al_2O_3.6SiO_2.2H_2O$.

Mica possesses the following physical characteristics

Specific gravity	2.80 to 2.85
Oil absorption	75.00
Refractive index	1.58

India occupies a unique position in supply of mica to the world. The bulk of the India's production comes from the mica belts of Bihar, Rajasthan and Andhra Pradesh. Its use in paints is based on the property of the particles to leaf or to orientate themselves parallel with a paint surface and to overlap. This property confers improved moisture resistance and antipenetrating properties and in some cases, hard settlement of the pigments in the liquid paint is prevented.

Silica

In addition to the numerous minerals composed of silica *(SiO_2)* in combination with metallic oxide, it occurs in the free state in a variety of forms, *e.g.* quartz, ground flint, diatomaceous earth, amorphous silica etc. As the refractive index of silica approximates to that of linseed oil, all varieties are practically transparent in oil vehicles. The specific gravity varies from 2.8 in the case of ground quartz to 2.2 for the hydrated type. The low gravity of this type combined with its fine texture renders it suitable as a suspending agent in paints.

Talc

Talc, also known as french chalk has the formula $MgH_2(SiO_3)_4$. It is used in paints for its flatting and anti-setting properties. It is a chemically inert substance and is not sensitive to water. It has the following physical properties.

Specific gravity	2.65
Oil absorption	30
Refractive index	1.59

Abbestine

Asbestine is a ferro-magnesium silicate with formula $MgCa\,(SiO_3)_4$ and has the following physical properties.

Specific gravity	2.9
Oil absorption	27 to 30
Refractive index	1.62

It is a good anti-setting agent in paints, because of its fibrous nature. It gives extra mechanical strength, chemical inertness and resistance to water.

Red Pigments

A wide variety of naturally occuring and synthetically prepared, red inorganic pigments are used in paint industry. The more important pigments include

(1) Red Iron Oxide
(2) Red Lead Oxide and Orange Lead.
(3) Cadmium Red
(4) Antimony Red etc.

Red Iron Oxide

The red iron oxide pigments can be divided into two classes depending upon their origin.

(a) Red Pigments of Natural Origin

This class of pigments include

(a) Spanish Red, the ore of which contains 76 to 92 percent of ferric oxide and the popularity of this pigment is due to its colour and staining power.

(b) Persian Gulf Réd, a fine oxide of soft texture and expectionally good colour.

(c) Indian Red, this name is now generally used for the darker shades of pure manufactured oxides. The average iron oxide content of this is 64 percent.

(d) Red Ochres, which contain 15 to 50 percent iron oxide.

(e) Burnt Ochres, is a light red pigment with comparitively lower staining power, with an iron oxide content of from 10 to 20 percent.

(f) Burnt Sienna, is reddish-orange in colour and has a high oil absorption. It is practically transparent in colour and is mainly used as a glazing and tinting colour. Natural iron oxide pigments are used in exterior, anti-corrosive, durable and protective paints, Persian Gulf red is used specially for permanence and high stability of colour and undertone.

(b) Red pigments of Synthetic Origin

This class of pigments include

(a) Pure iron oxide - calcined,
(b) Pure iron oxide - precipitated
(c) Venetian Red etc.

Synthetically prepared iron-oxide pigments can be classified as under

(i) Turkey Red, including all the higher shades up to full scarlet, produced by calcining at temperatures up to 850°C.

(ii) Indian Reds, including all the darker shades prepared at temperatures up to 900°C.

(iii) Purple Brown, including the degraded reds produced at temperatures upto 1000°C.

The Venetian Red includes, blended red oxides, Mars Red and Tuscan Red.

Properties and Applications

The iron oxide pigments are cheap, non-toxic, light fast and solvent resistant. However they have poor acid resistance. they are very fine and uniform in texture, and possess great spreading and hiding power.

Synthetically prepared pigments are apt to contain traces of basic sulphate unless the process is carefully controlled. This is important in the preparation of paints for iron and steel, as traces of basic sulphates act as carriers of oxygen to the metal and promote corrosion.

Oxides of venetian red type, containing a large proportion of calcium sulphate, are unsuitable for exterior paints, as the solubility of calcium sulphate in water causes disintegration and promotes rusting.

Iron oxide pigments are extensively used in the preparation of paints for exterior work, on account of their low cost and protective value. The precipitated pigments have excellent hiding power owing to their high Fe_2O_3 content and small particle size. They are used in enamel finishes where the dull colours are required or mixed with extender for use in low-cost paints, metal primers etc.

2. Red Lead

Pure red lead is a bright orange colour pigment having the chemical composition Pb_3O_4, but commercial grades contain 2-15 % Pbo. Commercial red lead is available in both types, regular and fumed, and in four gardes 85%, 95%, 97%, and 98%. The presence of free litharge *(PbO)* has an important influence on the properties of the pigment. A high proportion causes it to react to such an extent with linseed oil that the mixture rapidly sets almost solid and dries rapidly forming a very hard film. As a pigment it is useless for paint manufacture but is used as a mastic for joining pipes and similar other purposes.

The red lead pigments are used almost exclusively in corrosion inhibiting primers for iron and steel. Red lead is not generally used in primers for aluminium or the non-ferrous alloys because these metals tend to reduce red lead into metallic lead.

The red lead pigments show low oil absorption *(5-9)* and very low bulking value, have specific gravity in the range of 8.8 to 9.0. Red leads reacts with fatty acids in paint vehicles to form lead soaps.

Orange Lead

Orange lead is more free from litharge than red lead, and is in a finer and more uniform state of division. It has low specific gravity averaging 6.9. It is paler in colour than red lead and has a higher oil absorption.

Orange lead is employed rarely as a pigment by itself, but is extensively used as a base for striking opaque red lakes.

3. Cadmium Red

The so called *'Cadmium colours'* range light yellow through to red and maroon. Pure cadmium colours may be made by reacting the cadmium sulphate with hydrogen sulphide to precipitate water-insoluble cadmium sulfide. Water soiuble selenium salts are included to impart colour. The ratio of cadmium to selenium for various colours is as follows :

Cd	:	Se	Colour
100	:	12	Orange
100	:	15	Orange-Red
100	:	20	Light-Red
100	:	25	Bright-Red
100	:	30	Dark-Red
100	:	33	Maroon-Red
100	:	40	Dark Maroon

Properties and Uses

The cadmium colours have only fair resistance to acids, but they are not affected by hydrogen sulphide. All the cadmium colours have excellent heat resistance they are calcined at high temperature during manufacture. The cadmium reds and maroons are very much brighter in colour than iron-oxide reds. They have excellent light resistance in mass tone but are poor in tints particularly in the presence of moisture. In exterior finishes they show fairly rapid chalking and usually fail by cracking.

Cadmium colours have excellent resistance to ultravoilet light alone but they fade considerably in exterior paints because of the presence of moisture and air. The combination of ultravoilet rays, moisture and air causes oxidation of the cadmium sulphide to cadmium sulphate. The incorporation of selenium improves this situation and the dark reds have somewhat better resistance. It is found that discolouration does not occur until the film has broken down sufficiently to expose the pigment to oxidation. For this reason it is important to use binders of maximum durability for exterior applications using cadmium colours. Paints containing cadmium colours should not be applied directly to galvanized iron, because cadmium is deposited under such conditions by electrolytic action. They are also used for colouring rubber.

4. Antimony Red

It is the synthetically prepared antimony sulfide (Sb_2S_3). It has considerable opacity and staining power and an oil absorption of 40. It almost invariably contains a smaller proportion of free sulphur and on this account is objectionable as a paint pigment.

Yellow and Orange Pigments

The important pigments in this group are mainly the chromates of lead, zinc, barium and strontium and yellow oxide of iron.

1. Lead chromates

The pigments in this group, which range from pale primrose to scarlet, derive their colour from chromium. They all contain lead chromates either alone or co-precipitated with other lead salts. Some of the important lead chromes are the following

Primrose Chrome

This pigment consists of mixtures of lead chromate, lead sulphate and alumina. Primrose chrome is a greenish yellow and the palest of the lead chromes.

Lemon Chrome

This pigment consists of a mixture of lead chromate and lead sulphate. The depth of colour of this pigment can be adjusted by varying the ratio of lead sulphate to lead chromate in the precipitate. An increase of lead sulphate leads to paler shades. lemon chrome is a redder yellow than the primrose and has a monoclinic crystalline form.

Middle Chrome

It is pure lead chromate $PbCrO_4$, and is deeper and redder than lemon chrome and has a monoclinic crystalline form.

Orange Chrome

It consists of a mixture of lead chromate and lead hydroxide. It is a basic lead chromate and its shade can be varied by altering the ratio of lead chromate to lead hydroxide. Increase of lead hydroxide leads to deeper shades.

Scarlet Chrome

It consists of a mixture of lead chromate, lead molybdate and lead sulphate . Scarlet chrome is prepared by co-precipitation of lead chromate with lead molybdate. It is a deep orange pigment of exceptional brilliance and opacity.

Properties and Uses

There is an increase in depth and redness of colour in passing from the greenish-yellow primrose through lemon and middle chrome to the very reddish orange chrome. Scarlet chrome occupies a rather unique position. It is brighter and cleaner than the orange chromes and possesses much greater tinting strength.

The lead chromes possess the following physical characteristics

Specific gravity	5.9 to 6.2
Oil absorption	12 to 16
Refractive index	2.4

They are all bright pigments with good opacity, and high tinting strength. Their general durability is good. When exposed to open atmosphere, however, they are darkened by the presence of hydrogen sulfide and tend to blacken when exposed to sulfur dioxide.

Lead chromes are non-reactive towards paint media and compatible with most other pigment. The lead chromes are all non-toxic. They have a decided property of inhibiting the corrosion of metals and are, therefore, efficient as anticorrosive primers.

2. Zinc Chromes

There are two zinc chromate pigments which are more generally used in the paint industry today, zinc chrome and zinc tetroxy chromate. The former can be regarded as a zinc potassium chromate and the latter as a basic zinc chromate.

Zinc Chrome

Zinc chrome is a complex, having a formula $4ZnO.4CrO_3.K_2O.3H_2O$. It is a greenish, yellow pigment with poor opacity. It has the following physical characteristics

Specific gravity	3.4 to 3.5
Oil absorption	14 to 18

It has lower hiding power and poor chemical resistance because it is reactive with both acids and alkalies. It can be used in corrosion- resistant meta primers for both light alloys and steel.

Zinc Tetroxy Chromate

It has the chemical structure $ZnCrO_4$. $4Zn(OH)_2$.It has poor colour and hiding power. It is free from soluble salts and is much less soluble in water than is the normal zinc chrome.

The main use of the pigment is in etch primers although it is sometimes used in conventional primers for steel-work. It is also used in corrosion-resistant primers.

3. Barium Chromate

This pigment has the formula $BaCrO_4$. It is a very weak, greenish-yellow pigment and is used in stoppers for use on light alloys.

4. Strontium Chromate

Strontium Chromate is brighter in colour than its barium analogue. It has been found very suitable for use in water-soluble stoving primers for application by spray, dip or electrodeposition.

5. Cadmium Yellow

The paler colours most often than not consist of cadmium sulphide *(CdS.)*. It possesses the following physical characteristics.

Oil absorption	32 to 35
Specific gravity	4.2 to 4.3

In all cases, 95 percent of the particles of this pigment are below 5μ in mean diameter. They are bright colours with good light fastness and excellent heat resistance. Cadmium pigments are insoluble in all paint media and solvents and are resistant to alkalies.

Cadmium yellow is used for high class decorative work such as coach painting, in heat-resisting paints, plastics & inks but are expensive.

Yellow Oxides of Iron

1. Ochres

These pigments are actually clays and consist of mixtures of hydrated oxide of iron with mineral silicates. The colour of the pigment is described as yellow but is dirtier and redder than the yellow of the paler lead chromes.

In iron oxide pigments, properties such as tinting strength and opacity vary with the iron oxide content. The latter figure for ochres can range from 16 to 60 and there is therefore a vary wide variation in pigment properties. The specific gravity averages 2.8 to 3.0 but the oil absorption ranges from 20 to 40.

Ochre is mainly used in paint industry in its micronized form as a stainer for gloss paints, undercoats and emulsion paints where it confers a pleasent reddish cream tint.

2. Umbers

These are dark brown in colour and contain upto 15 percent manganese dioxide and 30 to 50 percent iron oxide. It is semi-transparent in oil and in micronized form it is used in paint stainers.

3. Ferrite Yellows

It is also known as yellow oxide of iron. The pigment is dull golden-yellow in colour, very soft in texture, with a high oil absorption. Its staining power is several times greater than that of the finest natural ochre. It forms a very useful pigment on account of its high staining power and freedom from grit. It is used as a stainer in gloss paints, undercoats and aqueous paints.

Green Pigments

The most important green pigments in use in the paint industry are the chrome greens, and the oxide and hydrated oxide of chromium.

1. Chrome Green Pigments

Chrome green pigments are available in a wide range of clean, bright colours which vary from light-yellow green to very deep blue green. Since they are co-precipitates of chrome yellow and iron blue, they inherit both the strong and weak features of these pigments.They have excellent hiding power and tinting strength.

Chrome greens are quite sensitive to alkali but are resistant to mild acids. They should not be used in combinations with pigments which have an alkaline reaction. Such as calcium carbonate extender. Since they contain a lead compound they darken if exposed to atmosphere containing sulphur compounds. Mixtures of cadmium yellow and iron blue are satisfactory for fume resistance and lead free requirements but cadmium pigments are considered toxic and their cost is higher. Light greens have a tendency to become yellower on storage in oxidizing paint because of the reduction of the blue. When dark greens are simply mixed with a highly oxidizable oil such as linseed and allowed to stand overnight, the blue may be reduced or the oil oxidized to such an extent that considerable heat is developed and spontaneous combustion may occur. However, if the paste is given atleast one grind, Sufficient air will be eliminated to prevent combustion. Chrome greens do not bleed in solvents, oil or water.

Chrome greens are used in a wide range of industrial paints and will withstand normal stoving conditions. In building paints they are used where toxicity is no risk but they are unsuitable for use on alkaline surfaces such as lime plaster and cement, or in distempers.

Chromium Oxide Green

Chromium oxide is a sage-green colour and is dull and chalky compared with the chrome greens. It is composed almost entirely of chromium oxide, Cr_2O_3. It possesses the following characteristics

Specific gravity	5.2
Oil absorption	10

Their opacity is very high as is also the resistance to light, heat, acids and alkalies. It is extremely durable and is used under such conditions where resistance is more important than a bright colour. It can safely be used in water paints and distempers and finds wide use in colouring concrete and roof-tiles, plastics, printing inks and ceramics.

Guignet's green or Virdian

It is a hydrated oxide of chromium and is generally assigned the formula $Cr_2O_3.2H_2O$.

Guignet's green is a much brighter pigment than chromium oxide and possesses the following characteristics

Specific gravity	3.2
Oil absorption	63

It has very poor opacity but is fast to light, alkali and all types of paint media. Its resistance to acids and heat is not as high as that of chromium oxide. It is unaffected by cold mineral acids. Lack of opacity and rather high cost limit its use in paints but it is a satisfactory stainer for water paints and distempers.

Cobalt Green

Cobalt green or zinc green is a compound of the oxides of zinc and cobalt. Its averages composition is

Zinc oxide, ZnO	71.93%
Cobalt oxide, CoO	19.15%
Phosphoric anhydride P_2O_5	8.22
Ferric oxide, Fe_2O_3	0.01%
Sodium oxide, Na_2O	0.69%

Cobalt green is rather yellowish in tone and dull in appearence. It is coarse in texture and its staining power is not very great; its specific gravity is 5.69. it is a perfectly stable and inert pigment, unaffected by light and heat, and not attacked by alkalies or weak acids.

Blue Pigments

There are only three blue inorganic pigments of importance in this class — ultramarine blue, prussian blue and cobalt blues.

1. Ultramarine Blue

Ultramarine blue is a complex alumino-silicate which has a crystalline structure containing sulphur. Ultramarine blue is quite different in colour from the two other major blue pigments.

Ultramarine blue has a specific gravity of 2.35 and an oil absorption of 30 to 35. It is available in a range of tones which probably correspond to variation in composition. It is one of the reddest blues available and the colour is not easily matched with other pigments. Its heat resistance is excellent and it is insoluble in all paint media and solvents. It is fast to alkali but is readily attacked by mineral acids. Acids discharge the colour and produce hydrogen sulphide, a precipitate of sulphur and a residue of siliceous matter. Ultramarine is fast to light and reasonably permanent on exposure to the atmosphere under normal conditions.

Ultarmarine blue is largely used for the preparation of washable water paints and similar products as it is fast to light and will with stand the action of lime and alkaline media. It is also used for adding in small proportion to white pigments to correct the colour to standard by making any traces of yellowness due to impurities. It is used extensively in other industries for a similar purpose, particularly in laundry work and paper-making.

Prussian Blues

These are iron compounds of the ferrocyanide radical *$[Fe(CN)_6]$* and contain also an alkali metal or ammonia. They are also known as Iron Blues.

Two types of Prussian Blues are known

(i) Potash or non-bronze blues, usually considered to be a ferric potassium ferro-cyanide, KFe $[Fe(CN)_6]$.

(ii) Ammonia-Soda or bronze blues, Fe $NH_4[Fe(CN)_6]$.

Properties and Uses

Prussian blue is extensively used on account of its brilliance and strength of colour. Ths specific gravity of prussian blue is 1.97 and the oil absorption, which is related to particle size, varies from 70 tò 160. The extreme finemess of the particles, of this pigment results in a high tinting strength but its opacity in paint media is poor. It pòssesses good light fastness and is resistant to solvents and resins. Prussian blue is resistant to mineral and organic acids but is decomposed by alkalies. Prussian blue is therefore unsuitable for use in paints to be applied to alkaline surfaces such as lime plasters and cements, or in water paints.

Non-bronze blues have been used extensively in the manufacture of chrome or brunswick greens.

3. Cobalt Blue

Cobalt oxide forms solid solution with some other metallic oxides. These are highly coloured and possess great resistance to heat, light and chemicals.

Cobalt blue is sometimes known as *'Thenard's blue'* and is a solid solution of cobalt and aluminium oxides.

Properties and Uses

It has the following composition

Cobalt oxide, CoO.	15 percent
Alumina, Al_2O_3	81 percent
Water of hydration, H_2O.	4 percent

It is very bright and clean in colour and almost transparent when dispersed in paint media. It is valued for its colour but more light, heat, acids and alkalies, but is expensive.

Cobalt blue is used occasionally in paints but is too expensive and lacking in opacity for general use. It is used as a pigment for artist's paints.

Black Pigments

The bulk of the black pigments used in the modern paint industry consists of amorphous carbon black either in a fairly pure state *(carbon and vegetable blacks)* or in admixture with inorganic matter *(bone blacks)*.

1. Carbon Blacks

The carbon blacks, prepared from channel process are more common in the paint industry. They have specific gravity ranging between 1.8 to 2.0 and oil absorption 80 to 150. A range of grades is available classified according to intensity of blackness and this appears to be related to particle size. Generally, price increases intensity of blackness.

Carbon blacks are hygroscopic and if exposed to a moist atmosphere they can absorb up to 15 percent of moisture. This renders them difficult to disperse in organic media. They are amorphous and have an extremely small particle size and high oil absorption. As a result of the almost total light absorption and the fine particle size, carbon blacks have very high opacity. They are very fast to light and chemicals *(with the exception of concentrated nitric acid)* and when reduced with white produce greys with a brownish tint. They are therefore widely used for tinting purposes and for this the bluer vegetable black is preferred. When dispersed in paints, carbon blacks tend to absorb materials from the medium. Thus a black paint tends to lose its drying properties on storage as a result of the absorption of part of the drier metals by the carbon black. In some paints, especially undercoats, it can cause an increase in viscosity due to absorption of lower molecular weight polymers.

Carbon blacks can safely be used in all types of paints with the possible exception of some alkyd-type undercoats. They are very extensively used in rubber and links.

Vegetable (Lamp) Black

The term Vegetable Black was originally given to the product obtained by burning vegetable oils in a limited supply of air.

Vegetable black has a specific gravity of 1.8 to 1.9 and an oil absorption of 90 to 150. It is dull and grey in comparison with carbon black. However, on reduction with white it gives a much bluer and cleaner tint and is preferred as a stainer. It is a fast to light, paint media and chemicals *(except ntric acid).*

It is extensively used as a stainer in paints. Other uses are in rubber and inks.

Graphite

This material is a crystalline form and is obtained from natural sources or manufactured from a high carbon type coal.

Graphite is dark grey material with a metallic lustre and a characteristic slippery feel. The specific gravity of graphite varies from 2.5 of natural occurring to 2.25 of manufactured one. It has good opacity and its plate-like structure and characteristic surface give it great spreading power. When made into paint the particles leaf with their planes parallel to the surface with overlapping. The film then possesses high resistance to moisture penetration. Graphite also has a tendency to grip metal surfaces, resulting in good adhesion.

Graphite is used in maintenance paints for structural steel work and also in corrosion inhibiting primers. Graphite is also used in lubricants and pencils.

Bone Black

This pigment is produced by calcination of degreased bones and animal refuse. The product quality is assessed on carbon content and varied with type of bones.

Properties and Uses

The carbon content of Bone Black can vary from 5 to 20 percent, the balance being calcium phosphate and a little calcium carbonate. It has specific gravity of 2.6 to 2.8 and an oil absorption of 30 to 40. The colour and tinting strength of bone black is variable and depend on the carbon content. It mixes more readily with oils and water than do the carbon black but it is similar to carbon balck in its absorption properties.

Thus in paint it tends to absorb driers from the medium and it is sometimes used in water to absorb colouring matters.

Bone black is used in fillers and in cheaper types of black undercoats.

2. Black oxide of Iron

It is synthetically prepared pigment, having the approximate composition equivalent of magnetic iron oxide. It is a fine powder, strongly magnetic, which turns to a dark red colour on calcination. It has a specific gravity of 4.7 and an oil absorption of 28 to 30. It has a fine soft texture and moderate tinting strength. It is used in undercoats, where carbon black can lead to increase in viscosity, and in oil-type finishes, It has good fastness and satisfactory heat resistance for normal stoving conditions.

Organic Pigments

Organic pigments are principally employed in top coats in architectural finishes and also in finishing coats, undercoats and primers. These pigments are also used extensively in industrial finishes including structural or maintenance paints and decorative finishes. The importance of organic pigments have increased to a considerable extent owing to the new fashion trends and increasing aesthetic sense among the people. In consequence, demand has changed from the dull functional shades obtainable with inorganic pigments to the brighter, more varied hues only provided by the use of organic pigments. The organic pigments offer a wider range and a greater variety of shades than do the inorganics.

Organic pigments may be divided into three main groups according to their composition.

(i) Pigments Dyestuffs
(ii) Toners
(iii) Lakes

(i) Pigment Dyestuffs

Pigment dyestuffs are wholly organic water-insoluble compounds, produced by a wide variety of chemical reactions. They can be burnt off leaving virtually no residue. Pigment dyestuffs are produced in one operation from the treated intermediates *e.g.* Helio Red and Hansa Yellow.

Some of the important pigment dyestuffs are described as follows :

1. Toluidine Red *(Helio Red)*

Helio Red is the most widely used red organic pigment. These are fine toluidine reds which are bright rich reds with a limited range in colour. They are produced from the diazonium salt of m-nitro-p-toluidine and Beta-naphthol. The general reaction may be as follows :

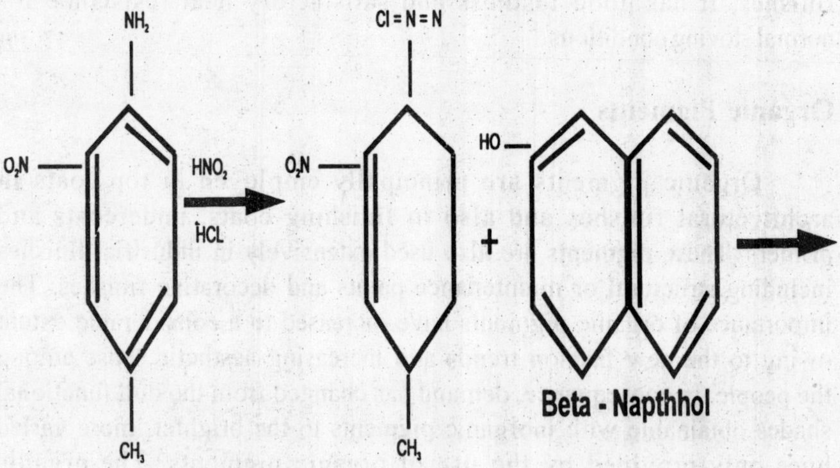

m-niro - p-toluidine

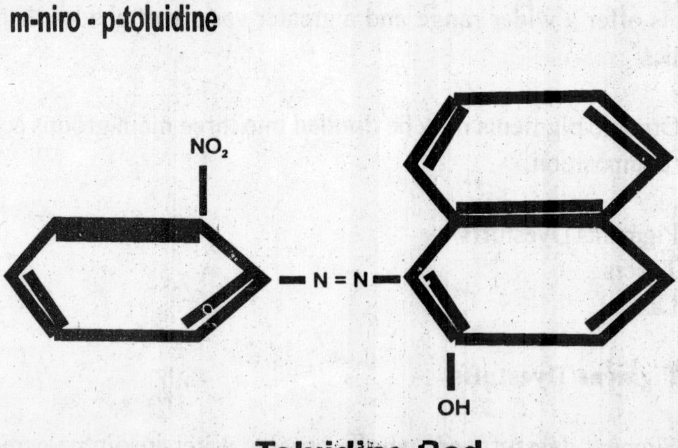

Toluidine Red

All toludine reds have the following common characteristics

Specific Gravity	1.45 to 1.50;
Ease of grinding	Excellent;
Hiding Power	Good;
Transparency	Poor; Permanence,
Mass	Excellent;
Baking stability	Good;
Alkali Resistance	Excellent;
Acid Resistance	Excellent.

Uses

Toluidine reds are widely used in exterior finishes because of their colour and permanence of light, but not used in exterior tints. Their heat stability makes them satisfactory for industrial baking finishes, which are baked at temperatures of 250-300°F. Toluidine reds have good acid and alkali resistance and may be used in chemical-resistant finishes. They have satisfactory alkali-resistance for use in latex paints.

Gloss enamels made with toluidine reds tend to develop a slight haze on their surface after drying. This applies to air dry oleoresinous enamels and also to alkyd-animo resin baking enamels. The cause of the haze has not been detrmined precisely, but it may be related to the slight solubility of toluidine reds in the solvent used in these enamels.

2. Toluidine Maroons

Several variations of toluidine maroon pigments are available commercially. They are similar to Toluidine Reds in that they are prepared from m-nitro-p-toluidine but the beta-naphthol is replaced by m-nitro-anilide of beta-Oxynaphthoic acid. Its chemical formula is

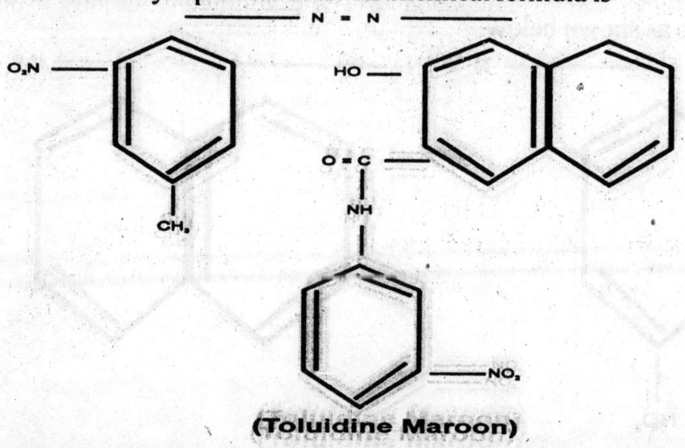

(Toluidine Maroon)

Both toluidine red and maroon are Azo (-N=N-) colours of insoluble types. The maroon has a larger molecular structure than the red which is frequently though not always a criterian of deeper colours. They have the following characteristics

Sp. gravity	1.28 to 1.42
Pounds/gallon	10.66 to 11.83
Gallons/100 lb.	9.38 to 8.46

The toluidine maroons are sensitive to bleed in various solvents. The type of solvent and extent of bleed varies with the individual pigments. It has good resistance to both acids and alkalies. They are quite permanent to light in mass tone, but they should not be used in tints.

They are durable in exterior finishes but the particular pigment vehicle combination should be selected carefully.

3. Para Reds

Para reds are available in a more wider range of colours than the toluidine reds. It occurs in ÿ and ß form. The para red of ÿ type is lighter and yellower than the deep para red of ß type, which has a bluer tone. The simplest modern Para Red is a combination of para-nitroaniline and ß-naphthol R. When it was first introduced it was considered to be a great advancement on the dyes previously available, particularly as regards durability and it rapidly attained popularity for use as a pigment. By varying the conditions of preparation the tone of the colour can be modified to produce a range of red pigments which have been used extensively for many years owing to their brilliancy, staining power and fastness to light. As a paint pigment, however, Para red has the defect of bleeding badly when used in oil vehicles, and it has now been largely superseded for this reason by other pigments. The chemical structure of Para red is as shown below

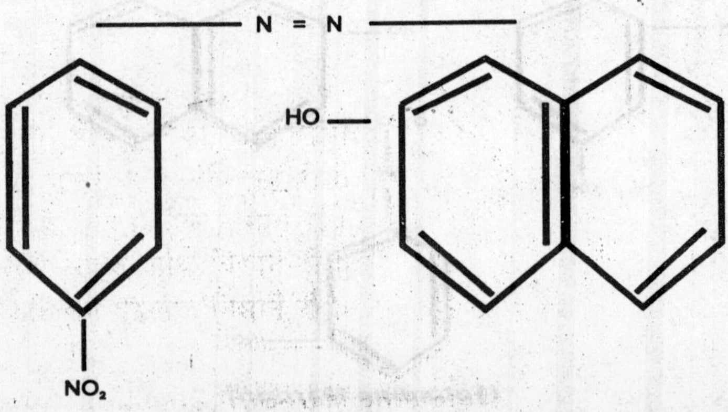

4. Naphthol Reds

A group of azo insoluble colours may be made by replacing Beta-naphthol in the coupling reaction with various derivatives of ß-naphthol. These colours include the toluidine maroons. More recently series of reds have been produced which are referred to as *'naphthol-reds'*. They are bright reds, more expensive than toluidine and para reds, but they are quite resistant to alkali and to soap.

A soap of so called *"naphthol AS"* derivatives may be made by condensing amino-compounds with ß-oxynaphthoic acid. A typical example is

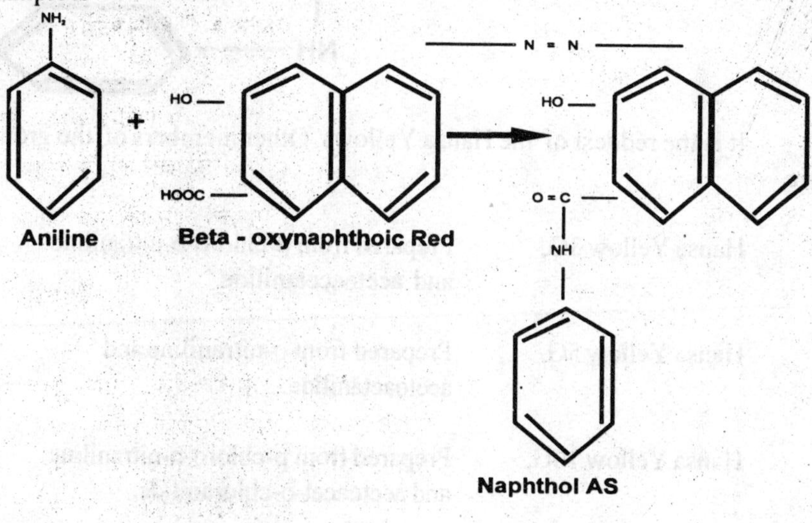

The particular naphthol AS derivatives used in commercial naphthol reds generally are not disclosed.

The naphthol reds are durable colours, but they are not as permanent to light as the Para reds or the toluidines. Their excellent resistance to alkali and soap makes them suitable for such applications as latex paints and soap wrapper inks.

5. Hansa Yellows

These are prepared by coupling diazotized amines with acetoacetlnuilide or its derivatives under weakly acid conditions. Thus Hansa Yellow G is prepared from diazotized m-nitro-p-toluidine by coupling with aceto-acetanilide suspended in dilute acetic acid.

A typical composition is

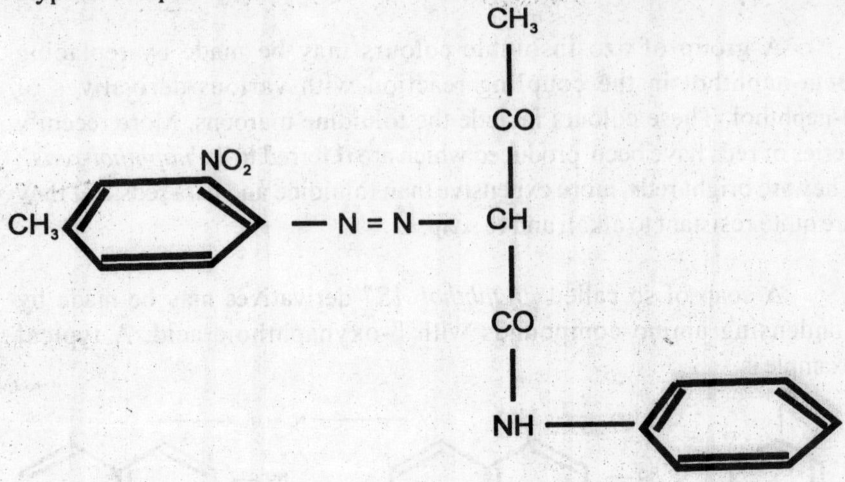

It is the reddest of the Hansa Yellows. Other members of the group are

Hansa Yellow 3G,	Prepared from p-chloro-o-nitraniline and acetoacetanilide.
Hansa Yellow 5G,	Prepared from o-nitraniline and acetoactanilide.
Hansa Yellow 10G,	Prepared from p-chloro-o-nitraniline and acetoacet-o-chloranilide.

Uses and Properties

Generally there is a gradation of properties fr om the reddest and strongest Hansa Yellow G to the greenest and weakest Hansa Yellow 10G. At the same time the light fastness increase in passing from the G to the 10G.

They are all bright and soft pigments and their light fastnes is of a high order. Their resistance to heat is only moderate. They are hydrophobic and flush readily from aqueous dispersion into organic media. Their main uses are for making very bright greens with phthalocyanine blue and as stainers. When used for the latter purpose in emulsion paints they should be converted to the hydrophilic condition to avoid flushing.

6. Benzidine Yellows

These are prepared by coupling tetrazotized benzidines with acetoacetnilide or its derivatives. The most commonly used base is 3:3'-dichlorobenzidine. This is tetrazotized and coupled with aceto-acetanilide to give benzedine yellow.

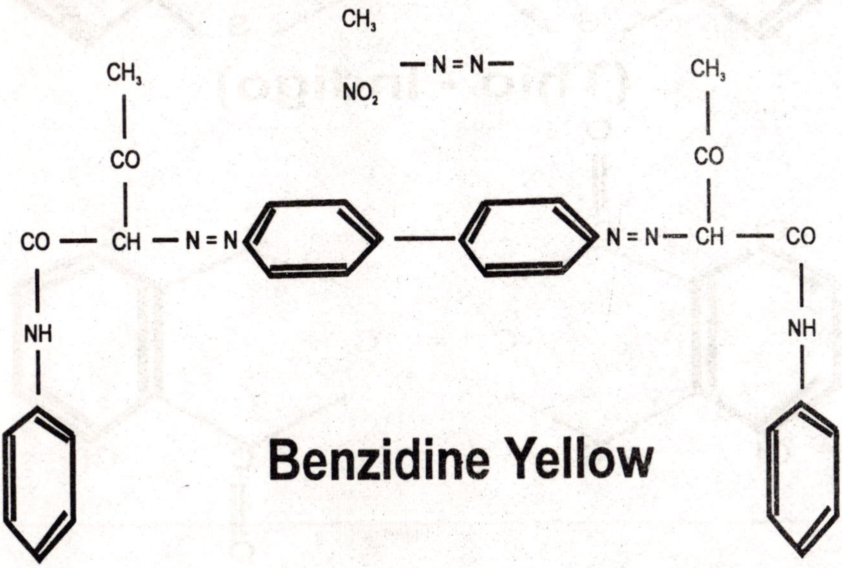

Benzidine Yellow

Properties and Uses

These yellows possess fair opacity compared with chrome yellow and they have greater tinting strength than Hansa Yellow. It has good resistance to acid and alkali and it does not bleed in oil or water.

Benzidine yellows are used instead of chrome yellow in coating which are required to have alkali resistance, fume resistance, and to be lead-free.

7. Thio-Indigo

These contain the chromophore which is of most interest as providing vat dyes for cellulosic fibres but in recent years derivatives have become important as pigments. These comprise a range of colours from pink through red to vioilet and they all contain chlorine atoms in the molecule.

The structure is given below

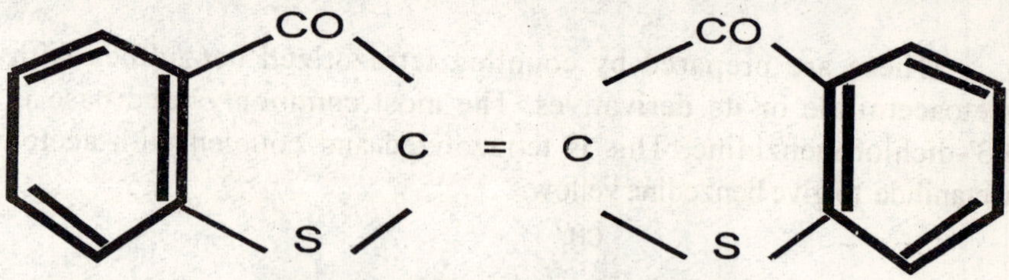

(Thio - Indigo)

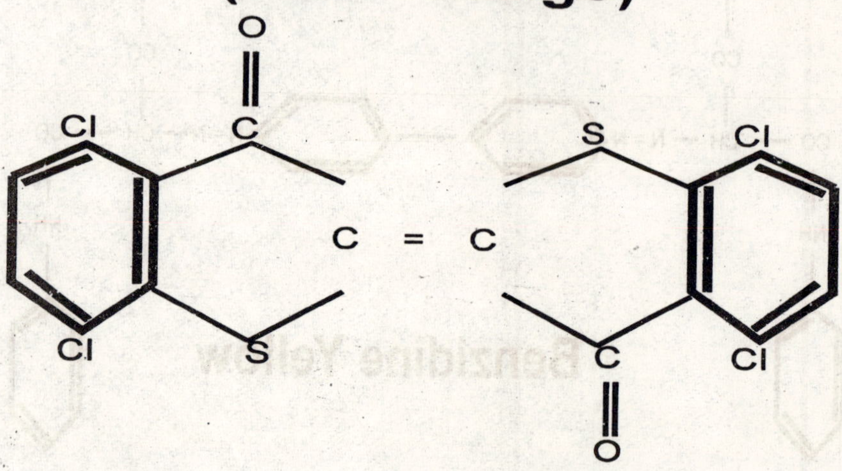

(Thio - indigo Bordeaux)

Uses

This dyestuff is still used in dyeing of cotton goods. The parent substances have quite a large number of derivatives, some of which have excellent physical and tinctorial properties for pigments. Synthetically prepared indigo itself is not a satisfactory pigment because of its interior brilliance, low strength and lack of covering power. So their derivatives like Thio-Indigo are found more useful in commercial practice but are little costly.

8. Phthalocyanine Pigments

The phathalocyanine comprise an important class of pigments ranging in colour from deep blue to yellowish green. The introduction of these pigment dyes was a remarkable achievement in the dyes industry; their constitution being markedly different from anything previously produced.

Phthalocyanine Blue

The structure of Phthalocyanine Blue is as shown below:

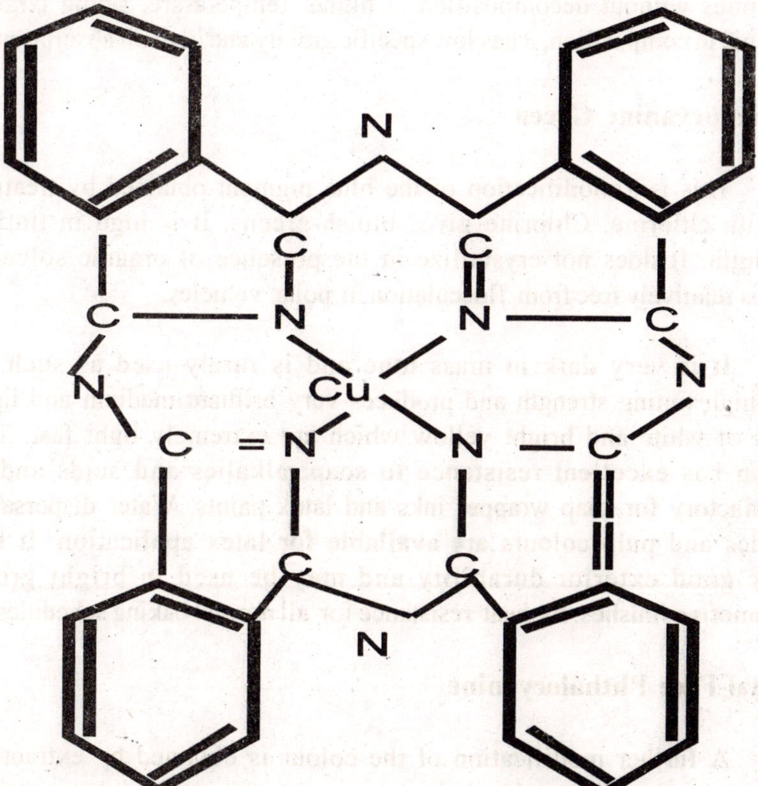

It was first introduced in 1935 by the British Dyestuffs Coroporation under the proprietary name of *'Monastrel Fast Blue'*. It is a highly complex compound containing copper in the molecule.

Phthalocyanine blue may be prepared by reacting phthalic anhydride with a copper salt in the presence of urea.

The pigment has attained considerable popularity on account of its exceptional combination of properties. It is insoluble in water and in the drying oils and thinners normally used in paint formulations so that paints made with it are free from any tendency to bleeding. It is fast to light, and not attacked by either acids or alkalies; the colour, therefore, is not discharged or degraded by exposure to urban atmospheres, or in contact with new cement or plaster surface; it will also stand temperatures up to 200°C without change of colour, and it sublimes without decomposition at higher temperature. Being largely organic in composition, it has low specific gravity and high oil absorption.

Phthalocyanine Green

This is a modification of the blue pigment obtained by treating it with chlorine. Chlorine gives bluish-greens. It is high in tinting strength. It does not crystallize in the presence of organic solvents and is relatively free from flocculation in polar vehicles.

It is very dark in mass tone and is rarely used as such. It has high tinting strength and produces very brilliant medium and light tints of white and bright yellow which are extremely light fast. The green has excellent resistance to soap, alkalies and acids and is satisfactory for soap wrapper inks and latex paints. Water dispersable grades and pulp colours are available for latex application. It has very good exterior durability and may be used in bright green automotive finishes. Its heat resistance for all normal baking schedules.

Metal-Free Phthalocyanine

A further modification of the colour is obtained by extracting the copper from the molecule by transparent with acid, giving a purely organic substance; this is bluish green in colour, intermediate between the blue and green copper compounds.

It possesses very good fastness to water, acid, alkali, lime, oil, heat etc., and is suitable for use wherever their valuable properties come into consideration. It is particularly suitable for the production of high class printing inks. It is also particular interest in paper coating and wall paper trades, where there are special demands for pigments of non-poisonous metal content and in manufacture of oil paints and enamels, distempers and water paints. It is not recommended for use in the colouring of nitrocellulose lacquers.

12

VARNISHES

Introduction

Varnishes are clear unpigmented coatings, made by dissolving a resin or the reaction products of a resin and a drying oil in a suitable solvent. The term varnish is applied to a class of clear liquids of 2 to 3 poise viscosity which, when exposed to the air in thin coatings dry to touch glossy films. Drying of a varnish may be due to evaporation, oxidation and polymerization of its constituents. Not being pigmented, varnishes are less resistant to light than are paints, enamels and pigmented lacquers. They furnish, however, a transparent film, which accentuates the texture of the surface coated. There are two major classifications for varnishes.

(i) Oil varnishes
(ii) Spirit varnishes.

Oil Varnishes

Oil varnishes are combinations of drying oils and resins which are thinned to application viscosity with volatile solvent. Driers are incorporated to catalyse the drying process which us controls largely by the amount of oil present or the ratio of oil to resin. This ratio of oil to resin, by weight, is known as oil length and can be varied considerably. Oil varnishes may be classified according to oil-lenght as :

(a) Long oil length varnishes
(b) Medium oil length varnishes
(c) Short oil length varnishes.

Some times oil lengths are expressed in gallons of oil per 100 lb resin. The *'oil length'* largely controls the properties of the varnish. A short varnish will possess faster-drying properties to a harder and more brittle film, whereas the long varnishes possess more weather-resistant, pliable film. Some oil lengths of typical varnishes are as follows :

Short type (6-15 gal.)	:	Floor and furniture varnishes.
Medium type (20-30 gal.)	:	General-purpose varnishes.
Long type (35-60 gal.)	:	Spar varnishes

A hard resin is preferably used in order to attain the following characteristics:

(i) Shorten the drying time.
(ii) Increase the hardness of the film
(iii) Improve the gloss
(iv) Improved water and chemical resistance
(v) Increase in durability in some cases.

Oil-varnishes contain the following four ingredients :-

1. Resins

Resins provide the hardness and gloss to the film. In general, the higher the proportion of resin in a varnish, the harder and more brilliant but the less durable it is *i.e.*, both hardness and gloss increase with resin content but the durability decreases. Both natural and synthetic resins are used, including copals, estergum, limed rosin, pure and rosin-modified phenolics, maleics and coumarones and many other synthetic resins. Rosin-modified phenolics are replacing others due to their low cost.

2. Drying Oils

Drying oils provide elasticity, toughness and durability to the film. These properties improve with increasing oil content but differ from one oil to another. Drying oils used include linseed *(as varnish linseed oil, stand oil, and enamel oil)*, tung *(wood oil)*, dehydrated castor oil, tobacco seed oil, sova and oitiaica oils.

3. Driers

Driers are usually added in varnishes as they catalyse the conversion of the oil to the solid conditions. Strictly speakings, driers regulate the drying of the film. Frequently used driers include naphthanates and octates of lead and cobalt and sometimes maganese.

4. Thinners

The function of thinners is to adjust the consistency of the varnish for application; after application they must evaporate fairly rapidly and at a uniform rate. Thinners commonly employed include white spirit, dipentene, naphtha and xylol distillates and other petroleum hydrocarbons.

Manufacturing. Procedure

The oleoresinous varnishes may be considered solutions of a resin, natural and synthetic, in a drying oil to which has been added driers and thinners. The procedure used in manufacturing varies widely, depending upon types of oil or resin used. In the case of natural resins, which are insoluble in oil, the resins must be depolymerised by heating, a process called *'running'*. The drying oil is also preheated before adding. In the case of synthetic resins, the preheating is omitted and the oil and resins are heated together until a homogenous solution of correct viscosity is obtained.

Manufacture of Varnishes from Fossil Resins

The varnish-making operation consists of the following successive steps :

(a) Disintegration or size reduction of the resin.
(b) Running the resin
(c) Addition of the drying oil
(d) Cooling, dilution with thinners and addition of driers
(e) Clarification and maturing

Disintegration or Size Reduction of the Resin

The resin is first as far as possible and graded for quality. It is then broken up into pieces of approximately the size of walnuts.

Running the Resin

This process is carried out in open varnish pots or kettles fitted with lids connected to an exhaust-system. These pots vary in capacity but a common size is about 20 inches diameter and 40 inches high. Very considerable frothing can take place during the runing and a suitable charge for a pot of this size is 60 lb. of resin.

Stainless steel is the most satisfactory metal of construction. The resin charge is introduced into the kettle and the latter placed in position over an oil or gas burner. Heating must be uniform and for this purpose, a jacketed vessel is always preferred, with continuous stirring. At the same time the approximate amounts of drying oil heated gradually to a temperature of 130-150°C. The resin is heated rapidly to 300-325°C when depolymerization occurs and the fumes are led off and condensed. The charge is kept stirred to prevent local overheating and charring and the contents of the pot ultimately become fluid. Temperature control is important and long stem mercury-in-steel thermometer or recording thermemeters are usually employed. The temperature is maintained until all frothing ceases and the mass in a clear liquid condition.

Addition of Drying Oil

This process is also known as *'oiling out'*. The hot drying oil is added slowly and in stages to the molten resin, which is kept stirred. The temperature is allowed to fall to 250-180°C and maintained at this point with uniform stirring until a drop placed on glass plate remains clear when cold. Any cloudiness indicates that combination is not complete, and heating must be continued until the cold bead is clear. This test must be applied after addition of each portion of oil, and after the last test a sample is checked for white spirit solubility.

Thinning

After completion of the cooking process the pot is removed from the fire and taken to the thinning chamber, where it is allowed to cool to 160-180°C. The thinner is then added in small quantities at a time with constant stirring. Appreciable loss of solvent takes place during the process and it must therefore be carried out in a location well away from any open flames. After addition of all the thinner, the requisite driers are added as such or in the form of other oil-soluble salts. The varnish is then pumped to storage tanks for maturing and may also be clarified.

Maturing

The so prepared varnishes inevitably contain small quantities of foreign matter, and when freshly prepared are in a state of unstable equilibrium. They are therefore tanked for as long a period as possible. During this period the impurities gradually settle out and the varnish reaches a state of uniformity and stability.

The insoluble matter from varnishes can be removed by filtering or centrifuging.

Filteration is generally affected by a plate and frame type filter press. The mucilage present in a number of varnishes is often difficult to filter and this is coagulated by addition of a filter aid to the varnish. Materials such as diamaceous silicas are commonly used for this purpose.

Centrifuging is an effective methos for the removal of insoluble matter and the action serves to ensure a homogenous product.

Varnishes from Fused and Esterified Copals

The process of manufacture of these varnishes is much simple as these materials are directly soluble in drying oils on heating. The fused resin can either be heated until it melts and oil is then added, or the resin can be added to the heated oil. Varnishes from copal ester can be made by heating a portion of the oil, dissolving the resin in it and then adding the rest of the oil. Bodying of the varnish is carried out by maintaining the temperature at about 250°C, and the cooling and thinning are then carriod out.

The drying times of these varnishes varies with the oil length, the long oil types taking from 16 to 20 hours and the short oils from 1 to 2 hours.

Copal varnish is used as a best quality varnish for decorative purpose. Long oil types are used for exterior work and medium oil types for interior decoration.

Tung Oil Ester Gum Varnish

Natural rosin is melted in an aluminium pot and glycerol equivalent to about 10% of its weight is added. It is heated to a temperature of about 200°C until acid value of about 5 is obtained. Temperature is then raised, tung oil is then added with constant stirring. When the combination is complete, mellt is allowed to cool and thinner is added to it. In the case of synthetic resins the preheating is omitted and the oils and resins are heated together until a homogenous solution of the desired viscosity is obtained. The solution of resin in oils is frequently chilled back with a small amount of oils, and cooled, and the thinners and driers are added.

Types of Oil Varnishes

Many different types of varnish can be produced by combining different resins or mixtures of resins with various proportions of oil, thinners, and driers. Drying times and durability depend on both oil length and composition.

1. Exterior Varnishes

The primary requirement is durability and this is obtained by using hard resins such as copal or hard modified phenolics in a long oil combination. They are relatively slow drying but should be sufficiently hard to tape a second coat in 16 to 20 hours.

2. Interior Decorator's Varnishes

Decorative value is the important property, durability being of less importance. Hard resins of the copal or modified phenolic types are used at a medium oil length. This gives greater gloss and hardness. These varnishes usually surface dry in 4 to 6 hours and are hard dry overnight *(about 16 hours)*.

3. Church Oak Varnish

It is used for seats and other church furniture. It must dry hard but must not soften and become stickly with the heat of the body. Short oil types are used based on hard resins such as copals or hard modified phenolics.

4. Floor Varnishes

It should be quick drying, hard and tough. They are short oil types based on hard resins and often contain a proportion of ethyl cellulose.

5. Flating Varnish

It must dry rapidly to a hard film is capable of being rubbed down without clogging the paper within a few hours of application. Durability is immaterial and they are short oil types based on hard resins.

6. Flat Varnishes

For some decorative purposes, varnishes are required which dry to a matt finish rather than the usual high gloss. The matting effect was formerly obtained by the use of waxes but the modern metthod employs very finely divided precipitated silicas of high oil absorption. The varnish used is the medium oil type.

7. Gold Size

It is a short oil length varnish containing the maximum amount of driers. It is often used on copal and used as a binder for fillers and stoppers as well as an adhesive for gold leaf.

8. Mixing Varnishes

These are used as media for paints and are ususlly of long oil length with low acid value to avoid feeding with basic pigments. Modified phenolics, ester gums and sometimes copal esters are used in conjuction with linseed tung oil. These varnishes were formerly used in hard gloss paints but their use is now confined to undercoats where they are frequently blended with alkyl resins. Mixing varnishes based on tung oil and rosin derivatives are used in machinery enamels; tung oil-coumarone varnishes are used in alkali-resistant primers and in metallic paints.

9. Stoving Varnishes

It is commonly known as stoving lacquer. Some of the short oil types of varnishes are used in the protection and decoration of cans. The varnish is applied to the flat sheet, before fabrication, by roller coating or other means and is then stoved Stoving times and temperatures depend on circumstances and vary from 30 minutes to 1 hour at 120 to 150°C. The films obtained are tough, very adherent and elastic.

Some Typical Formulations for Varnishes

Furniture Varnishes

(a) High-grade Rubbing Varnish

Modified phenolic resin	100 lbs
Tung oil	8 gal
Linseed, body	4 gal
Mineral spirit	30 gal

Cooking Procedure

Heat the resin and 4 gal. of tung oil to 550°F. Add 4 gal. of tung oil and reheat to 550°F. Check with 4 gal. of linseed and hold at 550°F for required body. Cool to about 450°F and reduce with mineral spirits. Add naphthenate driers to give the following percentages by weight of metal to oil in the varnish : 0.3% pb; 0.015% Co; 0.015% Mn.

(b) Furniture Rubbing Varnish

Maleic modified rosin resin	100 lbs
Tung oil	8 gal
Linseed, body	4 gal
Mineral spirit	4 gal

Cooking Procedure

Heat resin and tung oil to 450°F to complete solution, then continue heating to 575°F. Hold about 5 min., then check with linseed oil to 500°F and hold for required body. Cool to about 450°F and reduce with mineral spirits. Add soluble driers to give the following percentages of metal to oil in the varnish : 0.5% pb; 0.005 Co.

(c) Mixed Resin-Mixed Oil Rubbing Varnish

Phenolic-modified Penta-ester gum	66.6 lbs
100% Phenolics resin	33.4 lbs
Linseed, alkali refined	2 gal
Tung oil	8 gal
Mineral spirit	33 gal
Toluol	7 gal

Cooking Procedure

Heat resins and oils to 565°F, and allow to reach 575°F. Cool to 450°F and reduce with mineral spirits followed by toluol. Add soluble driers to give 0.5% Pb; 0.005% Co as metal to oil in varnish.

This varnish is fast drying and gas-proof, and it illustrate the addition of a 100% phenolic resin to the modified phenolic resin to improve water and solvent resistance. The small amount of linseed oil assists in solubilizing the resins in the cooking process.

Metal-Primer Varnishes

Medium-oil-length varnishes are used as vehicle for air-drying and baking primers for metal finishing. Usually, they are pigmented with corrosion-inhibiting pigments, but they may also be pigmented with white pigments for use under white enamels.

(a) Medium-oil, Modified Phenolic Varnishes

Modified phenolic resin	100 lbs
Linseed, body	10 gal
Dehydrated castor oil	15 gal
Mineral spirit	46 gal

Cooking Procedure

Heat resin and 10 gal. of bodied linseed oil to 580°F and hold for a clear cold pill on a glass plate. Add the 15 gal. of bodied dehydrated castor oil and reheat to 580°F. Hold for a clear, cold pill on glass and required body. Cool to 450°F and reduce with mineral spirits and add driers as usual. This varnish is fast air-drying or baking and has excellent toughness and adhesion and good water resistance.

(b) Medium-oil, modified phenolic Varnish (Gas-proof at low Temperature)

Phenolic-modified Penta-ester gum	100 lbs
Tung oil	25 gal
Mineral spirits	41 gal
Turpentine	4 gal

Cooking Procedure

Heat resin and oil to 475°F, hold for 45 minutes, cool to 450°F, and reduce with mineral spirits and turpentine. Add soluble driers to give 0.5% Pb; 0.05% Co, and 0.05% Mn, as metal to oil. Care should be taken not to exceed 475°F in the processing. The holding time will vary somewhat with the grade of oil. and it may be necessary to lower the holding temperature to 450°F for large batches. The addition of anti-skinning agent. ASA, will reduce the tendency to skin in the container. Usually 0.5% of ASA on varnish solids is sufficient.

If lower cost primer vehicles are required, the modified phenolic resin may be replaced entirely or in part by ester gum with the hard oil, or by penta-modified ester gum with soft oils. The cooking time will be increased, and the varnishes will be slower drying and have less resistant films.

Varnishes of Maximum Water Resistance and Durability

For the combination of maximum water resistance and exterior durability, it is necessary to use medium to long oil varnishes made with

100% phenolic resins and tung oil, or a mixture of tung and linseed oils. In general, resins are more water-resistant than oils; therefore, short oil varnishes are more water-resistant than longer oil varnishes. However, short-oil varnishes are not flexible enough for exterior durability.

(a) Heat-resistant, Non-reactive Phenolic Varnish

100% Phenolic resin (Based on p-phenyl phenol)	100 lbs
Tung oil	25 gal
Mineral spirit	30.5 gal

Cooking Procedure

Heat resin and 12.5 gal. tung oil to 560°F in 30-35 minutes, hold at this temperature for 15 minutes and add remainder of the oil. Reheat to 450°F, hold for about 60 min. for body, reduce with mineral spirit and add soluble driers to give 0.4% Pb, 0.05% Co, 0.02% Mn, metal to oil. This varnish is gas proof, non-reactive with zinc oxide, has no skins in the skinning test in two weeks, passes 110% Kauri reduction, fails at 120%. The dried film shows no failure after immersion in 55 NaOH solution for 24 hours.

(b) General Utility Varnish

100% Phenolic resin (Heat-reactive) type	25 lb
W.W. Rosin	10 lb
Ester gum	65 lb
Tung oil	20 gal
Linseed oil, bodied	5 gal
Mineral spirits	44 gal

Cooking Procedure

Heat rosin, ester gum, and tung oil to 400°F. Remove fire and add phenolic resin, and stir continuously until complete dispersion is obtained. Heat to 560°F in about 20 minutes: check at once with linseed oil. Cool to 450°F in about 35 minutes, and reduce with mineral spirits. Add soluble driers to give 0.5% Pb, 0.05% Co, and 0.02% Mn as metal to oil. Add

0.2% anti-skinning agent by volume of varnish.

The varnish is gas proof, is moderatly reactive with zinc-oxide, does not skin in two weeks, passes 70% Kauri reduction, but fails at 80%. The dried film shows no failure after immersion in 5% NaOH for 4 hours.

Alkali-Resistant Varnishes

For maximum alkali resistance a short oil varnish must be used but of course, this advantage cannot be obtained without a sacrifice of flexibility. However, flexibility is not important on many rigid surfaces. The following varnish gives excellent result in alkali-resistant finishes.

(a) Heat-non-Reactive phenolic Varnish

100% phenolic resin (Based on p-phenyl phenol)	100.0 lbs
Tung oil	12.5 gal
Xylol	27.5 gal

Cooking Procedure

Heat oil and resin to 450°F in 30 minutes, hold for about 25 minutes for body, reduce with xylol, and add soluble driers to give 0.05% Pb, 0.006% Co as metal to oil.

The varnish is gas-proof, does not skin in 2 weeks, is not reactive with zinc oxide and fails at 0% in the Kauri reduction test. The film is resistant to 5% NaOH for 96 hours.

(b) Coumarone-Indene Varnish

Coumarone-Indene Resin	100 lbs
Tung oil	16 gal
Cobalt naphthenate (6%)	12.02
Mineral spirits	28 gal

Cooking Procedure

Heat oil very quickly to 400°F, and add 75 lb. of resin and continue heating rapidly to 550°F. Take kettle off the fire, allow temperature to rise to 570-575°F, check with 25 lb. of resin and water, cool the outside of the keetle to a batch temperature of 500°F. Hold for body between 450-500°, reduce and add drier.

Alkyd Resin-short Oil Varnish

The resin composition of the ingredients in the reaction kettle will be as follows :

	Parts by weight
Phthalic anhydride	200
Glycerine	140
linseed oil } Glycerine } (50-50 parts)	200

Procedure for Resin Making

At the start linseed oil fatty acids are poured with glycerine into the reaction kettle. The temperature is raised to 250°C gradually upto 280°C.

To keep the atmosphere inert, either Co_2 or N_2 is blown in, which creates minor stirring. Also the whole mass is stirred very slowly by stirrer. When good temperature is attained inside the kettle as required, phthalic anhydride is added. The time of addition of phthalic anhydride is taken as zero and at regular interval of time a sample of the resin is taken out and tested for acid value. Continuous heating and stirring is carried on to the time when the acid value is reduced to below 20. Agitation is stopped and the batch is allowed to cool to 150°C.

The time taken for the preparation of resin is about 2 hours. The resin is dissolved in solvents like xylene, benzene, toluene, or turpentine called thinners. The quantity of the thinner added is about 3/4th of that of the resin content. A small amount of the thinner is kept for dissolving the driers that are to be added after thorough stirring.

The driers used are mostly naphthenates, linoleates, and rosinates of lead, cobalt and manganese. Their percentage as the ratio of metal content to resin *(solids)* present for best combination of driers is given as :

Cobalt	0.05% As metal
Lead	0.5% As metal
Manganese	0.01% As metal

The mixture of driers is mixed with small quantity of the thinner that is kept away as a paste from the total thinner required.

The driers are dissolved in thinner or partially dissolved *(heat slightly if necessary)* and added into the ketle and agitation by stirrer is contained for 5-10 minutes. The varnish is now ready for use.

Precautions during Manufacture

1. The temperature conditions are to be strictly followed as required and mentioned.

2. Before adding the thinner, the temperature should be brought low, and it should be kept at about 100°C.

Spirit Varnishes

It includes those varnishes which consist of a simple solution of resin in a solvent. Plasticizers may also be present and the films dry entirely by evaporation. The preparation of these varnishes involve no complicated cooking process.

Among the spirit varnishes may be included, solutions of shellac; or bleached shellac soft monila, oxidized rosin, phenol and urea-formaldehyde resins and modified phenolic resins in industrial alcohol; and solutions of coumarone, damar, limed rosin, rosin and copal esters, modified phenolics, maelic and other synthetic resins in hydrocarbons.

The treatment of these varnishes during their production depends upon the chemical properties of the resins, the amount and form of the insoluble matter, and the viscosity of the final product.

Spirit Mania Varnishes

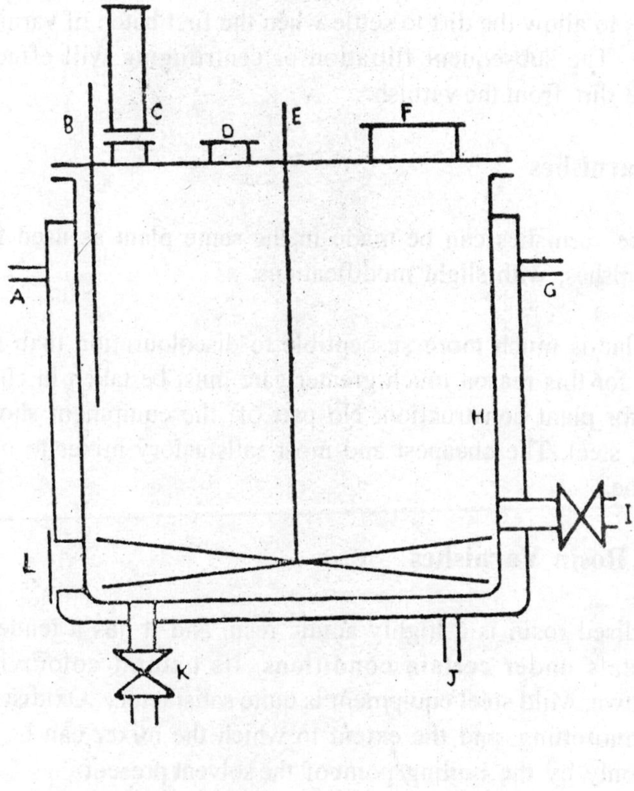

Under normal circumsatnces, more spirit or soft manila is used in spirit varnishes on an industrial alcohol base than any other alcohol soluble resin, with the possible exception of rosin.

Spirit manila is an acidic resin, having an acid value of the order of 140. It varies in hardness and many contain dirt, mineral matter, bark, twigs, etc. Its solubility is likely to vary considerably. All these special features require careful consideration in designing the ideal plant.

A steam jacketed mixer is employed for the manufacture of spirit varnishes. The mixer is fitted with a stirrer. The temperature of the mix is allowed to risen only 20 to 30°C above room temperature. Higher temperatures are not advisable beacuse of the relatively low boiling point of alcohol. Low-pressure steam, therefore, serves as a good heating medium. The most economical procedure to adopt for dirt treatment is to allow the dirt to settle when the first batch of varnish has been made. The subsequent filtration or centrifuging will effectively remove the dirt from the varnish.

Shellac Varnishes

These varnishes can be made in the same plant as used for the manila varnishes, with slight modifications.

Shellac is much more susceptible to discolouration than manila copal, and for this reason much greater care must be taken in choosing materials for plant construction. No part of the equipment should be made mild steel. The cheapest and most satisfactory mixer to use is a wooden one.

Oxidized Rosin Varnishes

Oxidised rosin is a highly acidic resin and it has a tendency to attack metals under certain conditions. Its natural colour is dark reddish brown. Mild steel equipment is quite satisfactory. Oxidised rosin is not thermosetting, and the extent to which the mixer can be heated is limited only by the boiling point of the solvent present.

Phenolic Rosin Varnishes

These fall into two classes, those involving pure unmodified resins, and those involving the highly rosin modified types.

The former are both sensitive to heat and to darkening in contact with iron. The latter are affected by these conditions to a much diminished extent. Both are similar in that they do not need any special cleanising.

Urea-formaldehyde Rosin Varnishes

These resins should not be made to go into solution by the action of heat, and except for this mixer as used for spirit manila varnish is satisfactory. No provision need be made for dirt romoval or special cleanising.

Varnish Formulations

Formulation No. 1

Gum cauri	100 kgs
Linseed oil, boiled	200 litres
Manganese resinate	4 kgs
White spirit	450 litres

Formulation No. 2

Manila gum	50 kgs
Copal gum	50 kgs
Linseed oil	200 litres
Litharge	5 kgs
Manganese dioxide	2.25 kgs
Methylated spirit	450 litres

It is a cheap type varnish and can be used in both exterior and interior coatings.

Formulation No. 3

Cauri gum	100 kgs
Linseed oil	150 litres
Turpentine oil	50 litres
White spirit	150 litres
Drier	1 Kg

Formulation No. 4

Copal gum	100 kgs
Linseed oil, boiled	250 litres
Cobalt acetate	2.25 kgs
White spirit	500 litres

Some Typical Formulations of Spirit Varnishes

Formulation No. 1

Shellac	2.25 kgs
Methylated spirit	10.0 litres
Benzon	0.5 kg

Formulation No. 2

Bleached shellac	4 kgs
Methylated spirit	25 litres

Formulation No. 3

Shellac	90 kgs
Turpentine oil	3.5 kgs
Methylated spirit	360 litres

Formulation No. 4

Sandarac	15.9%
Mastic	14%
Turpentine oil	1%
Aloe	7.0%
Methylated spirit	66.1%

Formulation No. 5

Shellac	82 kgs
Yellow resin	28 kgs
Methylated spirit	260 litres
Wood naphtho	250 litres

Formulation No. 6

Sandarac	16.6%
Mastic	3.4%
Turpentine oil	3.4%
Methylated spirit	63.2%

Formulation No. 7
(Floor Varnish)

Manila copal	12 parts
Shellac	16 parts
Turpentine oil	12 parts
Spirit (96%)	250 parts

Formulation No. 8 *(Electrical Insulating Varnish)*

(i)	Xylenol	45 parts
	Para-formaldehyde	10.75 parts
	Triethanolamine	1.5 parts
	China Wood oil	47.75 parts
	Solvent Naphtha	8.0 parts
	White Spirit	16.0 parts

(ii) Flexible Insulating Varnish

	I	*II*
Phthalic anhydride	213 parts	235 parts
Glycerol	129 parts	118 parts
Succinic Acid	456 parts	235 parts
Ethylene Glycol	242 parts	230 parts
Rosin	200 parts	200 parts
China wood oil	80 parts	80 parts

Formulation No. 9 (Exterior Varnish)

(a) Water-Resisting Varnish (spar varnish)

	% by weight
Glyptal solution	66.0
Low body oxidised linseed oil	22.0
High flash naphtha	10.5
Lead naphthenate (24%)	1.0
Cobalt naphthenate (6%)	0.5

(b) Glycerol-phthalate Spar Varnish

	% by weight
Glyptal solution	75.0
Petroleum spirit	23.7
Dipentane	1.0
Cobalt drier (6%)	0.3

Formulation No. 10

Bitumen Varnishes

		parts by weight
(a)	Bitumen from Petroleum (m.p. 80-90°C)	55.0
	High flash naphtha	10.0
	White spirit	35.0

Bitumen is first heated to 200°C. The temperature is then allowed to fall to 170°C. At this stage, all the thinners are added.

		parts by weight
(b)	Natural Bitumen	28.0
	Tung oil	28.0
	Litharge	2.0
	White spirit	41.0
	Cobalt naphtha (6%)	1.0

Tung oil and bitumen are heated together to 250°C. Litharge is then added and the temperature is raised to 280°C. Keep the mix at 280°C for some time. Cool it to 180°C and add white spirit and driers.

Formulation No. 11

Epoxy-phenolic Primer Varnish

	Kgs	*Litres*
Phenolic Resin	75.0	83.2
Epoxy Resin	25.0	25.1
Tung oil	97.7	124.0
Linseed oil	97.7	125.7
White spirit	241.6	372.0
	537.0	730.0

Process

Both Epoxy and phenolic resins are mixed together and the temperature is raised to 450°F in 30 minutes. This temperature is maintained for 30 minutes and then linseed oil is added. The temperature is then raised to 565°F in 15 minutes and maintained for 30 minutes. Tung oil is now added and the temperature is kept constant for sufficient time to obtain the desi product of desired viscosity.

Formulation No. 12

A typical *'long-oil'* alkyd based on linseed oil would have the following composition

Linseed oil fatty acids (LOFA)	70.0 parts by weight
Glycerol	15.3 parts by weight
Phthalic anhydride	14.7 parts by weight

British Standards Institution gives the following definition of long and short oil alkyds:

Long-oil alkyds	60 percent oil, or more
Short-oil alkyds	40 percent oil, or less

'Long-oil' alkyds are based on drying or perhaps semi-drying oils. Commercial products vary fairly widely in composition but the majority of them give acid values in the range 10-30 mg KoH per gram of resin. Long-

oil alkyds are commonly dissolved in white spirit and applied by brushing. They dry relatively slowly in approximately 4-8 hours, giving comparitively soft films with good exterior durability. A typical application would be in decorative house paints, where their colour is an advantage compared with oleoresinous varnishes. Compared with simple linseed oil paints, their drying is rapid, and their films are hard.

'Short-oil' alkyds are based on drying oils. Acid values of this varnishes vary usually between 20 and 40 mg KoH per gramme of resin. These alkyds are generally dissolved in xylene and applied by spraying. If dipping techique is used, a less volatile solvent is needed but it must still have a high aromatic content to dissolve the resin. These alkyds dry rapidly in about 1-2 hours, giving fairly hard films. In general, durability of these alkyds tends to be somewhat lower than that of long-oil types. A typical application is in general purpose metal primers. Major performance requirements include good adhesion to metals, good corrosion resistance and rapid film formation. Films are often stoved.

13

PAINTS FORMULAES

Introduction

Industrial finishes are used for protection and decoration of industrial, commercial and household items. These finishes are highly varied and usually specific formulas are developed to meet the various requirements of performance, method of application and drying schedule. They are used on wide variety of substrates including metal, wood, plastics, textiles, paper, leather and rubber. They are normally applied by spraying but other methods of application are also sometimes used to obtain maximum efficiency and lowest cost and to comply with particular characteristics of the item being finished, they are usually force dried at 120-180°F or baked at 200-400°C. Force drying and baking are done under closely controlled temperature and time conditions.

White Finishes For Metals

Introduction

A list of major items which are given white finishes include refrigerators, washing machines, lighting fixtures, hospital equipments, kitchen cabinets *etc*. The formulation of paint for each application is different because of the different levels of acceptance in performance requirements and cost consideration. The refrigerator finishes should have brilliant whiteness and scratched proof, marproof and non-yellowing qualities. Hospital equipments should have high stain resistance. In washing machines retention of whiteness is not as important as resistance to alkali and soap. In lighting fixtures, colour retention at somewhat elevated temperatures is important. The painting system consists of priming, surfacing, undercoating and finishing steps; each steps involving a different formulation.

Priming

The priming coat is usually white and only sometimes clored. It should have maximum adhesion and toughness. These primers are mostly based on medium oil alkyds for white primers and may be used on dehydrated castor oil alkyds for white or coloured primers. Primers based on epoxy esters are used for better adhesion, and moisture and chemical resistance. Melamine or urea formaldehyde resins can be incorporated for better hardness. On galvanized steel, wash or etch primers are used. Stoving schedule for these primers is usually 120°C for 30 minutes or 150°C for 20 minutes.

Stoving Primer White *(Best Quality)*

Titanium Dioxide (Anatase)	20.350
Zinc Oxide	18.460
Soya Medium Oil Alkyd (50% solids)	40.420
Mineral Turpentine Oil (M.T.O.)	14.340
Butanol	2.115
Pine Oil	1.115
Cobalt Naphthenate (9% Co)	1.100

Stoving Primer White

Wetting and Antisettling Agent	0.400
Titanium Dioxide	18.350
Barytes	15.460
China Clay	5.230
Whiting	3.540
Soyabean Medium Oil Alkyd (50% solids)	45.760
Mineral Turpentine	9.160
Butanol	1.000
Cobalt Drier (1% Co)	1.100

Stoving Primer White *(based on D.C.O. Alkyd)*

Titanium Dioxide	17.940
Wetting and Antisettling Agents	0.320
Barytes	14.650
China Clay	4.250
Whiting	4.250
D.C.O.Medium Oil Alkyd (50% solids)	45.540
Urea Formaldehyde	4.000
Mineral Oil	4.460
Petroleum Solvent	2.330
Butanol	1.450
Cobalt Naphthenate (1% Co)	0.810

Stoving Primer *(based on D.C.O. Epoxy Ester)*

Wetting Agent	0.230
Titanium Dioxide	16.380
Barytes	8.430
China Clay	8.430
D.C.O. Epoxy Esters (50% solids)	53.380
Petroleum Solvent	5.650
Mineral Turpentine	5.650
Butanol	1.850

Surfacing

Surfacers are of two types — ***paste filler*** and ***spray filler***. The Paste filler is used to fill coarse dents on the surface and spray filler is used to uniformly level the surface. Paste Fillers are grey or off white. They consist of pigments and extenders like barytes and whiting and titanium di-oxide or along with zinc oxide. They should be quick drying and hard settling. Therefore the medium is usually rosinated alkyds or coumarone indene resins. In spray fillers medium oil alkyds are used to get hard and wrinkle free finish on stoving.

Sometimes surfacers can replace undercoatings and undercoatings can replace surfacers because the function of both is more or less same *i.e.* to impart eveness on the surface and provide hard and adherent base for the finishing coat.

Paste Filler Grey

Titanium Dioxide	7.460
Barytes	33.130
Whiting	27.800
China Clay	9.250
Limed Rosin Stand Oil Varnish (40% oil length, 60% solids)	22.500
Carbon Black	0.070
Mineral Oil	1.000
Pine Oil	0.290
Manganese Drier (1% metal)	0.500

Knifing Grey Filler *(Superior Quality)*

Zinc Oxide	8.430
Titanium Dioxide	8.336
Barytes	31.993
Whiting	27.700
China Clay	3.155
Coumarone Resins (45% solids)	22.500
Mineral Turpentine	1.286
Manganese Naphthenate	0.200

Spraying Filler off-White

Antisettling and Wetting Agent	0.250
Titanium Dioxide (Anatase)	15.620
China Clay	7.960
Asbestine	7.960
Whiting	8.210
Medium Oil Linseed Alkyd (50% solids)	47.300
Mineral Turpentine Oil (M.T.O)	8.000
Pine Oil	1.600
Butanol	1.600
Manganese Naphthenate	1.500

Undercoating

Undercoating is done to increase the build-up of painting system. the only difference in composition of the undercoating and finishing coat is the pigmentation percentage which is lower in undercoating.

Finishing Coats

In refrigerators and hospital equipment where whiteness and stain resistance and non-yellowing property are of prime importance, a combination of alkyd and amino resins is used. The combination provides a low baking schedule, excellent scratch hardness, mar resistance and very good water, alkali and solvent resistance, durability and colour retention. The pigments used should be neutral in character; basic pigments like zinc oxide require higher baking temperature and time. Coconut oil short alkyds are usually used. These resins are non-yellowing type and act as plasticizer for amino resins and produce a film which has excellent adhesion.

For lighting fixtures, colour retention at elevated temperature is of utmost importance. Here a combination of amino and alkyd resins is used. Although coconut oil alkyd is preferred, in certain cases to reduce the cost, castor oil or dehydrated castor oil alkyds can replace coconut alkyd partially or fully. The dehydrated castor oil alkyds is cheaper than coconut oil alkyd and its use also permits lower requirements of amino resin in D.C.O alkyd-amino resin combination as against, in coconut alkyd-amino resin, because D.C.O. alkyds being drying type give the same hardness as coconut alkyds at lower percentage of amino resins. A further reduction in costs can be accomplished by replacing 50% of melamine resins by urea-formaldehyde resins.

In washing machine where colour is not as important as resistance to water, soap and alkali, epoxy ester resin in conjuction with melamine resin is recommended.

Stoving Enamel for Refrigerators

Antisettling and Wetting Agent	0.250
Ultramarine Blue	0.054
Titanium Dioxide (Rutile)	27.846
Coconut Alkyd-Short-Oil (50% solids)	41.746
Melamine Formaldehyde Resin (62% solids)	21.302
Xylene	4.808
Butanol	1.902
Pine Oil	2.000
Triethylamine	0.092
Weight per Litre	1.18 (± 3%) Kg
Viscosity by Ford Cup No. B-4 at 30°C	60 ± 5 seconds
Stoving Schedule	120°C/30 minutes

Stoving Enamel for Regrigerators *(with Improved Adhesion)*

Antisettling and Wetting Agent	0.250
Ultramarine Blue	0.080
Titanium Dioxide (Rutile)	20.700
Coconut Alkyd-Short-Oil (50% solids)	43.210
D.C.O Alkyd-Short-Oil (60% solids)	5.300
Melamine Formaldehyde Resin (62% solids)	18.530
Xylene	8.380
Butanol	1.250
Pine Oil	2.200
Triethylamine	0.100
Weight per Litre	1.16 (± 3%) Kg
Viscosity by Ford Cup No. B-4 at 30°C	75 ± 5 seconds
Stoving Schedule	120°C/30 minutes

Stoving Enamel for Hospital Equipments

Wetting Agent	0.200
Ultramarine Blue	0.070
Titanium Dioxide(Anatase)	20.356
Coconut Short-Oil (50% solids)	24.255
D.C.O. Alkyd-Short -Oil (50% solids)	24.255
Melamine Formaldehyde Resin (60% solids)	20.150
Toluene	7.250
Butanol	1.409
Pine Oil	2.050
Weight per Litre	1.16 (± 3%) kg
Viscosity by Ford Cup No. B-4 at 30°C	75±5 seconds
Stoving Schedule	120°C/30 minutes

Low Cost Stoving Enamel for Light Fixture, Hospital Equipments, Washing Machines and Kitchen Cabinets.

Wetting Agent	0.250
Ultramarine Blue	0.075
Titanium Dioxide (Anatase)	20.136
Coconut Alkyd-Short-Oil (50% solids)	20.135
D.C.O. Alkyd-Short-Oil (50% solids)	35.365
Melamine Formaldehyde (50% solids)	6.500
Urea Formaldehyde Resin (50% solids)	6.500
Toluene	8.539
Butanol	1.500
Pine Oil	1.000
Weight per litre	1.16 (± 3%) kg
Viscosity by Ford Cup No. B-4 at 30°C	75±5 seconds
Stoving Schedule	120°C/30 minutes

Lost Cost Stoving Enamel for Lighting Fixtures

Wetting Agent	0.150
Ultramarine Blue	0.060
Titanium Dioxide (Anatase)	17.350
Castor Oil-Short-Alkyd (50% solids)	8.936
D.C.O. Alkyd-Short-Oil (50% solids)	45.350
Urea Formaldehyde Resin (50% solids)	15.430
Toluene	9.324
Pine Oil	1.700
Butanol	1.700
Weight Per Litre	1.13(± 5%) kg
Viscosity by Ford cup No.B-4 at 30°C	75±5 seconds
Stoving Schedule	120°C/30 minutes

Very Low Cost Stoving Enamel for Lighting Fixture

Wetting Agent	0.100
Ultramarine Blue	0.050
Titanium Dioxide (Anatase)	16.750
D.C.O. Short-Oil-Alkyd (50% solids)	61.380
Urea Formaldehyde Resin (50% solids)	8.360
Cobalt Naphthenate (5% Co)	0.500
Toulene	10.860
Butanol	2.000
Weight per litre	1.12 (± 5%)kg
Viscosity by Ford Cup No. B-4 at 30°C	90 ± 5 seconds
Stoving Schedule	120°C/30 minutes

Several other white finishes which can be used on refrigerators, kitchen cabinets, washing machines, and lighting fixtures can be made from epoxy resins or epoxy esters in combination with polyamide, melamine, urea formaldehyde and acrylic resins.

White Baking Enamel Based on Epoxy Ester-Melamine Formaldehyde Resin

Wetting Agent	0.150
Titanium Dioxide (Rutile)	16.530
D.C.O. Epoxy Ester (50% solids)	47.142
Melamine Formaldehyde Resin (50% solids)	15.918
Toluene	16.630
Butanol	3.630
Weight per litre	1.13 (± 5%) kg
Viscosity by Ford Cup No. B-4 at 30°C	90 ± 5 seconds
Stoving Schedule	120°C/30 minutes

Baking Enamel Based on Epoxy -Urea Formaldehyde Resin

Wetting Agent	0.130
Ultramarine Blue	0.050
Titanium Dioxide (Rutile)	24.630
Epikote 1007 (50% solids)	39.482
Urea Formaldehyde Resin (50% solids)	14.778
Toluene	10.130
Xylene	7.400
Butanol	3.400
Weight per litre	1.18 (± 3%) kg
Viscosity by Ford Cup No. B-4 at 30°C	75 ± 5 seconds
Stoving Schedule	130°C/30 minutes

White Enamel based on Epoxy-Polyamide Resins
(Two Pack System)

Component I

Wetting Agent	0.120
Ultramarine Blue	0.050
Titanium Dioxide (Rutile)	21.650
Araldite PLZ	34.380
Toluene	15.200
Xylene	20.400
Methyl Isobutyl Ketone	8.200

Component II

Hardner PLZ	34.300
Xylene	60.320
Cellusolve	5.300

Mixing Ratio = Component I : Component II
1:3

White Enamel based on Acrylic Resin

Titanium Dioxide	20.356
Ultramarine Blue	0.023
Acrylic Ester Resin (Indofil, 40% solids)	76.200
Xylene	3.421
Stoving Schedule	$120^{o}C$/30 minutes

This enamel gives extremely white finish. It may be noted however, that the use of acrylic resins in paint systems in India is very much limited because of their high cost.

Machinery and Furniture Finishes

Machinery and furniture are major consumers of paints. Cost is the major consideration in the formulation and selection of ingredients for the manufacture of paints for furniture inspite of the fact that appearance is a major criteria in sales appeal. The paint should give very good finish and gloss, its durability is not very important because these items are generally not subjected to exterior exposure and corrosive atmospheres. However, even in these finishes a certain degree of hardness, mark proofness, mar resistance and water proofness is desirable. These finishes can be air drying type, stoving type or air drying-cum-stoving type.

In the formulation of paint it is necessary to consider the me of application that will be adopted during use. Since these items not subjected to corrosive enviroments. their surfaces are genera not given any passivating treatment. In general the first coat spra is of an anticorrosive primer having very good adhesion beca it forms the ground for whole of the painting system. Then a co of surfacer or knifing paste filler is given in order to cover uneveness of the surface and to cover rivets and welding spots. This is follow by two coats of finishing paint to get a smooth, uniform and glo finish. In some cases semi-glossy finish is also desired.

The finishing coats are mostly applied by spraying, althou dipping technique is also sometimes used. The mediums used different for dipping and spraying systems. For dipping systems medium must have very good flow and stability in dipping ta for longer period. In these systems a lot of aeration occurs du movement of articles in and out of the tank resulting in incre in viscosity and skinning tendency. Therefore, the medium shou have antiskinning properties and solvents should have low evaporatio rates.

Mediums for furniture and Machinery Finishes

Low Cost Medium for First Cost

Estergum	30.000
Stand Oil Linseed (60-90 poises)	30.000
Mineral Turpentine Oil (M.T.O)	35.000
Pine Oil	5.000

Heat resin and the oil to 260°C for 2 hours or more until the Ford Cup No. B-4 viscosity after thinning with 40% mineral turpentine oil is about 120 seconds.

Cheaper Quality Medium For First Coat

Rosin	30.000
Lime Slaked	1.500
Stand Oil Linseed (60-90 poise)	28.500
Mineral Turpentine	38.000
Pine Oil	2.000

Heat rosin to 230°C and start adding lime in small lots at a time. After the complete addition of lime raise the temperature to 260°C and maintain the temperature to get clear pill. Cool the limed rosin to 200°C. Add stand oil and again raise the temperature to 250°C-260°C to get the desired viscosity. Cool to 140°C and thin down with solvent.

Medium for First Coat *(Medium Quality)*

Maleic Resin	35.00
Dehydrated Castor Stand Oil	25.00
Mineral Turpentine Oil (M.T.O)	35.00
Butanol	2.00
Pine Oil	3.00

Heat maleic resin and dehydrated castor stand oil to get the desired viscosity at 250-260°C and after cooling down to 140 to 150°C thin it down with solvent.

Medium for First Coat

Medium Oil Linseed Alkyd (100% solids)	30.000
Estergum	20.000
Mineral Turpentine Oil (M.T.O)	47.000
Butanol	3.000

Heat estergum to 160°C and add medium oil alkyd till both the ingredients are homogenous. Then thin it with solvents.

Medium for Finishing Coat

Rosinated Dehydrated Castor Oil Alkyd (100% solids)	40.000
Mineral Turpentine Oil	50.000
Butanol	5.000
Pine Oil	5.000

Medium for Finishing Coat

Long Oil Linseed Penta Alkyd (100% solids)	60.000
Mineral Turpentine Oil (M.T.O)	35.000
Butanol	3.000
Pine Oil	2.000

All these mediums form the basis of all plain finishes. Selection of the medium is made on cost and performance considerations. Other mediums required can be based upon rosin modified phenolics and linseed stand oil or D.C.O. stand oil. The particular illustrations are given below. The combinations can be changed depending upon drying time and flexibility *etc.*

Medium Oil Modified Phenolic Varnish

Linseed Stand Oil (60-90 poises)	30.000
Rosin modified Phenolics	30.000
Mineral Turpentine Oil (M.T.O)	38.000
Pine Oil	2.000

Heat linseed stand oil and phenolics to 250°C and cook at this temperature until the desired viscosity is attained. Cool to 150°C and thin it with solvents.

Modified Phenolic Varnish

Rosin Modified Phenolics	30.000
Linseed Stand Oil (60-90 poises)	10.000
D.C.O. Stand Oil (40-60 poises)	20.000
Mineral Turpentine Oil (M.T.O)	38.000
Butanol	2.000

Modified Phenolic Varnish

Rosin Modified Phenolics	40.000
D.C.O. Stand Oil (40-60 poises)	20.000
Mineral Turpentine Oil (M.T.O)	37.500
Butanol	2.500

Othern mediums can be formulated for specific requirements like chemical resistant coating for machinery used in chemical industry.

Primers

Red Oxide Primer Air Drying-cum-Stoving (Low Cost)

Aluminium Stearate	0.240
Indian Red Oxide	40.770
China Clay	9.500
Limed Rosin Stand Oil Varnish (60% solids)	38.870
Lead, Cobalt and Manganese Naphthenates	1.540
Mineral Turpentine Oil	9.080
Viscosity by Ford Cup No. B-4 at 30°C	60 ± 5 seconds
Weight per litre	1.45 kg
Pigmentation	50.27%
Surface Drying Time (SDT)	30 minutes
Hard Drying Time (HDT)	3 hours
Stoving Schedule	120°C/30 minutes

Synthetic Red Oxide Primer

Anti-settling Agent	0.250
Indian Red Oxide	41.320
China Clay	8.760
Rosinated D.C.O. Alkyd (60% solids)	30.950
Lead, Cobalt and Manganese Naphthenates	1.500
Pine Oil	1.220

Butanol	1.450
Mineral Turpentine Oil	14.450
Weight per litre	1.43 kg
Viscosity by Ford Cup No. B-4 at 30°C	60 ± 5 seconds
Pigmentation	50.08%
Surface Drying Time	30 minutes
Hard Drying Time	2 hours
Stoving Schedule	120°C/30 minutes

Red Oxide Zinc Chromate Primer (IS : 2074)

Antisettling Agent	0.250
Indian Red Oxide	18.780
Synthetic Red Oxide	18.780
Zinc Chromate	8.450
Long-Oil-Linseed Penta Alkyd (60% solids)	35.320
Lead, Cobalt and Manganese Naphthenates	1.420
Mineral Turpentine	14.450
Pine Oil	1.350
Butanol	1.200
Viscosity by Ford Cup No. B-4 at 30°C	60 ± 5 seconds
Weight per litre	1.415 kg
Stoving Schedule	120°C/30 minutes
Surface Drying Time	45 minutes
Hard Drying Time	2.5 to 3.0 hours
Pigmentation	46.01%

Red Oxide Primer (Medium Quality)

Anti-settling Agent	0.200
Indian Red Oxide	46.600
China Clay	4.350
Rosinated Linseed Alkyd (60% solids)	38.450
Lead, Cobalt and Manganese Naphthenates	1.350
Mineral Turpentine Oil (M.T.O)	6.550
Pine Oil	1.250
Weight per litre	1.46 Kg
Viscosity by Ford Cup No. B-4 at 30°C	75 ± 5 seconds
Pigmentation	50.95%
Surface Drying Time	20 minutes
Hard Drying Time	2 hours
Stoving Schedule	20°C/30 minutes

Surfacers

Low Cost Knifing Grey Filler

Titanium Dioxide (Anatase)	9.945
Slate Powder	19.350
Whiting (off-colour)	49.850
Malenized Rosin Stand Oil Varnish (60% solids)	15.380
Turpentine Oil	3.200
Mineral Turpentine Oil	2.200
Lead, Cobalt and Manganese Naphthenates	0.570
Surface Drying Time	20 minutes
Hard Drying Time	2 hours
Stoving Schedule	120°C/30 Min
Pigmentation	78.65%

Low Cost Spraying Grey Filler

Titanium Dioxide (Anatase)	8.830
Slate Powder	18.450
Whiting (off-colour)	18.450
Malenized Rosin Stand Oil Varnish (60% solids)	24.350
Rosinated D.C.O. Alkyd (60% solids)	20.450
Mineral Turpentine Oil	7.470
Pine Oil	1.200
Lead, Cobalt and Manganese Naphthenates	0.900
Weight per litre	1.21 kg
Viscosity by Ford Cup No. B-4 at 30°C	75 ± 5 seconds
Surface Drying Time	30 minutes
Hard Drying Time	3 hours
Pigmentation	45.63%
Non-volatiles	27%

Kniffing Paste Filler Grey (Top Quality)

Silicone Oil Solution (10% Solids)	0.263
Carbon Black	0.020
Whiting	29.730
Barytes	25.000
Zinc Oxide	2.336
Titanium Dioxide (Anatase)	10.430
China Clay	5.135
Coumarone resin (40% solids)	24.300
Triethylamine	1.245
Mineral Turpentine Oil	1.245
Pine Oil	0.300
Stoving Schedule	120°C/30 minutes
Surface Drying Time	20 minutes
Hard Drying Time	1 hours

Synthetic Spraying Filter Grey

Anti-settling Agent	0.630
Titanium Dioxide (Anatase)	6.750
China Clay	20.630
Barytes	20.630
Rosinated D.C.O. Alkyd (60%)	33.650
Rosinated Linseed Alkyd (60%)	6.430
Lead, Cobalt and Manganese Naphthenates	0.680
Mineral Turpentine Oil	9.400
Pine Oil	1.200
Weight per litre	1.121 kg
Viscosity at 30°C by Ford Cup No. B-4	90 ± 5 seconds
Surface Drying Time	20 minutes
Hard Drying Time	2.5 hours
Stoving Schedule	120°C/30 minutes
Pigmentation	48.01%
Non-volatiles	24.08%

Finishes

The most common shades used in furniture finishes are olive green and greys. General formulations of these shades are given below. Some adjustment in composition may be made for specific requirements.

Low Cost Air Drying-cum-Stoving Olive Green Enamel

Wetting and Anti-settling Agent	0.433
Natural Yellow Ochre	14.300
Carbon Black	0.225
Phthalocyanine Blue	0.140
Pigment Grade Red Oxide	0.430
Middle Yellow Chrome	1.600
Rosinated Dehydrated Castor Oil Alkyd (60% solids)	48.340
Limed Rosin Stand Oil Varnish (60% solids)	21.480

Mineral Turpentine Oil	10.052
Butanol	1.500
Lead, Cobalt and Manganese Naphthenates	1.500
Weight per litre	1.03 (± 3% kg)
Viscosity by Ford Cup No. B-4 at 30°C	75±5 seconds
Surface Drying Time	45 minutes
Hard Drying Time	4 hours
Stoving Schedule	120°C/30 minutes
Pigmentation	16.7 %
Non-volatiles	41.9 %

Olive Green Stoving Enamel

Titanium Dioxide	0.372
Natural Yellow Ochre	11.285
Lemon Chrome	9.350
Phthalocyanine Blue	0.300
Carbon Black	0.150
Medium Oil D.C.O. Alkyd (60% solids)	60.430
Urea Formaldehyde Resin (50% soilds)	6.350
Manganese Naphthenate (6% Mn)	0.250
Butanol	1.163
Mineral Turpentine Oil	4.200
Pine Oil	1.250
Toluene	3.750
Weight per litre	1.01 Kg
Viscosity by Ford Cup No. B-4 at 30°C	60±5 seconds
Stoving Schedule	120°C/30 minutes

Smoke Grey Air Drying-cum-Stoving Enamel

Wetting Agent	0.385
Titanium Dioxide (Anatase)	11.075
Phthalocyanine Blue	0.320
Carbon Black	0.068
Rosinated D.C.O. Alkyd (60% solids)	68.300
Pine Oil	1.125
Butanol	1.125
Mineral Turpentine Oil	14.902
Lead Naphthenate (18%)	1.230
Cobalt Naphthenate (6%)	0.670
Manganese Naphthenate (6%)	0.800
Viscosity by Ford Cup No.	
B-4 at 30°C	65±5 seconds
Weight per litre	1.0 (± 3% kg)
Pigmentation	11.463 %
Surface Drying Time	30 minutes
Hard Drying Time	3 hours
Stoving Schedule	120°C/30 minutes
Non-volatiles	40.98 %

Light Grey Air Drying-Cum-Stoving Enamel

Wetting Agent	0.402
Titanium Dioxide (Anatase)	8.934
Carbon Black	0.033
Phthalocyanine Blue	0.064
Yellow Ochre	0.450
Red Oxide (Pigment Grade)	0.040
Rosinated D.C.O. Alkyd (60% solids)	70.350
Pine Oil	1.550
Butanol	1.550
Mineral Turpentine Oil	14.357
Lead Naphthenate (18%)	1.030
Cobalt Naphthenate (6%)	0.510
Manganese Naphthenate (6%)	0.730
Viscosity by Ford Cup No.	
B-4 at 30°C	65±5 seconds
Pigmentation	9.59 %

Weight per litre	0.955 Kg
Surface Drying Time	30 minutes
Hard Drying Time	3 hours
Non-volatiles	42.1 %

Steel Grey Air Drying-cum-Stoving Enamel

Wetting and Anti-settling Agent	0.235
Titanium Dioxide (Anatase)	7.239
Yellow Ochre (Natural)	9.356
Pigment Grade Red Oxide	2.653
Carbon Black	0.195
Phthalocyanine Blue	0.008
Rosinated D.C.O. Alkyd (60% solids)	68.850
Mineral Turpentine Oil	7.320
Butanol	1.530
Dipentene	1.530
Lead, Manganese and Cobalt Naphthenates	1.084
Weight per litre	1.10 (± 3% kg)
Viscosity by Ford Cup No. B-4 at 30°C	75±5 seconds
Surface Drying Time	45 minutes
Hard Drying Time	3 hours
Stoving Schedule	120°C/30 minutes
Pigmentation	19.451 %

14

VARNISHES FORMULAE

Introduction

A varnish is defined as a clear unpigmented syrupy liquid having a viscosity of 2 to 3 poise when applied in the form a thin coating dries into a tough and glossy film either by exposure to air or elevated temperatures. Varnishes are prepared by dissolving a resin or the reaction products of a resin and a drying oil in a suitable solvent. Drying of a varnish may be due to evaporation, oxidation, or polymerization of a part of its constituents. Not being pigmented, varnishes are less resistant to light than paints, enamels, and pigmented lacquers. They produce, however, a transparent film which accentuates the texture of the surface coated. They are classified into two major categories — ***Oleoresinous varnishes*** and ***Spirit varnishes.***

Oleoresinous Varnishes

Introduction

Oleoresinous varnishes are combination of drying oils and resins which are thinned to application viscosity with volatile solvents. Driers are incorporated in these resins to catalyze the drying process which is controlled largely by the amount of oil present or the ratio of oil to resin. The ratio of oil to resin by weight, in paint industry, is known as oil length and can be varied considerably. The oil length largely controls the properties of the varnish. A short oil varnish possesses faster drying properties and forms a harder and more brittle film and a long oil varnish forms more weather resistant, pliable film. A hard resin is preferably used to shorten the drying time, increase the hardness of the film, improve gloss, improve water and chemical resistance, and increase durability in some cases. Oleoresinous varnishes, as already indicated above, consist of four ingredients-resins drying oils, driers and thinners (solvents).

Resins provide hardness and gloss to the film. In general with increasing proportion of resin, the hardness and gloss of the varnish film increases but durability decreases. Both natural and synthetic resins are used including copals, ester gum, limed rosin, pure and rosin modified phenolics, maleics and coumarones and many other synthetic resins. Rosin-modified phenolics are replacing other resins in their use because of their low cost. Drying oils provide elasticity, toughness and durability of the film. These properties improve with increasing oil content but their contribution differs from oil to oil. Drying oils used include linseed *(as varnish linseed oil, stand oil and enamel oil)* tung *(wood oil)* dehydrated castor oil, tobacco seed oil, soyabean oil etc. Driers are usually added in varnishes to catalyze the conversion of oil to the solid conditions. Strictly speaking, driers regulate the drying of film. Driers commonly used are naphthenates and octoates of lead, cobalt and manganese. The function of thinners is to adjust the consistency of the varnish for application and evaporate fairly rapidly at a uniform rate after application. Thinners commonly employed are white spirit, dipentene, naphtha and xylol distillates and other petroleum hydrocarbons.

The manufacturing process of oleoresinous varnishes varies widely depending upon the types of oil and resin used. In the case of natural resins which are insoluble in oil, the resins are depolymerized by heating - a process called *"running"*. The drying oil is also heated before adding. In the case of synthetic resins, the pre-heating is not required the oil and resin are heated together until a homogenous solution of correct viscosity is obtained. The mixture is cooled and thinned with solvents and filtered to remove any solid particles present.

Different types of varnishes can be made by varying the type and quantity of resins, drying oils, solvents, and driers. Their classification can be done from several points of view.

Furniture Varnishes

Furniture varnishes are low cost finishing materials with fast drying, casy rubbing, sanding, and polishing characteristics. In finishing of wooden furniture filler and sealer coats are applied before the application of finishing coat. All these operations involve lot of rubbing and polishing. To reduce the cost, the varnish should be such that it can be easily applied and the furniture quickly packed or wrapped. The furniture varnish should be quick drying, print resistant, hard and mar proof and of reasonable durability.

Furniture Varnish (Low Cost)

Rosin	50.000
Hydrated Lime	2.100
Zinc Oxide	1.500
Linseed Stand Oil (90-120 poise)	16.700
Mineral Spirit	28.900
Lead Naphthenate (18%)	0.400
Cobalt Naphthenate (6%)	0.400

Heat rosin to 260°C and cool to 240°C. Introduce a mixture of hydrated lime and zinc oxide slowly, maintaining the temperature at 240°C. Increase the temperature of rosin to 260°C and maintain till a clear drop of rosin. Lower the temperature to 200°C and add stand oil. Again raise the temperature to 260°C and maintain until a hard pill or drop is obtained on cooling. Cool the mix to 140°C and thin it with mineral spirit. Add drier.

Furniture Varnish (Better Quality)

Malenized Rosin	55.450
Linseed Stand Oil (90-120 poise)	14.500
Mineral Turpentine	29.500
Lead Naphthenate (18%)	0.300
Cobalt Naphthenate (6%)	0.250

Heat the rosin and stand oil to 260°C and maintain the

temperature to get a hard pill and clear drop on cooling. Cool it to 160°C and thin it with mineral turpentine and add driers.

Furniture Varnish (Low Cost Quality)

Maleic Resin	52.300
Linseed Stand Oil (90-120 poise)	8.700
Mineral Turpentine	21.000
Lead Naphthenate (18%)	0.400
Cobalt Naphthenate (6%)	0.300
Dehydrated Castor Oil (D.C.O) Stand Oil (45-60)	7.300

Heat resin and oil to 250°C till a clear, hard and firm pille is obtained. Cool it to 160-180°C and thin it down with mineral turpentine and add driers.

Water Resistant Furniture Varnish

Modified Phenolic Resin	40.000
Maleic Resin	10.000
Mineral Turpentine	30.000
Linseed Stand Oil	14.500
Lead Naphthenate (18% Pb.)	0.300
Cobalt Naphthenate (6% Co)	0.200
Pine oil	5.000

Heat resins and oil to 280°C and hold at this temperature to get firm drop. Cool it down to 180°C and thin it with mineral turpentine. Then add driers and finally pine oil. This varnish is slightly brownish in color but has good water and alkali resistance. It gives quite hard and easy rubbing finish.

Furniture Varnish

Modified Phenolic Resin	30.000
Penta Ester Gum	20.000
Linseed Stand Oil (90-120 poise)	9.000
D.C.O. Stand Oil (45-60 poise)	8.000
Mineral Spirits	28.400
Butanol	2.000
Pine Oil	2.000
Lead Naphthenate (18% Pb)	0.350
Cobalt Naphthenate (6% Co)	0.250

Heat resin and oils to 270°C and hold it at this temperature to get the desired voscosity and firm pill. Then cool it to 160-180°C and add solvents and finally the driers. This varnish is fast drying, gas proof and has good water resistance and solvent resistance.

Aluminium Paint Varnishes

Varnish for making aluminium paints should have low acid value and should not be highly bodied. The finish should dry principally by evaporation of solvent. Some applications for aluminium paint require lead-free composition, therefore, for such paints the varnish used should not contain any lead even in the form of a drier. Highly bodied oils increase the viscosity of the system and may hinder the orientation of leafing properties of aluminium, therefore, they are not used. In no case, butanol is used because it hampers the finishing property of aluminium paints.

Varnish for Aluminium Paint

Modified Phenolics	40.000
Dehydrated Castor Oil	10.000
Alkali Refined Linseed Oil	10.000
Mineral Turpentine	35.600
Dipentene	2.000
Pine Oil	2.000
Coabalt Naphthenate (6%)	0.400

Heat rosin and linseed oil to 270-280°C and hold at this temperature for about 30 minutes. Add dehydrated castor oil and maintain the temperature at 250°C for about an hour till a string of 16 to 18 inches length is obtained when it is pulled from cold drop. Cool it to 160°C and add thinners and driers. This varnish is suitable for aluminium paint for exterior use. It has good water resistance.

Varnish for Aluminium Paint for Interior Use

Pentabased Rosin Estergum	40.000
Linseed Stand Oil (30 Poise)	20.000
Mineral Turpentine Oil (M.T.O)	37.500
Pine Oil	2.000
Cobalt Naphthenate (6%)	0.500

Heat resin and Linseed oil to 240-260° to get a string of 10-12 inch long when drawn from a cold drop. Cool it to 160°C and thin with solvent and add drier and pine oil. This varnish is useful for interior use where durability is not very important.

Low Cost Varnish for Aluminium Paint for Interior Use

Penta based Rosin Ester gum	35.000
Linseed Stand Oil (30 Poise)	10.000
Dehydrated Castor Oil (15-20 poise)	15.000
Mineral Turpentine Oil	37.400
Dipentene	2.000
Cobalt Naphthenate (6%)	0.600

Heat resin and linseed oil at a temperature of 260-270°C to a clear drop and cool it to 220°C. Add dehydrated castor oil and heat to 250-260°C to get a string of 14 inches length when drawn from a cold drop. Cool it to 180°C and thin it with solvents and add drier. This varnish is slow drying but has better durability.

High Grade Varnish for Aluminium Paint

Courmarone Resin	30.000
Linseed Stand Oil (25-30 Poise)	30.000
Mineral Turpentine Oil	35.000
Pine Oil	4.300
Cobalt Naphthenate	7.000

Heat oil to about 250°C. Add resin and maintain this temperature till the resin is dissolved in the oil. Cool the batch to 180°C and thin it with mineral turpentine oil (M.T.O). Add drier and pine oil. This varnish gives excellent results both in interior and exterior use and at elevated temperatures because of very low acid value resin used.

Decorative Varnish for Tin

Decorative varnishes for tins are used as clear coatings generally known as silver stoving varnish. Stoving is done to get better hardness and quick drying. Second use of varnish in this case is for making pigmented coatings which are used for printing sheet metal which is cut and shaped into containers and bottle caps and collapsible tubes. Varnish for tins are made for two purposes— one for general packing tins and the other for food packaging tins. The varnish for good cans should be tasteless, odourless, and non-toxic. It should be reisitant to food acids and any solvent present in the food. In their composition lead should not be there even in the form of a drier.

In general varnishes for tin containers should be non-yellow type to maintain desired finish and shade. Manganese drier should be used only in pigmented varnishes of dark colour. To improve mar resistance silicone additives are used. Use of wax reduces the gloss of the finish. Modified phenolics, maleic resins, pentaestergums alongwith dehydrated castor oil, Kardi seed oil, or soyabean oil give best results.

Metal Decorating Varnish

Modified Phenolic Resin	25.000
Dehydrated Castor Oil	35.000
Mineral Turpentine Oil	38.000
Pine Oil	1.400
Cobalt Naphthenate/Octoate	0.300
Zinc Naphthenate/Octoate	0.300

Heat resin and dehydrated castor oil to 260°C-270°C until a viscosity of 60 poise is observed. Cool to 180°C and add mineral turpentine slowly and then add driers and pine oil. The stoving schedule of this varnish is 30 minutes at 120°C.

Metal Decorating Varnish

Modified Phenolic Resin	15.000
Penta Maleic Resin	15.000
Dehydrated Castor oil	30.000
Mineral Turpentine	37.400
Pine oil	1.000
Butanol	1.000
Cobalt Naphthenate	0.300
Zinc Naphthenate	0.300

Heat resins and oils to 260°C and maintain this temperature to get a viscosity of 900 seconds in Ford Cup No. 4 at 30°C. Cool to 160-180°C and thin it down with solvents. Add driers and pine oil.

Decorating Varnish (Non-Yellowing Metal)

Maleic Resins	30.000
Kardi Seed Oil	15.000
Dehydrated Castor Oil	15.000
Mineral Turpentine Oil	36.400
Pine Oil	2.000
Butanol	1.000
Zinc Octoate	0.300
Cobalt Octoate	0.300

Heat resin and Kardi seed oil to 270°C and maintain this temperature for two hours, then add dehydrated castor oil and heat at 250-260°C to get clear drop and desired viscosity. Cool to 160-180°C and add solvents, driers and pine oil.

Varnishes for Metal and Wood Primers

In metal primers medium oil length varnishes are used in both air-drying and stoving finishes. In wood primers long oil varnishes are used because of the porous surface of wood, there is a lot of absorption of solvent. In such coatings, maximum amount of solvent is used. Varnishes for wood are highly bodied. For metals, medium oil varnishes made from phenolics and ester gums, linseed oil, dehydrated castor oil, and linseed oil and dehydrated castor oil combinations are used. For wood primer varnishes linseed oil alone or along with modified phenolics, maleics, and ester gums are used.

Varnish for Metal Primers (Air Drying-cum-Stoving)

Modified Phenolics	33.000
Dehydrated Castor Oil	12.000
Linseed Stand Oil (25-30 poise)	15.000
Mineral Turpentine Oil	38.400
Butanol	1.000
Lead Naphthenate (18%)	0.300
Cobalt Naphthenate (6%)	0.150
Manganese Naphthenate (6%)	0.150

Heat resin and linseed oil at 260°-270°C for about 45 minutes. Add dehydrated castor oil and maintain the temperature at 240-250°C till desired viscosity is maintained. Cool to 180°C and add solvents and driers.

Low Cost Varnish for Metal Primers

Penta Estergum	38.000
Dehydrated Castor Oil	10.000
Linseed Oil (25-25 Poise)	15.000
Mineral Turpentine Oil	35.100
Pine Oil	1.000
Lead Naphthenate (18%)	0.400
Cobalt Naphthenate (6%)	0.250
Manganese Naphthenate (6%)	0.250

Medium Quality Varnish for Metal Primers

Modified Phenolics	20.000
Penta Estergum	15.000
Linseed Oil	15.000
Dehydrated Castor Oil	10.300
Mineral Turpentine Oil	37.300
Butanol	1.000
Diepentene	1.000
Lead Naphthenate (18%)	0.300
Cobalt Naphthenate (6%)	0.200
Manganese Naphthenate (6%)	0.200

Varnish for Wood Primers

Modified Phenolics	20.000
Linseed Stand Oil (60-90 Poise)	40.000
Mineral Turpentine Oil	36.800
Pine Oil	1.000
Butanol	1.000
Lead Naphthenate (18%)	0.800
Cobalt Naphthenate (6%)	0.400

Heat resin and linseed oil to 260 to 270°C to get the desired viscosity of the order of 75 to 90 seconds by Ford Cup NO. 4 at 30°C when thinned to 40% solids with mineral turpentine oil. Cool to 160 to 180°C and add solvents and driers.

Water Resistant Varnishes

Phenolic resins in combination with linseed and dehydrated castor oil give maximum water resistance. 100% oil soluble phenolics can be used as the water resistance of oil is not as good as that of phenolics. These varnishes are generally short oil length type.

D.C.O. — Phenolic Water Resistant Varnish

100% Oil Soluble Phenolics	40.000
Dehydrated Castor Oil	20.000
Mineral Turpentine Oil	37.400
Butanol	1.000
Pine Oil	1.000
Lead Naphthenate	0.300
Cobalt Naphthenate	0.150
Manganese Naphthenate	0.150

Heat resin and dehydrated castor oil to 270°C to 280°C for about 1 hour to get the viscosity desired. Cool to 180-200°C and add solvents and driers. This varnish has excellent water-resistance and can be used in air drying as well as stoving finishes.

The following varnish has better air-drying properties than the above varnish but it does not give as hard films as the above varnish.

Water Resistant Varnish

100% Oil Soluble Phenolics	35.000
Dehydrated Castor Oil	10.000
Linseed Stand Oil (25-40 poise)	15.000
Mineral Turpentine	37.400
Pine Oil	1.000
Butanol	1.000
Lead Naphthenate(18% pb)	0.300
Cobalt Naphthenate (6% Co)	0.150
Manganese Naphthenate (6% Mn)	0.150

Heat oil resin for about 90 to 120 minutes at 260-270°C to get the desired viscosity. Cool to 180°C and thin with solvents and add driers.

Water Resistant Varnishes

100% Phenolic Resin	40.000
Linseed Oil	20.000
Mineral Turpentine Oil	37.000
Butanol	1.000
Pine Oil	1.000
Lead Naphthenate	1.000
Cobalt Naphthenate	0.300
Manganese Naphthenate	0.200

Alkali Resistant Varnishes

In alkali resistant varnishes again short oil length mediums are used because resins have better alkali resistance than oils. Mediums based on dehydrated castor oil and tung oil have better resistance to alkalies than mediums based on linseed oil. Resins like estergum and maleics are attacked by alkalies and phenolics. Coumarone indene resins have better alkali resistance.

Phenolic —D.C.O.— Alkali Resistant Varnish

Phenolic Resin (100%)	30.000
Dehydrated Castor Oil (D.C.O)	20.000
Mineral Spirits	45.300
Butanol	2.000
Pine Oil	2.000
Lead Naphthenate (18% Pb)	0.300
Cobalt Naphthenate (6% Co)	0.200
Manganese Naphthenate (6% Mn)	0.200

Heat oil and resin to 250°C for about 3 hours to get desired viscosity. Cool to 180°C, thin with solvents and add driers and pine oil.

Linseed—D.C.O.— Phenolic Alkali Resistant Varnish

Phenolic Resin (100%)	35.000
Dehydrated Castor Oil (D.C.O)	10.000
Linseed Stand Oil (30-40 poise)	10.000
Mineral Turpentine	35.000
Toluene	8.100
Butanol	1.000
Lead Naphthenate	0.400
Cobalt Naphthenate	0.250
Manganese Naphthenate	0.250

Heat linseed, dehyrated castor oil, and phenolic resins to 260-270°C and maintain until desired viscosity is reached. Cool to 160-180°C. Thin it with mineral turpentine oil and butanol and add driers. Further cool to 90°C and add toluene.

Linseed —— D.C.O.—Coumarone Resin Varnish

Coumarone Resin	30.000
Linseed Stand Oil (25-40 poise)	15.000
D.C.O. Stand Oil (15-30 poise)	15.000
Mineral Turpentine Oil	37.000
Pine Oil	1.000
Butanol	1.000
Lead Naphthenate (18%)	0.500
Cobalt Naphthenate(6%)	0.250
Manganese Naphthenate (6%)	0.250

Heat resin and oils to 250-260°C in 30 minutes and cool to 230-240°C and maintain this temperature till desired viscosity is attained. Cool to 160-180°C, thin with solvents and add driers.

D.C.O. — Linseed—— Coumarone— Phenolic Resin Varnish

Coumarone Resin	15.000
Phenolic Resin (100%)	5.000
Dehydrated Castor Oil	20.000
Linseed Stand Oil (25-40 poise)	10.000
Mineral Turpentine Oil	38.800
Toluene	8.000
Butanol	2.000
Lead Naphthenate (18% Pb)	0.600
Manganese Naphthenate (6% Mn)	0.300
Cobalt Naphthenate (6% Co)	0.300

Heat Phenolic resin and oil to 230-240°C for about 1 hour. Add coumarone resin and maintain the temperature at 250-260°C till desired viscosity is attained. Cool to 160 to 180°C and thin with solvents and add driers.

Spar Varnishes

Spar varnishes are applied on surfaces which are required to have very good water resistance. The best medium for these varnishes is a combination of pure phenolic resin with medium oil length varnish. All formulations discussed under alkali resistant varnishes except those in which coumarone resins are used are also suitable for this purpose. Modified phenolics with dehydrated castor or linseed oil give satisfactory results.

Pure Phenolic — D.C.O.—— Linseed Spar Varnish

Phenolic Resin (100%)	20.000
Dehydrated Castor Stand Oil (15-20 poise)	20.000
Linseed Stand Oil (45-60 Poise)	10.000
Mineral Turpentine Oil (M.T.O)	47.300
Pine Oil	2.000
Lead Naphthenate (18%)	0.300
Cobalt Naphthenate (6%)	0.200
Manganese Naphthenate (6%)	0.200

Heat resin and linseed stand oil to 260°C and cook for 30 minutes. Add dehydrated castor stand oil and maintain the temperature at 240-250°C, until desired viscosity is attained. Cool to 160°C, thin it with solvents and add driers.

Modified and Pure Phenolic——D.C.O. Varnish

Modified Phenolics	15.000
Pure Phenolics	15.000
D.C.O. Stand Oil	30.000
Mineral Spirits	37.200
Butanol	2.000
Lead Naphthenate (18% Pb)	0.400
Cobalt Naphthenate (8%)	0.200
Manganese Naphthenate (6%)	0.200

Heat oil and modified phenolics to 260°C for about 2 hours. Add pure phenolics and maintain the temperature at 240-250°C till desired viscosity is reached. Cool it to 160°C, thin it with solvents and add driers.

Floor Varnishes

The floor varnish should be quick drying and should give hard, tough and elastic film having good resistance to water and alkalies. The short-oil length varnishes have good water, alkali and abrasion resistance but their elasticity is poor. Long oil-length varnishes have good elasticity but they are not quick drying and lack in some other desirable properties also. Therefore, a compromise is made and medium-short oil length combinations are used. Pure phenolics with linseed and dehydrated castor oil are used.

Pure Phenolic Resin	27.500
D.C.O. Stand Oil (25-30 poise)	12.500
Linseed Stand Oil (45-60 poise)	10.000
Mineral Spirits	41.400
Butanol	3.000
Pine Oil	5.000
Lead Naphthenate (18% Pb)	0.400
Cobalt Naphthenate (6% Co)	0.200

Heat phenolic resin and linseed stand oil to 260°C for one hour. Cool to 200°C and add D.C.O. stand oil. Raise the temperature to 240-250°C and maintain it to get a viscosity of 120 seconds by Ford Cup No. 4 at 30°C when it is thinned to 50% solids in mineral spirits. Cool to 160-180°C, thin it with solvents, and add driers.

Insulating Varnishes

Insulating varnishes, as the name implies, are used in electrical industry for insulation purposes. These varnishes provide protection from current leakage as well as provide safety from atmospheric and enviromental detriments to electrical equipments and accessories. These varnishes are required to have high dielectric strength, poor surface conductivity and high insulation resistance. They should have good resistance to water, oils,. solvents, acids, alkalies, conductor material. The film of the varnish should dry uniformly. It should be unaffected at elevated temperatures. Their thermal expansion and contraction should be the same as conductors on which they are used. The polymeric base of the varnish should have maximum stability to heat. It should have very low thermoplastic characteristics. The coatings should not be flammable.

Insulating varnishes are classified into different categories according to their upper temperature limit-in use as follows :

Class of Insulation	Maximum Temperature Limit
Y	90°C
A	105°C
E	120°C
B	130°C
F	155°C
H	180°C
C	Above 180°C

Insulating varnishes should have very good flow properties, so that they can penetrate deep into the interior of windings and form uniform coating. They should have very goos adhesion and flexibility so that during winding they do not chip off or crack. They should be hard and abrasion resistant. Insulating varnishes can be based on oleoresinous base or spirit base. According to their application they can be classified into four categories —

1. *Impregnating varnishes*
2. *Core plate varnishes*
3. *Wire enamels and*
4. *Finishing varnishes*

Impregnating varnishes are used for insulation of coils. They penetrate or impregnate into the interior of the coils and fill voids. On drying they bind the loops of the coils. These varnishes can be air-drying type or stoving type. Air drying varnishes, although satisfactory, take a long time to dry since in the interior of coils there is considerably less exposure to air. The stoving type insulating varnishes give better performance as on stoving they dry into tough rubbing solid films.

Core plate varnishes are applied on core plates of transformers for insulation against flow of eddy currents. They are applied by either dipping or roller coating.

Wire enamels are used for coating of winding wires. As the wires are wound after coating, these enamels should have maximum flexibility, mar resistance, hardness and abrasion resistance.

Finishing varnishes are decorative finishes used on electrical equipment not only for insulation but also for decor.

Insulating Varnish (Impregnating and Core Plate)

Antifoaming Agents	0.020
Cashew Nut Shell Liquid	34.321
Formalin	0.446
Gilsonite	3.392
Dehydrated Castor Oil	13.372
Mineral Turpentine Oil	47.760
Hexamine	0.669

Heat cashew nut shell liquid, hexamine dissolved in formalin, and antifoaming agent to 80-90°C. Maintain this temperature till the smell of ammonia in the vapours die out. Then slowly raise the temperature to 200°C and maintain for 1 hour then increase the temperature to 260°C and cook it at this temperature to get non-sticky drop on cooling. Then bring down the temperature to 200°C and add dehydrated castor oil and raise the temperature to 250-260°C and cook to get again a non-stickydrop after cooling. Cool to 180°C and thin it down with mineral turpentine. Add lead, cobalt and iron naphthenates to get 0.4% lead, 0.05% cobalt and 0.5% iron on CNSL and DCO. To improve gloss and flow pine oil to extent of 5% of the weight of total varnish may be added. This is an air-drying-cum-stoving varnish which gives better results if stoved.

Air Drying Insulating Varnish

Antifoaming Agent	0.020
Cashew Nut Shell Liquid	24.321
Maleic Resin	10.000
Bisphenol	0.670
Hexamine	0.669
Formalin	0.446
Dehydrated Castor Oil	14.392
Mineral Turpentine Oil	43.302
Pine Oil	4.500
Lead naphthenate (18%)	0.600
Cobalt Naphthenate (6%)	0.400
Iron Naphthenate	0.600

This varnish has better water and oil resistance.

Clear Finish Insulating Varnish

Long Oil Linseed Penta Alkyd	30.500
Rosin Modified Phenolic	9.500
Mineral Turpentine Oil	2.500
Pine Oil	54.500
Butanol	1.500
Lead naphthenate (18%)	0.600
Cobalt Naphthenate (6%)	0.300
Zinc Naphthenate (6%)	0.600

Heat phenolic resin to 200-230°C and add long oil linseed alkyd. Continue to heat until a homogenous mass is obtained. Cool to 160-180°C, thin it with solvents and add driers.

Insulating Varnish (Better Quality)

Silicone resin	0.010
Oil soluble Pure Phenolics	15.000
D.C.O. Stand Oil (30-45 poise)	30.000
Mineral Turpentine Oil	50.040
Butanol	3.500
Lead Naphthenate (18%)	0.600
Cobalt Naphthenate (6%)	0.350
Zinc Naphthenate (6%)	0.500

Heat phenolic resin and DCO stand oil to 260°C to get the desired viscosity. Cool it, thin it with solvents, and add driers and silicone resin solution.

Spirit Varnishes

Introduction

Spirit varnishes consist of simple solutions of resins in solvents. In these varnishes plasticizers may also be present. These varnishes form dry films entirely by evaporation. The preparation of these varnishes does not involve any complicated cooking processes. The treatment of these varnishes during their production depends upon the chemical properties of the resins, the amount and form of the insoluble matter and the viscosity of the final product.

The most important resins used in spirit varnishes include shellac, spirit soluble malenised rosin, spirit soluble phenolics, polyvinyl acetate etc. The choice of resin depends upon the quality of varnish required. Shellac gives films of poor water resistance brittle in nature with poor flexibility. Spirit soluble maleic resins give films of good water resistance but they also lack flexibility although they have definitely better properties than shellac. Spirit soluble phenolics, modified or pure give best results. Polyvinyl acetate gives water white films but they have poor water resistance and flexibility. The most common solvents are industrial methylated spirit and methyl alcohol since these solvents have very fast evaporating rates, they are often mixed with slow evaporating solvents like butanol and isopropyl alcohol.

As most of the spirit soluble resins produce brittle films, plasticizers are incoroporated to impart flexibility to the film. Generally dibutyl phthalate, dimethyl phthalate, tricresyl phosphate and methyl cyclohexanol are used. Their percentage is generally 5 to 10% by weight of the resin. Certain additives are used to improve the properties of spirit varnishes. Ethyl methyl cellulose is used to improve the water resistance of films. As most spirit soluble resins have high acid values, they tend to react with the metallic containers in which they are packed, stored or handled. Therefore, materials like triethanolamine and ethyl aniline phosphate are added in small quantities to check this tendency.

A steam-jacketed mixer is employed for the manufacture of spirit varnishes. The mixer is fitted with a stirrer. The temperature of the contents is allowed to rise by only 20-30°C above room temperature. Higher temperatures are not advisable as the alcohols have relatively low boiling points. Low pressure steam, therefore, serves as a good heating medium. The most economical procedure toadopt for dirt treatment is to allow the dust to settle when the first batch of varnish has been made. The subsequent filtration or centrifugation will effectively remove the dirt from the varnish.

Material of Construction

Shellac is much more susceptible to discolouration than manila copal. and for this reason much greater care must be taken in choosing materials for plant construction. No part of the equipment should be of mild steel construction. The cheapest and most satisfactory mixer is of wooden construction. *Oxidized rosin* is a highly acidic resin and it has tendency to attack metals under certain conditions. Its natural colour is dark reddish brown. Mild steel equipment is quite satisfactory. Oxidized rosin is not thermosetting, and the extent to which the mixer can be heated is limited only by the boiling point of the solvent used. *Phenolic resins* fall into two classes, those involving pure unmodified resins and those involving the highly rosin modified types. The former are sensitive to both heat and darkening in contact with iron. The latter are affected by the conditions to much lesser extent. Both are similar in that they do not need any special cleaning plant. Urea formaldehyde resins should not be made to go into solution by the action of heat. No provision need be made for dirt removal or special cleansing.

Shellac Varnishes

Interior Decorative Varnish

Shellac	40.500
Ethyl Cellulose	1.500
Dibutyl Phthalate	2.250
Industrial Spirit	56.750

This above varnish dries quickly and has sufficient water resistance and hardness.

Shellac Varnish with Improved Water Resistance

Shellac	30.000
Ethyl Cellulose	1.250
Spirit Soluble Phenolics	10.000
Dibutyl Phthalate	2.500
Industrial Methylated Spirit	56.250

French Polishes

Low Cost Shellac French Polish

Shellac	35.000
Dibutyl Phthalate	2.500
Industrial Methylated Spirit	62.500

French Polish with Improved Water Resistance

Shellac	20.000
Spirit Soluble Phenolics	15.000
Dibutyl Phthalate	3.000
Industrial Methylated Spirit	57.000
Butanol	5.000

Colourless or White Water Resistant and Durable Polish

Bleached and Dewaxed Shellac	25.000
Dibutyl Phthalate	2.100
Ethyl Cellulose	0.500
Spirit Soluble Phenolics	5.000
Industrial Methylated Spirit	65.000
Butanol	2.400

Insulating Varnish

Electric Insulating Varnish

Xylenol	45.00
Para-formaldehyde	10.75
Chinawood Oil	47.75
Solvent Naphtha	8.0
White Spirit	16.0
Triethanolamine	1.50

Flexible Insulating Varnish

Phthalic Anhydride	213.00
Glycerol	129.00
Succinic Acid	456.00
Ethylene Glycol	242.00
Rosin	200.00
Chinawood Oil	80.00

Flexible Insulating Varnish

Phthalic Anhydride	235.00
Glycerol	118.00
Succinic Acid	235.00
Ethylene Glycol	230.00
Rosin	200.00
Chinawood Oil	80.00

Industrial Varnish (Fast Air Drying)

Spirit Soluble Phenolics	20.000
Spirit Soluble Maleics	10.000
Industrial Methylated Spirit	45.000
Butanol	3.000
Isopropyl Alcohol	22.000

The varnish is fast air drying type with maximum water and oil resistance but has poor flexibility. The flexibility of this varnish can be improved by using 0.5 to 2% by weight of dibutyl phthalate depending upon the degree of flexibility required. THe varnish is prepared by cold cutting the resins with solvents.

Insulating Varnish based on Shellac

Silicone Resin	0.010
Dewaxed Shellac	30.000
Spirit Soluble Phenolics	10.000
Industrial Mehtylated Spirit	46.000
Butanol	2.000
Isopropyl Alcohol	12.400

15

IMPORTANT FORMULATIONS OF READY-MIXED & STIFF PAINTS

Ready Mixed Paints

1. White Ready-Mixed Paint

	Parts
Zinc oxide	35
White lead	8.8
Lithopone	.7.0
Stand oil	19.0
White spirit	22.0
Naphthenate drier	0.2
Raw oil	0.5

2. Ready-Mixed Paint Finishing Oil Gloss For Exterior purposes (Colour white)

	Pounds
White Lead	275
Zinc oxide	75
Raw linseed	90
Stand oil	60
Mineral Turpentine	25

3. Azure Blue Ready-Mixed Paint

	Parts
Talc	3.8
Barytes	66
Raw oil	7
Drier paste	3

Mix the above ingredients and add :

Boiled oil	2.2
White spirit	0.2
Liquid toner	17.0

4. Oxford Blue

	Parts
Ultramarine blue	3.1
Prussian blue	1.3
Barytes	47.0
Talc	8.0
Raw oil	8.0

Mix the above ingredients and then add :

Boiled oil	23.0
Stand oil	7.0
White spirit	3.0
Naphthenate driers	0.6

5. **Ready-mixed Paint Finishing oil Gloss For exterior purposes (Red oxides and chocolate colours)**

	Pounds
Red oxide	260
Double-boiled linseed oil	140
Stand oil	50
Mineral turpentine and driers	25

6. **Ready-Mixed Paint, Brushing, Finishing, Semi-Gloss**

For general purposes

Manufactured or natural Red oxides of iron	57%
Oil of turpentine	5%
Linseed oil	35%
Liquid driers and tinters	3%

7. **Ready-mixed Paint, Brushing, Finishing, Semi-Gloss (Brown)**

	Pounds
Manufactured, natural or mixture of both of red oxides of iron	24
Whiting, barytes,blanc fixe etc.	36
Turpentine, white spirit or mixture of both liquid drier	5

8. Ready-mixed Paint, Brushing, Finishing, Oil-Gloss For general purposes (Golden-brown)

	Pounds
Manufactured or natural or mixture of both of red oxides of iron	12
Lead chrome	8
Argillaceous matter	5
Whiting	5
Barytes, blanc fixe, other extenders and stainless	30
Turpentine or white spirit	5
Linseed oil, stand oil, or mixture of both plus dehydrated castor oil	30
Linseed driers	5

9. Brown Ready-Mixed Paint

	Parts
White lead	40.0
Yellow ochre	23.0
Gold chrome	2.0
Raw oil	15.0
Double-boiled oil	16.0
Mineral turpentine	4.0

10. Yellow Ready-Mixed Paint

Lithopone	2.5
Gold chrome	2.5
Chalk	7.0
Barytes	63.0
Double-boiled oil	20.0
White spirit	2.5
Naphthenate drier	0.5

11. Ready-Mixed, Finishing Oil Gloss For general purpose (Green)

	Pounds
Zinc oxide	30
Barytes	150
Boiled linseed oil	135
Stand oil	45
Mineral turpentine and driers	21
Green colouring matter	90

12. Dark-green Ready-Mixed Paint

	Parts
Lithopone	15.0
Prussian blue	1.0
Lemon chrome	4.0
China clay	18.0
Barytes	31.0
Varnish	22.0
White spirit	8.0
Driers	1.0

13. Ready-Mixed, Finishing Oil Gloss For general purpose (Grey and allied colours)

	Pounds
White lead	98
Zinc oxide	98
Barytes	58
Double-boiled linseed oil	135
Stand oil	45
Mineral turpentine and driers	21
Tints	40

14. Ready-Mixed, Finishing Oil Gloss For interior purpose (Grey and allied colours)

	Pounds
Zinc oxide	150
Barytes	110
Tints	30
Double-boiled linseed oil	125
Stand oil	40
Mineral turpentine and driers	20

15. Post-Office Red

		Parts
(a)	Fast scarlet-red	3
	China clay	5
	Barytes	52
	Raw oil	8
Mix and then add boiled oil		22
	Mineral turpentine	2
	Manganese drier	0.5
	Stand oil	6
	White spirit	2
(b)	Red pigment	0.5
	Chalk	7.5
	Barytes	67.0
	Double-boiled oil	22.0
	White spirit	3.0
	Driers	1.0

16. Ready-Mixed Paint, Spraying, Finishing
For railway under Frames (Block)

	Pounds
Carbon black	6
Argillaceous matter	8
Barytes and whiting	38
Linseed oil	23
Stand oil	8
Mixing varnish	6
Liquid driers	5
Turpentine or white spirit	10

17. Ready-Mixed Paint Undercoating for Interior Purposes

	Pounds
Zinc oxide	162
Barytes	120
Colouring substances	8
Boiled linseed oil	114
Stand oil	45
Mineral turpentine and driers	25

18. Ready-Mixed Paints, Brushing, Finishing, Semi-Gloss
For General Purposes (Black)

	Pounds
Carbon black	10
Argillaceous matter	8
Whiting	10
Barytes	22
Oil of turpentine	5
Linseed oil	43
Liquid driers	2

19. Ready-Mixed Paint Undercoating for Exterior Purposes

	Pounds
White lead	220
Barytes	74
Colouring substance	9
Double-boiled linseed oil	117
Stand oil	45
Mineral turpentine and driers	25

Stiff Paints

1. White Stiff Paint

	Parts by weight
Lithopone	10
Barytes	35
Talcum	7
China clay	18
Whiting	19
Medium refined oil	11

2. Zinc-Stiff Paint

	Parts by weight
Zinc oxide	87.5
Refined oil	12.5
Fatty acid	0.5

3. White Stiff Paint for Interior Purposes

	Pounds
Zinc oxide	336
Barytes	112
Raw linseed oil	65

4. Green-Stiff Paint

	Parts
White lead	25.0
Dark chrome green	5.0
Light chrome green	5.0
Barytes	50.0
Talc	4.0
Raw oil	11.0

16

INSULATING VARNISHES AND WIRE ENAMELS

Introduction

A good insulating varnish is of prime importance in the construction of electrical equipment, the life and performance of which depends to a great extent on the efficiency of the total insulation. Due to the hygroscopic nature of many of the materials used for general insulation. It is necessary by varnish impregnation to render them proof against moisture and in certain cases, from the action of oils, acids and alkalies. Insulating varnish is also necessary to bond the conductors especially in rotating machines, and in addition heat dissipation from the windings is improved by replacement of air by varnish solids between the separate conductors.

It is 80 years since the first oleoresinous insulating varnish was first developed by *James Todd* in America and such varnishes are still in limited use today, although they have largely been susperseded by the new thermal setting types. The oil-modified synthetic resin varnishes were first introduced in 1932 and are in use until today. Black varnishes are becoming less popular day by day. The development of new resins such as epoxy, silicon *etc.,* has provided the varnish manufacturer with great incentive to improvement, and although it takes a long time to evaluate fully and safely, new insulating varnishes, synthetic resin chemistry is advancing so rapidly that oil modified synthetic varnishes are expected to be used for a long time in future.

The function of insulating varnish is to maintain efficient protection against electrical stresses. Since insulating varnishes are used as film forming material on various substrates in addition to good electrical properties, they should possess certain mechanical, thermal and physio-chemical properties. The essential properties of insulating varnishes are as follows :-

A. Electrical Properties

(1) Dielectric strength is defined as the voltage gradient at which electrical failure occurs. It is stated as the voltage required to puncture the insulation, divided by the film thickness of the sample. Hence it is expressed as volts per mm. For impregnating as well as finishing varnishes dielectric strength must be of a higher order.

(2) Dielectric constant is a measure of the relative capacity of a material to store static electrical energy relative to vacuum 1 and air 1,006. Most organic materials have good dielectric properties and even under high humid conditions continue to have good dielectric properties.

(3) Insulation resistance is measured at 500 volts between two pairs of electrodes, each pair being connected in parallel while the specimen is in a controlled atmosphere. The reading is taken after 1 minute electrification and shall be not less than 1000 megohms.

(4) *Surface conductivity* — Generally, even good insulators break down on the surface due to moisture deposition *etc.* While the body of the insulation may be good, the breakdown may occur on the surface.

(5) Arc Resistance is the ability of a material to withstand the discharge across its surface of a specified intermittent and then continuous arc of high voltage and low current.

(6) *Ionisation loss or corona affect — CORONA*— When the electrostatic flux density in the air exceeds a certain value, a pale violet light appears near the adjacent metal surface. In the regions where corona appears, the air is electrically broken down and ionised so that it becomes a conductor of electricity. This discharge is called electrostatic corona. When the voltage is increased still furhter, a

discharge takes place until the whole thickness of the dielectric is broken down.

(7) *Voltage endurance* — Many insulators behave extremely well at low voltage but at higher voltage, they wil break down.

(8) *Power factor and dielectric loss* — As applied in insulation technology, power factor has a different meaning from that used in electrical engineering. It is the ratio of that part of the input of energy in water, which is lost as heat to the total input. At higher voltage this loss tends to increase. Low power factor is essential. It is effected by temperature, humidity and frequency.

B. Mechanical Properties

(1) All insulating varnishes should be capable of good penetration and must give uniform and even coating.

(2) Impregnating varnishes must be able to bind the coils into co-herent mass and not permit the coils to hang loose.

(3) Abrasion Resistance of all insulating and finishing varnishes must be good.

(4) Flexibility, toughness and good aging properties are essential for good insulating varnish.

(5) Good mechanical strength is essential since the electrical machines such as motors are subjected to high centrifugal forces.

(6) All insulating varnishes should have good moisture resistance and ability to seal the fibrous caoillaries of the coverings on the conductors.

(7) *Hardness and toughness* — Insulating varnishes must be sufficiently hard and must have high toughness.

(8) Insulating varnishes must stand heavy impact.

(9) Resistance to vibration and breakdown under conditions of vibration and certain stresses and frequencies is necessary.

C. Chemical Properties

(1) *Water Resistance*— avoidance of polar groups in insulating materials such as COOH — OH— NH — NH_2— RSO_3— CO, SH_2 — $NHCH_2$—NCS—COR—COOR—NO_2 will ensure water resistance.

(2) Resistance to acids and alkalies or other chemicals. In hydro carbons —C—OC S— C— C *etc.* linkages are generally good resistance excepting for the action of oxidising acids.

(3) Resistance to deterioration by impurities and contaminants.

(4) Resistance to corrosive vapours and solvents and oils.

(5) Through drying and cure in depth.

(6) By itself non-corrosive to copper and other conductors.

D. Thermal Properties

(1) *Thermoplasticity* or softening under heat — Good dielectrics *(insulators)* lose some or all of their insulating properties when they become fluid, just as metals which are very good conductors under normal conditions are relatively poorer conductors in their molten condition.

(2) *Thermal expansion and contraction*—Very high thermal expansion or contraction will result in eventual breakdown of the insulation.

(3) *Aging under heat*— All organic materials tend to degrade under high temperatures.

(4) Good thermal emissivity is desirable.

(5) Thermal conductivity and electrical conductivity so often go hand in hand. Good thermal conductivity commensurate with good electrical insulation properties is very much sought after.

Types of Insulating Varnishes

Insulating varnishes may be divided into following groups —

(a) Baking-type insulating varnishes.
(b) Air-drying insulating varnishes.
(c) Other types of insulating varnishes.

Baking Type Insulating Varnishes

1. Oleoresinous Varnishes

Oleoresinous varnishes are one of the earliest types of insulating varnishes used in the electrical industry. They are manufactured from natural resins with various types of vegetable oils and depend for cure largely on oxidation after the evaluation of the solvent constituent of the varnish under the influence of heat, a fair *'gel'* in mass is obtained. The films, however, of this type of varnish have excellent electrical strength and moisture resistance. Oleoresinous varnishes are used on static electrical equipment where bonding strength is not of prime importance. Even today, a considerable amount of this type of varnish is used by transformer manufacture and the varnishes of this type have to be taken great care of to keep the acidity of the varnish to a very low limit, because varnish of high acidity can contribute to the phenomenon of *"greeving"* in conjuction with cotton covered copper conductors.

Natural resins, with asphalt, cooked with drying oils, have been extensively used to produce black baking varnishes, not only for applications by impregnation alone but also for producing black varnished cloth. Both yellow and black oil varnished cloths are widely used as insulation in the electrical industry, although alkyds, silicones and other synthetic types are being developed for coating purposes where high temperature resistance and insulation are required.

2. Oil-Modified Synthetic Resin Varnishes

The advent of synthetic resin capable of being oil-modified

and cure in depth under the influence of heat, proved invaluable to the electrical industry. Oil-modified synthetic resin varnishes do not rely on oxidation for this curing but set by polymerisation after evolution of the solvent. Gel formation is, however, often assisted by the presence of atmospheric oxygen. By careful blending and cooking with various oils, varnishes from the flexible to the rigid, hard type can be produced. This type of varnish is now the general purpose varnish for the electrical industry, finding numerous applications from oils, where a certain degree of flexibility is required to vaccum cleaner armatures where bonding at high speed and elevated temperature is essential.

3. Amine/Alkyd Varnishes

The main function of this type of varnish is for the production of varnish for finishing purposes, although these varnish can also be used for impregnation in depth. The outstanding characteristic of the material is its excellent *'anti-trecking'* properties. This is of immense value for the crating of terminal boards, bushings and the like. A further advantage of this material is that it requires shorter stoving time and lower temperature than those normally required by the oil-modified synthetic resins of the phenolic type, but the use of powerful solvents such as xylol/butanol is involved, which is not regarded as favourable in contact with enamelled wire.

4. Epoxy Resin Varnishes

These Varnishes have marked chemical resistance. They can be plasticized to give flexible varnishes or can be fastened to give a tough film and are capable of being cured in depth under the influence of heat. They are normally not used with drying oils but can be esterified to produce both air-drying and stoving varnishes. Epoxy resin varnishes have great resistance to the synthetic transformer cooling mediums of the chlorinated diphenyl type, the new cutting oils and the high temperature ester lubricants. At present, their high cost seem to preclude their use in place of the phenolics for general use.

5. Silicone Varnishes

For continuous performance under the influence of heat the silicone varnish has no equal. The majority of organic varnishes of the phenolic type are only capable of working continuously at temperatures of not more than 150°C. Modified silicone varnishes can be produced to withstand temperatures upto 180°C, but for continuous temperatures above this straight silicone varnishes are unequalled. In conjuction with glass fabric asbestos, and mica, the silicone materials provide the highest class of the insulation.

Air-Drying Insulating Varnishes

1. Spirit Varnishes

The term spirit varnish is mainly used for solutions in methylated spirit of such natural resins as shellac, manila etc. They are quick drying and provide a smooth and glossy finish, of which the black type is extremely popular particularly with the repair trade. Their moisture resistance and heat inductance, however, are not particularly good.

2. Oleoresinous Varnishes

This type is similar to that already described under baking varnishes, being formulated with driers to produce air-drying films which are flexible and have excellent resistance to moisture absorption. They require longer air drying time than the spirit type, and can be pigmented to produce red and grey enamels having excellent filling properties, and good heat endurance. Normal uses includes finishing bakelite tubes, boards and windings etc.

3. Alkyd Varnishes

Alkyds, whether styrenated or straight, have proved to be excellent finishing varnishes. They can be modified to give flexible films of hard rigid films, and in general the styrenated alkyds dry much quicker than the straight alkyds. Both these types of varnishes dry in depth and possess good water and chemical resistance for machines operating under normal condition. The alkyd varnishes can be pigmented, and are particularly suitable for application to windings, make excellent paints for all classes of electrical equipment.

4. Varnishes for Tropical Finishing

This type of varnishes are oil modified phenolic type and contain a small amount of fungicide. they are designed to give protection to electrical equipment under moist conditions and insect attack and fungus growth usually associated with tropical conditions. Although they require a long drying time, they are the best finishing varnishes used in the electrical industry.

Other Types of Insulating Varnishes

1. Solventless Varnishes

These type of varnishes are used in deep windings requiring no solvent retention and risk of attack on enamelled wire. These varnishes may require to be heated during applicatio.ı to lower viscosity suitable for impregnating purpose. They can be used to best advantage in lightly wound compounds using fine wire, and multilayer interleaving to prevent excessive draining. Its application must be followed by four or three of an envelope varnish which may be type of solventless varnish which, after dipping, stays on the component with minimum of draining, or a more conventional solvent-bearing varnish.

2. Core Plate Varnishes

Core plate varnishes are used as surface coating on laminated elecrtical stampings to prevent eddy currents in the finished transformer core *etc*.

The coatings are applied by rollers and cured in flash bake ovens. Here the varnished stampings are passed over naked gas flames which ignite the varnish solvents, producing sufficient heat to cure the varnish.

3. Casting Resins

They are also solventless in nature but require a small amount of catalyst to promote the chemical change necessary for complete cure. They are available in solid and liquid forms. The solid form is heated to melt and then the catalyst is added. Both types of resins require slight heating after the addition of catalyst or may be cold set.

4. Super Enamels

Copper wire enamels must possess excellent flexibility, adhesion and mar resistance and a high dielectric strength. The phenomenal advances in high polymer chemistry and advances in this field naturally synchronised resulting in the development of super enamels.

5. Mica Sticking Varnishes

Mica is one of the most widely used electrical insulator generally in conjuction with a varnish type binder. For many years, shellac has been widely used for this purpose, typical examples being sheet micanite for part purposes and flexible mica folium for slot insulation and slot are wrapping. For large machines and turbo-alterators a black bonding bituminous varnish is also in general use. There are many other types of mica sticking varnishes for special purposes such as those based on spirit manila for mica tapes, silicon and alkyd types for heat resisting and phenolic types for moulding etc.

Formulation of Insulating Varnishes

Electrical Insulating Varnishes

Rosin 1000, metallic aluminium a little quantity, glycerine 50-150, anhydride of sodium sulphide 5-30, and tung oil 1,500 which has been previously stirred up with 0.1 to 0.5% of anhydride of sodium sulphide, are mixed together and heated at 240-260°C. When they have sufficiently reacted upon themselves, the mixture is properly diluted with a solvent, *e.g.* turpentine oil.

Flexible Insulating Varnish :

	I	*II*
Phthalic anhydride	213 Parts	235 Parts
Glycerol	129 Parts	118 Parts
Succinic acid	456 Parts	235 Parts
Ethylene glycol	242 Parts	230 Parts
Rosin	200 Parts	200 Parts
China wood oil	80 Parts	80 Parts

The ingredients are mixed and heated to 480°F quickly and kept at this temperature until the resin becomes clear.

Insulating Varnish :

Bakelite varnish	24 litres
Naphtha 140-220°F	6 litres
Ethylene dichloride	12 litres

Electric Insulation :

Electric insulating coating compositions are prepared on a base of urea formaldehyde resin, mixed with materials with which solid solutions are formed.

Example : 33 parts of a 46% solution of urea formaldehde resin in n-butyl alcohol are mixed with a solution of nitrocellulose, blown castor oil 30, and rosin 6 parts in ACOBU 25, ethyl alcohol 75, and phenyl methyl 75 parts by weight. Coatings of this composition are very adherent, elastic and durable after drying for 8 hours at 75°C. They are resistant to mineral acids, and to the action of transformer oils at high temperatures.

Electrical Insulation :

The following composition is suitable for transformers, capacitors, cables etc.

Crude scale wax	80
Patrolatum	10
Mineral Oil	10

Electrical Insulating Compound :

The following formula may be used as a covering or for moulding into forms.

Nitrobenzol	100 gms
Manganese resinate	50 gms
Molasses	18 Kgs

The amount in above formula may varied to produce different consistencies.

Electric Insulating Tape :

Tape is treated with following at 165°C.

Carnauba-montan wax	40-50
Rosin	32-40
Castor oil	10-28

Insulating Composition, Coil Impregenation :

Rosin	70
Asphalt	30

Apply at 160-175°C.

Formulation for an Insulating Varnish :

Coumarone resin	30 Parts
Ester gum	16 Parts
Wood oil	114 Parts
White Spirit	132 Parts
Kerosene	57 Parts
Linseed oil	48 Parts
Cobalt acetate	0.05 Parts

Silicone Type Insulation

The exceptional heat stability of silicones is especially valuable when they are use as insulating materials in conjuction with glass cloth, asbestos, mica. When glass cloth became available to replace cambric, silk, and paper for coated insulating tapes and windings, it was found that glass cloth would withstand higher temperatures than the standard organic insulating varnishes. This spurred the development of silicone resins for coating glass and asbestos cloth for bonding mica sheets. Silicon resins are also used for impregnating coils and windings for motors and other elecrtical equipment. The silicone-type insulation makes possible the safe operation of motors and other equipment at temperatures which would destroy the previous organic insulation.

The silicone insulation resins meet the AIEE requirements for class H materials. Equipment with this type of insulation can operate about 100°C higher than that with class B materials, and has a longer life. Silicone varnishes are used to impregenate glass and asbestos fabrics and to bond together mica splittings and other finely divided particles. The fabrics are often coated by drawing them through a bath of the varnish, removing the excess by squeeze rolls, and drying the coating by passage up a tower drier. Several coats may be applied continuously by multiple arrangement of baths and tower driers. The coils, *etc.*, may be dipped followed by careful baking to avoid air holes from bubbles. They may also be placed in a chamber from which the air is evacuated and the varnish then drawn in. The resins have a wide range of hardness and flexibility to meet various requirements. They also vary in the temperature required for proper cure.

Some Insulating Materials

The following table gives the specific inductive capacity of a number of insulating materials :

Asphaltum	2.68
Paraffin	2-2.3
Rosin	1.8-2.6
Shellac	3-3.7
Porcelain	4.4-6.8
Paper	2-2.5
Mica	5.7-7
Sulphur	3.6-4.3
Castor Oil	4.6-4.8
Turpentine	2.2-2.3
Bakelite	5.7-6.8

Polystyrene

Electrical Properties

Polystyrene resins have excellent insulating properties which are claimed to be comparable with those of mica and superior to those of shellac. Ellis states that polystyrene has greater insulating power than any other synthetic resin. When it is necessary to plasticize polystyrene, hydrocarbon plasticizers such as diphenyl naphthalene are recommended in order not to diminish its electrical properties.

Asphaltum

Good electrical insulating properties have prompted their incorporation in every in every type of black insulating varnish, whether for the production of empire insulating cloths or for the impregnation of coils, rotors or transformers. Other electrical uses as sealers for accumulators and condensers.

Coumarone Resin

In insulating varnishes coumarone resin is a popular choice because its low acidity prevents corrosion of copper wire which might occur during stoving or on ageing. Furthermore, it has a satisfactory dielectric strength. Electrical restivity is claimed is claimed to be higher than that for shellac. It is used increase the viscosity of hydrocarbon oils for impregnation of insulating paper for cables. Coumarone is a suitable resin whether used in the long oil type used for the manufacure of insulating tape or in the short oil type of insulating varnish for impregnation of coils. Varnishes for coil impregnation will be based on wood oil with coumarone alone or in admixture with estergum, limed rosin or pure and modified phenol formaldehyde resins.

Acrylic Resins

Acrylic and methacrylic are very useful for electrical purposes. The breakdown volatile of polymethyl-methacrylate resin is given as 280,000-340,000 volts per cm. Their power factor is higher than that of polystyrenes. Other facts which make these types of resin invaluable for electrical work have been enumerated, as non-tracking, reduction of power factor with increase of temperature, high melting point and resistance to substances likely to be encountered in electrical work such as mineral oils and ozone.

Shellac

Shellac has good insulating properties, and is not suspectible to tracking. Pure shellacs only be used in insulating compositions and they should be should be free of orpiment and rosin. Shellacs are used in the production of moulded components; in micanite from mica dust, for wire enamels, for laminated paper tubes, and for impregnating and finishing varnishes for coils, cotton and paper.

Waxes

Most waxes possess valuable electrical properties. In addition, their water repellant properties make them particularly suitable. They are used for electrical insulation where the maximum working temperature of the plant is comparitively low, and where there is no chance of contact with organic liquids such as transformer oils.

Chlorinated Rubber

Chlorinated rubber is highly resistant to acids and to alkalies, even when these are highly concentrated. It is also resistant to softening and penetration by mineral oils, but lacks strong resistance to animal or vegetable oils and can not be recommended for use in environments where these oils are likely to be present. Chlorinated rubber films have desirable electrical qualities. The following typical data have been recorded on clear, unplasticized films :

Specific surface resistance	2000×10^{-10} ohms
Dielectric strength (A.S.T.M. Method)	2,300 volts per mil
Electric constant at 25°C and 1000 cycles	3.1
Power factor at 25°C and 1000 cycles	0.0015 to 0.0030

Insulating Varnish from CNSL

The present invention relates to electrical insulation made from cashew-nut shell liquid. It provides electrical insulation which, has a higher dielectric value than insulation made from oils such as linseed oil and tung oils and the like. It also provides and electric insulation which has a high heat resistance.

Another object of the invention is to provide an electrical insulation which when it is in place about a conductor, is insoluble in oils such as machine oil, castor oil, petroleums such as gasoline, kerosene, and so on. The dried films, impregnations and moulded compositions made with cashew nut shell liquid are impreviously to water and moisture, and can be successively and repeatedly heated to temperatures as high as 500°F and higher, and cooled wothout lowering their dielectric value.

One method of making insulation film according to the present invention is as follows :

100 kgs. of cashew nut shell liquid is brought up to about 580°F and cooled to room temperature. As the temperature is lowering an equal volume of solvent vehicles such as gasoline or varnoline is added at about 300°F. At room temperature, 2-5 kgs. of formaline is added. The mixture

is then heated to about 235°F to drive off the water and then cooled. This solution can be thinned with more solvent vehicle if desired. Electrical coils or fabrics, paper, and so on dipped in or coated with this solution and heated at about 285°F for about one hour will dry to a firm film which has the advantageous properties above said.

An air-drying varnish is made as follows :

Heat 100 kgs. of comercial cashew nut shell liquid to about 450°F and add 2.5% to 5% of manganese resinate which dissolves therein and allow to cool to about 300°F and add an equal volume of varnoline or gasoline, then cool to about 140°F and add formaline *(40% water solution of formaldehyde),* in about 10% of the cashew nut shell liquid used, raise the temperature to about 190°F, preferably under a reflux condenser, and hold for about one to two hours, then raise to about 235°-240°F to drive off water and any excess formaldehyde. Add another volume of solvent and cool. Dippings and coatings made of this will dry in air at room temperature in about five to eight hours.

An example of obtaining a liquid for dipping or coating is as follows :

100 kgs. of commercial cashew nut shell liquid is heated to 570°Fand allowed to cool. At 140°F, 3 kgs. of hexamine added and temperature raised to about 265°F and then allowed to cool. This latter temperature is suitable for small batches, for large batches lower temperatures would need to be used depending on the rate of cooling after the heating. The reaction product is a liquid at normal temperatures. Dippings and coatings made of this liquid product when set at a temperature of 285°F give a film which is water and moisture proof, is resistant to petroleum solvents, to acids and alkalies, and has a comparitively high dielectric value. This material can be applied with a solvent such as gasoline, varnoline, benzol. The drying or setting time, when a solvent is used, is longer than when none is used.

An example of a method for making and applying an impregnating compound for electric coils is given as follows :

100 kgs. of commercial cashew nut shell liquid is heated to 570°F and allowed to cool. At 450°F about 1 kg. of manganese resinate is added and allowed to cool to room temperature. Now 3 kgs. of hexamine is added and the mixture is heated to 195°F to dissolve the hexamine Coils to be impregnated are heated for about two hours at about 225°F, and placed in an autoclave and the air with drawn therefrom, the suction being held for about one-half hour after maximum vacuum is obtained. The above prepared impregnating liquid is then charged into the autoclave without breaking tha vacuum and the vacuum held for another half hour after charging with the impregnating liquid. Now the vacuum is released and pressure is applied of about 60 to 80 pounds for about one-half hour, to drive the liquid into the coils, the temperature being kept around 125°F. At the end of this period the coils are removed from the autoclave, drained, and are baked in an oven at about 225°F for about twelve hours to set the impregnating liquid. At the exposed surfaces the said liquid has a comparitively hard, smooth film, and inside the surface the impregnating liquid has set into a firm, binding mass.

The cashew nut shell liquid can be used with natural oils such as linseed oil; or china wood oil with gums or resins such as coumarone, copal, East India gum; with pitches, mineral, animal or vegetable; or with any number of said materials, to make insulation. Such an example is as follows :

300 kgs. of cashew nut shell liquid and 150 kgs. of linseed oil are heated to about 600°F, when this temperature is reached heating is discontinued and cold linseed oil, 150 kgs. is added, as the mix reaches about 550°F, in cooling, one percent of litharge is added as a drier and the mix held at this temperature for about 15 minutes and then allowed to cool further to 450°F, and one percent of manganese resinate is added. In making coating material, dilute with thinner. This preparation, with or without the solvent is useful in making electrical insulation coatings, dippings, impregnations, and moulded compositions. In making moulded compositions the preparation can

be provided with fillers such as wood pulp, slate dust, barytes, asbestos, zinc oxide, portland cement, lime and so on. The preparation will dry or set at about 285°F, and at higher and at lower temperatures.

The above examples are given merely as such and are not to be considered as limiting the use and application of the methods and products of the invention because variations in percentages of the materials used, in the time and temperatures of the different heating steps, and in the sequences these steps, and in the mode of application and use of the products of reaction can be made by one skilled in the art to suit different needs.

The CNSL used can be raw and unheated, or it can be preheated, as, for example, in the open or in a closed container. The preheating speeds the rate of reaction with the hexamine. Usually the CNSL, when preheated, is cooled or allowed to cool before the hexamine is added, because the CNSL and hexamine reacts at a rapid rate at elevated temperatures.

The products of reactions CNSL and hexamine can be made to go through various states of consistency from the liquid, through a plastic, or rubbery state, and to a solid state; and the reaction products can be used and applied in any of these states. The former or harder states are obtained by the application of heat or by the aid of driers or catalizers, or with the latter or heat. The amount of hexamine is regulated to control the rate of reaction of the products; the greater the amount of hexamine used, the quicker is the setting. As is well known in the production of chemical reactions with the aid of heat, the length of time and temperature to which the CNSL and hexamine are heated are regulated and controlled to suit the mass or quantity of these agents because larger bodies retain heat for a longer period after the source of heat is removed than do smaller bodies.

An example for making coating, dipping, or impregnating material is as follows :

200 kgs. of commercial cashew nut shell liquid and 100 kgs. of stearine pitch are mixed and heated together to about 575°F and allowed to cool, 6 kgs. of hexamine is added at 240°F slowly with stirring and reacted at

265°F for desired viscosity with different size batches, the hexamine is added at different temperatures, to suit the rate at which the mass can be cooled. A solvent is added at about 240°F.

Coatings of this material on paper and cloth dry to a smooth, flexible and strong film in twenty minutes at about 285°F. For some purposes, such as for impregnations, the solvent is omitted; and the hexamine is not added until the CNSL stearin pitch mixture has reached a lower temperature than that given above, for example, at 195°F, this for the purpose of slowing down or delaying the setting of the material and keeping it at an optimum state of fluidity until it has been forced into the material and structure to be impregnated.

Manufacturing of Insulating Varnish

A particular example of the making of electrical insulation is as follows:

200 kgs. of the cashew nut shell liquid is heated to about 580°F and then allowed to cool, and drier is added consisting of litharge and manganese resinate each in amount about 1% of the weight of the cashew nut shell liquid used. The drier can be added at any time, 450°F being found to be practical for handling the materials. The prepared composition can be applied as it is, either at room temperature or at higher remperature, and it can be applied with a suitable solvent vehicle. The composition, however applied, is suitable for use for electrical insulation in many ways such as a coating or varnish; as an impregnation. The composition above described can be set or dried in a film on paper or cambric at about 285°F in about one-half hour.

The insulation practice suitable for bare conductor, for enamelled conductors, for conductors covered as, for example, with a cotton braid for conductors which have been enamelled and then covered with a braid and for use generally for making coils or a multiplicity of turns or layers of either rigid bars of flexible wires. An example of the material suitable for the practice is as follows:

Equal parts by weight of shellac *(e.g. delta shellac)* and the residue obtained by distilling cashew nut shell liquid (CNSL) with steam to remove about fifty percent of the weight of the cashew nut shell liquid are heated together to about 300°F whereupon application of heat is discontinued. The temperature will rise about five degrees and the material is stirred thorughly, poured into hollow pans hollow pans and when cooled, broken up and pulverized.

The cashew nut shell liquid residue — shellac product made as described above and pulverized can be dissolved cold in a mixture of equal parts of normal butyl alcohol and toluol to the extent of about 47% solids, and this solution can be thinned with high flash naphtha, for example six parts of said solution and about one part of high flash naphtha, by weight.

This material can be applied to bare, enamelled, braided, or enamelled and braided wire by running the wire through the solution to pick up a coating and running the coated wire through an oven at about 250°F, at a rate that will give the coated wire a heating for one minute. This coated wire is then wound tightly into coils and baked at about 250°F for about 20 hours during which the coating material softens and forms an integral mass which binds the coil of wire together. This heating also gradually brings about a setting of the material to a state in which it is infusible at the baking temperatures and also at higher temperatures, high enough to prevent softening of the binder at temperatures which will give a substantial safety factor for temperature above normal operating temperatures.

A Superior Electrical Varnish from CNSL :

The method for making a superior grade electrical insulation varnish with high electric strength as compared with conventional varnishes prepared from cashew-nut shell liquid formaldehyde resin. One of the methods is as follows :

Cashew nut shell liquid *(1 part)* and formaldehyde in the form of either formalin *(40%, 0.25 part)* or paraformaldehyde *(0.05 to 0.1 part)* are initially condensed by heating from 90° to 105°C to obtain the cashew formaldehyde resin. The resin if prepared from formalin, is first dried by heating under reduced pressure. After cooling, fusel oil titanate/silicate *(0.01 to 0.25 part)* is added, the mixture again heated up slowly from 100 to 150°C and the fusel oil distilled off under reduced pressure. One part of this product and a drying oil *(1 to 3 parts, such as linseed oil double- boiled)* are cooked at 220° to 250°C till the viscous product on cooling gives a string of 3 to 4 inches. It is then allowed to cool to about 150°C and is diluted with mineral solvents such as mineral turpentine and xylol, and cobalt and/or manganese naphthenate is added. The varnish is cured by baking at 110°C for two to four hours.

Methods of Use

Skill and care must be applied when using an insulating varnish so that the function for which it is designed is a success. To obtain maximum protection and insulation, the windings must be completely impregnated. Care must be exercised on viscosity control, and the oven used must be uniform in temperature, well ventilated, and preferably a few degree hotter than the prescribed baking temperature.

Adequate ventilation in baking ovens is essential so that the impregnated component is not *"stewed"* in the solvent which is being removed. High viscosity can cause incomplete penetration of the varnish, and failure of the varnish to dry out satisfactorily under the prescribed baking temperature and time or on the other hand, the deposit of solid varnish may be inadequate if the varnish is over thinned.

There is a particular procedure to be followed in every operation for successful results. The steps to be followed in logical sequence are :

(i) Initial drying
(ii) Impregnation or application by any other means,
(iii) Hardening and
(iv) Finishing.

Initial Drying :

The coils or windings are dried in an oven at 110°C for at least one hour depending upon the size and shape of the coils to ensure that all free moisture is driven out before impregnation. If any free moisture is left in the coils it will lead to premature breakdown. If there is facility for application of high vacuum, the coils may be subjected to high vacuum at this temperature for a very short period to remove all traces of moisture.

(a) Impregnation by Dipping

This is the easier process. The coils, as soon as they are taken out of the drying ovens, are dipped in a tank filled with the varnish. This prevents further absorption of moisture. The coils are dipped from one hour to six hours depending upon the job. Then the coils should be allowed to drain completely in a separate tank, preferably, and the filtered varnish can be added back to the impregnating tank.

(b) Impregnation by Vacuum

The coils are held at 110°C, then transferred to the vaccum tank where it is held for 1/2 to 1 hour under a vaccum of 749 mm to 762 mm of mercury. The varnish is drawn into the tank until the coils are completely submerged. The vacuum is released, the varnish held under the high pressure of the order 3,515-4,218 kgs. per sq. cms. for an hour or so. The varnish is pumped back to the reservoir and a vacuum of 381 to 508 mm of mercury applied for about an hour. The coils are further cured in a curing oven.

Curing and Hardening

Through drying of the insulating varnish occurs on account of the high residual reactivity of the varnish. The drained coils are at first kept at a temperature of 60°C or in that neighbourhood in a well-ventilated oven so that the solvents may be removed. The oven is then slowly raised in temperature and curing is proceeded with gradually. The coils should never be subjected to sudden thermal shock as this will act prejudicially in the long run. Radiant heat or convention type of heating are equally well suited.

Finishing

It is a common practice to impregnate the coils twice in order to obtain a satisfactory appearence. Others prefer to apply an air-drying clear or pigmented varnish by dipping, or brushing as a finish coat. This serves to give a greater measure of protection than the single coat.

Care and Maintenance

From time to time the viscosity of the varnish should be adjusted. To bring the varnish back to a specific viscosity, the relative thinners are to be fradually added with constant stirring. Any sudden addition will produce a colloidal shock resulting in a worthless jelled mas. All tanks containing varnish should be kept covered when not in use. Smoking and open flames should be avoided near the tanks. In emptying out the tanks, men should not enter the tank unless there are others also present to be handy in case the person in the tank happens to be suffering from a fit of giddiness which may occur rarely. The tanks should be cleaned periodically taking all the precautions referred to. Any sludge formation due to gel particles in the varnishes should be removed by filtration.

Wire Enamels and its manufacturing process

Wire enamels are unpigmented compositions used for insulating electrical winding; the film produced are compact flexible and hard with chemical and thermal stability and high dielectric strength. Coated wires possess several advantages over wires insulated with cotton, silk and paper which need to be impregnated with insulating varnishes to render them proof against moisture, oils, acid and alkalies.

Conventional wire enamels are oleoresinous formulations containing tung oil with modified phenolic resins. Varnishes based on polyvinyl formaldehyde resins possess satisfactory dielectric strength and give films with good flexibility and toughness; they are used with phenol-formaldehyde resins for improving surface hardness, abrasion, resistance to solvents and thermal stability. Polyvinyl formal wire enamels are graded as *A class* insulation. Varnishes based on polyurethanes, silicones and vinyls are also used.

Following wire enamels are in general use.

(i) Oleoresinous Wire Enamels

An excellent combination of tung oil and resin modified phenolic resin has resulted in the development of a continuous process whereby enamel is applied in 6-8 very thin layers. The process offers a great advantage in carrying out a thorough curing through oxidation and polymerisation. Every time the enamel is applied, excess enamel is wiped out by felt pads or metallic dies suspended on wire and then it is baked at very high oven temperature of 350° to 400°C in a very short time varying from 1 second to 1 minute depending on the length of the oven, speed of wire, diameter of wire and thickness of the covering *etc.*

(ii) Wire Enamels Based on polyvinyl Acetal

This enamel is based on a combination of polyvinyl formal *(P.V.F.)* and phenol formaldehyde resin. P.V.F. is a linear high molecular weight polymer and as such it gives a very thick solution even at low solid content. Because of the very high viscosity it is not possible to obtain concentric coating with P.V.F. based wire enamels with felt pad wiping arrangement. Excess wiping has to be done with the help of metallic dies suspended on wires. It gives good flexibility and toughness but exihibits poor thermal and chemical resistance. Therefore, it is usually used in combination with phenol formaldehyde resin, which improves surface hardness, abrasion resistance, resistance to solvents and imparts higher thermal stability. These enamels are easy to apply and the wires insulated with these enamels withstand the high stresses occuring in the use of enamelled wires. As all products with improved temperature ratings that have been developed later do not have these properties to the same extent, they have not succeeded in replacing PVA completely.

(iii) Wire Enamels Based on Polyurethanes

Wire enamels based on polyurethanes were mainly developed in Germany. Polyisocyanate combines with residual hydroxyl group of a polyester to give polyurethanes. Polyurethanes have excellent cohesion and hence give very tough films. Consequently, the adhesion to copper cannot be very high. Therefore, with the usual polyester polyurethane one cannot get an improvement in adhesion. Flexibility of the film can be improved by the addition of another high polymer such as polyamide.

(iv) Wire Enamels Based on Terephthalic Polyesters

Wire enamels based on tere phthalic polyesters have been by far the best developments in the recent years. They are capable of withstanding a temperature of 155°C permanently; abrasion resistance is better than that of P.V.F. The adhesion to copper is inferior but it can be improved by proper combination with poly-alcohols. It is also chemically inert to most of the aromatic solvents. Polyesters have low resistance to thermal shock.

(v) Wire Enamels Based on Other Plastics

Besides the above mentioned plastics, wire enamels based on polyester imides, polyamidoimides and polyhydantoins have also been developed. Enamels based on these materials are costly and still in the experimental stage.

Polyester imides show better resistance to thermal shock than polyester. They show some some deficiences in flow properties which present problem in applications to the critical round wire diameter *(0.22 mm. and 1.5 mm)* as well as to flat and profiled wires; in addition there is difficulty of combining high softening temperature and good solvent resistance with good flexibility and high thermal shock.

Polyamidomides are used dissolved in N-methyl pyrolidone. They give high hardness and resistance to solvent attack and abrasion and show good resistance to termal shock and good hermetic properties. However, with it also levelling is not without problems. On the other hand, polyhydantoins show good levelling properties. They have high softening temperatures, good flexibility and good resistance to thermal shock and hence, are suitable for flat wires. They also show good compatibility with other raw materials. Both polymidoimides and polyhydantoins are soluble in cresol.

Formulations of Wire Enamels

Electric Wire Lacquer

Material	*Parts by wt*
Cellulose Acetate	100
Tetrachlorethane	100
Alcohol	20
Triacetic	3

Adhesiveness may be increased by incorporating talc and opacity by zinc oxide

Enamelling of Iron

Formula No. 1

Dip Cleaned iron articles in

Nickel sulphate	60.0 gm
Boric acid	1.8 gm
Water	1.0 lt

For 30 min. at 70-80°C

Wash in 1/2% soda ash solution and then in 1/5% trisodium phosphate solution and dry at 100-150°C.

The following mixture, 50 parts, is ground and made into a paste with water, 40 parts, applied to iron and baked at 870-890°C.

Sand	25.1 Gm
Borax	32.9 Gm
Felspar	20.2 Gm
Soda ash	7.0 Gm
Potassium nitrate	3.8 Gm
Flourspar	3.3 Gm
Zinc oxide	2.1 Gm
Antimony	5.6 Gm
Clay	4.0 Gm
Zirconia	4.0 Gm

Formulation No. 2

The process of enamelling requires a more or less elaborate equipment. The black or raw metal shape or sheet as it comes into the enamel departmental has grease, oil, dirt and so on they are gathered by the press, lathe or drill which must be removed. A boiling caustic solution in a steel or lead-lined tank is used and requires about 10 to 15 minutes. The pieces are then lowered into an adjoining tank of following clear water, raising and lowering the crate several times to assure a good rinsing.

The next and important step is the *"pickling"* of the pieces which are now lowered, in the same crate, into a sulphuric acid solution of 5 to 6% strength, or a muriatic acid solution of 11 to 12%. The former is used hot at 150°F, while the latter is used cold. The time required is about 10 to 20 minutes. When properly pickled, the crate is again lowered into the next rinse tank, after which it is lowered into a neutralizer tank for 3 to 5 minutes at 150 to 160°F and finally the crate is quickly rolled into a steam heated driers. With the aid of a roller conveyer, the crate is brought to the inspector's section where the pieces are looked over and passed on to the applier's department. An overhead trolley and electric hoist, are used to move the crates along the line from cleaner to dryer.

The porcelain enamel used is composed of borax, feldspar, quartz, soda ash, flourspar, bone ash, cryolite and oxide of tin, manganese, iron cobalt etc.

Two typical formulaes are as follows :

For the base Coat :

Borax	120 lb
Soda ash	32 lb
Saltpeter	48 lb
Flourspar	48 lb
Quartz	60 lb
Manganese oxide	18 lb
Iron oxide	1 lb
Cobalt oxide	1 lb

In the mill to each 100 lb. of frit add :

Clay	8 lb
Carbonate of magnesia	60 oz

For a white cover coat mixs the following :

Borax	132 kgs
Soda ash	26 kgs
Cryolite	100 kgs
Flourspar	3 kgs
Feldspar	130 kgs
Quartz	130 kgs
Saltpeter	6 kgs

In the mill to each 100 kgs. of frit add :

Clay	6 kgs
Tin oxide	8 kgs
Water	30 %

For making coloured enamels, oxides of whatever colour desired are used. The oxides are added to the mill in the proportion to produce correct shade.

Formula for an Insulating Enamel :

	Kilograms
Rosin	50.0
Alkyd Resin	150.0
Perilla Oil	205.50
Fish Oil	15.00
China wood oil	73.50
Manganese resinate	0.30
Ferrous resinate	0.45
Cobalt acetate	0.25
Zinc resinate	1.00

17

TESTING & EVALUATION OF PAINTS

Introduction

From the point of view of production and quality control, it is essential that the final product and several other intermediates are subjected to certain tests designed to ensure that the product conforms to a pre-determined standards or set of values. Generally, samples are drawn at various stages of manufacture and tested by standard methods for the following characteristics of the product, namely, viscosity, brushability, covering power, opacity, drying time, volatile content and the flash point. Some of the common testing methods are described below.

1. Viscosity

Viscosity is an important characteristic of paints and varnishes and it is responsible to a great extent for the performance of the product. For example, the ease of brushing and spreading rate of a paint are influenced by its visosity. Flat wall paints, which must spread easily, are made at a relatively low viscosity *(2 to 3 poise)* while one-coat brushing enamels which depend on high build for their opacity are made at much higher viscosities *(about 5 poise)*. A number of methods are in use for viscosity determination.

(a) Efflux Cup

This is the simplest method and consists of measuring the time required for a standard volume of paint to flow through an orifice of prescribed dimension. It can be used only with paints which possess good flow properties such as industrial finishes and the conventional types of decorative enamels.

The two types of cup used in paint testing are described in *B.S. 1733* and are designated types A and B. In use, the cup is placed in the holder, levelled and filled with the paint, the orifice being closed with the finger. The finger is removed and a stop-watch started at the same time. With type A cup, the time is recorded for 50 milli litres to be collected in a graduated cylinder; with type B cup the time taken to the first break in the emergent stream. The orifice sizes can be varied and are quoted in viscosity figures, *e.g.* Type B-4 cup. Viscosity is greatly affected by temperature and the determination is usually carried out 25+ 0.5°C.

Efflux cups cannot be used for paints which exhibit thixotropy, and a rotational type of viscometer is best suited for these. Rotational viscometers can be used with both newtonian and non-Newtonian liquids and the following are the commonest forms.

(b) The Roto Thinner

It is a dual purpose instrument used both as a thinning mixture and as a viscometer.

Using the rotothinner, a given amount of paint is placed in a 1/2 pint tin on the turntable and the stirrer lowered. The torque transmitted through the liquid, exerts a twist on the turntable, the base of which is marked off in poiser and a fixed pointer indicates the viscosity. Thinners can be added from a graduated cylinder until the desired viscosity is reached.

(c) The Ferranti Portable Viscometer

This is a co-axial cylinder instrument, the outer cylinder being rotated. The inner cylinder is connected through a spring to a dial and this shows the torque transmitted through the liquid by the rotation of the outer cylinder. Three speeds are used and sets of cylinders of different sizes are supplied to cover a range of viscosities.

This instrument is useful not only for assessing the degree of thixotropy in a paint but, the rate is more important in practice of recovery of gel structure.

The stormer Viscometer and the Brookfield Viscometer are the other common types of rotational viscometers employed for the purpose.

2. Brushability

Although the viscosity figures can afford a guide to the ease of brushing or suitability for spraying, other factors are involved which appear only during the application process. Brushability test of decorative paints are made by application to areas of about 2 feet square to one side of which a piece of moulding is attached. The later shows the behaviour of the paint on sharp edges and in hollows. Yet another method of qualitative assessment of brushability is given in *B.S.3900*.

A quantitive assessment of brushability is usually obtained by B.K. Brushability Recorder. This consists of a spring-loaded table to which a panel can be fixed. This table is attached to a recording mechanism whereby displacement of the table can be recorded on moving graph paper. The table displacement results from brush drag when paint is applied to the panel, and the graph obtained is compared with that of a *'standard'* paint.

3. Covering Power

Covering power, often referred to as spreading rate, is expressed in square yards or square feet per gallon and represents the area which can be covered by a coat of paint under normal application conditions. It can be measures by application of sufficient paint to cover a given area *e.g.* a *Morest Chart*, the amount of paint used being determined either by weighing the chart before and after application or by the difference in weight of container and brush. More accurate figures are obtained by painting larger areas, and with spray paints if it is necessary. The spreading rate of an average decorative enamel is 80 to 90 square yards per gallon.

4. Opacity

Opacity or hiding power is the ability of a paint to hide or obliterate the surface. It essentially depends on the light scattering and absorption properties of the dispersed pigments and on the thickness of the film. Opacity measurement are usually made on dry films of known thickness but occasionally the need arises for measurement on the liquid paint. This is best carried out by the use of the Pfund cryptometer.

Pfund Cryptometer

The Pfund Cryptometer is made in two forms :

(i) The recess type which is suitable for whites and tints only,

(ii) The black and white type which can be used for all colours in addition to the white and is more widely used.

The constituent parts of the recess type cryptometer are the base of black glass A, the groove B, the steel distance strip C and the thin glass plate D. A linear scale is engraved on the surface of the base. A wedge-shaped layer od white paint is formed between the base and D and this becomes *'infinetly thick'* at B. As long as opacity is not compiete the edge of the groove is visible. By sliding the wedge to the left a point is reached when it is impossible to see the edge. The scale reading is taken at the re-appearence of the edge. The accuracy is of the order of 5 percent. From the scale reading and a knowledge of the wedge angle it is possible to calculate the critical thickness of paint above the edge of B.

The black and white Cryptometer has a base consisting of blocks of white and black glass fused together. The operation is the same as with the recess type but scale marking are made on both sides of the finding line so that readings can be taken both with the wedge in position and in the reverse position.

Opacity of the dry paint film is generally required for most specification work and is ususally determined by the *Contrast Ratio Method*, described in brief below.

Contrast Ratio Mehtod

A film of uniform thickness is cast on a thin sheet of cellulose acetate by fixing this on a plane surface under two steel shims of 2 mils. thickness. The paint is spread over the surface with a doctor blade and allowed to dry.

The opacity or contrast ratio is obtained by measuring the total reflectance from the film when placed over a white and then over a black substrate. The difference is a measure of the amount of light which penetrates the film and is absorbed by the black.

The substrate consists of blocks of white and black glass fused together. The reflectance characteristics of these are first measured by reference to a magnesium carbonate standard. The paint film is placed on the white surface and the reflectance measured by means of the opacity head.

The opacity head essentially comprises a lamp and photoelectric cell. It is connected to a galvanometer and the latter reading, with the opacity head and film on the white substrate, is set at 100. The film and opacity head are then placed on the black plate and the galvanometer reading noted. After making the correction for the surface reflectances the opacity or contrast ratio of the paint is expresses as a percentage.

5. Drying Time

The drying time of a paint is the time required for the film to change from liquid condition as applied, to a solid film. The drying process is characterized by two periods known as surface drying time and hard drying time. A film is surface dry when it is free from tackiness. It is also sometimes known as *tack-free*.

There are several definitions of hard dry. It is defined as the film condition when a further coat can be applied without damage to the film.

Various methods are available for determining the surface drying time and hard drying time. However, the B.K. drying Tester, is probably the most common appartus for determining the drying time of paints.

The B.K. Drying Tester

It provides information on the whole process. Films of definite thickness are cast on long strips and by means of a moving carriage a vertical round-ended needle is drawn slowly through the paint film. The speed can be choosen so that the glass strip is traversed in 4,8,16 or 24 hours. In the early period of drying, the paint flows round the needle and no record remains. As the paint sets, the needle and no record remains. As the paint sets, the needle cuts a groove and the appearence of this groove gives information on the relative speeds of surface and through-drying. Rapid surface drying is shown by tearing of the skin. Too-slow surface dry is accompanied by an extended groove. When the paint film is hard dry, the needle rides on the surface and leaves little or no record.

6. Density

Density of paints is expressed in pounds per gallon and is determined using a weight per gallon cup. This cup, which is made to hold 100, 50 or 25 ml., is filled with the paint and used in the same way as a specific gravity bottle. The weight per gallon is a useful check on composition and is necessary for transport and shipping.

7. Volatile Content

The volatile content is a useful check on composition and is often required in specification work. It is determined by weighing out 2 to 3 grams of paint into a flat-bottomed dish or tin-lid *(which is disposable)* and heating for about 3 hours in an oven at 105°C. It is cooled, weighed, and reheated for a further 1/2 hour to check that the weight is constant. The volatile content is expressed as a percentage of the original paint.

8. Flash Point

This is required for transport and shipping regulations. The majority of paints flash below 120°F and the Abel *(Closed cup)* method is used. The use of this apparatus is described in detail in British Standard 3442.

9. Colour Assesement

Colour assessment is usually done visually using either dry or wet standards. Dry standards are panels or patterns which are compared with the sample after the latter has been applied to a suitable panel and allowed to dry. The comparison should be made in a *"north light"*.

With a wet standard, this should be applied to a panel alongside the sample and the panel allowed to dry before comparison in a *"north light"*.

Changes in the standards can be guarded against by recording the colour by means of a spectrophotometer or calorimeter.

Test on Dry Films

1. Gloss

Paint films can exhibit any degree of gloss from high gloss *(98 to 100 percent reflectance)* to dead mat *(no reflectance)* but it is customary to refer to five categories — high gloss, semi-gloss,egg-shell gloss, egg-shell flat and mat. In the absence of any universally accepted standard off gloss, however, it is not feasible to quote gloss values for any except the high gloss. The measurement of gloss values above 50 percent is usually carried out as follows :

A film of uniform thickness is cast on a plane glass surface by means of 2-mill shims and a doctor blade. The film is allowed to harden up for seven days. The gloss determination is carried out using a gloss head connected to a galvanometer. The instrument is standardized on a glossy black tile and the galvanometer set at 100. The gloss head is placed on the sample and several readings taken at right angle to each other, the means of the values obtained being taken on the gloss reading.

With high gloss enamels retention is as important as the initial gloss and the panel is therefore examined at weekly intervals over a period. The loss of gloss should not exceed 10 percent in the first 4 weeks.

2. Hardness

(a) Scratch Test

This test is widely employed for testing the hardness of dry paint-film. The paint is applied to clean abraded tin-plate, allowed to dry for the appropriate time and fixed in a horizontal position in a slide in the apparatus. Fixed over the slide is a pivoted counter-balanced arm to which is attached a needle with a hemisperical hardned steel point, 1 mm. in diameter. This arm can be lowered so that the needle, which can be weighted, is vertical when in contact with the paint film.

In use the weighted needle is lowered gently on to the paint surface and the slide pulled out causing the needle to move along the paint film. This may produce a sceatch through the metal, cut a groove in the paint, or the paint may be unaffected. The result recorded is the maximum load which can be applied to the needle before bare metal is visible through the scratch. Good adhesion between paint and metal is essential for consistent results.

(b) Pencil Hardness Test

This is a very simple and useful test which is used for assessing the hardness of industrial finishes. Pencils of decreasing hardness are drawn across the surface until one found which leaves a black line. The method involves a number of variables but is very useful when experience in its use has been acquired.

In addition to the above, a number of manual and automatic forms of apparatus are available for testing the hardness of paint films. Some of the other common testers include Sward Hardness Rocker and Persoz Pendulum.

3. Flexibility and Extensibility

These properties are of importance on metal substrates which are subject to temperature fluctuations. The following methods of assessment are in common use but in each case the test also indicates the degree of adhesion.

Bend Test

The paint is applied to a strip, 4 in. by 2 in., of 30 s.w.g. chromatic-dipped soft aluminium and allowed to harden for the specified time. The panel is then placed, paint-side outermost under a mandrel of prescribed diameter embodied in a hinge. The panel is bent through 180° in one second, removed, and the bend examined for cracks and loss of adhesion. Mandrels are in use ranging from 1 inch to 1/8 inch in diameter.

Erichsen Test

This test measures the extensibility of a paint film when a portion of the substrate is extended into a dome-shaped mound. The paint is applied to a prepared deep-drawing steel panel and when ready for test is fixed against a steel plate containing a wide orifice. The painted side is against the orifice. A hemisperical hardened steel tool is placed against the back of the panel in line tool and the painted panel is slowly distorted to form a dome. The machine is stopped at the first sign of rupture in the paint film and the distance traversed by the tool is noted. The result is known as the Erichsen Depth. The dome is also examined for loss of adgesion. A piece of Scotch tape is presses on the surface and then sharply pulled off.

4. Adhesion

The adhesion of a paint to a surface depends on good wetting and therefore on the cleaniliness of the surface. A large number of methods have been suggested for the measurement of adhesion but in many cases the precise significance of the results is not evident. In the *Scratch Bend and Erichsen* tests described above, adhesion is involved and expressed in a qualtative manner, *i.e.*, good, fair, or bad.

The Adhesive Tape Method

This method is widely used in one or other forms. In one form, a piece of pressure-sensitive adhesive tape is applied to a painted panel and the urea covered by the tape cut round and through the metal with a sharp blade. The end of the tape is then pulled sharply at right angles to the panel and any film removal is noted. This test is made qualtative in the *Gardner Tensiometer* using linen tape and epoxy adhesive.

The Hounds Field Tensiometer Test

The paint is applied to the ends of two cylinders of the appropriate substrate and these are then glued together, end to end. The composite specimen is placed in the tensiometer and the two cylinders drawn apart. The force required to pull the paint from the surface in noted. The precise significance of the results provides an interesting speculation.

5. Film Thickness

(a) Wet Films

The most successful instrument for this purpose is the Wet Film Thickness Gauge. It consists of two solid metal disks and between them is mounted a slightly smaller third disk which is eccentric to the other two, and at one point the three circum ferences are in the same plane. This point is marked ***O*** and the point opposite is marked ***4*** — the difference in diameter *(in mills.)* between the centre and outside disks.

To use gauge it is placed on the film with point 4 downwards and then rolled along. The point at which paint is picked up on the centre disk is noted and the corresponding marking on the outer disk gives the thickness of the film.

(b) Dry Films

Either destructive or non-destructive methods are employed according to the nature of the substrate. The former must be used on non-metallic substrates, and the principle methods are the following.

Dial Thic' ;ess Gauge requires the removal of a small area of paint from the substrate. The gauge has two legs which rest on the film and between them is the spring-loaded probe which rest on the exposed substrate. The film thickness is then indicated on the dial.

In *Microscopic* method a portion of the paint film is mounted vertically on the microscope stage and the thickness determined using a suitable graticule. The destructive methods can, of course, be used for paints on metallic substrates but for these non-destructive methods are preferred.

The non-destructive methods used on metallic substrates utilize electrical effects with differences for ferrous and non-ferrous metals.

18

PROJECT PROFILES

1. ALUMINIUM PAINTS
2. BITUMIN BASED INDUSTRY
3. CEMENT PAINT (DRY) (SNOWCEM TYPE)
4. CLEAR TRANSPARENT LACQUER FOR COATING ON BRASS BANGLES
5. CEMENT PAINT
6. DRY DISTEMPER
7 EMULSION PAINTS
8. EPOXY RESIN BASED PRIMER (PUTTY)
9. HAMMERTONE PAINTS
10. HEAT CHAMBER PAINTING
11. NAPHTHA BASED THINNER
12. N.C. THINNERS USED IN AUTO PARTS

13. N.C.PUTTY (CAR PUTTY)

14 OIL BOUND DISTEMPER

15. PAINT INDUSTRY PRIMER

16. PAINTS INDUSTRY

17. PAINTS FOR AUTO VEHICLES

18. PUTTY AND WATER PROOFING PAINT

19. PAINT BRUSHES

20. PAINT DRIERS

21. PUTTY (METAL CASEMENT PUTTY) (ASIAN PAINTS TYPE)

22. PAINT REMOVERS

23. POWDER SPRAY PAINTING WORKSHOP

24 STOVING PAINTS

25. THINNERS

26. VARNISH AND PAINTS INDUSTRY

27. WIRE ENAMELS (POLY VINYL BUTYRAL BASED)

28. WOOD PRIMER FOR PAINTS

PLANT ECONOMICS OF
ALUMINIUM PAINT

Rated Plant Capacity = 1000.00 KGS./day

LAND & BUILDING

(Land Required 1000 Sq. Mt.)	Rs. 14,30,000.00

PLANT & MACHINERY

M.S. ball mill with reduction gear motor belt conveyor, cylinder etc. M.S. Varnish kettle Electrically heated with accessories, Planetary mixer, Triple roll mill Paint storage tanks, Solvent storage tank, Laboratory testing equipment Semi Automatic, can filling & sealing machine, Miscellaneous tools, pipes & pipe fitting, Zig fixture screens etc.

TOTAL	**Rs. 7,75,000.00**
OTHER FIXED ASSETS	Rs. 6,05,000.00

WORKING CAPITAL REQUIREMENT/MONTH

RAW MATERIALS

1. Aluminium paste
2. Coumarone resin
3. Linseed stand oil
4. White spirit
5. Solvent Naphtha
6. Cobalt Naphthenate
7. Tin containers for Aluminium paste
8. Tin container for Varnish
9. Miscellaneous.

TOTAL	**Rs. 18,15,928.00**

TOTAL WORKING CAPITAL/MONTH

1.	RAW MATERIAL	Rs.	18,15,928.00
2.	SALARY & WAGES	Rs.	72,125.00
3.	UTILITIES & OVERHEADS	Rs.	78,100.00
	TOTAL	**Rs.**	**19,66,153.00**

TOTAL CAPITAL INVESTMENT

TOTAL FIXED CAPITAL	Rs.	24,95,000.00
TOTAL WORKING CAPITAL	Rs.	58,98,459.00
TOTAL	Rs.	83,93,459.00

TURN OVER/ANNUM

Receipt by sale of Aluminium paint
3,00,000 kgs Rs. 2,85,00,000.00

PROFIT SALES RATIO = Profit / Sales x 100 = 37.16 %

RATE OF RETURN = Operating profit / T.C.I x 100 = 37.16 %

BREAK EVEN POINT (B.E.P) = 44.54 %

PLANT ECONOMICS OF
BITUMIN BASED INDUSTRY

Rated Plant capacity = 0.50 MT/day

LAND & BUILDING
(Land Required 1000 Sq. Mts) Rs. 10,00,000.00

PLANT & MACHINERY

Mild steel ball mill, 4 ft. 500 litre capacity with 10 H.P. motor, Planetary mixer/edge runner basket size 48" no with reduction gear and other accessories, Paint storage tank Capacity 1 tonne, Heating kettle 50 litre capacity with all accessories, Miscellaneous

TOTAL **Rs. 4,20,000.00**

OTHER FIXED ASSETS Rs. 1,92,000.00

WORKING CAPITAL REQUIREMENT/MONTH

RAW MATERIALS

1. Bitumen 6250 kg.
2. Pigment 375 kg.
3. Driers and Drying oil 400 kg.
4. Solvent litre xylol 6000 kg.

TOTAL **Rs. 3,46,250.00**

TOTAL WORKING CAPITAL/MONTH

1.	RAW MATERIAL	Rs.	3,46,250.00
2.	SALARY & WAGES	Rs.	45,811.00
3.	UTILITIES & OVERHEADS	Rs.	40,000.00
	TOTAL	**Rs.**	**4,32,061.00**

TOTAL CAPITAL INVESTMENT

TOTAL FIXED CAPITAL	Rs.	16,12,000.00
TOTAL WORKING CAPITAL FOR 3 MONTHS	Rs.	12,96,183.00
TOTAL	**Rs.**	**29,08,183.00**

TURN OVER/ANNUM

1.	By sale of Bituminous paints 150 tonnes	Rs.	78,00,000.00

PROFIT SALES RATIO = Profit / Sales x 100 = 22.99 %

RATE OF RETURN = Operating profit / T.C.I x 100 = 62.34 %

BREAK EVEN POINT (B.E.P) = 40.03 %

PLANT ECONOMICS OF

CEMENT PAINT (DRY) (SNOWCEM TYPE)

Rated Plant capacity = 2.00 TON/day

LAND & BUILDING

(Total land required 600 sq. mt.) Rs. 6,40,000.00

PLANT & MACHINERY

Paint Mixers, Edge Runner Mills, Grinding Unit, Ball Mills or Pebble Mills, Screening Equipments, Weighing Machine, Packaging Unit, Laboratory and Quality Control, Instruments, Miscellaneous equipments, Conveying unit, pumps, etc.

TOTAL **Rs. 5,55,000.00**

OTHER FIXED ASSETS Rs. 1,95,000.00

WORKING CAPITAL REQUIREMENT/MONTH

RAW MATERIALS

1. Portland Cement 33500 kgs
2. Hydrated Lime 12,300 kgs
3. Zinc Sulphide 2000 kgs
4. Aluminium Stearate 500 kgs
5. Calcium Chloride 2500 kgs
6. Essential Oil
7. Packing Charges for 50,000 kg Cement Paint

TOTAL **Rs. 1,21,900.00**

TOTAL WORKING CAPITAL/MONTH

1.	RAW MATERIAL	Rs.	1,21,900.00
2.	SALARY & WAGES	Rs.	35,500.00
3.	UTILITIES & OVERHEADS	Rs.	48,100.00
	TOTAL	**Rs.**	**2,05,500.00**

TOTAL CAPITAL INVESTMENT

TOTAL FIXED CAPITAL	Rs.	13,90,000.00
TOTAL WORKING CAPITAL FOR 3 MONTHS	Rs.	6,16,500.00
TOTAL	**Rs.**	**20,06,500.00**

TURN OVER/ANNUM

600 Tonnes of Cement Paint	Rs.	39,00,000.00

PROFIT SALES RATIO = Profit / Sales x 100 = 21.01 %

RATE OF RETURN = Operating profit / T.C.I x 100 = 40.33 %

BREAK EVEN POINT (B.E.P) = 55.31 %

PLANT ECONOMICS OF

CLEAR TRANSPARENT LACQUER FOR COATING ON BRASS BANGLES

Rated Plant Capacity = 100.00 KGS./day

LAND & BUILDING

(Land Area required 50 sq.mts.) Rs. 1,50,000.00

PLANT & MACHINERY

Mixing Vessel with agitator & motor Cap: 150 kgs, Raw material storage vessel Cap: 500/- kgs., Production storage vessel Cap: 200 kgs., Filling sealing & packaging m/c., Miscellaneous, Testing Equipments Pipe fillings etc.

TOTAL **Rs. 1,64,000.00**

OTHER FIXED ASSETS Rs. 33,500.00

WORKING CAPITAL REQUIREMENT/MONTH

RAW MATERIALS

1. 1/2 second nitro-cellulose wet.with 35% Ethyl Alcohol, 445 kgs.
2. Dibutyl phthalate, 148.28 kgs.
3. Ethyl Acetate, 470.75 kgs.
4. Butyl Acetate, 322 kgs.
5. Butyl Alcohol 322 kgs.
6. Toluol, 768.25 kgs.
7. 4 lb. cut refined wax-free shallac in alcohol 23.75 kgs.
8. Packaging material
9. Miscellaneous.

TOTAL **Rs. 1,73,259.33**

TOTAL WORKING CAPITAL/MONTH

1.	RAW MATERIAL	Rs.	1,73,259.33
2.	SALARY & WAGES	Rs.	38,061.00
3.	UTILITIES & OVERHEADS	Rs.	17,350.00
	TOTAL	**Rs.**	**2,28,670.33**

TOTAL CAPITAL INVESTMENT

TOTAL FIXED CAPITAL	Rs.	3,47,500.00
TOTAL WORKING CAPITAL FOR 3 MONTHS	Rs.	6,86,010.99
TOTAL	**Rs.**	**10,33,510.99**

TURN OVER/ANNUM

Receipt by sale of Clear Transparent Brass Lacquer 30,000 kgs.	Rs.	36,00,000.00

PROFIT SALES RATIO = Profit / Sales x 100 = 17.51 %

RATE OF RETURN = Operating profit / T.C.I x 100 = 61.43 %

BREAK EVEN POINT (B.E.P) = 44.13 %

PLANT ECONOMICS OF
CEMENT PAINT

Rated Plant capacity = *1.00 TON/day*

LAND & BUILDING		
(Total land required 300 sq.mts)	Rs.	3,10,000.00
PLANT & MACHINERY		
Edge Runner, Ball Mill, Weighting balance, Laboratory equipments		
TOTAL	**Rs.**	**1,15,000.00**
OTHER FIXED ASSETS	Rs.	40,000.00

WORKING CAPITAL REQUIREMENT/MONTH

RAW MATERIALS

1. Portland Cement (19650 Kgs.)
2. Hydrated Lime (7590 Kgs.)
3. Zinc Sulphide (1350 Kgs.)
4. Calcium Stearate 60 Kgs.
5. Calcium Chloride 1350 Kgs.

TOTAL	**Rs.**	**55,737.00**

TOTAL WORKING CAPITAL/MONTH

1. RAW MATERIAL	Rs.	55,737.00
2. SALARY & WAGES	Rs.	21,328.00
3. UTILITIES & OVERHEADS	Rs.	27,400.00
TOTAL	**Rs.**	**1,04,465.00**

TOTAL CAPITAL INVESTMENT

TOTAL FIXED CAPITAL	Rs.	4,65,000.00
TOTAL WORKING CAPITAL FOR 3 MONTHS	Rs.	3,13,395.00
TOTAL	**Rs.**	**7,78,395.00**

TURN OVER/ANNUM

300 Tons of Cement Paint	Rs.	19,50,000.00

PROFIT SALES RATIO = Profit / Sales x 100 = 27.04 %

RATE OF RETURN = Operating profit / T.C.I x 100 = 67.23 %

BREAK EVEN POINT (B.E.P) = 43.26 %

PLANT ECONOMICS OF
DRY DISTEMPER

Rated Plant Capacity = 1.00 Tonne/day

LAND & BUILDING
(Land 700 Sq.Mts.) Rs. 17,75,000.00

PLANT & MACHINERY

Mild steel ball mill cap: 200 Kgs/hr with 10 H.P. motor., Edge runner (basket size 72") with reduction gear & other accessories., Mixer (M.S.) cap: 200 Kgs. with 5 H.P. motor & other arrangements., Vibrating screen of (size 5' X 5') of 100 mesh made of M.S. with other necessary arrangements., Weighing balance, plate form type., Laboratory equipments., Pulverizer, cap: 200 Kgs/hr., Powder packing machine (Semi-automatic)., Miscellaneous pipe fitting valve, jigs & fixtures etc., Conveyor belt & other material handling equipments., Storage tanks (M.S.) for raw materials, cap: 500 Kgs.

TOTAL **Rs. 7,40,000.00**

OTHER FIXED ASSETS Rs. 2,20,000.00

WORKING CAPITAL REQUIREMENT/MONTH

RAW MATERIALS

1. Paris white 13.75 Ton .
2. Lactic casein 2.5 Ton
3. Barytes, 6.25 Ton
4. Slacked lime, 1.5 Ton
5. Borax 1 Ton
6. Pigments, preservative & anti foaming agents.
7. Packaging materials.

TOTAL **Rs. 3,15,250.00**

TOTAL WORKING CAPITAL/MONTH

1.	RAW MATERIAL	Rs.	3,15,250.00
2.	SALARY & WAGES	Rs.	50,125.00
3.	UTILITIES & OVERHEADS	Rs.	62,250.00
	TOTAL	**Rs.**	**4,27,625.00**

TOTAL CAPITAL INVESTMENT

TOTAL FIXED CAPITAL	Rs.	27,35,000.00
TOTAL WORKING CAPITAL FOR 3 MONTHS	Rs.	12,82,875.00
TOTAL	**Rs.**	**40,17,875.00**

TURN OVER/ANNUM

300 Ton of dry distempers	Rs.	75,00,000.00

PROFIT SALES RATIO = Profit / Sales x 100 = 18.13 %

RATE OF RETURN = Operating profit / T.C.I x 100 = 33.34 %

BREAK EVEN POINT (B.E.P) = 53.17 %

PLANT ECONOMICS OF
EMULSION PAINTS

Rated Plant Capacity = 500.00 KG/day

LAND & BUILDING

(Land Required 300 Sq. Mt.) Rs. 2,70,000.00

PLANT & MACHINERY

Ball Mills-Driven by 3 phase 440 V, 3 H.P. Motor at 25 R.P.M. Capacity of Mixing 300 Kg/per running, Hard Cast Iron Balls 2000 Kgs., Li-Kneader Mixer of made by Mild Steel. Capacity of mixing 100 Kg Powder, attached 4 H.P. Motor Moveable Balance Automatic Bagging Machine

TOTAL Rs. 1,90,000.00

OTHER FIXED ASSETS Rs. 95,000.00

WORKING CAPITAL REQUIREMENT/MONTH

RAW MATERIALS

1. White Cement
2. Hydrated Lime
3. Titanium Dioxide
4. Calcium Stearate
5. Calcium Chloride

TOTAL Rs. 96,683.50

TOTAL WORKING CAPITAL/MONTH

1. RAW MATERIAL	Rs.	96,683.50
2. SALARY & WAGES	Rs.	19,968.00
3. UTILITIES & OVERHEADS	Rs.	33,100.00
TOTAL	**Rs.**	**1,49,751.50**

TOTAL CAPITAL INVESTMENT

TOTAL FIXED CAPITAL	Rs.	5,55,000.00
TOTAL WORKING CAPITAL FOR 3 MONTHS	Rs.	4,49,254.50
TOTAL	**Rs.**	**10,04,254.50**

TURN OVER/ANNUM

1,50,000 Kg. Emulsion Paints	Rs.	25,50,000.00

PROFIT SALES RATIO = Profit / Sales x 100 = 21.12 %

RATE OF RETURN = Operating profit / T.C.I x 100 = 53.13 %

BREAK EVEN POINT (B.E.P) = 47.30 %

PLANT ECONOMICS OF

EPOXY RESIN BASED PRIMER (PUTTY)

Rated Plant Capacity = 500.00 Kg./day

LAND & BUILDING

(Total Land Area 1000 Sq. Mts.) Rs. 14,25,000.00

PLANT & MACHINERY

Mixing Tank made of M. S. 1000 Kg., Tripple Roll Mill, Blending Tank, Storage Tanks, Diesel Generator Set (25 KVA)

TOTAL Rs. 7,40,000.00

OTHER FIXED ASSETS Rs. 6,80,000.00

WORKING CAPITAL REQUIREMENT/MONTH

RAW MATERIALS

1. Zinc Phosphate 5000 Kg.
2. Titanium Dioxide 1170 Kg.
3. Talc 1030 Kg.
4. Bentone 540 kg.
5. n-Butanol 235 kg.
6. Epoxy Resin (70%) Solution in xylol 2000 kg.
7. Methylethyl Ketone 1320 Kg.
8. Toluol 1300 Kg.
9. Pigments & Chemicals
10. Packing Materials

TOTAL Rs. 5,82,320.00

TOTAL WORKING CAPITAL/MONTH

1. RAW MATERIAL	Rs.	5,82,320.00
2. SALARY & WAGES	Rs.	87,960.00
3. UTILITIES & OVERHEADS	Rs.	30,730.00
TOTAL	**Rs.**	**7,01,010.00**

TOTAL CAPITAL INVESTMENT

TOTAL FIXED CAPITAL	Rs.	28,45,000.00
TOTAL WORKING CAPITAL FOR 3 MONTHS	Rs.	21,03,030.00
TOTAL	**Rs.**	**49,48,030.00**

TURN OVER/ANNUM

Epoxy Resin Base Primer 150 MT.	Rs. 1,08,00,000.00

PROFIT SALES RATIO = Profit / Sales x 100 = 11.41 %

RATE OF RETURN = Operating profit / T.C.I x 100 = 24.78 %

BREAK EVEN POINT (B.E.P) = 58.27 %

PLANT ECONOMICS OF
HAMMERTONE PAINTS

Rated Plant Capacity = 1.00 MT/day

LAND & BUILDING

(Total Land Required 500 Sq. Mt.) Rs. 3,40,000.00

PLANT & MACHINERY

1. Grinder of 10 HP
2. Ribbon blender
3. Ball Mill of 200 kg. capacity
4. Mixer to adjust viscosity of paint
5. Weighing Balance platform type
6. Lab. equipments
7. Heating equipment with burner firnace (either gas or coal fired)
8. Stainless Steel Reaction Kettle with ammeter, stirrer, electric meter (2 H.P. etc.)
9. Storage tank
10. Others - Filter press, Tanks, Vacuum Pump
11. Edge Runner

TOTAL **Rs. 5,05,000.00**

OTHER FIXED ASSETS Rs. 95,000.00

WORKING CAPITAL REQUIREMENT/MONTH

RAW MATERIALS

1. Butylated Urea Formaldehyde
2. Short Oil D.C.O. Alkyd 17.00 tonnes
3. Non Leafing Al Paste 0.50 tonnes
4. Xylol 1.25 tonnes
5. N - Butanol 0.70 tonnes
6. Miscellaneous - pigments, finishing matter.

TOTAL **Rs. 6,35,050.00**

TOTAL WORKING CAPITAL/MONTH

1.	RAW MATERIAL	Rs.	6,35,050.00
2.	SALARY & WAGES	Rs.	27,000.00
3.	UTILITIES & OVERHEADS	Rs.	18,400.00
	TOTAL	**Rs.**	**6,80,450.00**

TOTAL CAPITAL INVESTMENT

TOTAL FIXED CAPITAL	Rs.	9,40,000.00
TOTAL WORKING CAPITAL FOR 3 MONTHS	Rs.	20,41,350.00
TOTAL	**Rs.**	**29,81,350.00**

TURN OVER/ANNUM

300 Tonnes of Hammertone Paint Rs. 1,11,00,000.00

PROFIT SALES RATIO = Profit / Sales x 100 = 19.09 %

RATE OF RETURN = Operating profit / T.C.I x 100 = 71.04 %

BREAK EVEN POINT (B.E.P) = 32.09 %

PLANT ECONOMICS OF
HEAT CHAMBER PAINTING

Rated Plant Capacity = 5000.00 NOS/day

LAND & BUILDING

(Total Land Required 500 Sq.Mt.) Rs. 5,00,000.00

PLANT & MACHINERY

1. High pressure jet scrubber (equipped with accessories)
2. Stainless steel storage tank
3. Conveyor system, hanger and accessories
4. Stoving heater (equipped with air and free drying general purpose system)
5. Electrostatic spraying machine

TOTAL **Rs. 4,96,000.00**

OTHER FIXED ASSETS Rs. 1,26,200.00

WORKING CAPITAL REQUIREMENT/MONTH

RAW MATERIALS

1. Alkali solution 1500 litres (NaOH/KOH)
2. Zinc phosphate 300 kg.
3. Dilute Acid rinse mixture 250 litres (Chromic acid and phosphoric acid)
4. Primer surfacer 200 kg. (Red Oxide/epoxy type)
5. Fine abrasive paper 100 kg.
6. Stoving synthetic 125 kg. (Containing nitrocellulose)
7. Sealer 125 kg.
8. Paint 1520 kg. (According to requirement)

TOTAL **Rs. 2,98,050.00**

TOTAL WORKING CAPITAL/MONTH

1.	RAW MATERIAL	Rs.	2,98,050.00
2.	SALARY & WAGES	Rs.	22,750.00
3.	UTILITIES & OVERHEADS	Rs.	20,200.00
	TOTAL	**Rs.**	**3,41,000.00**

TOTAL CAPITAL INVESTMENT

TOTAL FIXED CAPITAL	Rs.	11,22,200.00
TOTAL WORKING CAPITAL FOR 3 MONTHS	Rs.	10,23,000.00
TOTAL	**Rs.**	**21,45,200.00**

TURN OVER/ANNUM

By painting 5000 vehicles Rs. 58,75,000.00

PROFIT SALES RATIO = Profit / Sales x 100 = 19.79 %

RATE OF RETURN = Operating profit / T.C.I x 100 = 54.19 %

BREAK EVEN POINT (B.E.P) = 41.06 %

PLANT ECONOMICS OF

NAPHTHA BASED THINNER

Rated Plant Capacity = 1000.00 LITRES/day

LAND & BUILDING

(Total Land Required 500 sq. mts.) Rs. 7,40,000.00

PLANT & MACHINERY

1. ***DISTILLATION UNIT*** :
   Comprising reboiler reflux condenser for distillation or crude naphtha into (cont.)
2. Pure solvent naphtha distillation capacity 200 litres/8hr=25 litrs/hr
3. Blending vessel/mix (SS) with agitator cap. 1500 litres
4. Body boiler steam generating cap: 50 Kg/hr process control and equipment
5. Lab equipment
6. Storage tanks for crude naphtha cap: 15 MT
7. Storage tanks (M.S) CAP : 5 MT
8. Miscellaneous

TOTAL **Rs. 8,70,000.01**

OTHER FIXED ASSETS Rs. 2,35,000.00

WORKING CAPITAL REQUIREMENT/MONTH

RAW MATERIALS

1. Crude naphtha 10,000 litresre,
2. Toluene 2500 litre
3. Benzene, 5000 litre
4. White Oil, 10,000 litre
5. Packaging materials
6. 250 drum, 100 litres cap.

TOTAL **Rs. 3,85,000.00**

TOTAL WORKING CAPITAL/MONTH

1.	RAW MATERIAL	Rs.	3,85,000.00
2.	SALARY & WAGES	Rs.	61,122.00
3.	UTILITIES & OVERHEADS	Rs.	57,700.00
	TOTAL	**Rs.**	**5,03,822.00**

TOTAL CAPITAL INVESTMENT

TOTAL FIXED CAPITAL	Rs.	18,45,000.01
TOTAL WORKING CAPITAL FOR 3 MONTHS	Rs.	15,11,466.00
TOTAL	**Rs.**	**33,56,466.01**

TURN OVER/ANNUM

1. Naptha Based Thinner 300,000
2. Un-extracted Naptha Crude oil 45,000 ltr.

TOTAL **Rs. 85,50,000.00**

PROFIT SALES RATIO = Profit / Sales x 100 = 19.10 %

RATE OF RETURN = Operating profit / T.C.I x 100 = 48.16 %

BREAK EVEN POINT (B.E.P) = 46.31 %

PLANT ECONOMICS OF

N.C. THINNERS USED IN AUTO PARTS

Rated Plant Capacity = 1000.00 Ltr/day

LAND & BUILDING

(Land Area Required 500 Sq.Mts.) Rs. 3,95,000.00

PLANT & MACHINERY

1. Storage Tank
2. Mixing Vessels Cap. 500 ltr. with motor 3 H.P. & agitator
3. Ordinary filter Cap. 200 ltr./hr.
4. Filling & Packing machine
5. Weighing scale
6. Pump, motors, pipe fittings etc.
7. Miscellaneous

TOTAL **Rs. 2,26,000.00**

OTHER FIXED ASSETS Rs. 89,600.00

WORKING CAPITAL REQUIREMENT/MONTH

RAW MATERIALS

1. Nitrocellulose 1025 ltr. Grade 1/2 second
2. Butyl Acetate 425 ltr.
3. Butyl Alcohol 250 ltr.
4. Ethyl Alcohol 25 ltr.
5. Ethyl Acetate 300 ltr.
6. Benzene/Toluene 1575 ltr.
7. M.T.O. 2000 ltr.
8. Methanol 400 ltr.
9. Solvent Oils 4000 ltr.

TOTAL **Rs. 1,81,125.00**

TOTAL WORKING CAPITAL/MONTH

1.	RAW MATERIAL	Rs.	1,81,125.00
2.	SALARY & WAGES	Rs.	45,186.00
3.	UTILITIES & OVERHEADS	Rs.	9,900.00
	TOTAL	**Rs.**	**2,36,211.00**

TOTAL CAPITAL INVESTMENT

TOTAL FIXED CAPITAL	Rs.	7,10,600.00
TOTAL WORKING CAPITAL FOR 3 MONTHS	Rs.	7,08,633.00
TOTAL	**Rs.**	**14,19,233.00**

TURN OVER/ANNUM

1. 96,000 Ltr. Ordinary Thinner
2. 18000 ltr. of Medium Grade Thinner
3. 6000 ltr. of high grade Thinner

TOTAL **Rs. 43,50,000.00**

PROFIT SALES RATIO = Profit / Sales x 100 = 27.58 %

RATE OF RETURN = Operating profit / T.C.I x 100 = 84.03 %

BREAK EVEN POINT (B.E.P) = 32.52 %

PLANT ECONOMICS OF

N.C. PUTTY (CAR PUTTY)

Rated Plant Capacity = 200.00 Kgs/day

LAND & BUILDING

(Land Area Required 1000 Sq.Mts.) Rs. 8,00,000.00

PLANT & MACHINERY

1. S.S. Mixing Tank with Stirres& other accessories 3 H.P.Motor Cap. 1 cubic mt.
2. Blender for dry powders Capacity 50 Kgs/hr. with loading unloading arrangement
3. Kneader with closed chamber for mixing of pasty mass with loading & unloading arrangement Cap.50Kgs/hr.
4. Quality Control & Testing Lab. equipment
5. Semi Automatic Packaging unit consisting of weighing, filling & sealing unit for pasty mass
6. Misc. equipment
7. Pumps & Blowers
8. Safety Equipments
9. Weighing Scale - Cap.500 Kgs.

TOTAL Rs. 3,00,000.00

OTHER FIXED ASSETS Rs. 1,10,000.00

WORKING CAPITAL REQUIREMENT/MONTH

RAW MATERIALS

1. Titanuim Dioxide
2. Barytes
3. China Clay
4. Ground Asbestos fibre
5. Carbon Black
6. Phthalo Cyanine Blue
7. Coconut Alkyd

8. Nirtocellulose Cotton
9. Butyl acetate
10. Isopropyl alcohol
11. Butanol
12. Toluene
13. Pakaging material (plastic containers)

TOTAL	Rs.	2,04,288.00

TOTAL WORKING CAPITAL/MONTH

1. RAW MATERIAL	Rs.	2,04,288.00
2. SALARY & WAGES	Rs.	31,560.00
3. UTILITIES & OVERHEADS	Rs.	18,900.00
TOTAL	Rs.	2,54,748.00

TOTAL CAPITAL INVESTMENT

TOTAL FIXED CAPITAL	Rs.	12,10,000.00
TOTAL WORKING CAPITAL FOR 3 MONTHS	Rs.	7,64,244.00
TOTAL	Rs.	19,74,244.00

TURN OVER/ANNUM

60000 Kgs. of Car Putty	Rs.	42,00,000.00

PROFIT SALES RATIO = Profit / Sales x 100 = 16.78 %

RATE OF RETURN = Operating profit / T.C.I x 100 = 35.47%

BREAK EVEN POINT (B.E.P) = 49.38 %

PLANT ECONOMICS OF
OIL BOUND DISTEMPER

Rated Plant Capacity = 150 MT./Year

LAND & BUILDING

(Total Land Required 500 sq.mt)	Rs.	3,97,500.00

PLANT & MACHINERY

1. High Speed mixer complete with stirrer & 1 HP motor
2. Mixing Vessel Complete with stirrer & 0.33 HP motor
3. Mixer made of mild steel cap: 50 kg/batch complete with stirrer
4. Edge runner
5. Granite roller mill made of mild steel
6. Testing equipment (Penetormeter)
7. Miscellaneous tools and equipments etc.

TOTAL	**Rs.**	**1,34,000.00**
OTHER FIXED ASSETS	Rs.	50,000.00

WORKING CAPITAL REQUIREMENT/MONTH

RAW MATERIALS

1. Glue Flakes 166 kg.
2. Carboxy Methyl Cellulose 54 litre
3. Triethanolamine 18 kg.
4. Linseed stand oil 1014 kg.
5. Cobalt Naphthenate 44 kg.
6. Meta Cresol 9 kg.
7. Pine oil 25 kg.
8. Titanium dioxide 2125 kg.
9. Zinc oxide 350 kg.
10. Ultramarine blue 6.25 kg.

11. Barytes 3831.50 kg.
12. China Clay 2500 kg.
13. Sodium rosinate solution 187.5 kg.

TOTAL	**Rs.**	**2,67,583.00**

TOTAL WORKING CAPITAL/MONTH

1. RAW MATERIAL	Rs.	2,67,583.00
2. SALARY & WAGES	Rs.	36,625.00
3. UTILITIES & OVERHEADS	Rs.	48,500.00
TOTAL	**Rs.**	**3,52,708.00**

TOTAL CAPITAL INVESTMENT

TOTAL FIXED CAPITAL	Rs.	5,81,500.00
TOTAL WORKING CAPITAL FOR 3 MONTHS	Rs.	10,58,124.00
TOTAL	**Rs.**	**16,39,624.00**

TURN OVER/ANNUM

1. 50,000 of 1 kg. oil bound distemper paints
2. 25,000 packs of 2 kg. oil bound distemper paints
3. 10,000 packs of 5 kg. oil bound distemper paints

TOTAL	**Rs.**	**59,75,000.00**

PROFIT SALES RATIO = Profit / Sales x 100 = 22.70 %

RATE OF RETURN = Operating profit / T.C.I x 100 = 82.74 %

BREAK EVEN POINT (B.E.P) = 37.52 %

PLANT ECONOMICS OF

PAINT INDUSTRY PRIMER

Rated Plant Capacity = 3.00 Tonne/day

LAND & BUILDING

(Total Area Required 500 Sq. Mt.) Rs. 12,00,000.00

PLANT & MACHINERY

1. Edge Runer
2. Ball mill with capacity 1200 lits with 4 HP motor
3. Pulveriser
4. Mixer or Thinning tank with cap. 2 tonnes
5. Storage tank for finished product Mild steel construction complete with piping, cap. 4 ton.
6. Screening of filtration machine
7. Filling machine
8. Miscellaneous

TOTAL **Rs. 3,10,000.00**

OTHER FIXED ASSETS Rs. 1,90,000.00

WORKING CAPITAL REQUIREMENT/MONTH

RAW MATERIALS

1. Red Oxide (27 ton)
2. Zinc chromate (7.5ton)
3. Microtalc (2.25 ton)
4. Whiting (caco3) 1.125 ton
5. Cobalt Naphthenate 0.3 ton
6. Lead nephthenate 0.75 ton
7. M.T.O. 15.15 ton
8. Matie Varnish 21 ton
9. Miscellaneous

TOTAL **Rs. 9,32,125.00**

TOTAL WORKING CAPITAL/MONTH

1. RAW MATERIAL	Rs.	9,32,125.00
2. SALARY & WAGES	Rs.	37,686.00
3. UTILITIES & OVERHEADS	Rs.	77,700.00
TOTAL	**Rs.**	**10,47,511.00**

TOTAL CAPITAL INVESTMENT

TOTAL FIXED CAPITAL	Rs.	17,00,000.00
TOTAL WORKING CAPITAL FOR 3 MONTHS	Rs.	31,42,533.00
TOTAL	**Rs.**	**48,42,533.00**

TURN OVER/ANNUM

900 Ton of Red Oxide	Rs. 1,71,00,000.00

PROFIT SALES RATIO = Profit / Sales x 100 = 20.05 %

RATE OF RETURN = Operating profit / T.C.I x 100 = 71.25 %

BREAK EVEN POINT (B.E.P) = 33.54 %

PLANT ECONOMICS OF
PAINT INDUSTRY

Rated Plant Capacity = 100.00 Kgs/day

LAND & BUILDING *(Land Area Required 300 Sq.Mt)*	Rs.	2,14,000.00
PLANT & MACHINERY		
1. Grinder for grinding lime with porcelain balls, equipped with motor of 10 H.P.	Rs.	40,000.00
2. Ribbon blender		
3. Edge Runner for making dry distemper paste	Rs.	40,000.00
4. OIL DISTEMPER & ENAMEL PAINTS SEC: Edge Runner		
5. Ball Mill		
6. Mixer to adjust viscosity of paint		
7. Varnish Preparation Reactor		
8. Steel Ball Mill		
9. GENERAL EQUIPMENTS : Weighing Balances platform type		
10. Lab. Equipments		
11. ALKYD RESIN Heating eqpt with burner bhatties (either gas or fired)		
12. Stainless steel Reaction vessel fitted with thermameter, stirrer, electric motor (2 H.P.) etc.		
13. Other		
TOTAL	**Rs.**	**3,60,000.00**
OTHER FIXED ASSETS	Rs.	50,000.00

WORKING CAPITAL REQUIREMENT/MONTH

RAW MATERIALS

1. Phthalic Anhydride
2. Glycerine
3. Lineseed oil
4. Titanium dioxide
5. White antimony
7. Alkyd Resin

TOTAL	**Rs.**	**1,40,970.00**

TOTAL WORKING CAPITAL/MONTH

1. RAW MATERIAL	Rs.	1,40,970.00
2. SALARY & WAGES	Rs.	7,552.00
3. UTILITIES & OVERHEADS	Rs.	9,600.00
TOTAL	**Rs.**	**1,58,122.00**

TOTAL CAPITAL INVESTMENT

TOTAL FIXED CAPITAL	Rs.	6,24,000.00
TOTAL WORKING CAPITAL FOR 3 MONTHS	Rs.	4,74,366.00
TOTAL	**Rs.**	**10,98,366.00**

TURN OVER/ANNUM

1. 30,000 kg. Enamel Paint
2. 24000 kg. Oil Varnish

TOTAL **Rs. 25,80,000.00**

PROFIT SALES RATIO = Profit / Sales x 100 = 16.00 %

RATE OF RETURN = Operating profit / T.C.I x 100 = 37.59 %

BREAK EVEN POINT (B.E.P) = 47.13 %

PLANT ECONOMICS OF

PAINTS FOR AUTO VEHICLES

Rated Plant Capacity = 200.00 Kgs/day

LAND & BUILDING

(Land Area Required 500 Sq.Mts.)	Rs.	11,57,500.00

PLANT & MACHINERY

1. Heavy duty Pug Mixer made by Stainless
2. Solvent Storage Tanks 8 m3
3. Bal Mill 300 Kg.
4. Mixer to adjust the Viscosity of Paint
5. Stainless Steel Reactor Vessel fitted with thermometers electric motor 3 H.P.
6. Heating Equipment with Burners (either gas or oil fired)
7. Weighing Balance Platform type upto 500 kg.
8. Laboratory Eqipments
9. Other Office Equipments
10. Erection Commissioning & Transportation charges
11. Pre Operative Expenses
12. Pigment & Solvent Mixing Vessel

TOTAL	**Rs.**	**6,68,000.00**
OTHER FIXED ASSETS	Rs.	1,55,000.00

TOTAL WORKING CAPITAL/MONTH

1. RAW MATERIAL	Rs.	2,04,180.00
2. SALARY & WAGES	Rs.	10,625.00
3. UTILITIES & OVERHEADS	Rs.	97,300.00
TOTAL	**Rs.**	**3,12,105.00**

TOTAL CAPITAL INVESTMENT

TOTAL FIXED CAPITAL	Rs. 19,80,500.00
TOTAL WORKING CAPITAL FOR 3 MONTHS	Rs. 9,36,315.00
TOTAL	**Rs. 29,16,815.00**

TURN OVER/ANNUM

60,000 Kg. of Nitrocellulose Lacquer Paint	Rs. 76,80,000.00

PROFIT SALES RATIO = Profit / Sales x 100 = 39.28 %

RATE OF RETURN = Operating profit / T.C.I x 100 = 104.75 %

BREAK EVEN POINT (B.E.P) = 31.12 %

PLANT ECONOMICS OF

PUTTY AND WATER PROOFING PAINT

Rated Plant Capacity = 200.00 Kgs/day

LAND & BUILDING

(Land Area Required 1000 Sq.Mts.)	Rs.	8,00,000.00

PLANT & MACHINERY

1. S.S. Mixing Tank with Stirres& other accessories 3 H.P.Motor
2. Blender for dry powders
3. Kneader with closed chamber for mixing of pasty mass with loading & unloading arrangement
4. Quality Control & Testing Lab. equipment
5. Semi Automatic Packaging unit consisting of weighing, filling & sealing unit for pasty mass
6. Misc. equipment
7. Pumps & Blowers
8. Safety equipment
9. Weighing scale

TOTAL	**Rs.**	**3,00,000.00**
OTHER FIXED ASSETS	Rs.	90,000.00

TOTAL WORKING CAPITAL/MONTH

1. RAW MATERIAL	Rs.	0.00
2. SALARY & WAGES	Rs.	3,000.00
3. UTILITIES & OVERHEADS	Rs.	6,400.00
TOTAL	**Rs.**	**9,400.00**

TOTAL CAPITAL INVESTMENT

TOTAL FIXED CAPITAL	Rs. 11,90,000.00
TOTAL WORKING CAPITAL FOR 3 MONTHS	Rs. 28,200.00
TOTAL	**Rs. 12,18,200.00**

TURN OVER/ANNUM

60000 Kgs. of Putty	Rs. 45,00,000.00

PROFIT SALES RATIO = Profit / Sales x 100 = 88.42 %

RATE OF RETURN = Operating profit / T.C.I x 100 = 328.45 %

BREAK EVEN POINT (B.E.P) = 9.66 %

PLANT ECONOMICS OF

PAINT BRUSHES

Rated Plant Capacity = 78000 Dozen Brushes PER ANNUM

LAND & BUILDING

(Land Required 250 Sq. Mt.) Rs. 2,48,750.00

PLANT & MACHINERY

1. Circular Saw 10" dia with 1 H.P Electrical motor with electricals
2. Disc sander 12" dia
3. Multi cut bobbing wood working lathe (length of bed 3" and height of centre 41/2" dia)
4. Polishing and buffing machine with 1/2 H.P motor
5. Electric drying oven (air circulated chamber size 3'x 3' with shelf, temp. upto 1500°C
6. Hand press No.5
7. Ferrule folding and crimping Toggle press, capacity 2 ton
8. Dipping tank, hand tools, strictizer, weighing scale etc.
9. Electrification expenses
10. Erection commissioning installation etc.

TOTAL **1,45,000.00**

WORKING CAPITAL REQUIREMENT/MONTH

RAW MATERIALS

1. Bristles 800 kg.
2. Timber
3. PC.R.C. Sheets (22-24 s.w.g)
4. Polish for wooden handles and rubber vulcanising solutions
5. Nails etc.

TOTAL **2,84,000.00**

TOTAL WORKING CAPITAL/MONTH

1. RAW MATERIAL	Rs.	2,84,000.00
2. SALARY & WAGES	Rs.	50,687.50
3. UTILITIES & OVERHEADS	Rs.	16,000.00
TOTAL	**Rs.**	**3,50,687.50**

TOTAL CAPITAL INVESTMENT

TOTAL FIXED CAPITAL	Rs.	3,93,750.00
TOTAL WORKING CAPITAL FOR 3 MONTHS	Rs.	10,52,062.50
TOTAL	**Rs.**	**14,45,812.50**

TURN OVER/ANNUM

9,36,000 No. Paint Brushes	Rs.	65,52,000.00

PROFIT SALES RATIO = Profit / Sales x 100 = 30.05 %

RATE OF RETURN = Operating profit / T.C.I x 100 = 136.31 %

BREAK EVEN POINT (B.E.P) = 25.22 %

PLANT ECONOMICS OF
PAINT DRIERS

Rated Plant Capacity = 1000.00 KG/day

LAND & BUILDING

(Total Land Required 1500 sq.mts.) Rs. 26,02,000.00

PLANT & MACHINERY

1. (A) COBALT OCTOATE SECTION
   Reactor M.S F.R.P lining
2. Storage Tanks
3. Evaporator
4. Luotrumentation & Process Control Eqpt.
5. Miscellaneous *viz;* Pipe Fitting Pumps etc
6. (B) METAL(COBALT) NAPHTHENATE SECTION
   Diss Tank Equipment with Steam oil agitator
7. Plate & Frame Filter Press size 36"x 36" plate & having 28 plates
8. Iron Removal Tank
9. Cobalt Sulphate Solution Storage Tank
10. Soda Soap Kettle Equipped with agitator & other accessories
11. Precipitation Kettle equipped with Pumps & oil burner from from beneath
12. Cutting Tank equipped with mixing Tea, Circulating pump
13. Blending Tank Equipped with mixing adductor and circulating pump.
14. Product Storage Tank
15. Baby Boiler Steam generating
16. Calcium Sulphate Solution Tank
17. Pipes, fittings, pumps etc.
18. D.G. SET 100 KVA
19. LAB Equipments
20. Other miscellaneous

TOTAL **Rs. 30,80,000.00**

OTHER FIXED ASSETS	Rs.	8,00,000.00

WORKING CAPITAL REQUIREMENT/MONTH

RAW MATERIALS

1. (A) COBALT OCTOATE SECTION
   2-ethyl hexoic acid
2. Cobalt Hydroxide
3. White Spirit / Butyl alcohol
4. (B) METAL (COBALT) NAPHTHENATES
   Cobalt Hydroxide
5. Sulphuric Acid
6. Caustic Soda
7. Naphthenic Acid
8. Mineral Spirit Solvent
9. Other Chemicals
10. 5 kg packs

TOTAL	**Rs.**	**19,55,061.00**

TOTAL WORKING CAPITAL/MONTH

1.	RAW MATERIAL	Rs.	19,55,061.00
2.	SALARY & WAGES	Rs	96,250.00
3.	UTILITIES & OVERHEADS	Rs.	95,400.00
	TOTAL	**Rs.**	**21,46,711.00**

TOTAL CAPITAL INVESTMENT

TOTAL FIXED CAPITAL	Rs.	64,82,000.00
TOTAL WORKING CAPITAL FOR 3 MONTHS	Rs.	64,40,133.00
TOTAL	**Rs.**	**1,29,22,133.00**

TURN OVER/ANNUM

1. Cobalt Octoate 1,50,000 kgs
2. Cobalt Naphthenate 1,50,000 kgs

TOTAL **Rs. 3,45,00,000.00**

PROFIT SALES RATIO = Profit / Sales x 100 = 15.50 %

RATE OF RETURN = Operating profit / T.C.I x 100 = 41.22 %

BREAK EVEN POINT (B.E.P) = 44.16 %

PLANT ECONOMICS OF

PUTTY (METAL CASEMENT PUTTY) (ASIAN PAINTS TYPE)

Rated Plant Capacity = 200.00 KGS/day

LAND & BUILDING

(Total Area Required 700 Sq. mts) Rs. 7,00,000.00

PLANT & MACHINERY

1. Pug mill (Horizontal) (Alloy steel barrel & screw) fitted with screw conveyor for discharge of pasty mas
2. Mixing Tank (Rotating type) made of stainless steel and fitted with 2 H.P. motor cap: 50 kgs
3. Grinder/Pulverizer (for grinding of calcium carbonate) Cap: 35 kg/hr. along with vibrating screens
4. Centrifuge chemical type for separation of linseed oil from impurities after acid/alkali refining
5. Semi Automatic filling machine
6. Acid Treatmet Tank (MS(epoxy lined) fitted with agitator and motor 1H.P Cap: 0.5 MT
7. Sulphuric acid storage tank (M.S. epoxy lined) cap: 2 MT
8. Caustic lye storage tank (M.S. Epoxy lined) Cap: 2 MT
9. Baby boiler Cap. 100 kg/hr. steam generating capacity
10. Instruments & process controls, & Lab. Testing equipment
11. Pipes, fittings, pumps valves & other miscellaneous equipments

TOTAL Rs. 5,18,000.00

OTHER FIXED ASSETS	Rs.	1,60,000.00

WORKING CAPITAL REQUIREMENT/MONTH

RAW MATERIALS

1. Calcium carbonate
2. White Lead (lead caronate)
3. Talc
4. Soyabean oil
5. Linseed oil
6. Soya fatty acids
7. Mineral Spirits
8. Sulphuric acid
9. Caustic Soda
10. Packaging material for packing metallic containers

TOTAL	**Rs.**	**65,500.00**

TOTAL WORKING CAPITAL/MONTH

1. RAW MATERIAL	Rs.	65,500.00
2. SALARY & WAGES	Rs.	28,200.00
3. UTILITIES & OVERHEADS	Rs.	37,500.00
TOTAL	**Rs.**	**1,31,200.00**

TOTAL CAPITAL INVESTMENT

TOTAL FIXED CAPITAL	Rs.	13,78,000.00
TOTAL WORKING CAPITAL FOR 3 MONTHS	Rs.	3,93,600.00
TOTAL	**Rs.**	**17,71,600.00**

TURN OVER/ANNUM

60,000 Kgs. Metal Casement Putty Rs. 26,40,000.00

PROFIT SALES RATIO = Profit / Sales x 100 = 22.82 %

RATE OF RETURN = Operating profit / T.C.I x 100 = 34.00 %

BREAK EVEN POINT (B.E.P) = 56.31 %

PLANT ECONOMICS OF
PAINT REMOVERS

Rated Plant Capacity = 2000.00 LIT/day

LAND & BUILDING

(Land Required 500 Sq. Mts.)	Rs. 4,85,000.00

PLANT & MACHINERY

1. Storage tank for solvent.
2. Storage tank for co-solvent.
3. Storage tank for activator.
4. Corrosion inhibitors storage tank.
5. Storage tank for thickener.
6. Weighing balance.
7. Volume measuring device.
8. Mixing tank.
9. Laboratory equipments.
10. Miscellaneous & others.

TOTAL	**Rs. 4,20,000.00**
OTHER FIXED ASSETS	Rs. 1,55,000.00

WORKING CAPITAL REQUIREMENT/MONTH

RAW MATERIALS

1. Methyl ethyl ketone (co-solvent)
2. Toluene 1500 kg.
3. Methanol 3500 kg.
4. Wax 1500 kg.
5. Methyl Cellulose 1500 kg.
6. Activators 250 kg.
7. Corrosion inhibitor 250 kg.
8. Wetting agents 1500 kg.
9. Methylene chloride 37,500 kg.

TOTAL	**Rs. 18,97,500.00**

TOTAL WORKING CAPITAL/MONTH

1. RAW MATERIAL	Rs.	18,97,500.00
2. SALARY & WAGES	Rs.	27,694.00
3. UTILITIES & OVERHEADS	Rs.	1,32,200.00
TOTAL	**Rs.**	**20,57,394.00**

TOTAL CAPITAL INVESTMENT

TOTAL FIXED CAPITAL	Rs.	10,60,000.00
TOTAL WORKING CAPITAL FOR 3 MONTHS	Rs.	61,72,182.00
TOTAL	**Rs.**	**72,32,182.00**

TURN OVER/ANNUM

6,00,000 litre of Paint Remover Rs. 3,30,00,000.00

PROFIT SALES RATIO = Profit / Sales x 100 = 19.06 %

RATE OF RETURN = Operating profit / T.C.I x 100 = 88.12 %

BREAK EVEN POINT (B.E.P) = 29.55 %

PLANT ECONOMICS OF

POWDER SPRAY PAINTING WORKSHOP

Rated Plant Capacity* = *20,000 SQ.MTS.
SPRAY PAINTING
ON FERROUS AND
NON FERROUS
SURFACE PER ANNUM

LAND & BUILDING

(Total Land Required 300 Sq. Mts) Rs. 5,40,000.00

PLANT & MACHINERY

1. Spray Painting Compresses (Complete with compressor, motor, etc.)
2. Spray Gun with Complete Accessories
3. Stove Ovens (5' x 4' x 4')
4. Operating Tables (Steel)
5. Fluidizing Hoppers
6. Over Spray Collection Hopper
7. Screen Board for Painting Booths
8. Quartz envelope infra-red lamp for heating & drying
9. Sander, Compressed air driven checker coating thickness
10. Room heating equipment
11. Hand Tools
12. Miscellaneous

TOTAL **Rs. 1,54,500.00**

OTHER FIXED ASSETS Rs. 45,000.00

WORKING CAPITAL REQUIREMENT/MONTH

RAW MATERIALS

1. Coating Powder of different colours 250 Kgs.
2. Miscellaneous like soap & other cleaning materials, paint remover etc.

TOTAL	**Rs.**	**42,500.00**

TOTAL WORKING CAPITAL/MONTH

1. RAW MATERIAL	Rs.	42,500.00
2. SALARY & WAGES	Rs.	42,561.00
3. UTILITIES & OVERHEADS	Rs.	23,600.00
TOTAL	**Rs.**	**1,08,661.00**

TOTAL CAPITAL INVESTMENT

TOTAL FIXED CAPITAL	Rs.	7,39,500.00
TOTAL WORKING CAPITAL FOR 3 MONTHS	Rs.	3,25,983.00
TOTAL	**Rs.**	**10,65,483.00**

TURN OVER/ANNUM

Powder spray painting on ferrous & non-ferrous metals 20,000 sq.mts.	Rs.	18,00,000.00

PROFIT SALES RATIO = Profit / Sales x 100 = 14.57 %

RATE OF RETURN = Operating profit / T.C.I x 100 = 24.83 %

BREAK EVEN POINT (B.E.P) = 67.23 %

PLANT ECONOMICS OF STOVING PAINTS

Rated Plant Capacity = 1.00 Ton/day

LAND & BUILDING

(Land Required 750 Sq. Mts.) Rs. 18,00,000.00

PLANT & MACHINERY

1. Weighing Balance Electronic platform type
2. Small Weighing Balance
3. Ball Mill (M.S.body,S.S.lined) with steel balls
4. Strainer (S.S. make)
5. Stainless steel storage drums
6. Laboratory testing equipments
7. Pipes, pumps, tanks, structures, tools, jigs, fixtures etc.

TOTAL **Rs. 15,81,000.00**

OTHER FIXED ASSETS Rs. 6,05,000.00

WORKING CAPITAL REQUIREMENT/MONTH

RAW MATERIALS

1. FOR BLACK STOVING PAINT:- Linseed Alkyd Resin
2. Urea Formaldehyde Resin
3. Carbon Black
4. Xylene
5. Zinc Naphthenate (8% metal)
6. Cobalt Naphthenate (6% Cobalt)
7. n-Butanol
8. FOR WHITE STOVING PAINT:- Titanium Dioxide (Anatase)
9. Castor Alkyd Resin
10. Urea-formaldehyde Resin
11. Xylene
12. n-Butanol
13. Packaging container (M.S.Tin)

TOTAL **Rs. 13,96,905.00**

TOTAL WORKING CAPITAL/MONTH

1. RAW MATERIAL	Rs.	13,96,905.00
2. SALARY & WAGES	Rs.	66,750.00
3. UTILITIES & OVERHEADS	Rs.	1,60,500.00
TOTAL	**Rs.**	**16,24,155.00**

TOTAL CAPITAL INVESTMENT

TOTAL FIXED CAPITAL	Rs.	39,86,000.00
TOTAL WORKING CAPITAL FOR 3 MONTHS	Rs.	48,72,465.00
TOTAL	**Rs.**	**88,58,465.00**

TURN OVER/ANNUM

1. Black Stoving Paint (For Bicycle) 150 MT,
2. White Stoving Paint (For refrigerator) 150 MT

TOTAL **Rs. 2,55,00,000.00**

PROFIT SALES RATIO = Profit / Sales x 100 = 15.02 %

RATE OF RETURN = Operating profit / T.C.I x 100 = 43.24 %

BREAK EVEN POINT (B.E.P) = 46.06 %

PLANT ECONOMICS OF
THINNERS

Rated Plant Capacity = 1000.00 LTR/day

Based on below formulation :
(1) Toluene - 10 %
(2) Benzene - 20 %
(3) Solvent Naptha - 30 %
(4) White Oil - 40 %

LAND & BUILDING

(Land Area Required 1000 Sq. Mt.) Rs. 8,25,000.00

PLANT & MACHINERY

1. Raw materials storage Tanks. Cap: 5000 Nos.
2. Mixing Vessels & stirrers
3. Ordinary filter
4. Filling & Packing
5. Miscellaneous

TOTAL Rs. 5,05,000.00

OTHER FIXED ASSETS Rs. 90,000.00

WORKING CAPITAL REQUIREMENT/MONTH

RAW MATERIALS

1. Toluene 2500 litres
2. Benzene 5000 litres
3. Solvent naphtha 7500 litre
4. Special Denatured Spirit 10,000 litre (White Oil)

TOTAL Rs. 2,17,500.00

TOTAL WORKING CAPITAL/MONTH

1. RAW MATERIAL	Rs.	2,17,500.00
2. SALARY & WAGES	Rs.	29,280.00
3. UTILITIES & OVERHEADS	Rs.	24,500.00
TOTAL	**Rs.**	**2,71,280.00**

TOTAL CAPITAL INVESTMENT

TOTAL FIXED CAPITAL	Rs.	14,20,000.00
TOTAL WORKING CAPITAL FOR 3 MONTHS	Rs.	8,13,840.00
TOTAL	**Rs.**	**22,33,840.00**

TURN OVER/ANNUM

3,00,000 litres of Thinners	Rs.	42,00,000.00

PROFIT SALES RATIO = Profit / Sales x 100 = 10.52 %

RATE OF RETURN = Operating profit / T.C.I x 100 = 19.77 %

BREAK EVEN POINT (B.E.P) = 64.23 %

PLANT ECONOMICS OF
VARNISH AND PAINTS INDUSTRY

Rated Plant Capacity = 500.00 KGS/day

LAND & BUILDING

(Total Area Required 400 Sq.Mts.) Rs. 9,05,000.00

PLANT & MACHINERY

1. Cooking Kettle, filted with stirrer Capacity 500 kgs.
2. Running Kettle with stirrer, capacity 500 kg.
3. Filter press, wooden
4. Aging tanks
5. Instrumentation
6. Pipe fittings & valves etc
7. Storage tanks
8. Lab. Testing equipment
9. Depolluting equipment
10. Miscellaneous

TOTAL **Rs. 2,83,000.00**

OTHER FIXED ASSETS Rs. 1,05,000.00

WORKING CAPITAL REQUIREMENT/MONTH

RAW MATERIALS

1. Oleoresins 1750 kgs.
2. Turpenture oil 7700 litres
3. Linseed oil 3850 liters
4. Other chemicals 40 kgs.

TOTAL **Rs. 1,71,700.00**

TOTAL WORKING CAPITAL/MONTH

1. RAW MATERIAL	Rs.	1,71,700.00
2. SALARY & WAGES	Rs.	43,625.00
3. UTILITIES & OVERHEADS	Rs.	67,200.00
TOTAL	**Rs.**	**2,82,525.00**

TOTAL CAPITAL INVESTMENT

TOTAL FIXED CAPITAL	Rs.	12,93,000.00
TOTAL WORKING CAPITAL FOR 3 MONTHS	Rs.	8,47,575.00
TOTAL	**Rs.**	**21,40,575.00**

TURN OVER/ANNUM

1. 75000 Tin of 1 kg. each of paints
2. 75000 Tins of 1 kg. each of varnishes

TOTAL **Rs. 52,50,000.00**

PROFIT SALES RATIO = Profit / Sales x 100 = 24.59 %

RATE OF RETURN = Operating profit / T.C.I x 100 = 60.62 %

BREAK EVEN POINT (B.E.P) = 46.18 %

PLANT ECONOMICS OF

WIRE ENAMELS (POLY VINYL BUTYRAL BASED)

Rated Plant Capacity = 100.00 KGS/day

LAND & BUILDING

(Land Area Required, 500 Sq. Mts.)	Rs.	7,00,000.00

PLANT & MACHINERY

1. Reaction vessel, steam jacketed (S.S) with conical bottom with agitator & motor. Cap: 200 Kgs
2. Boiler, 100 Kgs/hr. vertical type, oil fired.
3. Storage tanks (M.S) Cap: 500 Kgs.
4. Filling & packing machine
5. Miscellaneous, *viz*. pipe, valve, pumps, weighing machinery etc.

TOTAL	**Rs.**	**5,60,000.00**
OTHER FIXED ASSETS	Rs.	1,40,000.00

WORKING CAPITAL REQUIREMENT/MONTH

RAW MATERIALS

1. Poly Vinyl Butyral Resin, 416.5 Kg.
2. Cresol-formaldehyde resin, 208.5 Kg
3. Cresylic acid, 625 Kgs.
4. High-flash Naphtha, 1250 kgs.
5. Packaging Material

TOTAL	**Rs.**	**1,31,037.50**

TOTAL WORKING CAPITAL/MONTH

1. RAW MATERIAL	Rs.	1,31,037.50
2. SALARY & WAGES	Rs.	35,400.00
3. UTILITIES & OVERHEADS	Rs.	26,840.00
TOTAL	**Rs.**	**1,93,277.50**

TOTAL CAPITAL INVESTMENT

TOTAL FIXED CAPITAL	Rs.	14,00,000.00
TOTAL WORKING CAPITAL FOR 3 MONTHS	Rs.	5,79,832.50
TOTAL	**Rs.**	**19,79,832.50**

TURN OVER/ANNUM

30,000 kgs. Enamel (Poly Vinyl Butyral based)	Rs.	36,00,000.00

PROFIT SALES RATIO = Profit / Sales x 100 = 21.05 %

RATE OF RETURN = Operating Profit / T.C.I. x 100 = 38.28 %

BREAK EVEN POINT (B.E.P) = 52.48 %

PLANT ECONOMICS OF
WOOD PRIMER FOR PAINTS

Rated Plant Capacity = 500.00 Kg/day

LAND & BUILDING

(Total Land Area 100 Sq. Mts.) Rs. 12,00,500.00

PLANT & MACHINERY

1. Mixing Tank M.S. Cap. 1000 Kg.
2. Tripple Roll Mill
3. Blending Tank
4. Storage Tank
5. Diesel Generator Set (25 KVA)
6. Laboratory Equipments
7. Instrumentation & Process Control Equipments
8. Miscellaneous Equipments

TOTAL **Rs. 9,10,000.00**

OTHER FIXED ASSETS Rs. 3,70,000.00

WORKING CAPITAL REQUIREMENT/MONTH

RAW MATERIALS

1. Non-Leafing Aluminium Paste
2. Solvent Naphtha 1000 Kgs.
3. Medium (60% Solids) [Alkyd Resin in Turfoil + Phenolic Resin]
4. Cobalt Naphthenate (6%) 25 Kgs.
5. Pigment
6. For Packaging 6250 Kgs. Tin Packs (1/2 by cobalts required 12,500 Nos
7. For Packaging 6250 Kgs. Tin Packs (1 Kg Cobalt required 6250 Nos.)

TOTAL **Rs. 7,02,250.00**

TOTAL WORKING CAPITAL/MONTH

1.	RAW MATERIAL	Rs.	7,02,250.00
2.	SALARY & WAGES	Rs.	76,875.00
3.	UTILITIES & OVERHEADS	Rs.	42,250.00
	TOTAL	**Rs.**	**8,21,375.00**

TOTAL CAPITAL INVESTMENT

TOTAL FIXED CAPITAL	Rs.	24,80,500.00
TOTAL WORKING CAPITAL FOR 3 MONTHS	Rs.	24,64,125.00
TOTAL	**Rs.**	**49,44,625.00**

TURN OVER/ANNUM

Wood Primer 150 MT.	Rs. 1,27,50,000.00

PROFIT SALES RATIO = Profit / Sales x 100 = 11.59 %

RATE OF RETURN = Operating profit / T.C.I x 100 = 30.22 %

BREAK EVEN POINT (B.E.P) = 56.36 %

19

SUPPLIERS OF PLANT, EQUIPMENTS & MACHINERIES

* Paint Machineries
* Pigment Machineries
* Varnish Machineries
* Lacquer Machineries
* Packaging Machineries
* Testing Instruments
* Powder Coating Equipments

1. **Advanced Packaging Industries**
1-33, Indira Nagar, Meerpet,
Moula Ali Housing Board,
Near Community Hall,
Hyderabad - 500 040 (A.P)
Tel : 7123128
Fax : 040-7120892
(Automatic Pouch Packing Machines to Pack Paints Etc.)

2. **Anu Rasayan Udhyog**
184, DSIDC Sheds,
Okhla Industrial Area -I,
New Delhi - 110 020
Tel : 6813624
(Chemical Plants & Eqpts.)

3. **Bhuvaneshwari Co. Ltd.**
13, Old Trunk Road,
Chennai - 43 (Tamil Nadu)
Tel : 401767/401716
(Sigma Mixers, Powder & Mass Mixers, Double Cone Blenders, Ribbon Blenders, Dryers,Pulverizers,Colloid Mills, Liquid Filling Machine, Powder Filling Machine Etc.)

4. **Chemach Engineering Works**
30, DSIDC Scheme-III,
Okhla Industrial Area-II,
New Delhi - 110 020
Tel : 6838943
(Chemical Plants)

5. **Chitra Engineers**
23, Narnmada Estate,
NH No.8, Odhav,
Ahmedabad
(Gujarat) - 382415
Tel : 2876516
(Mixer, Drier, Granulater etc.)

6. **Classic Scientific Works**
Rz-1B/1, Gali No.3,
Main Sagarpur, Palam Road,
New Delhi - 110 046
Tel : 5505423
(Powder Coating Booths, Industrial Oven etc.)

7. **D. Nath & Company**
WZ-845, Rishi Nagar Lane,
Rani Bagh, Shakur Basti ,
New Delhi
Tel : 7028828,7017947
(Electroplating Plants, Suspenders (Jigs), Titanium Coil & Basket, Industrial Heaters, Heater use Porcelain Goods, Oven furnace)

8. **Dhopeshwar Chem-tech Group**
A-16, Co-op. Industrial
Estate, Bala Nagar,
Hyderabad - 37 (A.P)
Tel : 040-270267, 271579
Fax : 040-291492
(Complete Plants on Turnkey for S.S.I : Blenders, Tanks, Vessels etc.)

9. **D.S Panchal Engg. & Welding Works**
1017/342, Gali No.4,
Anand Parbat Indl. Area,
New Delhi - 110 005
Tel : 5715549,5745549
(Complete Electroplating Plant, Transformer plain Tanks, Caustic, Polish & Plating Barrel, Mechanical rotary switch 1PH & 3 PH, Rubber, PVC & Lead Lining)

10. **Dayline Spray Systems**
Private Limited
C-176/2,

Okhla Industrial Area -I,
New Delhi - 110 020
Tel : 6811694
(Powder Coating Plants & Powder Coatings)

11. **Dry Conn Engg. Pvt. Ltd.**
B-4, Sidco Industrial Estate,
Chennai - 600 049 (T.N)
Tel : 626 2989
(Manufacturers of Chemical Pharamaceutical & Food Processing Equipmenmts Like Reactors, Blender, Heat Exchanger, Kettles, Sterlizer, Ball Mill, Planetary Mixer & Industrial Driers, Ovens, Made out of MS & SS, FRP & Rubber & Lead Linning Also Undertaken)

12. **Esco Powder Products**
C-63/3, Okhla Indl. Area - II,
New Delhi - 110 020
Tel : 6849157, 6827263/
011-6849157, 6827263
(Powder Coating Equipments)

13. **Ferricon Engineers Pvt. Ltd.**
4/16, Kamaruddin Nagar,
Nangloi, New Delhi - 110 041
Tel : 5476760
(Fabrication of Chemical Paints Equipments)

14. **Flowink Industries (P) Ltd.**
D-15, Commercial Complex,
Prashant Vihar,
New Delhi- 110 085
Tel/Fax : 7267006/07/
011-7267007
(Process Reactors, Auto Claves, Distillation Units, Fractionating Columns etc.)

15. **Ferro Tech Engineers**
P.O.Box 7078,
Pratap Bhawan,
Ground Floor, 5,
Bahadur Shah Zafar Marg,
New Delhi - 110 002
Tel : 3313670, 3351830,
3351848, 8-302394
Fax : 3739855, 3324082
(Dough Sigma Mixers, Wet Mixers, Kneaders, Sand Mills, Attritora, Bead Mills, Pug Mixers, Shrouded Ball, Rotary Valves, Ribbon Blenders, Ball Mills, Tripple Roll Mill, Planetary Mixer, Reaction Kettles, Resin Kettles, Glue Kettles, Sand Mullers, Edge Runner, laddles, Drying Ovens, Vulcanizers, Auto claves, Sterilizers.)

16. **Frigmaires Engineers**
P.O.Box No. 16353,
Janta Industrial Estate,
Lower Parel,
Mumbai - 13
Tel : 4941694
Fax : 2186046
(Tripple Roll Mill, Sigma Mixer, Sand Mill, Pulveriser, Ball Mill)

17. **Gallys Engineering Company**
140/1, Benaras Road,
Salkia, Howrah - 711106
(West Bengal)
Tel : 6658762
(Filter Press)

18. **GMA Enterprises**
B-122, Patparganj Village,
New Delhi - 110 091
Tel/Fax : 2716737
011 - 2258799
(Plating, Anodizing Plants,

Chemical Pumps, Indl. Ovens, Powder Coating Plants, Sand Blasting)

20. **Hi-Tech Engg. Works**
98-A, Tehkhand, Okhla Industrial Area - I,
New Delhi - 110 020
Tel/Fax : 6818150
(Continuous Galvanising Plants, Sitting Lines, Pickling & Annealing Plants etc.)

21. **Instrumentation & Engineering Enterprises**
B/H, ITI, Mehrauli Road,
Faridabad (Haryana)
Tel : 8-322346
(Steel Fabrication of Special Type Chemicals)

22. **JetPac Sadguru Sai Packaging Industries**
MIG-35, Apllc Colony,
Kamla Nagar
Hyderabad - 62 (A.P.)
Tel : 7127194
Fax : 040-7120892
Internet : http : www. metroindia.com/jetpac
(Automatic Form Fill & Seal Machines used for Pouch Packing of Paints & allied Products)

23. **Kasish Spray Systems**
330, Jawahar Colony,
Faridabad (Haryana)
Tel : 234586
(Powder Coating Plants)

24. **Kelleys Engg. Works**
24-B/6, Industrial Area,
Faridabad -121 001
Tel/Fax : 233251, 233261/ 0129-241912,233251
(Industrial Washing Machines, Pickling Phosphating Plant, Paint Booth & Oven, Inds. Blower)

25. **Kovai Finishing Systems Private Limited**
79 A, Taskant Nagar,
Coimbatore - 641014
Tel : 827088
Fax : 827088
(Spray Guns, Ovens & Paint Booths)

26. **Kinetics Technology India Limited**
B-22, Okhla Indl. Area - I,
New Delhi - 110 020
Tel : 6813262
(Tailor made process equipments for Chemical, Fertilizer, Pharmaceuticals)

27. Khushboo Scientific Pvt. Ltd.
132, Princess Street,
Govind Building,
Mumbai - 400002
Tel : 2081346, 2052822, 2067618
Fax : 91-22-2081023
(Specilists in Paint Testing Instruments : Digital Salt Spray Corrosion Cabinet, Paint Corrosion Cabinet, Digital Coating Thickness Gauge, Wire Bar Coater, Digital Gloss Meter, Autom atic Scratch Hardness tester,Flowcup Viscometer, Falling Block Impact Tester, Hegman Gauge, Film applicators, Electronic Balance, Brookfield Viscometer.)

28. **Machino Medicina Pvt. Ltd.**
WZ-12, Phool Bagh,
Ram Pura Morh,
New Delhi - 110 035
Tel : 5447399
(Liquid Filling & Sealing machines)

29. **M.D.Engineering Company**
117, M.I.E., Bahadurgarh,
Haryana - 124507
Tel : 91-311431
Fax : 91-314546
(Manufacturers of Reactors, Heat Exchanger, Blender Mixer, Autoclave, Chimney etc.)

30. **Marvel Engineers**
140, Anna Salai,
Chennai -15 (Tamil Nadu)
Tel : 2352863
(S.S.Vessels, Tanks, Mixers, Blenders etc.)

31. **Master Mach Industries**
D-25, Sahibabad,
Ghaziabad (U.P)
Tel : 771654
(Fabrication of Paint & Chemical Plant)

32. **Mathesis Chem Project Engineers Pvt. Ltd.**
7-1-50/C, F-4, Pleasant Apartment, AmeerPet,
Hyderabad - 500016 (A.P.)
Tel : 040-290134
Fax : 040-293 647
(Dryers & Other Paint Equipments)

33. **Membrane India**
347, Udyog Vihar, Phase - II,
Gurgaon (Haryana)
Tel : 341159, 342765/ 0124-342714
(Chemical Process equipment, Pressure vessels, Heat Exchanger, shell & tube, plate welding, gasketed types)

34. **Mills & Metals Corporation**
3621-22 Chawri Bazar,
Near P.T.College,
New Delhi - 110 006
Tel : 2927940
Fax : 2510364
(Sieves, Screens, Filters)

35. **Murzello Metal Finish Systems Pvt. Ltd.**
Raji Commercial Complex,
Lokhande Marg,
Chembur, Mumbai - 89
Tel : 5280682
(Manufacturers of Shot Blasting, peening Equipments, Airless Spray/ Powder Coating Equipment)

36. **Narang Scientific Works**
C-255, Mayapuri Industrial Area-II, New Delhi - 110 064
Tel : 540 2609
Fax : 5492491
(Trade Dryers, Drying Oven Etc.)

37. **Navyug Industries**
C-11/1, Mansarover Garden,
New Delhi - 110 015
Tel : 5432689
(Phosphating & electroplating Plants, Chemical Process & Storage Tanks & acid proof lining)

38. **Pisces Instruments**
Precision Plaza, 281,
Mount Road,
Chennai - 18 (T.N.)

Tel : 458834/458842
Works : 492 5274
Fax : 91-44-456223
(Tray Dryer, Autoclaves, Kettles Etc.)

39. **Plasto Pack Machiniries (India) Pvt. Ltd.**
B-15, Mugappair Industrial Estate (West),
Chennai - 58 (Tamil Nadu)
Tel : 044-656283, 6357736/ 044-6357249, 6253578
Tel/Fax : 044-655203, 6268666
(Automatic Form Fill Seal Machine to Pack Paints & Allied Products)

40. **Premier Engineering Works**
B-136, Phase -I,
Okhla Indl. Area,
New Delhi - 110 020
Tel : 6818210
(Mixer, Tripple Roll Mill, Filling Machine, Stirrers, Drying Oven, Storage Tanks, Ball Mills, Blender, Granulator etc.

41. **Process Equipment & Components**
82 A, Ibrahim Pure Road,
Jadav Pur, Calcutta - 110 032
Tel : 4123048, 4126209
Fax : 4126209
(Drier, Blender & General Fabricator of Chemical & Paint Equipment)

42. **Process Manufacturing Private Limited**
25/1, Jogindre Basak Road,
Calcutta - 26
Tel : 5571385
(Pressure Vessels & General Fabricators of Paint Equipment)

43. **Process Equipments**
F-11, Kavi Nagar,
Industrial Area,
Ghaziabad - 201 202 (U.P)
Tel/Fax : 702083, 702012/ 0575-702012
(FRP Storage tanks, PP/ FRP Reaction Vessels, Pickling Plants for M.S. & S.S., Effluent Pollution Control System, CPW/HCL Plants Chemical Plants.)

44. **Pugazh Industries**
L-36, Industrial Estate,
Chennai -58 (T.N.)
Tel : 652604
(Reaction Kettle, Filtration Equipment, Drying System & Custom Built Paint, Resin & Chemicals Plants Equipments)

45. **Quality Steel Fab (India)**
5A/131A, N.I.T,
Faridabad - 121 001
Tel : 91-216707
(Reaction Vessels, Heat Exchangers & Chem Process Equipment Mfrs. in M.S/S.S)

46. **Raja Industries**
C-210, Mayapuri Industrial Area, Phase - 2,
New Delhi - 110 064
Tel : 5400521
(D.O.P, Polyester Resin, Calcium Carbonate, Cement Plant, Furnace Equipment)

47. **Raj Shree Machinery Manufacturers Pvt. Ltd.**
106, Sidco Industrial Estate,
Chennai - 98 (T.N.)

Tel : 6250894/6260929
(Design, Manufacturer of Equipments, Like Reactors, Heat Exchangers, Pressure Vessels, Agitator, Distillation Column etc.)

48. **Ruby Auto & Rubber Industries**
B-241,
Naraina Inustrial Area - I
New Delhi - 110 028
Tel : 5792331
(Pressure Vessels, Filters, Softeners, Chlorinated Conveyors, rollers & special Fabricators)

49. **S.K.Engineering Company**
C-7/5, Bulandsahar Road, Industrial Area, Ghaziabad
Tel : 711111
(Chemical plant equipments & tank)

50. **Sefa Engineering Company**
D-162, Okhla Industrial Area, Phase - I, New Delhi - 20.
Tel : 6811883, 6811974
(Chemical Plants)

51. **Sheca Engineers**
D-7, Site - 4, Sahibabad, Ghaziabad (U.P)
Tel : 771764
(Chemical Tanks)

52. **Shivas Project India Private Limited**
C-71/7, Bulandsahar Road, Ghaziabad U.P)
Tel : 723146
(Chemical Processing Equipments)

53. **Shiv Shakti Engineering Works**
Opposite Azad Weigh Bridge, NH No.8,
Vapi - 396191 (Gujarat)
Tel : 31254/31652
(Manufacturer of polypropylene, Wooden & Cast Iron filter Press)

54. **Singhson Engineers**
B-8/1, Mayapuri Indl. Area, Phase - I, New Delhi - 64
Tel : 5142772, 5402526
(Chemical Plants, Storage tanks, Electric Poles, Heat exchangers, Thermal coils, & steel furniture)

55. **S.S.P. Private Limited**
13/4, Mathura Road,
19-DLF,
Faridabad - 3 (Haryana)
Tel/Fax : 277730, 275441, 0129-277441
(Vessels & Dairy Equipments, Food & Chemicals)

56. **Smid Engineering Co.**
25-A, Rama Park Bus Stop, Uttam Nagar,
New Delhi - 110 059
Tel : 5649063
(Tray Dryer, Heat Exchanger Steam/Thermax)

57. **Spray Tech India**
4th Floor,No. 15, Highway Towers, Mumbai Pune Road, Chinchwad, Pune -19
Tel : 0212-77-8685
(Suppliers of Spray Driers, Spin Wash, Tray Dryer Etc.)

58. **Sri Laxmi Engineering Works**
Gali No.1, Main Chowk, Samaipur,
New Delhi - 110 042
Tel : 7294981
(Ball Mill, High Speed Mixture, Low Speed Mixer, Kettles, Plant & Chemicals Machinery)

59. **Standard Engineers**
Sharda Sadan, 3rd Floor, 11 S.A.Brelvi Road,
Fort, Mumbai - 1
Tel : 2611916
Fax : 2626152
(Agitator, Stirrers, Blenders, Kettle & Mixing Eqpts.)

60. **Swastik Industrial Valves Pvt. Ltd.**
56A, Balaji Nagar,
Chennai - 50 (T.N.)
Tel : 6258243
(Manufacturers of Ball Mills etc.)

61. **Techmac Engineering Works**
325, Usha Kiran Bldg.,
Azadpur, New Delhi - 33
Tel : 7137027
(Mixer, Tray Dryer, Multimill, Coating Pan, Laboratory Equipments)

62. **T.R.Sharma Engg. Works**
A-156, Hari Nagar Clock Tower, New Delhi - 64
Tel : 5405269, 5745235
(Paint & Chemical Plants, Reaction Kettle, Ball Mills, Sand Grinders etc.)

63. **The Indure Ltd.**
45/1, Site-4, Sahibabad,
Ghaziabad (U.P).
Tel : 771835,36,37
(Gas Plants)

64. **United Technology & Systems**
L-56, Industrial Estate,
Chennai - 58 (Tamil Nadu)
Tel : 653457
(Agitators, Tanks, Reactor)

65. **Unitechna**
56, SMIE, 20/2, Mathura Road, Faridabad - 121 006
Tel : 282828, 232323
(Manual Semi-automatic & automatic botting equip ments for pharmaceuticals, distilleries, breweries, food products, inks etc. & also job work)

66. **Vibro-Tech Industries**
24-B/6, Industrial Area,
(Near Thermal Power House) Faridabad - 121 001
(Haryana)
Tel : 233251, 233261/ 0129- 241912, 233251)
(Blowers, Paint booth, Air Pollution Control Equipments, Powder Coatings Plants, Dust Collection Systems Etc.)

67. **Victory Engineering Enterprises**
A-10/12, Jhilmil Industrial Area, G.T. Road, Delhi.
Tel : 2270169, 2276705
(Powder Coating Plants, Powder Coating Spray Booth, Powder Coating oven in gas etc.)

20
SUPPLIERS OF RAW MATERIALS

* Paint Raw Materials
* Pigment Raw Materials
* Varnish Raw Materials
* Lacquer Raw Materials
* Resins Suppliers
* Enamel & Stoving Finishes
* Primers & Thinners etc.

1. **Aadhunik Rasayan Udhyog**
525, Ishwar Bhawan,
Khari Baoli, Delhi - 110 006
Tel : 3984001,3984002
Fax : 91-11-3984003
(Supplier of Titanium Di-oxide)

2. **Alka Minerals & Chemicals**
25 Jhilmil Indl. Area,
Delhi - 110 095
Tel : 2285 830
(All Kinds Paints)

3. **A Bhupendra Kumar & Company**
302, Dhan Mahal SV Road,
Malad West, Mumbai - 64
Tel : 8070922
(Contact : K.V.Shah)

4. **Acme Sales Corporation**
494, Maulana Azad Road, 3
Vithaldas House, Mumbai - 4
Tel : 3869597, 3852387, 4095741, 6291286
(Dls. of Decorative Furniture, Indl. Anti corrosive, Automo tive Janathacem Paints)

5. **Adarsh Chemicals**
24, bangaru Reddy Street,
Ayanavaram,
Chennai - 600023 (T.N)
Tel : 61 7591, 617592
Fax : 044 - 615790
(Acetone, M.E.K., Toluene, Xylene etc.)

6. **A. K. Enterprises**
CR - 254, Lalita Park,
Laxmi Nagar, Delhi - 110 092
Tel : 2249354
(Toluene, Methyl Ethyl Ketone, M.T.O. Etc.)

7. **Akerberally Sharefally Zaveri**
Ebrahim Rd., Botawala Bldg,
Mumbai - 3
Tel : 3761340

8. **Alfa Chemicals**
Goel Residency,
Nasik Phata,
Pune - 34 (M.S)
Tel : 779253
(Toluene, MEK, Ethyl Acetate, Xylene Etc.)

9. **Amar Enterprises**
2a Anand Nagar, K.K.Mrg.,
Juhu Tara, Mumbai - 49
Tel : 6126844
(Contact : Stanley Tauro)

10. **Amar Enterprises**
Hi View Indl Estate,
2nd FILBRSD, Mumbai - 86
Tel : 5171452

11. **Anil Roop Chemical Co.**
559, Katra Ishwar Bhagwan,
Khari Baoli, Delhi - 110 006
Tel : 2941 388
(Distr./Agent)

12. **Annu Chemicals**
2317,Gali Hinga Beg, Tilak
Bazar, Delhi - 110 006
Tel : 2916887
*(**Dist. :** Phthalic Maleic, Fumeric, Penta, Glycerine, Hexamine, Sodium formate, Bisphenol, Paraformal dehyde Deg, Meg, Toluene, Xylene, NBA, Ciba-IDI Pigment, Powder.*
***Mfr :** Alkyd Resin, M.F. Coconut, Short DCO.)*

13. **Anuradha Enterprises**
794, Joshi Path, Karol Bagh,
New Delhi - 110 005.

Tel : 7770 061
(Paint Raw Materials)

14. **Anticorrosive Chemical Industries**
6 Akash Deep Ram Maruti Road, Thane, Mumbai.
Tel : 5324005

15. **Anupam Colours & Chemicals Ind.**
145 Span Landmark AK Road, Mumbai - 93
Tel : 8362389
(Raw Material Traders)

16. **Anuvi Chemicals Pvt. Ltd.**
25 E/4 Model Town,
B.R.Road, West,
Mumbai - 80
Tel : 5645455
(Contact : Kanak Saxena)

17. **Aryan Chemicals**
Near Railway Line, Saijpur, Bogha,
Ahmedabad (Gujarat)
Tel : 816331/816332
Fax : 91-079-815441
(Industrial Solvents, Ben zene, Cyclohexanone, MEG, Toluene, CLX, Industrial Wax, Rosin, Titanium Dioxide, Acetone and Others)

18. **Aries Minerals Corpn.**
302, Dhan Mahal,
S.V.Road, Malad,
West, Mumbai - 64
Tel : 8070932
(Contact K.V.Shah)

19. **Aroon Mills**
H-3, Camal Indus. Est.
Goregaon, West
Mumbai - 63
Tel : 8730367
(Contact : Vinay Lal Mehta)

20. **Arti Paints & Chemicals Industries**
5, Jai Mahavir Indl. Estate,
Goregaon, East,
Mumbai - 72
Tel : 5126903
(Resin Manufacturers)

21. **Arun Udhyog**
B-3/7, Paschim Vihar,
New Delhi- 110 063
Tel : 5687 718
(Driers Ocatoates etc.)

22. **Ashok Chemical Co.**
Tvind Estate Skahire Marg,
Mumbai - 25
Tel : 4931148

23. **Asian Paints Ltd.**
Gaiwadi Indl. Est., S.V. Rd.,
Goregaon (West),
Mumbai - 62
Tel : 8881228
(Resin)

24. **Asiatic Trading Corpn.**
302, Dhan Mahal,
S.V.Road, Malad, West,
Mumbai - 64
Tel : 3758805
(Traders)

25. **Auto & Industrial Paints Corpn.**
42/Sleator Road,
Mumbai - 7
Tel : 3882691
(Manufacturers)

26. **Avishkar Coatings**
18, Pathare House, 1st
BhatWadi Gaum,
Mumbai - 4,
Tel : 3087788

(Contact : Nuthan C Shroff)

27. **A. K. G. Associates**
210 Kamalaya Centre 156 A
Lenin Sr., Calcutta - 13
Tel : 271319
(Paints & Resins)

28. **Anil Chemical Company**
9, Mangoe Lane, 3rd Floor,
Rm 8 & 9, Calcutta - 1
Tel : 2487920
(Paints & Resins, Raw Material)

29. **Anmol Rasayan**
33, Brabourne Road,
Calcutta - 1
Tel : 2433200
(Paints Mfg.)

30. **Aar Kay Paints**
Plot No. 7235, Street No. 2,
New Moti Nagar,
Ludhiana - 141 010 (Punjab)
Tel : 538452, 675181
(Specialist in Black Cycle Stoving Paints, Insulating Varnish, Paint Raw Material)

31. **Addison Paints & Chemicals Limited**
Sembiam, Chennai- 600 011
Off : 579, Industrial Area - B,
Ludhiana - 141003 (Punjab)
Tel : 535775
Brand : Addisons
(Manufacturers of Industrial & Decorative Paints, Enamels & Stoving Finishes)

32. **Amarson Paints**
Barwala Road,
Dera Bassi - 140507
(Punjab)
Tel : 566938
Brand : Amarson Hindrani, Amarlite
(Manufacturers of Indl. & Decorative Paints-Specially Stoving Paints & Primers)

33. **Amco Paints (India)**
1665, Street No. 16, Janak
Puri, Ludhiana - 141003
Tel : 662540, 530637
(Manufacturers of Industrial paints)

34. **Aristo Paints**
627-B, Partap Nagar, Street
No. 10,
Ludhiana - 141003
Tel : 490793 (PP)
(Manufacturers of Synthetic Enamels, Primer Stoving Paint, Varnish, Thinner, Resins etc.)

35. **Atul Paints**
2671, Street No. 1, New
Janta Nagar,
Opp. Arora Place,
Ludhiana - 141003
Tel : 490989
Brand : Silvy
(Manufacturers of Industrial & Decorative paints, Thinners, Varnishes & Enamels)

36. **A. C. Humidification Engineers Private Limited**
A-33/29, Gurunanak Pura,
Vikas Marg, Shakarpur,
New Delhi - 110092
Tel : 242 8282, 221 6935,
242 0624
Fax : 091-11-221 8282/
2283751
(Centrifugal Blowers, Azial Flow-fans, ManCoolers, Roof extractors, Spray Booths, Cyclone Separator, Fume Scrubber, Dust.Fume

Extraction, Dust Collector, Dust Proofing, Ventilation System, Aircooling System, Humidification System, Green house Ventilation)

37. **Bajrang Paints & Chemicals Private Limited**
P-16, South Extension -II,
New Delhi - 110 049
Tel : 641 7600
(Paints Mfg.)

38. **Bawa Enterprises Private Limited**
378/80 NarsiNatha St.,
Masjid, Mumbai - 9
Tel : 3422879, 3420939
(Mfr. of Insulating Varnishes & Synthetic resins)

39. **B.S.Chatterjee & B Choudhary**
7 Basanta Bose Road.,
Calcutta - 26
Tel : 485159
(Wholesaler of Spirit)

40. **Bharat Sales Agency**
P21/22, Radha Bazar Street,
Calcutta - 1
Tel : 2428690
(Paints & Resins)

41. **Casein (India)**
F-25, Bhangwadi Kalbadevi Road, Mumbai - 74
Tel : 5512270
(Contact : H.M.Chandwani)

42. **Chemitex Enterprises**
Appejay Bldg., B.S.Marg,
Fort, Mumbai - 1,
Tel : 2824084
(Trading in Raw Materials)

43. **Classic Chemicals**
14/59, Raj Nagar.,
Ghaziabad - 201 002
Tel : 9171 9433
(Mfr - Soya lecithin)

44. **Calcutta Paints & Trading Company**
242 B, B Ganguly Street,
Ist Floor, Calcutta - 12
Tel : 279722
(Paints & Resins)

45. **Camphor & Allied Products**
46 C, Chowringhee Road,
Everest House, Calcutta - 1
Tel : 2421518

46. **C.Dass Chemical Pvt. Ltd.**
Plot No. 287, Sec-24,
Faridabad - 121005
Tel : 91-233659/234659/ 234317
Fax : 91-234559
(Paint reducer of widest range : P.U., Acralic, Epoxy, Hr, Stoving, Electrostatic, Insulating)

47. **Chowdhry Rubber & Chemical Company**
1403, Pan Mandi,
Sadar Bazar,
Delhi - 110 006
Tel : 7773373, 7516098, 7534380
Fax : 91-11-6534153
{(Ethyl Vinyl Acetate, Rubber & Paint Chemicals, Industrial Chemicals, Pigment Powder, Fine Paste, Carbon Black, Silicone Rubber, Emulsion/ Oil, Rubber Blowing Agents, Blowing agents all Grades, Dispersing Agents, Foam stablisers, Stearic Acid & Glycerine,

Rubber To Metal, Bonding Agent, Chemlok 205/220 & All Grades, Stearate/Zinc Oxide, Dolphin, Silicone Products, ZInc Oxide (Swagat Brand))}

48. **D.C.Paints & Chemicals**
345/1, Shivaji Market,
Pitampura, New Delhi - 34
Tel :7010427
(ICI, Berger Asian)

49. **D.H.Exports**
4, Laxmi Niwas, Zaver Rd.,
Mind. (W), Mumbai - 80
Tel : 5604510

50. **D.Hemant & Co.**
198, Erskine Rd., Null Bazar,
Mumbai - 3,
Tel : 3764055
(Contact : Kashyap)

51. **Deep Jyoti Paint Industries**
S.V.Road Jawar Ngr., Gore Gaon, West, Mumbai - 62
Tel : 8724651
(Contact : Mr. Dharmesh Shah)

52. **Desai Varun Rasayan Private Limited**
D-16, Ansal Industrial Est.
Saki Naka, Mumbai - 72
Tel : 5783599
(Raw Materials Dealers)

53. **Dhaval Synthetic**
322, TV Indust., Est.,
Saki Naka, Mumbai - 72
Tel : 5783599
(Suppliers)

54. **Dhiraj Lal & Co.**
300-3, Jaojee Dadajee Rd.,
Nan Chowk, Mumbai - 7
Tel : 3866774, 3869330
Fax : 22-3879669
Telex : 011-73609
(Mfr. of "Sitolac" Brand Thinners Suitable for all paints)

55. **D.Sarkar & Brothers**
2 Maharshi Debendra Road,
Calcutta - 7
Tel : 2386391
(Paints & Resins)

56. **Deepali Paints**
Mankoo Market,
Focal Point Road, Sherpur
Ludhiana - 141 010
Tel : 673817, 676487
Pager : 9612-123817
(Deals in Bitumen & All Types of Bitumen & All types of Bitumen Products, Waxes & Indl. Chemicals)

57. **Eddy Chemical (P) Ltd.**
F-43-44, Phase VII,
Focal Point,
Ludhiana - 141 010 (Punjab)
Fax : 91-161-405639
(Lead Chromes)

58. **Elfine Chemicals**
Opp. Veena Beena Appartments,
A.D.Marg, Sewri (West)
Mumbai - 15
Tel : 4135131
(Dealers & Importers of Industrial Chemical solvents, acetone, D.O.P., MEK, Mallic Phthalic, Propylene etc.)

59. **Enkay Enterprises**
Happy Home Soc Vile Parle,
Mumbai - 57
Tel : 6142671
(Dls. of Raw Materials)

60. **Excel Coating India**
Mittal Est MV issanji Rd.,
Morol, Mumbai - 59
Tel : 8323967
(Paint/Resin - Raw Materials Mfrs.)

61. **Excel Organics Pvt. Ltd.**
17, Venkataroyen Lane,
Chennai -3 (T.N.)
Tel : 5352840,5343426
Fax : 91-44-5356553
(Sorbitol, Ethyl Acetate, Benzene, Aacetone, Stearic Acid, Castor Oil, Toluene, Xylene, MEK etc.)

62. **Fad Pharma**
Marg Darshan NS Phadke
Road, Mumbai - 69
Tel : 8349422

63. **Famous Minerals & Chemicals Comapny**
3/58 Sharda Topiwala Lgton
Road, Mumbai - 7
Tel : 3886089, 3871829
(Mineral Merchants & Mfrs of : Barytes, red Oxide, Silica, Calcite, China Clay, Whiting, Talc, Precipited, Barium, Sulphate, Precipi tated calcium, Carbonate Precipitated silica, Graphite)

64. **Fine Organics**
15/2, Neelkanth Market,
M.G.Road, Ghatkopar (East),
Mumbai - 400 077
Tel : 5116900, 5116902, 5124205
Fax : 022-5153215
(Anti-Settling Agents, Thickening Agents, Pigment Grinding Aids, Wetting and Dispersing Agents, Emulsifi ers, Defoamers (Non-Silicone), Anti-Mar Agents, Biocide, Anticorroson additives, Synthetic Waxes, Slip Agents)

65. **Fine Chemical & Solvent**
309, B.B.Ganguly Street,
Calcutta - 12
Tel : 264052
(Thinner, SOlvents, Redusr)

66. **Ganga Rasayanie Pvt. Ltd.**
1-45 Shivaji Ngr., Dr AB
Road., Worli, Mumbai - 25,
Tel : 4922942
(Raw Materials)

67. **Gayatri Enterprises**
5 Vinod Kh Shed Bh Coal
Cmpd. Bali Bzr.,
Mumbai - 70
Tel : 5115715
(Mfr. : Dklac NC Thinners Distt : Susliac Rubbing Compound)

68. **Gurukrupa Overseas Trading Corporation**
407, Vyapar Bha 49 PD
Mello Rd., Mumbai - 9
Tel : 3719190,3719205
(Leading Supplier : Micronised Extenders Like : Barytes, Talc China Clay, Calcite, Silicate, Etc. For Paint Industries.)

69. **Gwalior Oil Mills**
Ganga Vihar Poddar Rd.,
Cruz, Mumbai - 54
Tel : 6141155
(Contact : Arvind bhai N Patel)

70. **Gulab Paints**
98, Manik Talla, Main Road,
Calcutta - 54

Tel : 3515978
(Paints & Resins, Raw Material Suppliers)

71. **Hemant Kumar Paresh Kumar & Co. Pvt. Ltd.**
371/73, Narshi Natha Street, 2nd Floor, Mumbai - 9
Tel : 3247474/3442393
Fax : 3414611
(Dealers in All Solvents & Chems. Specilist in : Cyclohexanone, Methanol, Arsenic Trioxide, Rosin, Loban, Shellac Wax Etc.)

72. **Higrade Resins and Allied Products**
80, Marine Drive 10 Neelam Bldg.,Mumbai - 2
Tel : 2061793
(Contact : Amit Aggarwal)

73. **Hindustan Metal Industries**
1.7, Sai Niketan 345 M.T.Road, Mazgaon, Mumbai - 10
Tel : 3721208
(Contact : Gilroy Rodrigues)

74. **Hindustan Coatings**
1/1, Block - 41, Singh Sabha Road, Clock Tower, Subzi Mandi, Delhi - 110 007
Tel : 291-8947, 292-5356, 292-1188
Fax : 91-11-2923567
(Toluene, Solvent Oil, Benzene, M.T.O., Ethyl Acetate, Thinner Etc.)

75. **Hare Krishna Paints**
Post Box 176, 93 Beliaghata Main Road, Calcutta - 10
Tel : 500802
(Paints & Resins)

76. **Imperial Chemicals**
MB Hse., 79 Ghuga Street, Fort, Mumbai - 1,
Tel : 2870675
(Contact : D.F. Kotwal)

77. **Imperial Paints & Chemicals Company**
129, Latif Villa, Phalke Rd., Dadar (East), Mumbai - 14
Tel : 4110476
(Paint & Resin Mfrs Suppliers)

78. **Indiana Dyeing Chemicals**
228, Indl. Area-A, Ludhiana - 141003
Tel : 66040
(Dealers : D.E.G., M.E.G. Oils, Emulsifiers, Medium)

79. **Indraprastha Industrial Corporation**
B-70/7, DSIDC Complex, Lawrence Road, Delhi - 110 035
Tel : 7183612
(Mfrs. of Paints, Lacquers, Thinners etc.)

80. **Industrial Coatings & Adhesives**
A-689/A, Shastri Nagar, Delhi - 110 052
Tel : 7776612, 3551487
(Resins, Pigments, Chemi cals, Driers, Stearates & Adhesives)

81. **Indogem Paint Industries**
E-123, Focal Point, Ludhiana - 141010
Tel : 670067, 671240
Brand : Indolac
(Manufacturers of Indl. & Decorative Paints)

82. **Industrial Lube Chem**
118, Gupta Complex, Old Rohtak Road,
Delhi - 110 035
Tel : 541 5741, 541 5920
Fax : 91-11-5105599
(Titanium Dioxide - Indian & Imported)

83. **Jay Polychem India Private Limited**
A-32, Maya Puri Indl. Area, Phase - 1,
New Delhi - 110 064
Tel : 5131345, 5138601
Fax : 91-11-5493309/ 6843147
(Toluene, Titanium Diox--ide, Classical Organic Pigment Powders, Anti oxidant, Stabilisers etc.)

84. **J.B.Transmission Products**
88/15 Jawahar Nagar,
Gore Gaon,
Mumbai - 62
Tel : 8738924
(Contact : Rajni Bhai)

85. **Janathacem**
293/203 Shere Punjab Col
Andheri Est., Mumbai - 10
Tel : 8210778, 3712061
(Ultimate Wall Coating 200 Sq. Ft./Kg Coverage Supercedes Lime & White Cement Wash-Dry distemper)

86. **Jayant Oil Mills**
13 Sitafalwadi Mazgoan,
Mumbai - 10
Tel : 3738810
(Oils, Fatty acid, Dimer, Alkyds, POlyamides, Urethanes, Additives)

87. **Jaychem Corporation**
60/62, Varjivan Man
S.G.Marg,
Mumbai - 2
Tel : 2012798
(Paint & Resin Mfrs. Suppliers)

88. **Jayem Enterprises**
AGH Chambers 379/81 NN St., Mumbai - 9
Tel : 3422565,
(Contact : Shyam Sunder Jajodia)

89. **J.M.Chemical Co (Regd.)**
209, Tilak Bazar,
Khari Baoli,
Delhi - 110 006
Tel : 2529922
Fax : 11-2929933
(Emulsions, Solvents, Tio_2)

90. **Jog Colour Chem**
Ram Kishan Hse St. Rd.,
Bhandup (West)
Mumbai - 78

91. **Kannan & Co.**
127, Nainiappa Naicken Street, Chennai - 3 (T.N)
Tel : 5353558, 5354956
Fax : 5351174
(Formaldehyde, Acetone, MEK, Toluene, Xylene, Chloroform, Hexane etc.)

92. **Karwal Paints & Chemical**
15094, Street No. 2,
Guru Arjan Dev Nagar,
Near Military,
Ludhiana - 141003
Brand : Karwal
(Manufacturers of Industrial Paints)

93. **K Jivraj & Sons**
179 Samuel Street,
Mumbai - 9
Tel : 3753632
(Contact : Javendra J Parekh)

94. **Karan Dye Chem**
15 A/7 Sindhi Clny SIF
Colsion, Mumbai - 22
Tel : 4090076
(Contact : Sheela R Shah)

95. **Kohinoor Paints Works**
D-16, South Extension,
Part - II, New Delhi - 110 049
Tel : 643335
(Supp - Kohnr Pnts.)

96. **Krishna Chemicals**
Wagle Ind. Est., Thane,
Mumbai - 604
Tel : 4077627
(Raw Maerials for Paints & Resin)

97. **Kuber Trading Company**
2336, Tilak Bazar, Delhi - 06
Tel : 2510648
(Paints & Chemicals)

98. **Kundu Paint & Hardware Stores**
166F, A.P.C. Road,
Calcutta - 4
Tel : 5556527
(Paints & Reisns)

99. **Kundu Paint Stores**
180 A, A.P.C.Road,
Calcutta - 4
Tel : 5442577
(Delears of Berger, ICI, MRF Paints)

100. **Kundu Paint Supply**
5A, Library Road,
Calcutta - 26
Tel : 4640385
(Paints & Reisns)

101. **Lara Industries Pvt. Ltd.**
H-42, Bali Nagar,
New Delhi - 110 015
Tel : 5442729
(Paint Raw Mtrls)

102. **Lucky Paint Mart**
43,C.P.Tank Road,
Mumbai - 4
Tel : 3756038
(Asian, Berger, Nerolac, Gold, Pearl, Flou Pwd, Artist Brush)

103. **Lakshmi Paint Works Private Limited**
14/2, Old China Bazar Street,
Calcutta - 1
Tel : 2422286
(Manufacturing of Paint Prds.)

104. **Mamta Chemical & Rubber Industries**
237, Aden Building,
Oswal Road,
Industrial Area-A,
Ludhiana - 141003
Tel : 662798
(Dealer of Rubber & Paints Chemicals)

105. **Mangalia Hydrocarbon Ltd.**
7C, K.S.Roy Road,
Calcutta - 4. **Tel :** 2208839
(Paints & Resins)

106. **Magnus Impex Pvt. Ltd.**
516, Exp Tower Comercial Complex, Azadpur,
New Delhi - 110 033
Tel : 7224892
(Paint Raw Mtrls.)

107. **Makes Chem Industries**
123, Milan B Vashi Rd.,
Parle, Mumbai - 56
Tel : 6153043

108. **Manikant Brothers (Everest)**
257 N Natha St.,
Masjid (West),
Mumbai - 9
Tel : 3752881
(Contact : Mukesh Lodaya)

109. **Mayur Paints & Chemicals**
74, Shardhanana Marg,
Delhi - 110 006
Tel : 2523381
(Cont.: Mr.Tuli)

110. **Mohammed Plastics Private Limited**
Plot No. 2, C.I.E. Expansion,
Gandhi Nagar, Balanagar,
Hyderabad - 500 037
Tel : 3097181
Fax : 040-3098003
(All Purpose Plastic Containers For Paint Packaging)

111. **Multi Coats Pvt. Ltd.**
29/116, West Patel Nagar,
New Delhi - 110 008
Tel : 5741256
(Multi Coats)

112. **Narchem Industries**
7, Monica Apt.,
Panchpakhadi Th,
Mumbai - 602
Tel : Dlrs. of Raw Materials

113. **Noble Synthetics Ltd.**
314, TV Ind. Est., Worli,
Mumbai - 25
Tel : 4932347
(Suppl. of Raw Materials)

114. **Noida Chemicals**
C-10, Sec-7,
Noida - 201301 (U.P.)
Tel : 91-5718788/5727778/
522077/522088
Fax : 91-11-5735151
(Paint Raw Materials & Chemicals)

115. **Orbit Enterprises**
71 Lavina 52-A, Tagore Rd.,
Santa Crun'z (West),
Mumbai - 54
Tel : 5491498
(Mfrs. of Raw Materials)

116. **Orbit International**
19 Bhatia Niwas vadgadi,
Mumbai - 3
Tel : 3446167
(Contact : Nitin Mehta)

117. **Oxide and Chemical Industries**
12, Mullick Para Lane,
Calcutta - 55
Tel : 5511442
(Paints & Resins)

118. **Panex Overseas**
20/16, Rajinder Nagar,
New Delhi - 110 060
Tel : 5719546

119. **Paint Tech Consultants**
GovindAshram, 224 L.J.Rd.,
Dadar, Mumbai - 28
Tel : 4456214
(Suppl. of Raw Material)

120. **Parekh Chemicals Colour Company**
179, Samuel Street, Masjid,
Mumbai - 9
Tel : 3754556
(Suppl. of Raw Materials)

121. **PCL Enterprises Ltd.**
M-105, Cannaught Place,
New Delhi - 110 00 1
Tel : 3739191/92/93/94
Fax : 91-11-37113063

(Dealers & Importers : Toluene, Benzene, Thinner, Phenol, D.O.P., D.B.P. etc.)

122. **Perfect Plastics**
144, Guru Gobind Est., Gore Gaon, Mumbai - 63
Tel : 8731815
(Suppl. of Raw materials)

123. **Pooja Enterprises**
22, Khimji Meghji Hse., Vadgadi, Mumbai - 3
Tel : 3438634
(Resin - Raw Materials)

124. **Pragati Chemicals Limited**
Mittal Tower C, WingN Pt, Mumbai - 21
Tel : 2851402

125. **Process Instrumentation and Controls**
305, Galaxy Complex, Opp. Sarabhai Main Gate, Wadi Wadi, Baroda - 390 007
Tel : 435629, 482951
Fax : (0265) 430423
(Tin Coding Ink used for Paint)

126. **Protech Coatings Pvt. Ltd.**
C-31, Sec-57, Noida -201301 (Ghaziabad) (U.P.)
Tel : 91-527300
(Mfr. of Suppr Walcen)

127. **Paints & Industrial Coatings**
11 Moni Lal Chaterjee Lane, Calcutta -3
Tel : 6602151
(Paints Additives)

128. **Parekh Chemicals**
11B, BGanguly Street, 2nd Floor, Calcutta -3
Tel : 267827
(Paint Raw Material)

129. **Polle Colours & Pigments**
309B, BGanguly Street, Calcutta - 12
Tel : 263292
(Paint Raw Materials)

130. **Pure Chemicals Co.**
77, Perampur High road, Chennai - 600012
Tel : 6421532, 6422040, 6422152
Fax : 044-6422359
(Suppliers of Paint Raw Materials & Chemicals)

131. **Pushpab Chemicals**
65/1, Maharshi Debendre Road, Calcutta - 6
Tel : 2318197
(Paint)

132. **Rajeev Color & Varnish Limited**
28/2, ShakesPeare, Sarani, Calcutta -17
Tel : 2400792
(Paints)

133. **R.N.Sahni & Sons**
27/3, Shakti Nagar, Delhi - 110 007
Tel : 7227812, 7459390
Fax : 7243246
(Micronised Minerals, Pigments, Chemicals, Driers, Resins)

134. **Rajdeep Minerals & Chemicals Company**
179, Samuel St., Khojiagali, Mumbai - 9
Tel : 3750139
(Manufacturers of Raw Materials)

135. **Rajvanshi Traders**
Sh No.- 1 Sec - 5 Harola,
Noida - 201301 (U.P.)
Tel : 91- 555784
(Paints, Chems.)

136. **Rastogi Shell Oils Pvt. Ltd.**
5A/14,Ansari Road,
Daryaganj, New Delhi - 02
Tel : 3276075
(Mfr. of Cnsl & Crdnl)

137. **Reliable Paints**
276, Maulana Azad Rd.2,
Tank, Mumbai - 8
Tel : 3095420

138. **R.N.Sahni & Sons**
73, indira nagar,
Valasaravakkam,
Chennai- 600 087 (T.N.)
Tele/Fax : 4827315
Pager No. : 9632 702771
(Manufacturers of Industrial chemicals, All type of Fat Liquor Liquid Syntan, Treat ment Chemicals, Softeners, Dye Fixing Agents, Enzymes, Liquid Detergents, Solid Fuel, Bleaching Solutions & Silicon Antifoams for Sugar, Paper, Fertilizers, Paint, Soild Fuel, Food Industries Etc.)

139. **Rohini Paints Pvt. Ltd.**
65 B, Bay Samachar Marg,
Mumbai - 23
Tel : 2665297

140. **Rubber Mineral Products**
Shop No. 1418, Iqbal Market
Lane, Near Narain Market,
Gali Chulley Wali, Sadar
Bazar, New Delhi - 110 006
Tel : 737505, 520239
Pager : 9602407792
(Natural rubber, Rubber Chemicals, Reclaim Rubber, Silicone Rubber, Synthetic Emulsion & Oils, Foam Stablizer, Emlsolic Economy, Dispersale, Zinc Oxide, Titanium Dioxide, Stearic Acid, Carbon Black etc.)

141. **Sadana Thinners (P) Ltd.**
265, Basant Avenue,
Amritsar - 143 001
Tel : 222102
(Dealers in Thinners & All kinds of Industrial Solvents for Paint Industry)

142. **Sangeeta Enterprises**
Ansa Ind. Est, Sakinaka,
Andheri, Mumbai - 72
Tel : 5132776
(Traders of Raw Materials)

143. **Sangeeta Enterprises**
Binda Pur Road Crossing,
Main Matiala Road,
Uttam Nagar, New Delhi - 59
(All Kinds of Repairing and New Assembeling of Machin ery Job for Urea, Melamine, Unbreakable Powder Plant, Balmil, Reaxon Katrel, Mixture, Dryer, Pluf Grinder, Powder Cleaning, Jaal, S.S.Formal, Deite, Tank, Boiler S.S.Monoblock Pump)

144. **Shiva Chem**
14/71, Subash Nagar,
New Delhi - 110 027
Tel : 5141565
(Paint Chemicals)

145. **Shiva International**
21/2, Bally ganga Place,
Ground Floor, Calcutta - 19
Tel : 4408758
(Paints & Raw Materials)

146. **Sidhi Chem Corporation**
7 Raj Mohan Street,
2nd Floor, Calcutta - 73
Tel : 258776
(Raw Material Paint & Print Suppliers)

147. **Somani Oil Industries**
12/2, Sova Ram Bysack Street, Calcutta - 7
Tel : 2390470
Fax : 2397160
(Makers of Alkyd Resin, Stand Oil, DCO fatty Acid, RLO, DBLO, ARLO, Refine Castor,Tobacco, Soya Niger Oil & Acid Oil Etc.)

148. **Spectrum**
2 Inder Mohini Vr Rd
Santa Cruz West,
Mumbai - 54
Tel : 4114774
(Suppliers of Raw Materials)

149. **Shubham Dyes & Chemicals**
1/26, Roop Nagar,
Delhi - 110 007
Tel : 2933200/201/202
Fax : 2944202
(Toluene, NItrobenzene, Solvents & Chemicals Etc.)

150. **Shree Marketings**
5, G.N.C. Trust, 1413/1,
Nicholson Road,
Kashmere Gate,
Delhi - 110 006
Tel : 2921462/2929608
Fax : 2946870
(Zinc Oxide & Other Chemicals)

151. **Sri Sastha Chemicals**
81, Royapettah High Road,
Chennai -4 (T.N.)
Tel : 8549123, 8548879
(Toluene, Xylene, Benzene, MEK & Other Industrial Solvents)

152. **Sargodha Paints & Chemicals**
1274, Street No.3,
Simpla Puri,
Ludhiana - 141003
Tel : 491383
(Manufacturers of Water Proof Cements Paints & Dry Distempers)

153. **Tandon Solvents & Chemicals**
2529, Hudson Line Kingsway Camp, Delhi - 110 009
Tel : 7427437
(Cont : Mr. Tandon)

154. **Tripoot India Pvt. Ltd.**
559, Katra Ishwar Bhawan,
Khari Baoli,
Delhi - 110 006
Tel : 2947729 *(Chemicals)*

155. **Technico Enterprises Private Limited**
573, Block - N, New Alipore,
Calcutta - 53
Tel : 4780191
(Manufacturers of Paint & Printing Ink Driers)

156. **Uniflex Chemicals**
Neelam Apts., 61-B, Park Street, Calcutta - 16
Tel : 295555
(All Kinds of Paint Raw Materials, Phthalic & Maleic Anhydride)

157. **Ujwal Pharma Pvt. Ltd.**
1421, Maker Chamber V
Nariman Pt., Mumbai - 21
Tel : 2040232

20

DETAILS OF PLANT EQUIPMENT & MACHINERIES

Paint Machinery

Paint manufacture involves dispersing a pigment in a suitable vehicle using any or all of the following processes :

(a) Pigment mixing with a suitable vehicle and forming a paste of required consistency for grinding.
(b) Grinding the paste to break up the agglomerates.
(c) Reducing the viscosity of the paste by using some vehicle or solvents.
(d) Tinting and ready mixing the paint to required shade and
(e) Straining, filling and packing.

Paint Mixers

There are three general classes of mixers used in paint manufacture

(1) Mixers which mix the pigments and vehicle into a paste for subsequent grinding on a mill.
(2) Mixers which combine pigment vehicle mixing and grinding in the same piece of equipment.
(3) Mixers which mix the ground paste with the let-down materials to

produce finished paints. The machinery used for this purpose is of the following type.

1. Edge-Runner Mills

It is an efficient paste-mixer and has a definite grinding action. This machine has one or two heavy rolls attached to a vertical shaft which rotates on a flat grinding surface. The pan and roller are of cast-iron with polished surfaces and incase when iron contamination is undesirable, a mill with a granite roll and bed is used. The roll is mounted on a floating crank so as to allow it to rise according to the depth of mix. A positive driving gear ensures the revolving motion if the paste is slippery.

Grinding takes place due to the twist or the rolls. Edge-runner mill do the mixing and grinding simultaneously. Colours which have dried into cakes may be broken up in dry state or with solvent to form paste. It is very useful in blending of dry colours and in such cases the roll is tapered so as to make the operation more efficient. Paste distemper is prepared entirely on edge-runner.

Few typical specification of Edge-Runner are given below :

	Type I	*Type II*
Diameter of pan	2-1/2 ft.	4 ft.
Depth of pan	5 inch.	9 inch.
Size of the roller	15" x 4"	15' x 6"
B.H.P. required	4	7.5
R.P.M. of roller	20	25

2. Horizontal Paste-Mixer

They employ a combination of two or more actions of stretching, kneading and tearing. The mixer consists of a U-shaped trough in which a rotating mixer of the heavy duty-blades type, twin-blades type, or ribbon-blades type is used.

Heavy duty paddle mixer are used for very stiff pastes. They are of self-discharging type. In these mixers material is swept from one end of the trough to another constantly by the use of scrapers.

Twin-blade mixers produce a more intimate mix by the use of greater shear. They require a higher H.P. and are not fit for discharging stiff pastes.

Ribbon-blade mixer is used for mixing dry colours. They have vertical paddles and narrow vertical ribbons to prevent the local packing of solids and also give a constant slippage to the solids.

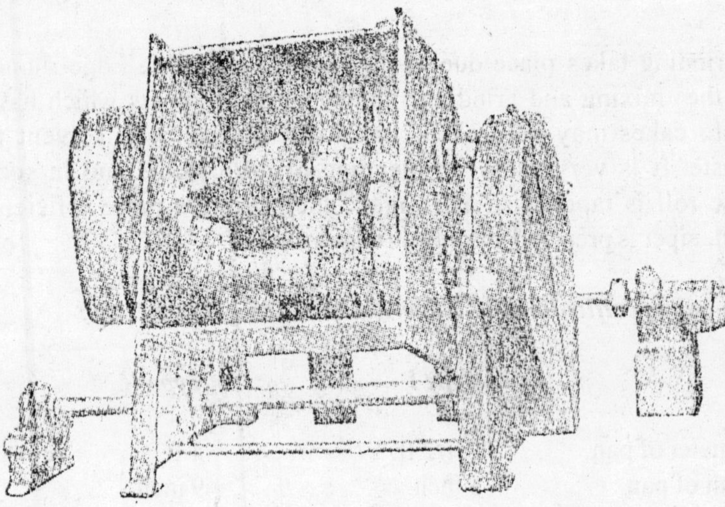

Horizontal Paste Mixer

In a specially designed, horizontal paste-mixer, known as Amalgamator, the cylinder is made of thick mild steel sheet and vertical shaft is of steel, fitted with steel beaters which rotate, in opposite direction to the other set of surrounding blades. A typical example of specifications is as follows

Sizer of cylinder	3' x 2'
Power required	3 H.P.
R.P.M.	100

3. Powder and Light Paste Mixers

There are many different models available either complete with motor or with pulleys for belt drive and are fabricated of either heavy gauge mild steel, stainless steel, monel metal, or of heavy gauge mild steel with sprayed non-contaminating lining *etc*. It can also be used as a dryer in addition to mixing and blending. For this purpose they are fitted with electric heaters and mild steel jackets. The capacity of this mixers from 3/4 cubic foot to 45 cubic feet.

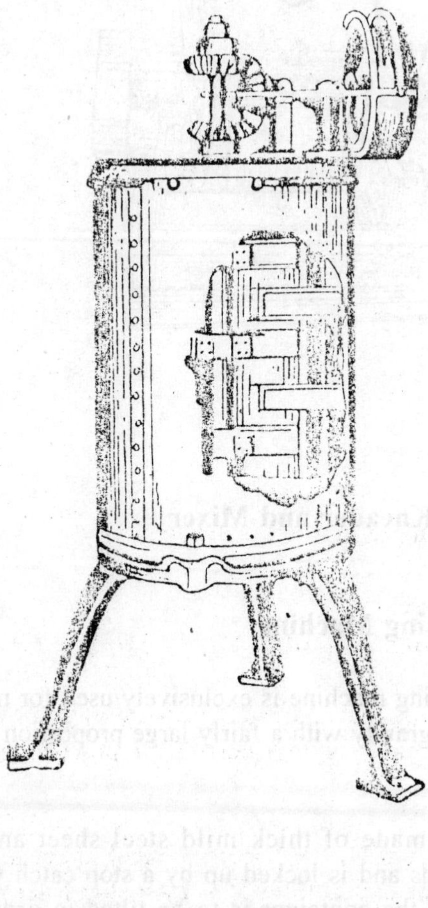

Amalgamator

4. Heavy Duty Paste Mixers

These machines are used in mixing pigments and medium at high consistencies. In addition to mixing putties, stoppers, and mastics, they are also used for the incorporation of pigments into cellulose nitrate and other binders in the so-called chip-process.

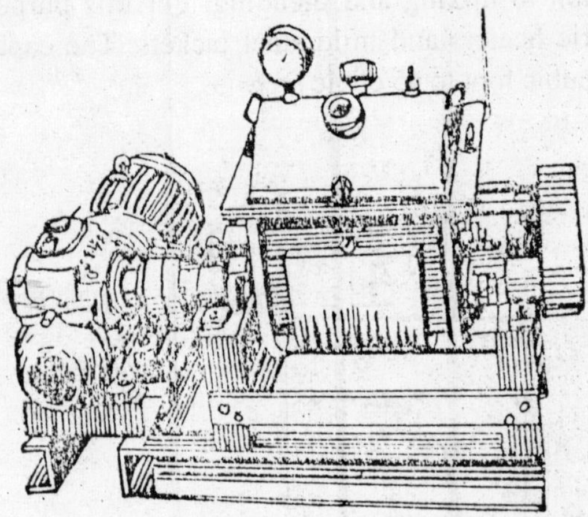

Kneader and Mixer

5. Kneading and Mixing Machine

Kneading and mixing machine is exclusively used for mixing the material of low specific gravity with a fairly large proportion of liquid medium.

The container is made of thick mild steel sheet and swings between two heavy stands and is locked up by a stop catch which can be easily released when the container is to be tilted in order to take out te mixed material. The strongly built stirrers rotate in opposite directions in such a manner as to prevent the contents of the container from gathering together into a ball of mass. It is especially suitable for mixing pigments and medium which do not require grinding.

Machines with the following specifications are available

Type A : Capacity 100 lbs. per batch, power drive
Type B : Capacity 75 lbs. per batch, power drive
Type C : Capacity 50 lbs. per batch, hand drive

Specially designed mixers and kneaders have been extensively used for mixing and kneading of stiff mass of any consistency of paints, enamels *etc*.

These kneaders have two *'Z'* type blades working with different speed ratios in opposite direction to each other to ensure perfect kneading. The container is often jacketed for either steam heating or water cooling and the kneader is fitted on leak-proof gland bearings. The discharging of material is facilitated by the tilting action of the container either mechanically or electrically. The working of the blades after tilting pushes out the material and thus quickens the process of discharging. These kneaders are fitted either directly with electric motor or with pulleys for belt drive and are fabricated from either mild steel, stainless steel, monel metal or mild steel with sprayed non-contaminating linings. The capacity of various models available ranges from 1/2 cubic foot to 45 cubic feet.

6. Pug Mixers

These types of heavy duty mixers are available in horizontal and vertical types. Horizontal pugs are used for the highest viscosity pastes and consists of a horizontal U-shaped steel trough fitted with two horizontal paddle shafts. These may be fitted with Z-blades or may be specially designed as the beken mixer. The bottom of the trough is designed to eliminate dead spots.

Vertical pugs comprise of a pan into which can be lowered a multi-bladed stirrer. This type of pug is used for pre-mixing pastes before processing on tripple-rolls or uniroll mills. It is not capable of handling the heavy pastes produced on the horizontal types.

7. Change Can Mixers

They employ blades which can be lowered and raised and are arranged off centre to sweep through the mix. They are used in mixing dry colours in solvents and thinners to give pastes of fine consistency.

The container can be of the stationary or rotating type. In the latter case the blades rotate in opposite direction. They give quick mixing and are used in small batch operations in units producing a large number of colours. They are normally used for handling small capacities. If required for handling a large volume of material at a time, they should be fitted with automatic lifting and handling devices.

8. High Speed Stone Mills

One mill contains two stones, a stator or stationary stone, and a rotor or rotating stone. The rotor revolves at high speed in a horizontal plane, and the pigment-vehicle mixture is passed between the two stones.

Dispersion is achieved by the shearing action developed in the material between the stones. The high speed of rotation tends to develop high shear. The paste must flow freely through this type of mill, therefore this is the limiting factor in the consistncy which can be used. Poor flow may cause overheating and excessive wear of the stones. The soild content of the vehicle of the grinding medium varies with the type of pigment and vehicle, but it should be fairly high to assure good flow and is usually in the range of 40-45. The paste should be mixed thoroughly before passing through the mill.

High speed stone mills are suitable for architectural paints and good production rates can be achieved because very fine dispersion is not required and the pigments are fairly easy to disperse.

Roller Mills

The most widely used roller mill in paint industry is the three roll mill but five roll, two roll and uniroll mills are also used.

(a) **Three Roller Mill**

Three-roller mill is widely used in paint industry . Each roller rotates in the opposite direction to the one adjacent and there is a differential in rotational speed among the rolls. The differential is about 3:1 between each roll on the three roller mill and about 2:1 on the five rolier mill.

Roll number	*1*	*2*	*3*	*4*	*5*
3 Roller mill r.p.m.	35	115	345	—	—
5 roller mill r.p.m.	25	50	100	200	300

The clearance between the rolls is of vital importance and a specific setting for each type of paste. Considerable experience is necessary to adjust the rolls correctly when starting the mill. A typical procedure for starting the mill is to move the back and the front roll in close contact with the centre roll. Before starting the mill the front-roll is moved slightly out of the contact with the centre-roll. Paste is then fed between the back and the centre-roll and mill is started. Front roll is then brought is close contact with the centre roll. In view of the differentials in speed among the rolls there must be more clearence between the back and the centre-rolls than that between the centre and the front rolls.

Tripple roll mill are effective in breaking down aggregates and dispersing the individual particles. No reduction in the ultimate particle size takes place. The capacity of a three-roll mill depends on the following factors.

(a) The rotational speed and speed differentials
(b) The clearance between rolls
(c) Physical dimensions of the rolls and
(d) Fluidity or stickiness of the paste

A tripple-roller mill has a number of limitations which, with the introduction of more efficient mills have resulted in a great decrease in their use in recent years. The following are the most important drawbacks.

(i) They are very slow and need constant attention.
(ii) They are unsuitable for media containing very volatile solvents.
(iii) There is not means of preventing foreign bodies from entering the nips. The shock is taken by springs but an emergency switch should

be located near the operators hand.

(iv) Cleaning is very hazardous the main danger lying at the contact of the back and centre rolls.

A triple roller grinding machine is specially suitable for working all sorts of tough pastes such as white lead oil, oil colours in general, lacquer colours, and paints of every consistency.

The rollers, through which the material comes out are highly polished and can be adjusted according to the fineness required. These machines are available in the following two varieties

(i) Machine with horizontal cast iron rollers without cooling device.

(ii) Machine with inclined cast iron rollers without cooling device.

Specifications of a Typical Machine

Size of the rollers	21" long X 8 dia
Power required	5 H.P.
R.P.M	150
Capacity	4 Cwt.

These mills are of robust construction throughout silent in operation and free from vibrations. These types of mills are availabe with finest quality chilled iron and granite rollers. Wide range of production models with rollers 8" X 18", 10" X 22", 12" X 24", 15" X 30" and 15" X 36" are used for paints enamels cellulose lacquers inks *etc.* at consistencies from stiff paste to liquids. These mills are available either motorised belt driven or as close coupled units.

(b) Five Roll Mill

In this mill there are five rollers, arranged just like in tripple roll mills. It is more effective than a tripple roll mill because it has one feeding interface and two grinding interface compared with one feeding and one grinding interface on the three roll mill. It runs at slower speed and the efficiency of shearing action is not as high as in tripple roll mill. The shearing efficiency is further reduced because the clearance among the back rolls on a five roll mill must be larger to permit sufficient paste to be fed to the front roll.

(c) Single Roll Mill

This is a less commonly used machine which can be used either for refining paint or for dispersing pigments. It is important to check the cleanliness of scraper blades in the mail because the ouput of the mill very much depends on correct scraping. Grinding paste must be removed and cleaned after each successive operation. Grease and oil must be used before it is returned to the mill.

The paint is carried under a bar fitted at the outlet of the hopper and the pressure on this bar can be adjusted to give the desired degree of refinement of dispersions.

(d) Two Roll Mill

It is often referred to as a ***'Rubber Mill'*** because it was used principally for dispersing chemicals and pigments in number of rubber stocks. The two roll mill is steam heated to soften hard polymers. A strong shearing force can be developed in mixtures in the mill.

Ball Mills or Pebble Mills

These mills consist basically of steel cylinders mounted horizontally and rotated about their axis. Ball mills are steel lined and contain steel balls pebble mills are lined with ceramic or silica blocks and are charged with steatite balls or Sea Washed pebbles. Generally pebble mills are used for white and light coloured paints and bali mills for dark coloured paints.

The mill is charged with pigment and medium, either separately or in the form of a pre mixed slurry and rotated at the appropriate speed. Dispersion takes place mainly by shear resulting from the relative movement of the balls, and to a lesser extent by impact.

The optimum working speed has been found by experience to be 50 to 60% of the critical speed. The critical speed is that minimum speed at which the balls are carried round by centrifugal force and is given by the expression.

$$\text{Critical Speed (Revolution/minute)} = \frac{54.18}{\sqrt{r}}$$

where

r = internal radius of mill in feet.

These mills are made in different diameters and lengths. Pebble mills are not usually water cooled except for grinding heat sensitive pigments. Steel ball mills should be water cooled in sizes over 90 gallons as they develop considerable heat.

Steel ball discolour white pigments and some dry colours. Porcelain and berylite mills are used where minimum discolouration is desired. Steel ball mills cause some contamination of iron and, since iron is a drier baking enamels seem shorter when ground in steel ball mills and the formula must be adjusted accordingly.

Grinding time in steel ball mills is about half that of pebble mills and Berylite mills grind white enamels nearly as fast as steel ball mills.

The consistency of the paint must be such that the balls or pebbles cascade freely inside the mill. The mills are equipped with lifter bars to aid the cascading of balls of pebbles.

Steel balls mill and Berylite mills cost nearly twice as mush as pebble mills because of their greater weight and have a much shorter operating life.

Factors Determining Output of Ball an Pebble Mills.

Some points should always be considered to attain good grinding result in ball or pebble mills. The recommended charge specification and mills speed are as follows

1. **Ball or Pebble Charge -- Weight**

Size Mill	*Pebble Charge*	*Steel Ball*
3' x 4'	939 lb	2,837 lb
4' x 5'	2,310 lb	6,281 lb
5 x 4'	2,954 lb	7,963 lb
5' x 6'	4,603 lb	11,904 lb

2. **Ball or Pebble Charge -- Size**

Diameter Mill-Feet Ball	Ball Charge of Porcelain Balls
1-2	1/2" -- 70%, 1" -- 30%
3-4	1/2"-- 30%, (1--1-1/2")-- 60%, (1-1/2" -- 2")-- 10%,
4-5	(3/4" -- 1") -- 85% (2" -- 2-1/2") -- 15%

In the case of pebbles, the size should be increased by 50% and the proportion of large pebble increased by 30-40%.

3. **Ball or Pebble Mill Speeds**

Internal Diameter of Mill (Feet)	6 1/2	5	4	3	2	1
R.P.M	17-18	19-21	20-22	25-26	30-32	49-52

4. Select the best wetting liquid ingredients for the grind. To increase the wetting properties of the liquids use wetting agents such as Lecithin or Zinc naphthenate.

5. Thin the vehicle to 25% solids, if possible.

6. Bring up the viscosity of the mill grinding base with pigment. In this way a maximum amount of pigment may be ground thus allowing a great deal off thinning down and subsequent higher yields.

The efficiency of a *ball mill* or *pebble mill* is influenced by the following factors

(a) Load of Pebbles or Balls

With pebbles the volume occupied should be 40 to 50% of the total volume of the mill but with steel balls 35 to 40%. High density materials give more rapid dispersion and ball mills are more efficient than pebble mills for grinding coloured pigments.

(b) Volume of Mill base

The optimum volume of mill base is equal to or slightly greater than the void space in the ball or pebbles.

(c) Composition of Mill Base

In ball mills, as in all batch mills the prime aim is the dispersion of the maximum amount of pigment per charge. In the early days of ball mill, mill base compositions were largely arrived at by empirical method until *Daniel* suggested a method whereby the optimum composition could be determined.

The power input peaks at the 50% gross volume loading and tapers off to zero for both the zero and 100% loadings. Since the dispersion effectiveness is directly related to power input, it follows that any ball charge which fills the mill to less or more than the half way mark results in a corresponding decrease in grinding output.

Advantages

1. No pre-mixing of pigment into vehicle is normally required. The vehicle is normally charged directly to the mill followed by the pigment charge.

2. Volatile loss and contamination is essentially nil, since the ball milling is carried out in a closed system.

3. No special skilled supervision or attention to the process is required since the ball mill equipment is so set and simple that labour costs for a ball mill operation are minimum.

4. Maintenance costs are low.

5. Ball mills are widely adaptable to the grinding to most paint dispersion and to all pigment whether soft or hard, fine or coarse. Only highly viscous systems are not amenable to ball mill grinding.

6. Standardization in ball mill is readly accomplished

Sand Grinders

This is a very simple machine consisting of a vertical water jacketted pot which contains graded sand (20 to 40 mesh) or glass bollotine of 0.5 to 1.0 mm diameter. It is agitated by a specially designed impeller comprising a vertical steel shaft to which steel disks are attached at intervals.

The pre-mixed pigments slurry is pumped in at the bottom of the container and rises through and sand which is kept in a fluid condition by rapidly rotating impeller. Dispersion of the pigment takes place as result of shear as it rises through the chamber, the rate of throughput being regulated by the speed of the pump. The majority of pigments are satisfactorily dispersed when they reach the top of the chamber and the dispersion passes out through a special mesh which retains the sand particles. With an adequate supply of premixed pigment slurry the process can be continuous and the great virtue of sand milling is the high output obtainable from a small mill.

Advantages

1. It has low power consumption small space requirement and low initial investment.

2. No special skilled supervision or attention is required due to safety and simplicity or the sand grinder equipment.

3. Flexibility in volume of output is afforded by the continuous nature of the process high production rates can be attained by use of proper mill base premix.

It is, however unable to handle highly viscous mill base or heterogeneous premixes containing large hard or oversize aglomerates.

Colloid Mill

Colloidal suspensions and emulsions, with particle or droplet sizes less than one micron are produced by wet grinding in a colloid mill. The mill consists or a stator and a rotor with conical working surfaces between which there is an adjustable clearance between 2-30 thousandth of an inch. The rotor speed is about 3000 - 15000 r.p.m. The suspension, consisting of particles is introduced through a funnel and it thrown outward by centrifugal action and size reduction is effected as it passes between the working surfaces.

Another form of mill which does not give quite such a fine product is a jet pulverizer in which the solid is pulverized in jets of high pressure superheated or compressed air supplied at pressures up to 500 lb/in^2. The pulverizing takes place in a shallow cylindrical chamber with a number of jets arranged trangentially at equal intervals around the circumference. The solid is thrown to the outside walls of the chamber and the fine particles are formed by the shearing action resulting from the differential velocities within the fluid streams. The jet pulverizer mill gives a product with a particle size between 1 and 10 microns.

In all colloid mills the power consumption is very high and the material should therefore be ground as finely as possible before it is fed to the mill.

Attrition Mill

The container is usually of stainless steel and the ceramics or stainless steel balls ranging in diameter from 1/8" to 1/2" according to the type of material being processed. It is more flexible than ball mill in operation over a wider range of viscosities.

The pigmented vehicle mixture is circulated by built in pumping systems. The pumping systems also serves also to charge with discharge the mill. The attritor is designed for producing very fine dispersion. It is suitable for industrial finishes.

Models	*Tank Capacity*	*Capacity Delivered*
0.1 S	750 CC	200-400 CC
1 S	1 Gallons	5 Pints
10 S	15 Gallons	8-10 Gallons
15 S	24 Gallons	12-15 Gallons
60 S	80 Gallons	30-35 Gallons
100 S	125 Gallons	60-80 Gallons

Kady Mill

It consists basically of a high speed rotor mounted at the end of a shaft and revolving in a closely fitting stator. Both rotor and stator are slotted so that material undergoing dispersion is drawn into the rotor and then ejected through the stator slots at high speed. Kady mill are made in a range of sizes and are used for the dispersion of *'soft'* pigments in both aqueous and nonaqueous paints.

High Speed Impellers

They are employed as premixers, as dispersers for *'soft'* pigments, as thinining and tinting mixers, and as dissolvers. A circular steel plate is attached to the end of a steel shaft and the periphery of the disk is cut and then bent to form an irregular edge. The disk is suspended in a pot which is usually jacketted for water cooling and for maximum efficiency. There is a definite relationship between the diameter for the disks and the dimentisons of the pot. When used as a premixer or disperser care must be taken to ensure the currect composition and consistency of mill base.

Mechanical factors affecting the efficiency of high speed impeller are the following mentioned.

1. Speed of rotation of impeller.
2. Ratio of impeller diameter to tank diameter.
3. Ration of height of liquid level to tank diameter.
4. Position of impeller in the mixture.

Refining

All paints are liable to contamination from materials such as skin, sack fibres etc. There are three ways of removing such extraneous matter.

(a) By the use of single roll mill which acts virtually as a very efficient strainer. All the coarse pigment particles are retained in the hopper, being unable to pass beneath the bar.

(b) By passing the paint through a very fine sieve. This improved technique has rendered the use of single roll mill unnecessary.

(c) By filtering through certain filteration equipment. Screening is often unsatisfactory for certain high grade finishes, for example automotive finishes and refrigerator finishes. In such cases a variable speed centrifugal classifier is required. Clear vehicles are clarified by means of centrifugal clarifier or filter press.

Packing

Packing also serves as an advertising medium. Packing sealing equipement is now available for almost any desired volume. The glueing and compression units are extensively used in paint industries.

ROLLING
114. NON-FERROUS FORGING
115. NON-FERROUS FOUNDRY
116. NON PRESSURE
117. INCANDESCENT LAMP
118. NUMBER COMBINATION LOCKS FOR LUGGAGES
119. NUTS & BOLTS
120. PAPER COATED ALUMINIUM AND COPPER WIRE
121. PETROMAX CONTAINER
122. PHOTO ETCHING OF STAINLESS STEEL PLATES
123. PIPE GALVANIZING PLANT
124. PISTON RING-AUTOMOBILE
125. PLANT PROTECTION EQUIPMENTS
126. PLATINUM LABORATORY APPARATUS
127. PRESSURE COOKER & ALUMINIUM UTENSILS
128. PRESSURE DIE CASTING
129. PRINTED ALUMINIUM COLLAPSIBLE TUBES
130. PRINTED TIN CONTAINERS
131. PRINTING PRESS (CYLINDER MACHINE)
132. PUMPS FOR CHEMICAL INDUSTRY (SPECIAL)
133. RAILWAY SLEEPERS (M.S.)
134. RAZOR TWIN BLADE
135. R.C.C SPUN PIPES
136. RE-ROLLING COPPER AND BRASS SHEET AND RODS
137. RE-ROLLING MILLS
138. RESIN COATED SAND
139. RESIN CORED SOFT SOLDER WIRES
140. ROLLER BEARING AND FORGING
141. ROLLING OF STAINLESS STEEL PATTA
142. RUBBER INSULATED PLIERS (HAND TOOLS)
143. RUBBING COMPOUND FOR AUTOMOBILES
144. SCIENTIFIC LABORATORY EQUIPMENTS
145. SECONDARY LEAD EXTRAC -TION BY SCRAP BATTERY PLATES,PIPES & SHEET
146. SEAMLESS M.S. TUBES & PIPES
147. SELF TAPPING STEEL SCREWS
148. SEWING NEEDLES
149. S.G. IRON & ALLOY STEEL CASTING
150. SHEET METAL PRODUCTS, (FERROUS/NON-FERROUS)
151. SHIP/MARINE CONTAINER
152. SHOCK ABSORBER
153. SHOE EYELETS
154. SHOT AND GRITS BY AUTOMIZATION PROCESS
155. SHOVELS
156. SILENCERS (MUFFLERS) EXHAUST & TAIL PIPE FOR ALL TYPES OF VEHICLES
157. SINTERED BEARING
158. SINTERED BUSHES
159. SINTERED METAL PRODUCT
160. SOFT AND HARD FERRITES
161. SPANNERS
162. SPARK PLUGS
163. STEEL PLANT (ELECTRIC ARC FURNACE BASED- EAF)
164. SPHERIODAL GRAPHITE CAST IRON
165. SPRAY DRYER
166. STAINLESS STEEL SHEET ROLLING TO PRODUCE STAINLESS STEEL UTENSIL
167. STAINLESS STEEL UTENSILS
168. STAPLE PINS,PAPER PIN , GEM CLIPS ETC.
169. STEEL CASTING
170. STEEL FOUNDRY
171. STEEL FURNITURES AND ELECTRICAL APPLIANCES
172. STEEL PLANT (MINI)
173. STEEL RODS AND COILS FROM SCRAPS
174. STEEL ROLLING MILL
175. STEEL STRIPS (COLD ROLLED) SILICON WITH GRAIN RIENTED FOR ELECTRIC USE.
176. STEEL TRANSMISSION LINE TOWERS & ROLLING MILL TO PRODUCE STEEL SECTION
177. STEEL FURNITURES AND ELECTRICAL APPLIANCES
178. STEEL WIRE DRAWING AND GALVANIZING
179. SUBMERGED ARC WELDED PIPES
180. SUBMERSIBLE PUMP MANUFACTURING
181. SUPER ENAMELLED COPPER WIRE
182. THREE WHEELERS
183. TIE-ROD ENDS
184. TIN CONTAINERS
185. TRACTOR TRAILERS
186. TRANSMISSION POWER FITTING
187. TUBULAR POLES
188. SUPER ENAMELLED COPPER WIRES
189. TUBULAR POLES FOR ELECTRICAL TRANSMIS- -SION (BY FABRICATION PROCESS)
190. TUBULAR POLES OF M.S. & HIGH TENSILE STEEL
191. VACUUM CLEANERS
192. VACUUM FLASK (STAINLESS STEEL)
193. VALVES FOR REFRIGERA TION AND AIR-CONDITION
194. VEHICLE WELDING & PAINTING
195. VENETION BLIND
196. WASHING MACHINES (AUTOMATIC AND COMPUTERISED)
197. WATER CONTROLLER (AUTOMATIC)
198. WATCH STRAPS/CHAINS/ BRACELETS/BELT BRASS & STAINLESS STEEL
199. WATER COOLERS
200. WELDED WIRE MESH
201. WICK STOVES

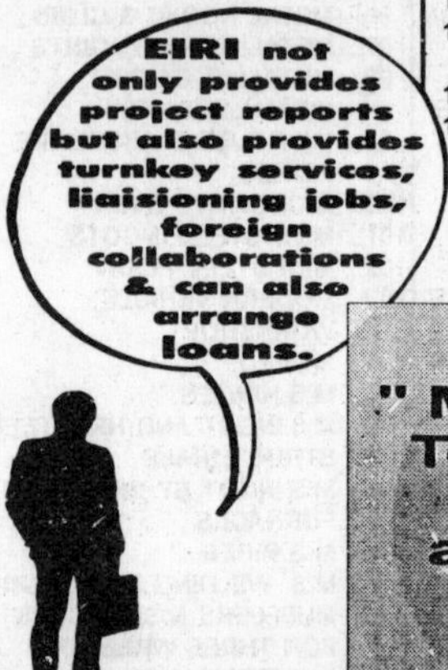

PATRONS

We can prepare " Market Survey cum Detailed Techno-Economic Reports" on any Item/Project as per your requirements.

COST : Rs. 6000/- ONLY (DELIVERY : WITHIN 20 DAYS)

Price Rs. 3000/- for each "Detailed Project Report" Payable in advance through Draft/Cash/M.O. in favour of *"ENGINEERS INDIA RESEARCH INSTITUTE"*. *OR Ask by V.P.P.* Ph : 291 8117, 291 6431, 292 0361 • Fax : 91-11-291 6431

LIME

273. CEMENT TILES (GLAZED)
274. DOUBLE FIRING (HEATING)
275. CHELATED ZINC (ZN EDTA)
276. CHEMICALS FROM PRAWN HEAD
277. CHLORAL HYDRATE

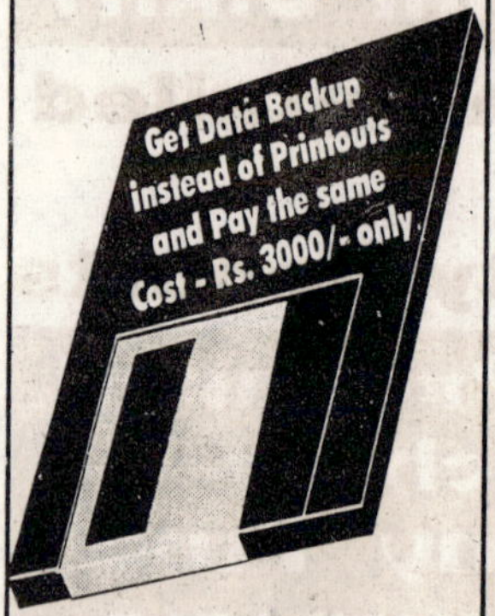

278. CHLORAMPHENICOL
279. CHLORINATED PARAFFIN WAX (C.P.W)
280. CHROMIC ACID
281. CEMENT PAINT & DISTEMPER
282. CITRIC ACID FROM MOLASSES
283. CLEANING OF COOLING SYSTEM AND BOILER
284. COBALT OCTOATE
285. COMPOST FOR MUSHROOM
286. COPPER OXYCHLORIDE
287. DE-NICKELING (ELECTROLYTIC PROCESS)
288. DEXTROSE MONOHYDRATE AND DEXTROSE ANHY DROUS POWDER FROM TAPIOCA STARCH
289. DI CALCIUM PHOSPHATE
290. DI ETHYL OXALATE
291. DI METHYL ORTHOPHTHALATE
292. DIOCTYL PHTHALATE (DOP)
293. DI PHENYL GLYCERINE
294. DI PHENYL OXIDE
295. DINITRO-CHLORO BENZENE
296. DISTILLED WATER
297. DODECYL BENZENE SULPHONATE
298. ELECTROLESS NICKEL PLATING ON PLASTICS
299. ENDOSULFAN
300. ETHYL ACETATE
301. ETHYL ALCOHOL (POTABLE LIQUOR)
302. ETHYL HEXANOL
303. FERRIC ALUM
304. FERRO CHROME LIGNO SULPHONATE
305. FERRO MANGANESE
306. FERRO SILICONE
307. FERRO VANADIUM FROM VANADIUM SLUDGE
308. FERROUS SILICATE
289. FERROUS SULPHATE
310. FLUORESCENT TUBE LIGHT POWDER
311. FORMALDEHYDE
312. FRACTIONAL DISTILLATION OF D.M.O (DEMENTHOLIZED OIL)
313. FRACTIONAL DISTILLATION OF ESSENTIAL OIL & MEDICINAL PLANT EXTRACT
314. FURFURAL FROM RICE HUSK
315. GASKET SHELLAC COMPOUND
316. GIBBERELLIC ACID
317. GLYCERINE
318. GOSSYPOL (POLY PHENOL) FROM COTTON SEED OIL
319. H - ACID
320. HEPTAL DEHYDE
321. HIGH CARBON FERRO CHROME
322. HYDRATED CALCIUM SILICATE BRICK
323. HYDRATED LIME FROM SEA SHELL
324. HYDROCHLORIC ACID
325. HYDRO FLUORIC ACID
326. HYDROGEN PEROXIDE (BY AUTO-OXIDATION PROCESS)
327. INDUSTRIAL ALCOHOL
328. INTEGERATED COMPLEX OF EASTER & ALLIED PRODUCT (D.O.P, D.B.P ETHYLACETATE WIRE ENAMEL & CABLE JELLY)
329. IRON OXIDE FOR MAKING FERITTES
330. LACTIC ACID FROM WHITE SUGAR BY FERMENTATION PROCESS
331. LEAD EXTRACTION FROM BATTERY SCRAP
332. LEAD OXIDE
(A) LEAD MONOXIDE
(B) LEAD TETRA OXIDE
(C) GREYLEAD OXIDE
333. LIQUID OXYGEN BOTTLING PLANT
334. LIQUID SHOE POLISH
335. LIQUID FLOOR POLISH
336. LUBE OIL VISCOSITY IMPROVED FOR P.P.G/P.E.G.
337 LUBRICANTS ASHLESS 100% COMBUSTION
338. MAGNESIUM CARBONATE AND MAGNESIUM BI-CARMONATE
339. MAGNESIUM HYDROXIDE POWDER
340. MAGNESIUM SILICATE
341. MAGNESIUM SULPHATE
342. MALEIC ANHYDRIDE
343. MANUFACTURING OF CARBON MONO-OXIDE WATER GAS
344. MENTHOL BOLD CRYSTALS FROM FLAKES
345 MENTHOL CRYSTAL AND MENTHA OIL
346. MERCURIC OXIDE
347. METAL PRE-TREATMENT CHEMICALS
348. METHANE GAS BY SODIUM ACETATE & SODA LIME
349. METHYL ACETYL RICINOLATE
350. METOL
351. METOL FROM HYDROQUI -NONE & METHYL AMINE
352. MICANITE
353. MICRO NUTRIENT MIXTURE
354. MINERAL WATER
355. MINI CEMENT PLANT (BY ROTARY KILN PROCESS)
356. MIXED FERTILIZER
357. MONO CHLORO ACETIC ACID
358. MONO CROTOPHOS TECHNICAL
359. MOSQUITO COIL
360. NICKEL SULPHATE
361. NICOTINE FROM TOBACCO WASTE
362. NICOTINE SULPHATE FROM TOBACCO WASTE
363. NITRO BENZENE
364. NITRO CELLULOSE SANDING SEALER/LACQUER
365. NITRO MUSK
366. NITROGEN AND OXYGEN GAS PLANT
367. NON-IONIC SURFACTANT (WETTING AGENT)
368. OCTANOL
369. ORTHO NITRO PHENOL
370. OXALIC ACID FROM MOLASSES
371. OXALIC ACID FROM TREE BARK
372. OXALIC ACID FROM WASTE VEGETABLES
373. OXYGEN GAS PLANT
374. OXYGEN GAS PLANT (AIR SEPERATION METHOD)
375. PARA-AMINO BENZOIC ACID
376. PARA-AMINO PHENOL
377. PECTIN FROM RAW PAPAYA
378. PHENYL
379. PHTHALIC ANHYDRIDE
380. PHOSPHORIC ACID FROM ROCK PHOSPHATE
381. PHOTO EMULSION FOR ROTARY SCREEN PRINTING
382. PHTHALOCYANINE BLUE
383. PLASTER OF PARIS BANDAGES
384. POLY VINYL ACETATE
385. POTASSIUM DICHROMATE/ BICHROMATE
387. POTASSIUM IODATE
388. POTASSIUM NITRATE
389. POTASSIUM PERMAGNATE
380. PTASSIUM PER SULPHATE
381. POTASSIUM PER OXY DI-SULPHIDE
382. POTASSIUM SILICATE

Price Rs. 3000/- for each "Detailed Project Report" Payable in advance through Draft/Cash/M.O. in favour of *"ENGINEERS INDIA RESEARCH INSTITUTE"* OR Ask by V.P.P. Ph : 291 8117, 291 6431, 292 0361 • Fax : 91-11- 291 6431

383. POWER ALCOHOL
384. PVC RESIN FROM ETHYL ALCOHOL
385. PYRIDINE & ITS DERIVATIVES
386. REACTOR (CHEMICAL)
387. RECLAMATION OF SPENT BLEACHING EARTH
388. RECLAMATION OF NICKEL SPENT CATALYST FROM VANASPATI INDUSTRY
389. RECTIFIED SPIRIT FROM MOLASSES & MAHUA FLOWERS
390. RECTIFIED SPIRIT FROM RICE STRAW
391. RED OXIDE PAINT/PRIMER (ANTI CORROSIVE) BASED ORGANIC RED PIGMENTS
392. REMOVAL OF ANTIMONY FROM LEAD SCRAP
393. RESORCINOL
394. SALICYLIC ACID
395. SANTONIN
396. SILICA GEL (BLUE SELF INDICATING PROCESS)
397. SILICONE EMULSION
398. SILICONE FROM RICE HUSK
389. SILICONE RESINS
390. SILICONE SPRAYSILVER BRAZING FOIL
391. SILVER EXTRACTION FROM WASTE HYPO SOLUTION
392. SILVER PARTS FOR CERAMIC CAPACITOR SINGLE SUPER PHOSPHATE & MIXED FERTILIZER (NPK)
393. SINGLE SUPER PHOSPHATE (S.S.P) & SULPHURIC ACID
394. SODA ASH
395. SODIUM ALUMINATE
396. SODIUM BI-CARBONATE (BAKING SODA) FROM SODA ASH
397. SODIUM CHROMATE SODIUM CYCLAMATE
398. SODIUM DI-CHROMATE
399. SODIUM DI-CHROMATE AND SODIUM SULPHATE AS BYE PRODUCTS
400. SODIUM HEXA META PHOSPHATE
401. SODIUM HYDROSULFITE SODIUM HYPO CHLORIDE (BLEACH LIQUOR)
402. SODIUM ISO-PROPYL XANTHATE
403. SODIUM LAURYL SULPHATE
404. SODIUM LAURYL SULPHATE AND SODIUM LAURYL ETHER SULPHATE
405. SODIUM NITRATE
406. SODIUM PETROLEUM SULPHONATE (EMULSIFIER)
407. SODIUM SILICATE FROM
   (1) PADDY SILK HUSK AND SILICA
   (2) SODIUM CARBONATE AND SILICA
   (3) CAUSTIC SODA AND SILICA
408. SODIUM SULPHATE (ANHYDROUS)
409. SODIUM SULPHIDE BY BARIUM SULPHATE PROCESS
410. SODIUM SULPHIDE FROM AMMONIA & SODIUM CHLORIDE
411. SODIUM SULPHITE
412. SODIUM TRI-POLY PHOSPHATE
413. SOFTENER (CATIONIC ANIONIC & NON-IONIC)
414. STANNOUS CHLORIDE
415. STERATES MANUFACTURE (CALCIUM, ZINC, ALUMINIUM, MAGNESIUM STEARATES)
416. SULPHUR FROM PYRITES AND SLAG
417. SULPHUR CRYSTALS/ LUMPS
418. SULPHURIC ACID
419. SULPHURIC ACID FROM D.C.D.A PROCESS
420. SUPER PHOSPHATE (S.S.P)
421. SYNTHETIC IRON OXIDE (YELLOW)
422. TARTARIC ACID
423. TRIMETHYL AMMONIUM CHLORIDE
424. TRIPHENYL PHOSPHITE (T.P.P)
425. UREA FORMALDEHYDE & MELAMINE FORMALDEHYDE POWDER
426. UNDECYLINIC ACID
427. VINYL ACETATE MONOMER
428. WIRE DRAWING LUBRICANT
429. WIRE ENAMEL
430. XANTHATES
431. ZINC CHLORIDE
432. ZINC OXIDE
433. ZINC PHOSPHATING IN COLD PROCESS
434. ZINC SILICATE
435. ZINC STEARATE
436. ZINC SULPHATE

DYES AND INTERMEDIATES

437. ACID BLACK
438. AURAMINE'O'
439. AZO DYES STUFF
440. DYE & DYE INTERMEDIATE
441. DYE INTERMEDIATES
442. MALACHITE GREEN
443. METHYLENE BLUE
444. PHTHALOCYANINE BLUE
445. PHTHALOCYANINE BLUE & GREEN
446. REACTIVE DYES
447. SULPHUR BLACK DYE
448. VAT DYES
449. WAX FLOOR POLISH

ELECTRICAL AND ELECTRONIC

450. AIR CONDITIONING
451. ALUMINIUM ALLOY CONDUCTOR
452. ALUMINIUM CABLE
453. ALUMINIUM ELECTROYTIC CAPACITORS
454. AUDIO CASSETTE ASSEMBLING & RECORDING
455. AUDIO CASSETTES DUPLICATING RECORDING
456. AUDIO CASSETTES & AUDIO STUDIO
457. AUDIO CASSETTES PLANE AND RECORDED
458. AUDIO MAGNETIC HEADS
459. AUDIO MAGNETIC TAPE
460. AUDIO/VIDEO CASSETTES
461. AUTO BULB/LAMPS
462. AUTOMATIC VOLTAGE STABILIZER
463. BATTERY PLATES
464. B/W TV & COMPUTER MONITOR PICTURE TUBE
465. BREAD BOARDS
466. CAMERA (35 MM)
467. CAPACITORS
468. CARBON ELECTRODE USED FOR BATTERY CELL
469. CARBON POTETIOMETERS
470. CEILING FAN
471. CERAMIC INSULATOR
472. CHOKE AND PATTI
473. CHOKE AND STARTER
474. CHOKE USED FOR FLUORESCENT LAMPS
475. COLOUR TELEVISION
476. COLOUR AND BLACK &

WHITE TELEVISION
477. COMPACT DISC
478. COMPACT DISC PLAYER (AUDIO/VIDEO)
479. COMPUTER ASSEMBLY
480. COMPUTER HARDWARE
481. COMPUTER KEYBOARD
482. COMPUTER PERIPHERALS
483. COMPUTER PRINTERS
484. COMPUTER RIBBON
485. COMPUTER RIBBON REINKING OR REFILLING
486. COMPUTER SOFTWARE
487. COMPUTER STATIONERY
488. COMPUTER STATIONERY & IMPORTED HARDWARE PARTS
489. COMPUTER TERMINALS
490. COMPUTERISED WASHING MACHINE (AUTOMATIC)
491. CONDENSER FOR MOTOR USING MPP FILM
492. CONTROL PANEL BOARD
493. COOLING COIL FOR AIR CONDITIONERS
494. COPPER STRIP COIL FROM SCRAP
495. CORDLESS TELEPHONES
496. D.C. MICRO MOTORS
497. D.G.SETS
498. DISH ANTENNA AND CABLE T.V. NETWORK EQUIPMENT
499. DISTRIBUTION TRANS--FORMERS AND REPAIRS
500. DOMESTIC ELECTRICAL APPLIANCES- ROOM COOLER, WASHING MACHINE, WATER HEATER, ELECTRIC ROOM HEATER
501. ELECTRIC ENERGY METER
502. ELECTRIC FANS
503. ELECTRIC HORN FOR AUTOMOBILE
504. ELECTRIC LAMP/GLS (INCANDESCENT LAMP)
505. ELECTRIC MIXER
506. ELECTRIC MOTORS
507. ELECTRIC MOTOR WINDING (FOR FAN, MIXIES, ETC.)
508. ELECTRIC STEAM IRON
509. ELECTRICAL APPLIANCES
510. ELECTRICAL FIXTURES
511. ELECTRICAL STAMPING
512. ELECTROLYTIC CAPACITORS
513. ELECTROMAGNETIC RELAY
514. ELECTRONIC BALAST/CHOK
515. ELECTRICAL CHOKE
516. ELECTRONIC DIGITAL WATCHES
517. ELECTRONIC DIGITAL WEIGHING MACHINE
518. ELECTRONIC FIRE ALARM
519. ELECTRONIC GAS STOVE LIGHTERS
520. ELECTRONIC PRESSURE INDICATORS, ELECTRICALS, ELECTRONIC LIQUID LEVEL INDICATORS, ELECTRONIC TEMPERATURE INDICATOR, DIGITAL TACHOMETER
521. ELECTRONIC TELEPHONE INSTRUMENTS
522. ELECTRONIC TOYS
523. ELECTRONIC WATCHES & CLOCKS
524. FAX MACHINES
525. F.H.P MOTORS
526. FLOPPY DISKETTES
527. FLUORESCENT LAMP STARTER
528. FLUORESCENT TUBULAR LAMPS WITH INTRODUC TION TO MERCURY VAPOUR LAMPS
529. GAS DETECTOR (L.P.G)
530. GENERATOR SET & PUMP SETS
531. GENERATOR (BATTERY OPERATED)
532. HARDWARE FITTING FOR TRANSMISSION LINE (OVERHEAD LINE MATERIAL
533. HEADERS FOR TRANSIS-TOR ICS SEMI CONDUCTOR
534. H.T & L.T INSULATORS
535. H.T & M.V INDUSTRIAL CUBICAL SWITCH BOARD
536. INFORMATION MOVING DISPLAY (L.E.D TYPE)
537. JELLY FILLED TELEPHONE CABLES
538. LAP TOP COMPUTERS
539. LEAD ACID BATTERIES
540. LEAD ACID BATTERY PLATES AND ASSEMBLING OF BATTERY
541. LIGHT EMITTING DIODES (L.E.D)
542. LINEAR ICS TRAINER KIT
543. LOUD SPEAKER
544. L.T TRANSFORMER REPAIRING
545. METAL FILM RESISTORS
546. METALLISED POLYPROPYLENE, POLYESTER FILM CAPACITOR
547. MICA BASE ELECTRONIC COMPONENTS
548. MICA PAPER WASTE PAPER FROM MICA WASTE
549. MICRO PROCESSORS TRAINER KITS BASED ON MICRO PROCESSORS
550. MINI COMPUTER (PERSONAL COMPUTER)
551. MINIATURE CIRCUIT BREAKER (M.C.B)
552. MINIATURE WATCH BATTERIES (BUTTON CELL)
553. MIXER/GRINDER (MIXI)
554. MONO CHROME COMPUTER MONITOR
555. MOTOR START ELECTROLYTIC CAPACITOR
556. MULTI LAYER P.C.B
557. MULTIPLE RELAY FOR LOW VOLTAGE
558. NEON INDICATOR
559. NEON SIGN MANUFACTURE
560. OPTICAL FIBRE CABLES
561. OPTO MECHANICAL & ELECTRICAL EQUIPMENTS
562. PHOTO COLOUR LAB
563. PICTURE TUBE (B/W)
564. PLAIN PAPER COPIER
565. PLASTIC FILM CAPACITORS
566. POLYESTER CAPACITORS
567. PORTABLE GENERATOR SET
568. PORTABLE TELEVISION(TV)
569. POWER CAPACITORS
570. POWER INVERTERS
571. POWER PLANT
572. POWER TRANSFORMERS UP TO 600 KVA
573. PRINTED CIRCUIT BOARD PUNCH CARDS
574. PVC WIRES & CABLES
575. RESIN CAST CT & PT (1 KV)
576. SEMI CONDUCTOR DEVICE
577. SEMI CONDUCTORS FOR TRANSISTORS AND DIODES
578. SETTING UP OF A VIDEO STUDIO
579. SMOKE DETECTORS
580. SOLAR CELLS
581. SOLAR MODULES
582. SOLAR PHOTO VOLTAIC SYSTEM
583. SOLDER FLUXES
584. SOLAR WATER HEATING PANELS
585. STEEL FURNITURE AND ELECTRICAL APPLIANCES
586. STEREO AMPLIFIERS
587. STEREO CASSETTE RECORDERS/PLAYERS
588. STREET LIGHT FITTINGS SURGE SUPPRESSOR
589. TANTALUM CAPACITORS

MIX)
690. INSTANT FOOD (INSTANT FOOD+FAST FOOD PARLOUR)
691. INSTANT NOODLES
692. INSTANT TEA
693. INSTANT TEA FROM BLACK TEA
694. INTEGERATED STARCH BAKING POWDER/YEAST INDUSTRY
695. IODIZED SALT
696. IODIZED SALT (ORDINARY MOISTURE-LESS/FREE FLOWING IN PLASTIC BAGS AND CONTAINERS)
697. JAM, JELLIES, FRUIT JUICE & ALLIED PRODUCTS
698. KATHA AND CUTCH
699. KHANDSARI SUGAR
700. KHANDSARI SUGAR & IMFL
700A. LACTIC ACID FROM WHITE SUGAR BY FERMENTATION PROCESS
701. LACTOSE & BY PRODUCTS PROCESSING FROM MILK
702. LIQUID GLUCOSE AND ITS BYE PRODUCTS
703. MACRONI AND VERMICILLI
704. MALT EXTRACTION FROM BARLEY
705. MANGO PROCESSING (MANGO PULP, JUICE & SLICES)
706. MAYUR BRAND TYPE CHEWING TOBACCO
707. MINERAL WATER
708. MILK PRESERVATION & MARKETING TO WHOLE SELLERS (INPOUCH PACKING BY UHT TECHNOLOGY)
709. MILK PROCESSING AND PACKAGING OF MILK PRODUCTS
710. MILK PRODUCTS (CASEIN, LACTOSE, GHEE & WHEY POWDER)
711. MILK TOFFEE
712. MINI FLOUR MILL
713. MINI SUGAR PLANT
714. MISRI (PEARL SUGAR CANDIES)
715. MODERN RICE MILL
716. MURABBA
717. MUTTON TALLOW
718. NON-BASMATI RICE FROM PADDY
719. OLEORESIN, ESSENTIAL OIL, DYES & POWDER OF SPICES
720. OLEORESIN EXTRACTION FROM DIPTERO-CARPUT TURMINATUS AND PINUS KHASYANA
721. OLEORESIN EXTRACTION FROM CHILLI
722. PAN MASALA AND POUCH MAKING
723 PAN MASALA, TOBACCO, ZARDA & KIMAM
724. PANEER FROM MILK
725. PAPPAD PLANT
726. PAPAIN FROM PAPAYA (PAPAYA LATEX)
727. PECTIN FROM MANGO PEEL PECTIN FROM APPLE POMACE
728. PICKLES AND SAUCES
729. PICKLES MURABBA ETC. (VEG. & NON VEG.PICKLES)
730. PIGGERY MEAT PROCESS
731. PINE-APPLE JUICE PREPARATION & PACKAGING
732. POTATO POWDER
733. POULTRY FEED
734. PROCESSED FOODS & SPICES (EOU)
735. PROCESSED READYMADE FOOD
736. PROCESSING OF FRUITS AND VEGETABLES
737. RASGULLAS MAKING AND CANNING IN METAL CANS
738. READY TO EAT SNACK FOOD (CRAX, ROLL & BALL TYPE)
739. RICE AND CORN FLAKES
740. ROASTED/SALTED/ MASALACASHEW-NUTS, ALMONDS & PEANUTS
741. ROLLER FLOUR MILL
742. SALT LICKS FOR CATTLE
743. SAUSAGES FOOD CASING
744. SOFT DRINKS
745. SOFT DRINKS ESSENCES
746. SOFT DRINKS (NON CARBONATED) MANGO, LICCHI, PINEAPPLE FLAVOURS- FROOTI TYPE IN TETRAPACK)
747. SOFTY ICE CREAM CONES (FULLY AUTOMATIC)
748. SOYABEAN PRODUCTS
749. SOYA MILK & PANEER
750. STARCH & ALLIED PROPDUCTS FROM BROKEN RICE
751. SUGARCANE JUICE PRESERVATION
752. SUGAR CUBES FROM CANE SUGAR
753. SUGAR PLANT(Rs.30Cr.Proj.)
754. SWEET AROMA BETEL NUT
755. SYNTHETIC TALLOW
756. TAMARIND JUICE POWDER
757. TEA & COFFEE PROCESSING & PACKAGING
758. TOFFEES, GOLIES, CANDY (HARD BOILED)
759. TOMATO PRODUCTS
760. TUITY FRUITY
761. VODKA FROM POTATOES
762. WINE, BRANDY, WHISKY AND CHAMPAGNE
763. YEAST FROM MOLASSES
764. ZARDA, KIMAM NO. 60,90,120,160,240,300 & 400 (TOBACCO)
765. ZARDA-ZAFRANI (BABA-CHHAP TYPE)

GUMS & ADHESIVE

766. ACRYLIC ADHESIVE
767. ADHESIVE (FEVICOL TYPE)
768. ADHESIVE BASED ON POLYURETHANE
769. ADHESIVE FOR BAND AID (JOHNSON & JOHNSON TYPE)
770. ADHESIVE INDUSTRIES (LAMINATED, STICKER,DDL & OTHER TYPES)
771. ADHESIVE FOR GASKET (LIQUID/PASTE)
772. GUAR GUM
773. GUM BOTTLE (PVC)
774. GUM FOR PASTING LABELS
775. OFFICE PASTE
776. RUBBER ADHESIVE
777. SURGICAL ADHESIVE PLASTER

LEATHER & LEATHER PRODUCTS

778. HANDMADE LEATHER
779. LEATHER BOARD FROM LEATHER WASTE
780. LEATHER FOR UPHOLSTRY (SOFA)
781. LEATHER GARMENTS
782. LEATHER GOODS
783. LEATHER SHOES
784. LEATHER SHOE & CHAPPAL
785. LEATHER SUITCASES, BRIEFCASES AND TRAVELLING BAGS
786. LEATHER GOODS AND GARMENTS
787. SHEEP SKIN PICKLING PLANT
788. SHOE UPPER
789. SPORT SHOES (PLASTIC)

MISCELLANEOUS PRODUCTS

790. AGARBATTI (INSENCE STICK)
790A AGARBATTI (Mosquito Repellent)
790B AGARBATI BAMBOO STICK
791. AGARBATTI SYNTHETIC PERFUMERY COMPOUND
792. AIR FRESHNER(ODONIL TYPE)
793. AIR TAXI
794. AMUSEMENT PARK
795. ANODIC ALUMINIUM LABEL
796. AQUACULTURE PRAWN FARMING (100% EOU)
797. AQUA CULTURE SHRIMP FARMING (100% EOU)
798. ARTIFICIAL FLOWERS
799. ARTIFICIAL JEWELLERY

800. ASBESTOS YARN
801. ASH TRAYS FOR MARUTI VEHICLE
801A AIR BUBBLE PACKAGING
802. ASPHALTIC ROOFING SHEET (METAL COMPONENTS)
803. AUTOMATIC BOOK BINDING
803A ALKYD RESIN
803B APPLE JUICE CONCENTRATE
804. BALL POINT PEN FEFILLS (JOTTER TYPE)
805. BANK BRANCH BUILDING
806. BANQUET HALL
807. BIO-COAL BRIQUETTES FROM AGRICULTURAL CELLULOSE WASTE
808. BOOT CREAM/POLISH
809. BUFFING & POLISHING COMPOUND
810. BRASS BADGES BY ETCHING
811. BRIQUETTED FUEL FROM AGRO WASTE
812. BRIQUETTING OF LIGNITE COAL
813. BUFFALO HORN TIP, HOOF
813A BANQUET HALL
814. BUTTON
815. CALCINED PETROLEUM (C.P) COKE
816. CANVAS SHOES
817. CANVAS SHOES, JUNGLE BOOTS
818. CARBON BRUSH, BRUSH HOLDER AND SLIP RING
819. CEMENT SHEETS WITH COIR FIBRE AND OTHER SEGMENTS
820. CERAMIC TILES (GLAZED) BY DOUBLE FIRING/ HEATING
821. CINNAMON
822. COAL BRIQUETTES
823. COLD STORAGE & ICE
824. COLD STORAGE FOR FRUITS AND VEGETABLES
825. COSTUME JEWELLERY/ IMITATION JEWELLERY
826. DECORATIVE LAMINATED SHEET (SUNMICA)
827. DIAMOND CUTTING AND EXPORTING
828. DRINKING STRAW FROM PROPYLENE
829. FASHION TECHNOLOGY INSTITUTE
830. FAST FOOD PARLOUR
831. FAST FOOD (INSTANT FOOD & FAST FOOD PARLOUR)
832. FIRE EXTINGUISHERS (SODA ACID TYPE)
833. FISH NET
834. FLORICULTURE (CUT FLOWER ROSE) WITH GREEN HOUSE
835. FLOOR COVERING SHEET
835A FILM STUDIO (VIDEO)
836. FLUSH DOOR, CHIP BOARD, WOOD WOOL & OTHER INSULATING BOARDS
837. GAS DETECTORS OF L.P.G
837A. GEMS MANUFACTURING
838. GLASS BOTTLE BY SCRAP
839. GOAT & SHEEP FARMING
840. GOLD ELECTROPLATING
841. GOLD JEWELLERY (E.O.U)
842. GOLD PLATED SILVER JEWELLERY & CUTLERY
843. GRANITE SLAB AND TILES
844. GREEN HOUSE
845. HARD CHROMIUM PLATING
846. HEALTH CLUB AND BEAUTY PARLOUR CUM HAIR SALOON WITH SONA BATH
847. HEALTH CLUB CUM BEAUTY PARLOUR TRAINING INSTITUTE
848. HORN TIP,HOOVE BUTTON
849. HOSPITAL
850. HOSPITAL (100 BEDS)
851. HOSPITAL (200 BEDS)
852. ICE MAKING PLANT
853. IMITATION AND COSTUME
854. JEWELLERY (NECKLACE, EARRINGS EAR TOP ETC.)
855. INITMATE SCENT CHEMICAL FROM ALL TYPES OF FLAVOUR
856. INVESTMENT CASTING
857. JUTE, COIR, GLASS ROPE/ SUTLI
858. JUTE TWINE
859. L.P.G BOTTLING PLANT
860. L.P.G REGULATOR (DOMESTIC PURPOSE)
861. LAMINATED PARTICLE BOARD & HARD BOARD
862. LAMINATED SAFETY AND TOUGHENED GLASS
863. LEASING & HIRE PURCHASE
864. LICHEN (CHARILA)
865. MANILA ROPES
865A MEDICAL COLLEGE
866. MATCH UNIT FROM WAXED PAPER
867. MEDIUM DENSITY FIBRE BOARD
868. MELAMINE CROCKERY
869. MINERAL WATER
870. MINI CEMENT PLANT
871. MIRROR SILVER, GOLDEN, PINK, BLACK & SMOKES
872. MODERN ADVERTISING AGENCY WITH DTP & FILM STUDIO
873. MOTEL/SMALL HOTEL
874. MULTI COLOUR PRINTING
875. MULTI STOREY COMMERCIAL COMPLEX ALONGWITH RESIDENTIAL AND DELUX FLATS FOR FOREIGN TOURISTS & REVOLVING RESTAURENT AT THE TOP
876. MULTIPLE LAMINATION INDUSTRY
876A. MUSHROOM GROWING AND PROCESSING (BY DEEP FREEZING METHOD)
877. NEWS PAPER PRINTING
878. NICKEL LINED INDUSTRIAL SCREEN
879. OFFSET COLOUR PRINTING PRESS (SIX COLOUR)
880. OFFSET PRINTING PRESS
881. P.C.C ELECTRIC POLES
882. PHOTOGRAPHIC DEVEL -OPER & FIXER
882A PVC EXTRUSION PROFILE
882B POP- CORN
882C PHOTO ETCHING OF S.S.
883. PRE STRESSES CEMENT CONCRETE PIPES
884. PILFER PROOF CAPS
885. PILFER PROOF CAPS AND CROWN CAP
886. POUCH MAKING AND GRAVURE PRINTING
887. POULTRY AND FISH FARMING (INTEGERATED UNIT)
888. PRINTING OF TIN SHEETS
889. READYMADE GARMENTS
890. RESTAURANT
891. ROSE PLANTATION AND ROSE OIL EXTRACTION
892. ROTOGRAVURE PRINTING
893. SAFETY BELTS
894. SAFETY MATCHES
895. SHOE LACES
896. SILK COCOON CULTIVATION (GROWING OF SILK COCOON WARM)
897. SILK SCREEN PRINTING FORMULATIONS FOR PLASTIC, PAPER & CLOTH
897A SPIKENARD (JATAMANSI)
898. STENCIL COATING SOLUTION
899. SUGAR CANDY (MISRI)
900. SUGAR CANE PLANTATION
901. SURAT ZARI
902. SYNTHETIC SHOES & SOLES
903. TEA PACKAGING INDUSTRY
904. TENNIS BALLS
905. THREE STAR HOTEL
906. TRAVELLING AGENCY
907. TRAYS, TROLLEYS FOR HOSPITAL WITH SCRATCHLESS COATING
908. WAX EXTRACTS (TANNING POWDER)
909. WIRE ROPE SLINGS
910. WOOD WOOL SLAB
911. WOODEN CANE FURNITURE WITH EXPORT POTENTIAL
912. WOODEN FURNITURE
913. WOODEN PANEL INCLUDING KILN SEASONING
914. WRIST WATCHES
915. ZEDOXY (KACHUR)

OIL FATS & WAXES

916. BEES WAX MANUFACTURE
917. CARDANOL FROM CASHEWNUT SHELL LIQUID
918. CASTOR OIL
919. CASTOR OIL DERIVATIVE OLEORESINS
920. CHILLI OIL

990. CAPSULE, TABLET & INJECTION WITH MODERN INSTRUMENTS
990A CASHEW FENI
991. CHLOROQUINONE PHOSPHATE (BULK DRUGS)
992. CLINICAL THERMOMETER
993. DENTAL GRADE EUGENOL
994. DEXTROSE MONOHYDRATE LIQUID GLUCOSE
994A DEHYDRATED ONION
995. DEXTROSE POWDER (ANHYDROUS FROM STARCH)
996. DEXTROSE SALINE SOLUTION
996A DISTILLERY (I.M.F.L)
997. DISPOSABLE NEEDLES FOR SYRINGES
998. DISPRIN
999. DISTILLED WATER
1000. EMPTY HARD GELATINE CAPSULES
1001. FILLING & PACKING OF CAPSULES
1002. GLUCOSE - D - POWDER
1003. GLYCERINE
1004. HOMOE & BIO-MEDICINES WITH MOTHER TINCTURE
1005. HOMOEPATHIC MEDICINES
1006. HYPODERMIC NEEDLES
1006A. I.V. FLUIDS
1007. IBUPROFEN
1008. INFUSION & TRANSFUSION SETS (I.V. SET)
1009. INJECTABLE FOR PHARMACEUTICALS
1010. INJECTION AMPOULES PACKAGING BOX
1011. INTEGERATED SURGICAL COTTON
1012. ICE MAKING PLANT
1012A ICE & COLD STORAGE
1013. LACTOSE & BY PRODUCTS PROCESSING FROM MILK
1014. LICHEN (JATAMANSI CHARILA)
1015. LIQUID GLUCOSE AND ITS BY-PRODUCTS
1015A L-LYSINE MONOHYDRO CHLORIDE
1016. LIQUID GLUCOSE FROM POTATOES
1017. MEDICAL COLLEGE
1018. NICOTINE FROM TOBACCO WASTE
1019. PHARMACEUTICAL AND FOOD GRADE GELATINE
1020. PHARMACEUTICAL INDUSTRY (TABLETS, CAPSULES, LIQUID, GEL, OINTMENT POWDER INJECTABLE)
1021. PHARMACEUTICAL UNIT (EOU) WITH FORMULA TIONS, INJECTABLES, ETC. PYRIDINE AND DERIVATIVES
1021A SALT (IODIZED SALT)
1022. SALINE & INJECTION WATER
1023. SALINE WATER & DEXTROSE SOLUTION (I.V.FLUID IN PLASTIC BOTTLES)
1024. SORBITOL
1024A STARCH (MAIZE)
1025. SURGICAL ADHESIVE PLASTER
1027. SURGICAL BANDAGES
1027A SURGICAL GLOVES
1028. SURGICAL COTTON
1029. SURGICAL COTTON AND BANDAGE
1030. SYNTHETIC CAMPHOR POWDER
1031. TABLETS & CAPSULES
1032. TISSUE CULTURE
1033. TINCTURE FROM RECTIFIED SPIRIT
1034. TRIMETHOPIME
1035. VETERENARY MEDICINES (ONLY FORMULATIONS)
1036. VITAMIN 'C', SORBITOL' ANHYDROUS DEXTROSE, STARCH

PULP, PAPER & STATIONERY

1037. AMMONIA PAPER
1038. AUTOMATIC BOOK BINDING
1038A ADHESIVE (FEVICOL TYPE)
1039. ALL PIN & GEM CLIPS
1040. CARBON PAPER
1041. CARD BOARD
1042. CELLPHANE PAPER
1043. COMPUTER FORMS & SECURITY PRINTING PRESS
1044. CORRUGATED BOARD & BOX (PRINTED & LAMINATED)
1045. CORRUGATED BOARD AND BOXES FROM FROM CARD BOARDS
1046. CORRUGATED CARTONS FROM PLAIN PAPERS
1047. CORRUGATRED PACKING AND MATERIAL (BULB AND TUBES PACKING)
1048. DESK TOP PUBLISHING
1049. D.T.P CUM OFFSET PRESS
1050. EGG TRAYS
1051. EXERCISE NOTE BOOK, REGISTER AND PAD
1052. FLEXOGRAPHIC INK
1053. GREETING CARD BY OFFSET PRESS
1054. HAND MADE PAPER
1055. HARD BOARD
1056. INJECTION AMPOULES PACKAGING BOXES
1057. KRAFT PAPER
1058. KRAFT PAPER FROM BAGASSE
1059. LAMINATED PACKAGING PAPER WITH PRINTING
1059A LAMINATION & COATING ON PAPER
1060. M.G. PAPER FROM WASTE PAPER
1061. MILL PAPER FROM WASTE PAPER
1062. MILL BOARD FROM RICE AND WHEAT STRAWS
1063. MILL BOARD FROM WASTE PAPER
1064. MINI PAPER PLANT
1065. MULTI WALL PAPER SACKS
1066. NEWSPAPER FOR CHILDREN
1067. NEWS PRINT PAPER FROM RICE STRAW BAGASSE
1068. NEWS PAPER CHILDRENS (DAILY)
1069. NEWS PRINT PAPER
1070. OFFSET AND TREADLE TYPE PRINTING PRESS
1071. MILL BOARD BASED ON RICE STRAW
1072. PAPER AND BOARD FROM STRAW
1073. PAPER & PAPER PRODUCTS
1074. PAPER BAGS FOR GENERAL USE
1075. PAPER BOARD CARTON
1076. PAPER CONES FOR LOUD SPEAKERS
1077. PAPER FROM AKRA
1078. PAPER FROM BAGASSE WITH CORRUGATED BOARD & BOXES
1079. PAPER FROM BAMBOO
1080. PAPER FROM RICE HUSK AND WHEAT HUSK
1081. PAPER FROM TREE BARK, EUCALYPRUS WOOD
1082. PAPER PRODUCTS
1083. PAPER PLATES, PAPER GLASS
1084. PAPER CUP FOR ICE CREAM
1085. PAPER TUBES SPIRAL WINDING COMPOSIT CONTAINER
1086. PARTICLE BOARD AND BLACK BOARD WITH SAND ING & LAMINATION OF PARTICLE BOARD
1087. PARTICLE BOARD FROM RICE HUSK
1088. POUCH FILLING & MAKING FOR TOMATO SAUCE
1089. POUCH MAKING & GRAVURE PRINTING
1090. PROCESSING OF PAPER FOR FEEDING IN COMPUTER
1091. PULP FROM BAMBOO AND WOOD
1092. SAND PAPER
1093. SANITRY NAPKINS
1094. SILICON COATED PAPER
1095. STENCIL PAPER
1096. STRAW BOARD AND GREY BOARD
1096A STRAW BOARD & MILL BOARD
1097. STRAW BOARD AND PAPER BOARD PLANT
1098. TISSUE PAPER FACIAL
1099. TISSUE MOIST TOILETERY CLEANSING TISSUE AND RELATED PRODUCTS
1100. TISSUE PAPER ROLLS
1101. TOILET PAPER ROLLS
1102. TOILET PAPER & NAPKINS
1103. WET FACE FRESHNER TISSUE
1104. WHITE WRITING & PRINTING

PAPER
1105. WRITING & PRINTING PAPER (PAPER MILLS)

RUBBER, PLASTIC & POLYMER

1106. ACRYLIC BEADS
1107. ACRYLIC COPOLYMER EMULSION
1108. ACRYLIC LATEX
1109. ACRYLIC SHEET
1110. ACRYLIC SHEET AND MOULDED PRODUCTS
1111. ACRYLIC TEETH
1112. AUTO TUBES
1113. AUTO TYRES & TUBES
1114. B.O.P.P. FILM
1115. B.O.P.P. PRESSURE SENSITIVE SELF ADHESIVE TAPE
1116. BABY NIPPLE (SILICON)
1117. BABY NIPPLE (BIG SIZE)
1118. BALLOON PLASTIC ADVERTISING
1119. BLISTER FILM PVC
1120. BLISTER PACKAGING & POUCH PAKAGING
1121. BLOW MOULDING PLASTIC CONTAINER
1122. COATING ON METALIZED POLYESTER FILM/ METALISED PAPER/ ALIMINIUM FOIL
1123. COATING ON PLASTIC (ELECTROLYSIS) & GLASS
1124. COIR FOAM (RUBBERISED)
1125. COLOUR COATING ON PLASTICS
1126. COLOUR MASTER BATCHES FOR VARIOUS PLASTICS
1127. CYCLE TYRES AND TUBES
1128. DISPOSABLE PLASTIC CUPS GLASSES, ETC.
1129. DISPOSABLE PLASTIC SYRINGES WITH NEEDLES
1130. DOUGH MOULDING COMPOUND (D.M.C)
1131. EPOXY RESIN
1132. EXPANDED POLYESTRENE MOULDING (THERMOCOLE)
1133. F.R.P AUTO,SCOOTER ROOFS & CEILINGS
1134. F.R.P PRODUCTS (HELMET, WASHBASIN SHEETS, ROOFING SHEETS)
1135. FIBRE REINFORCED PLASTIC (HIGH PRESSURE MOULDING WITH SMC BMC AND DMC)
1136. FIELD RUBBER CONVERTED TO THE 60% LATEX RUBBER
1137. FLEXIBLE P.U. FOAM
1138. FORMALDEHYDE CROCK -ERY AND OTHER ITEMS
1139. FORMALDEHYDE RESIN (UREA, PHENOL,MELEMINE)
1140. GASKET SHEET
1141. GUM BOTTLE (PVC)
1141A GLASS BEADS
1142. HDPE COATED PAPER SACK
1143. H.D.P.E. CONTAINERS
1144. H.D.P.E. CONTAINERS AND CARBON (BLOW MOULDING)
1145. H.D.P.E. JERRY CANS
1146. HDPE MANUFACTURING, FROM ETHYLALCOHOL
1147. H.D.P.E PIPE AND FITTINGS
1148. H.D.P.E. PIPES
1149. H.D.P.E PRINTED BAGS
1150. H.D.P.E TWINES AND ROPES
1151. H.D.P.E. & L.D.P.E PIPES AND FITTINGS
1152. H.D.P.E/PP BOX STRAPPING
1153. H.D.P.E/PP WOVEN SACKS USING PLAIN LOOMS
1154. H.M BAG PLANT WITH PRINTING UNIT
1155. HAWAI CHAPPALS (RUBBER)
1156. I.V PLASTIC BOTTLE
1157. ICE CREAM CUP (PLASTIC)
1157A INJECTION MOULDED AUTO COMPONENTS
1158. INJECTION & BLOW MOULDED PLASTIC PROD.
1159. INJECTION MOULDED PLASTIC PRODUCTS
1159A INTEGERATED COMPLEX ESTER'S & ALLIED PRODUCTS (D.O.P, D.B.P, & ETHYL ACETATE, BUYTL ACETATE, WIRE ENAMELS, JELLY CABLE COMPOUND)
1160. INTEGERATED SURGICAL RUBBER GOODS INDUSTRY
1161. L.D.P.E FROM ETHYL ALCOHOL
1162. LDPE MOULDED PRODUCTS
1163. LAMINATION OF CO-EXTRUSION MULTILAYER FILM IN ROLL FORM
1164. LATEX RUBBER
1165. LATEX RUBBER CONDOM
1166. MASTER BATCHES (COLOURED, P.V.C. L.D.P.E, H.D.P.E, ETC.)
1167. MELAMINE FORMALHYDE RESIN
1168. MOULDED LUGGAGE
1169. MULTI-LAYER (3 LAYER BAGS)
1170. MULTI-LAYER (3 LAYER) FILM WITH LAMINATION & PRINTING
1171. OIL SEAL
1171A PET BOTTLE/CONTAINERS
1172. PTFE COMPONENTS
1173. PU/PVC SOLE FOR SPORT SHOE BY IMPORTED M/C
1174. PVC BATTERY SEPARATOR

1175. P.V.C COMPOUNDS (FRESH)
1175A P.V.C COMPOUNDS (SCRAP)
1176. P.V.C ELECTRICAL INSULATING TAPE
1177. P.V.C FITTINGS
1178. P.V.C FLEXIBLE FUSIBLE POWDER HEAT FUSIBLE POWDER
1179. P.V.C GRANULES (FOR INSULATION & SHEETS GRADES)
1180. P.V.C GRANULES FROM PVC SCRAPS (WITH POLLUTION CONTROL)
1181. P.V.C HOSES
1182. P.V.C LEATHER CLOTH
1183. P.V.C FLEXIBLE PIPES
1184. P.V.C PIPES AND FITTINGS
1185. POLYTHENE BAGS (PRINTED)
1186. PVC PLASTICS FILM SHEET SOFT/RIGID
1187. PVC RESIN AND COMPOUND
1187A PVC RIGID PIPE
1188. PVC RULAR
1189. PVC STABLIZERS (SINGLE PACK SYSTEM)
1190. PVC WIRE AND CABLES
1191. PAPER BASED PHENOLIC SHEET FOR ELECTRICAL
1192. PHENOL FORMALDEHYDE RESIN
1193. PHENOLIC RESIN
1194. PLASTIC BEADS FROM PLASTIC SCRAPS
1195. PLASTIC BUTTONS
1196. PLASTIC CANS
1197. PLASTIC COLLAPSIBLE TUBE
1198. PLASTIC CORRUGATED SHEET & BOXES
1199. PLASTIC FILM AND SHEETS WITH PRINTING FLEXO & ROTO/LDPE/HDPE/PP/HM/ PVC
1200. PLASTIC GRANULES OR POWDER FROM PLASTIC SCRAP
1201. PLASTIC INJECTION MOULDED T.V. CABINETS
1202. PLASTIC ITEMS-MANUFAC TURE FROM POWDER MELAMINE
1203. PLASTIC GOODS
1203A PLASTIC SHEET FROM SCRAP
1204. PLASTIC PLANT (BLOW MOULDING & INJECTION MOULDING)
1205. PLASTIC PRODUCTS (GOLD, SILVER, NICKEL)
1206. PLASTIC TOYS
1207. POLYESTER BEADING
1208. POLYESTER FILM
1209. POLYTHENE BAGS & AUTOMATIC PRINTING
1210. POLYTHENE PRINTED BAGS
1211. POLYURETHANE FOAM AND ITS PRODUCTS
1212. PROPYLENE FILM (PRINTED) & BAG MANUFACTURING
1212A PLASTIC MATS
1213. RAINBOW COLOUR ON PVC FILM & SHEET
1214. RED MUD PVC PIPES AND FITTINGS
1215. RE-RUBBERISED OF SOLID TYPE
1216. RESIN COATED SAND REXINE
1217. REXINE CLOTH & ALLIED PRODUCTS
1218. RUBBER AUTO PARTS
1219. RUBBER BELTING
1220. RUBBER MOULDING UNIT INCLUDING LINING RUBBER SHEETING
1221. RUBBER RECLAIMING
1222. RUBBER ROLLERS FOR TEXTILE MILLS & PAPER INDUSTRIES
1223. RUBBER SHEET AND ALLIED HOSPITAL RUBBER GOODS
1224. RUBBERIZED PVC GASKET
1225. RUBBERISED COIR
1226. SAFETY BELTS
1227. SILVER AND GOLD PLATING ON PVC AND NYLON-6
1228. SPECTACLE FRAMES (PLASTIC)
1229. SPUNGE RUBBER
1230. SURGICAL EXAMINATION GLOVES
1231. SYNTHETIC PEARL COATING ON POLYSTY RENE BEADS
1232. TEFLON MANUFACTURING
1233. TEFLON TAPE
1234. TEFLON TAPES & CABLES
1235. THERMOCOLE SHEET AND MOULDED PRODUCTS EXPANDED POLYESTERENE EXTRUSION PROFILES
1236. THERFORMED PACKAGING (BLISTER PACKAGING AND POUCH PACKAGING)
1237. THERMOPLASTIC POLYURETHANE
1238. TOOTH BRUSHES
1239. TOY BALLOON, DECORA TIVE AND INDUSTRIAL BALLOONS
1240. TREAD RUBBER
1240A TYRE RETREADING (HOT)
1241. TYRE RETREADING BY COLD PROCESS
1242. TYRE TUBES & FLAPS
1243. UNSATURATED POLYESTER FOR REXINE
1244. V-BELT AND FAN BELT
1245. VINYL ASBESTOS AND PVC WALL PAPER
1246. VITON (FLUORO ELASTOMER)

SOAP, COSMETICS & PEFUMES

1247. ACID SLURRY, SYNTHETIC DETERGENT POWDER
1247A ACID SLURRY
1248. AGARBATTI SYNTHETIC, PERFUMERY COMPOUND
1249. AFTER SHAVE LOTION
1250. ANTISEPTIC CREAM
1251. BETA IONONE
1252. BLEACHING POWDER
1253. BLUE DETERGENT POWDER
1254. CLEANING POWDER (VIMTYPE)
1255. COLD CREAM
1256. COLOURED FLAME & PERFUMED CANDLES (RED, BLUE, GREEN FLAME)
1257. COSMETIC INDUSTRY (MODERN)
1258. COSMETIC INDUSTRY-SHAMPO, SPRAY PERFUME, TALCUM POWDER
1259. DETERGENT POWDER (ARIEL TYPE)
1260. DETERGENT POWDER (NIRMA TYPE) FULLY AUTOMATIC PLANT
1261. DETERGENT WASHING POWDER
1262. FISH OIL SOAP
1263. GLYCERINE TRANSPARENT SOAP
1264. HAIR REMOVING CREAM
1265. HERBAL COSMETICS
1266. HERBAL SHAMPO & CREAM
1267. HERBAL/AYURVEDIC COSMETICS UNIT
1268. INCENSE POWDER, INCENSE STICKS & INCENSE CAKE
1269. OPTICAL WHITENERS
1270. ROSE OIL EXTRACTION
1271. SHAMPOOS (COCONUT OIL BASED COLD PROCESS)
1272. SHAVING CREAM
1273. SINDUR (KUMKUM)
1274. SOAP COATED PAPER
1275. SPRAY DRIED DETERGENT POWDER
1276. STAIN REMOVER
1277. TALCUM POWDER (FACE & TOILET POWDER)
1278. TOILET AND HERBAL SOAP
1279. TOOTH PASTE & POWDER
1280. WASHING DETERGENT POWDER AND WASHING SOAP
1281. WASHING POWDER LIQUID DETERGENTS, LOTION & SHAMPOO

TEXTILE INDUSTRIES

1282. ANGORA RABBIT WOOL
1283. CERAMIC THREAD GUIDE
1284. COTTON BUDS/SWABS
1285. COTTON FROM WASTE YARN
1287. COTTON ROLLS
1288. COTTON SPIDERS FOR LOUD SPEAKERS
1289. DENIM CLOTH

1290. DENIM CLOTH (INTEGERATED UNIT WITH BLEACHING, DYEIN AND PRINTING)
1292 DISPERSENT FOR TEXTILE
1293. DYEING & BLEACHING
1294. EMULSIFIER FOR WOOL BATCHING OIL
1295. GARMENT DYEING, WASHING & STITCHING (JEANS, JACKETS, SKIRTS & SHIRTS)
1296. GOVES KNITTING
1297. GUNNY BAGS
1298 HDPE WOVEN SACKS
1299. HDPE TARPAULINS USING PLAIN LOOM WITH LAMINATION
1300. HDPE/PP WOVEN SACKS USING CIRCULAR LOOMS
1301. HOSIERY CLOTH (COTTON) PROCESSING (BLEACHING, DYEING, FINISHING OF CLOTH)
1302 HOSIERY CLOTH (COTTON) PROCESSING (BLEACHING, DYEING, FINISHING OF CLOTH)
1303. HOSIERY INDUSTRY
1304 HOSIERY MERCERISING
1305. HOSIERY PRODUCTS LIKE VEST, BRIEF, T-SHIRTS & SOCKS
1306 JACQUARD FABRICS
1307. JUTE COIR, GRASS ROPE/ SUTLI MAKING
1308 JUTE FELT
1309 JUTE TWINES
1310 KNITTED FABRICS
1311 LAMINATED JUTE BAGS
1312. LAMINATION OF HDPE WOVEN CLOTH (JUTE,COTTON, PAPER)
1313 NYLON YARN CRIMPING, DOUBLING AND BLEACHING
1314 PIGMENT BINDER FOR TEXTILE PRINTING
1315 POLYESTER RESIN FOR WIRE ENAMEL
1316 POLYESTER YARN FROM WASTE POLYESTER ZIP FASTENERS
1317 POWER LOOM
1318 READYMADE GARMENT AND HOSIERY
1319. READYMADE GARMENT MERCHANDISE
1320 RECOVERY OF NYLON FROM NYLON WASTE
1321. ROTARY PRINTING AND DYEING ON COTTON, SYNTHETIC TEXTILE
1322 SANITRY NAPKIN
1323. SCREEN PRINTING ON COTTON CLOTH
1324 SCREEN PRINTING ON COTTON, POLYESTER & ACRYLIC
1325 SHAWLS (WOOLLEN)
1326. SHOE LACES
1327. SILK FABRICS ON HANDLOOM
1328. SOCKS KNITTING
1329. SPINING, DOUBLING DYE ING, MERCERISING AND BLEACHING OF COTTON YARN
1330. STARCH BOOK BINDING CLOTH
1331. SURAT JARI
1332. SURGICAL COTTON & BANDAGE
1333. SYNTHETIC TEXTILE INDUSTRY (SUITING, SHIRTING, SAREES) TERRY CLOTH
1334. TOWELS, BED SHEET COVERS
1335. TERRY TOWEL
1336. TERRY FABRICS WEAVING UNIT
1337. TEXTILE AUXILLIARIES & CHEMICALS
1338. TEXTILE DYEING, BLEACHING FINISHING AND PRINTING OF COTTON FABRICS
1339. TEXTILE (HOSIERY)
1340. TEXTILE MILL
1341. TOWEL (TERRY)
1342. VELVET CLOTH BY FLOCKING PROCESS
1343. VISCOSE STAPLE FIBRE
1344. WADDING OIL (100%) FOR WADDING OF COTTON HOSIERY CLOTH IN THE DYEING PROCESS
1345. WEAVING OF DASUTI CLOTH WITH PRINTING, DYEING, EMBROIDERY AND FINISHING ETC.
1346. WORSTED WOOLLEN YARN CLOTH

OTHER NEW REPORTS

1347. HEENA POWDER REPACKING
1348. GINGER OIL & DUST
1349. TARPAULINS
1350. COMMUNITY HALL
1351. MEDICAL COLLEGE
1352. CALCIUM STEARATE
1353. P.C.B. WITH GRAPHITE AND SILVER COATING
1353. TEXTILE BLEACHING DYEING & FINISHING
1354. ELECTRIC ARC FURNACE AND ROLLING MILL
1355. DYEING (CANVAS) & WATER PROOFING
1356. TROUT CULTURE
1357. COMPACT FLUORESCENT LAMP
1358. GALVANISING PLANT FOR STRUCTURES FOR TOWER
1359 PORK PROCESSING & FARMING